Is Political Philosophy Impossib

Political philosophy seems both impossible to do and impossible to avoid. Impossible to do, because we cannot agree on a single set of political principles. Impossible to avoid, because we're always living with some kind of political system, and thus some set of principles. So, if we can't do the philosophy, but can't escape the politics, what are we to do? Jonathan Floyd argues that the answer lies in political philosophy's deepest methodological commitments. First, he shows how political philosophy is practised as a kind of 'thinking about thinking'. Second, he unpicks the different types of thought we think about, such as considered judgements, or intuitive responses to moral dilemmas, and assesses whether any are fit for purpose. Third, he offers an alternative approach – 'normative behaviourism' – which holds that rather than studying our thinking, we should study our behaviour. Perhaps, just sometimes, actions speak louder than thoughts.

Jonathan Floyd is a Lecturer in Political Theory at the University of Bristol. He has written widely on questions of method and justification in political philosophy and is co-editor of *Political Philosophy versus History* (Cambridge, 2011).

Contemporary Political Theory

Series Editor
Ian Shapiro

Editorial Board
Russell Hardin
Stephen Holmes
Jeffrey Isaac
John Keane
Elizabeth Kiss
Susan Okin[†]
Phillipe Van Parijs
Philip Pettit

As the twenty-first century begins, major new political challenges have arisen at the same time as some of the most enduring dilemmas of political association remain unresolved. The collapse of communism and the end of the Cold War reflect a victory for democratic and liberal values, yet in many of the Western countries that nurtured those values there are severe problems of urban decay, class and racial conflict, and failing political legitimacy. Enduring global injustice and inequality seem compounded by environmental problems, disease, the oppression of women, racial, ethnic and religious minorities, and the relentless growth of the world's population. In such circumstances, the need for creative thinking about the fundamentals of human political association is manifest. This new series in contemporary political theory is needed to foster such systematic normative reflection.

The series proceeds in the belief that the time is ripe for a reassertion of the importance of problem-driven political theory. It is concerned, that is, with works that are motivated by the impulse to understand, think critically about, and address the problems in the world, rather than issues that are thrown up primarily in academic debate. Books in the series may be interdisciplinary in character, ranging over issues conventionally dealt with in philosophy, law, history, and the human sciences. The range of materials and the methods of proceeding should be dictated by the problem at hand, not the conventional debates or disciplinary divisions of academia.

Other books in the series

Ian Shapiro and Casiano Hacker-Cordón (Eds.)
Democracy's Value

Ian Shapiro and Casiano Hacker-Cordón (Eds.)
Democracy's Edges

Brooke A. Ackerly
Political Theory and Feminist Social Criticism

Is Political Philosophy Impossible?

Thoughts and Behaviour in Normative Political Theory

Jonathan Floyd

University of Bristol

CAMBRIDGE
UNIVERSITY PRESS

CAMBRIDGE
UNIVERSITY PRESS

University Printing House, Cambridge CB2 8BS, United Kingdom

One Liberty Plaza, 20th Floor, New York, NY 10006, USA

477 Williamstown Road, Port Melbourne, VIC 3207, Australia

4843/24, 2nd Floor, Ansari Road, Daryaganj, Delhi – 110002, India

79 Anson Road, #06–04/06, Singapore 079906

Cambridge University Press is part of the University of Cambridge.

It furthers the University's mission by disseminating knowledge in the pursuit of education, learning, and research at the highest international levels of excellence.

www.cambridge.org
Information on this title: www.cambridge.org/9781107086050
DOI: 10.1017/9781316091081

First published 2017

Printed in the United Kingdom by Clays, St Ives plc

A catalogue record for this publication is available from the British Library.

ISBN 978-1-107-08605-0 Hardback
ISBN 978-1-107-45052-3 Paperback

Contents

Disclaimers and Debts

This book is written in a spirit that hovers somewhere between scepticism and fallibilism. That is, although I think there are truths to be had, as regards the issues under discussion, I do think it's very hard for us to have certainty about those truths, or at least for me to have them. Channelling Mill, I offer up my arguments as a contribution to a wider debate, in which I may well turn out to be wrong. Channelling Popper, I offer them up as claims we might learn something from, even if they are falsified.

I say this here because I often wonder about the gap between the research some people publish and the way they teach their students, given that the latter task requires one to do justice to the variety of views found in the discipline, and not just to the view of the teacher. I wonder of some people, how can you teach our subject as it stands, given what you say about the way it is standardly practised? How can you teach X, Y, and Z, given what you have said about them in A, B, and C? For my part, I will certainly continue to encourage, say, the analytical dissection and evaluation of concepts, as well as the working up and over of thought experiments, despite what I say in this book about (what I take to be) the limits of those experiments. I write here then, not just with a sense of fallibility about my own arguments, but also a great deal of respect for what might be called conventional analytical political philosophy, as well as a commitment to continue to teach it as it stands. Perhaps that is obvious, and such disclaimers are as unnecessary here as they are in, I suppose, many other books, given, as I say, the apparently comfortable gap between what other people write and what they teach. Nevertheless, lest these notes of fallibility and respect not be implicit in what follows, I make them explicit here.

Or one might put all of this quite differently. My hope is simply that the following book helps us to think about how we do, and how we ought to do, political philosophy, regardless of whether my own positions on these issues are either correct or widely adopted. A contribution to methodological clarity, then, offered up amongst a community of clever co-seekers for the truth – that is all I aim for.

Now for the more conventional bit. I have many people to thank here, starting with my wife, Rita Floyd, on whom I lean and from whom I learn. This book is dedicated to her, along with the son and daughter we've made together – marvellous Corin and delightful Arwen.

Outside of the private sphere, my thanks go far and wide. First, I want to thank my PhD supervisor, Alan Ryan, who watched over early work on this topic, and who was always kind, helpful, positive, and informed about whatever it was I was beavering away at (and writing too much about – a bad habit early on in my PhD thesis was to write, say, 30,000 words on a topic, only to end up shrinking that material down to around, in one case, about 2,000 words). Second, I want to thank the two figures who examined that thesis – Michael Freeden and John Horton. These again are generous and learned individuals – broadly interested, in a world that rewards specialisation, and always kind, in a world of too many prickly characters.

Third, I want to thank the many (many!) people who sat through one or more presentations on one or more parts of the argument of this book. This group includes audiences at various settings in Oxford, but also invited talks at ANU, the British Academy, Doshisha, Exeter, The Historical Institute, Keio, Kyoto, Leeds, the LSE, Sheffield, Sydney, UCL, and Yale, as well as the 2010 American Political Science Association annual convention, the 2012 International Studies Association annual convention, and the 2012 Manchester Political Theory workshops. Special mention goes to those whose comments and questions I remember receiving, whilst sincere apologies go to those whom I have forgotten altogether. As for the former, they are: Alice Baderin, Richard Bourke, Chris Brooke, Kimberley Brownlee, Dan Butt, Dario Castiglione, Jonathan Dean, Keith Dowding, Derek Edyvane, Stefan Eich, Sarah Fine, Miranda Fricker, Liz Frazer, Michael Freeden, Ed Hall, Iain Hampsher-Monk, Kei Hiruta, Matthew Humphries, Kimberley Hutchings, Jeremy Jennings, Rob Jubb, Rob Lamb, Seth Lazar, Andrew March, Shmulik Nili, Philip Pettit, Anne Philipps, Enzo Rossi, Quentin Skinner, Julia Skorupska, Matt Sleat, Graham Smith, Nicholas Southwood, Marc Stears, Ken Tsutsumibayashi, Laura Valentini, Daniel Viehoff, Jeremy Waldron, and Dominic Welburn.

Fourth, I want to thank those whose teaching left a considerable mark on me. In addition to being a guiding light to me as a theorist, the late Brian Barry was a kind and supportive advisor whilst I was at Columbia, as well as someone who once took me out for lunch just in order to encourage me to apply there in the first place. These kinds of efforts, invisible to line managers, as well as the many metrics by which we are now measured, really stick with you. Even more importantly, Peter Starie and Wolfram Kaiser, both of Portsmouth University, were instrumental in ensuring that I had any sort of career at all as a post-graduate, let alone one that led to this book. I am forever in their debt for the faith and support they offered me early on, at a time when I had only just found my vocation.

Fifth, I want to thank the two anonymous reviewers for Cambridge University Press whose positive, extensive, and searching comments helped make this book what it is today. If it is still not the book it could have been, then that is no fault of theirs, as they provided me with all the pointers and rebuttals I needed. Similarly, it is no fault of my editor, John Haslam. This is the second book of mine, and the first by my hand alone, that he has guided through the publication process. I am very grateful to him for his support, and especially so given that this book, unlike the first, arrived almost two years later than planned. This delay stemmed from the winning combination of a new home, a new job, and a new child, not to mention a long commute, and I am very grateful to John for not once rushing or pressuring me through this period. I hope such faith is rewarded, at least a little bit, by the pages that follow.

Sixth, I want to thank the Arts and Humanities Research Council, St. Hilda's College, Oxford, University College, Oxford, and especially the British Academy for funding different parts of the research process that led to this book. All of these institutions provided generous support and expected little in return by way of paperwork – a rare treat these days. I am grateful that they put their trust in me, and have tried to do justice here to the resources they invested.

Finally, I want to thank my students, both at Oxford and now Bristol. Provided one doesn't have too much of it at any one time, I relish teaching, and do genuinely learn, both from putting teaching material together, and from the responses students give to it. Perhaps I would learn less if I knew more, but I know little, and so learn lots.

Introduction

What Is This Book About?

Think how natural it is in philosophy to begin an argument about what we *should* think with a claim about how we *already* think. One example of such a beginning is the previous sentence. A second example is the inference that because we would save a boy drowning in a nearby pond if we could do so at little cost to ourselves, we should donate money in order to save starving children on the other side of the world. A third is the inference that because we do not think wealth and privilege should influence our choice of political system, we should live in whatever system would be chosen by an individual who did not know what place he or she would come to occupy within it. In this book I argue that the method expressed by these moves does not work, at least in political philosophy, because the pre-existing thoughts it tries to turn into political principles are too messy and inconsistent to be utilised and ultimately systematised in the desired fashion. There are, I claim, no hidden or buried political principles of the right type and pedigree expressed or entailed by the many twists and turns of human thinking. Instead, we should derive political principles from actions, not thoughts. Although I cannot say in this book that actions always speak louder than words, I do say that certain types of action, including certain types of political and criminal action, speak more clearly than any type of thought, and can be treated as grounds for political principles in much the same way as political philosophers currently treat the latter. This means that just as we would consult the diners and not the chef in order to assess the quality of a meal, political philosophers should pay more attention to the behaviour of real citizens than to the reflections of other political philosophers when assessing the quality of different political systems. It also means that rather than thinking about *what we think we would do* in different hypothetical choice situations, political philosophers should think about *what we already do* in different political environments (and note that the previous sentence invoked an analogy for illustration, not an inference for justification).

1

These claims, of course, provide only a partial flavour of the book, not a description. This is to be expected. Even the best descriptions are partial, which is why in this introduction I want to offer several. The first and best of these is also the most general. It runs as follows. This book is a work *of* and *about* political philosophy. It is a work *of* political philosophy just insofar as it provides an answer to the question 'how should we live?'. It is a work *about* political philosophy just insofar as its chief focus is the particular method by which political philosophers have traditionally attempted to answer that question. As far as descriptions go, that is a good one to be starting off with, even if it already begs a number of questions, including most obviously the question of why the question 'how should we live?' should be seen as the key one for political philosophy. But we will get to *that* question soon enough. If it helps, we can say for now simply that this is a book about both how politics should be organised and how political philosophers should argue about how it should be organised.

A second way of describing this book is to describe it in terms of its key ideas. There are three of these, with three chapters to match. The first of these is *the impossibility thesis*, the idea that political philosophy seems impossible to do despite being impossible to avoid. It *seems* impossible to do just insofar as it seems impossible to provide a convincing and meaningful answer to the question 'how should we live?'. It *is* impossible to avoid just insofar as it is impossible for groups of human beings to avoid living in accordance with one or other such answer, regardless of whether the principles expressed by that answer have been agreed upon, regardless of whether they have ever been made explicit, and regardless of whether they be libertarian or egalitarian, or anarchist or authoritarian in nature. Because we always live with other human beings, however distant those others might be, we are always living under one or other political system, regardless of how unsystematic that system might appear to be.

The second idea is *mentalism*, the idea that the right way of doing political philosophy involves, most fundamentally, the derivation of convincing and meaningful political principles from purported patterns in our normative thoughts, by which I mean patterns that are claimed to exist in the way that we think about both what should and should not be the case in the world and what should and should not be done within it. This idea is developed in the form of two arguments. The first of these is that mentalism is the dominant method in political philosophy. The second is that mentalism can never succeed because the thoughts it tries to turn into principles are too inconsistent both within and between different individuals. Taken together, these arguments serve to explain just why it is that political philosophy appears impossible to do in the manner described by the impossibility thesis.

The third idea is *normative behaviourism*. This idea holds that rather than trying to convert patterns in human thought into convincing and meaningful political principles, we should try to do the same with patterns in human behaviour, and in particular patterns involving insurrection and crime. What unites these two forms of behaviour, I claim, is the fact that, because they involve considerable personal risk, individuals only engage with them when they are deeply dissatisfied with their current political system, either in terms of the nature and policies of that system, or in terms of the ways of life that system makes available. This means, subject to a number of other arguments, that we should judge political systems that produce less of this behaviour as better than those that produce more, and the one that produces the least, a system I label 'social-liberal-democracy', as the best available. But still, the argument that attempts to apply normative behaviourism in order to prove the superiority of this political system is by no means the most important in the chapter. More important by some way are the arguments directed against the many objections this approach to political philosophy is likely to encounter. These objections, of which there are many, include the claim that normative behaviourism moves from an 'is' to an 'ought' and from 'facts' to 'principles' in an unacceptable manner, the claim that it implicitly relies on some deeper set of normative principles for which no adequate argument has been given, and the claim that it rules out any further political progress by restricting our options solely to those political systems that have already been historically tested.

A further way of describing this book would be to say something about how I arrived at these ideas. For the longest time I could not put my finger on it. Is there something about the subject matter of political philosophy (rights, justice, democracy, legitimacy, liberty, equality, and so on) that makes it impossible to resolve its central disagreements? Is the subject too complicated for any one person to be able to both see the full picture and convince us of the right position within it? Is the subject too young to deliver what we want it to deliver? Or is there something else going on? This book, clearly, is written in the conviction that there is something else, given that I am now convinced that political philosophy perpetually moves from one stalemate to another, which is to say one rationally interminable debate to another, on account of the method by which political philosophers reason to their conclusions. But it was not a conclusion reached overnight. It took years of false starts and wrong turns. It took, not just philosophical enthrallment with the depth and importance of this intractability, but also, if I am completely honest, some sort of political commitment to the idea of having relatively objective standards (if you can forgive the phrase) by which one could measure political ideals. It took a long and winding intellectual journey, as Chapter 1 attests, before I eventually realised that the problem was, fundamentally, not one of finding a new and magic set of principles – libertarian, egalitarian, democratic, etc. – but rather of the method political philosophers use to generate them.

Such reflections show that if one had to describe this book yet another way, and summarise it with a single term, then one should probably pick the m-word used twice in the previous paragraph: *method*. We might put it like this. Every day, in every part of the world, people argue about politics. Much of this argument is empirical in nature. That is, it is about whether this or that policy will work in the intended fashion. Will this budget boost economic growth? Will this treaty bring climate change under control? Will these measures reduce crime? But not all political argument is like that. The arguments that really bite, that really divide people, are not about whether or not a given policy is effective, where each side agrees what the right effects would be, but rather about whether or not the goals of those policies, and in particular the priorities those goals express, really are the right ones for us to be adopting[1]. This book is a contribution to that kind of argument in two ways. It provides, as noted earlier, an aid to that argument just insofar as it provides a particular set of priorities for us to adopt, along with an argument for why those priorities are the right ones, but that is not the most important thing. More important by far is the fact that it provides a new method, or model of enquiry, or, if you like, a new theory of how the kind of biting and dividing arguments described should be conducted, at least at the somewhat removed level of political philosophy – for I am certainly not insisting that every politician and citizen should always proceed, in every circumstance, in the strictest accordance with what I am calling normative behaviourism.

Finally, we might describe this book, not in terms of its arguments, or indeed the genesis of those arguments, but rather its intended audience. Who are *they*? Or indeed: Who are *you*? Most obviously, the arguments that follow are for political philosophers whose interests are broadly methodological, as well as those who feel intrigued, frustrated, or, like me, a mixture of both at the way arguments currently seem to run out of air in our field. But not just for them. Some readers, I imagine, will be scholars who say that political philosophy should be more political,

---

[1] I say 'priorities' here because sometimes we agree about the desirability of a given outcome – e.g. 'finding a cure for cancer' – without agreeing on the prioritisation implicit in a particular policy intended to realise that outcome – e.g. 'devote half of all government expenditure to finding a cure for cancer'. Similarly, one can approve of equality of opportunity, or even of outcome, as ideals, without wanting to pay the costs accrued in fully realising them, and thus prioritising them over all such costs.

or historical, or empirical. Some will be those who say that pluralism undermines political theory, or who say the same about the 'realities of politics'. Some will be intrigued by the relationship between facts and principles as well as the connection between that relationship and politico-philosophical argument. And so on and so forth. There are many strains of argument to which the arguments of this book connect, and many readers, at least potentially, accompanying them.

More generally, there will also be those who are simply looking for something new to get their teeth into after what they see as too many rehashed suppers – particular interpretive debates about Rawls revisited under 'global justice' and 'ideal theory', for example, or particular debates about value-pluralism reissued, all of a sudden, as debates about political realism. More generally still, there will be those who are here because they are frustrated, not just with the lack of progress towards consensus in political philosophy, but also by the fact that that lack encourages the almost complete absence of political philosophy from political practice. After all, how are political philosophers supposed to convince politicians of the right path if they cannot persuade each other? Naturally, like most authors, I would like to reach as wide an audience as possible, and who knows, given the way I try to work up from fairly clear propositions to rather more complex conclusions, perhaps some of my readers will be undergraduate or graduate students needing a single book to give them a taste of the field and (what I take to be) its flaws. Perhaps I'll even have a few philosophically curious members of the general public. Yet none of that is for me to decide. Getting to those audiences requires getting through the more particular and expert audiences already described, and that is no easy task.

This takes us, I think, to the limits of these kinds of descriptions, which is to say the limits of the various perspectives they afford. What we need now is to move beyond such descriptions of this book in order to provide a full, step-by-step synopsis of the arguments it contains. Clearly, my hope is that what has already been said will render more intelligible this synopsis, just as the synopsis should render more intelligible those arguments it distils, and which begin in full as soon as it is over. *And yet*, with all that being said, do bear in mind in what follows that this book, like any other of its kind, is a circle. This means that the answer it provides at the end to the question it asks at the beginning also carries with it an answer to the questions some might have thought begged by the initial enquiry. For example, just as my argument that political philosophy should be understood fundamentally in terms of the question 'how should we live?' cannot be rendered entirely convincing in the absence of an argument as to *how* that question should be answered, so can the significance and terms of the question 'can we provide an answer to that question in the form of convincing and meaningful political principles?' not be fully vindicated in the absence of providing *those* principles.

Synopsis of Chapter 1

The working title for Derek Parfit's recent magnum opus, *On What Matters*, was *Climbing the Mountain*. That phrase resonates here, and for at least two reasons. First, because what I want to do over the course of these three synopses, as well as in this book as a whole, is slowly take readers, step by step, to the summit of what must seem at the outset a rather improbable argument. Second, because it implies something that is required both of this argument and of any mountain, namely, that one has to start at the very bottom, which means in this case a very simple question: *what is political philosophy?*

Chapter 1 begins with my answer to this question, which is that political philosophy should be defined, not in terms of a concept, such as justice, or an institution, such as the state, but rather itself in terms of a question: *How should we live?* This definition, I believe, is both inclusive and exclusive in the appropriate fashion. It is inclusive just insofar as it does not rule out from the start any one particular approach to political philosophy, including, for example, those who would rather describe what they are doing as political *theory*. To take just a few examples, the 'how' and 'live' can be answered in anarchist or authoritarian terms, the 'we' in terms of all humanity or just twenty-first-century Germans, and the 'should' in terms of rationality or morality, or indeed something else altogether. Yet it is also exclusive, in just the way we would want it to be, given that it rules out any confusion of political philosophy with other subjects, such as moral philosophy, or the many social sciences – including political science – each of which we might further organise in terms of the questions 'how should *I* live?' and 'how *do* we live?'.

The only problem with this question-as-definition is that as soon as we try to answer it, we realise that we have unearthed an even trickier question, namely, *why should we live that way and not another?* This latter question I call political philosophy's 'foundational question' (FQ), in contrast to the former's status as what I call our 'organising question' (OQ). Let me clarify that distinction: whereas the organising question focuses our minds by delineating the relevant subject matter, without ruling out in advance any one way in which it might be approached, the foundational question directs our attention to what is in fact the real philosophical challenge. We might, after all, answer the first by saying something as simple as 'liberal-democracy'. The problem comes when someone asks 'why?'.

The question that truly organises this book, however, involves a third, though again related, formulation: *is it possible to provide a convincing and meaningful answer to political philosophy's organising question?* This question – our 'guiding question' (GQ) – is the question the rest of the book sets out to answer. We can explain this question by explaining its two key terms. Consider first of all that attempts to answer our organising question can be more or less precise and more or less persuasive. This means that when I say I want a *meaningful* answer, what I mean is that I want an answer capable of giving us a clear and reasonably full picture as regards how either a given society or set of societies, or indeed all societies, should regulate their collective political life. This does not mean that for an answer to be meaningful it has to set out for us every last detail of an ideal constitution. What it means is that, even if that answer comes, as it probably will, in the form of general political principles, those principles must be determinate enough to ensure that, when applied with local facts, and whatever concrete processes the particular principles require, a fairly clear picture of that constitution can be generated. Consider the same point from another angle. A useful rule of thumb here is that for an answer to OQ to be meaningful, it must at the least be able to distinguish between the leading answers to OQ put forward in our time, such as libertarianism and egalitarianism in political philosophy, and communism and fascism in political practice. For example, any answer that does nothing more than claim that the right answer to OQ is that all political systems should ensure clean water for everyone, will clearly have failed by the standard of comprehensiveness expressed by both this rule and the concept of 'meaningfulness' it represents.

By a *convincing* answer, in turn, I mean an answer that is rationally more compelling than any other offered answer. So, although I do not say that such an answer has to be demonstrably correct, I do hold that a convincing answer has to be demonstrably more attractive, and thus at least 'more' correct, than any other suggested answer. Consider once more the relationship between OQ and FQ. For an answer to OQ to convince us, it must be accompanied by a convincing answer to FQ. It must, that is, be able to convince us not just that a particular set of political principles is demonstrably more attractive in terms of some prior normative standard, but also that that standard is itself the most convincing one available. Our answer to OQ, therefore, is supposed to convince human beings of the attractiveness of a given set of political principles, which means, amongst other things, that it must be able to convince them of the merits of every step of argument it takes along the way, right from the very beginning, or, if one prefers a different metaphor, from the ground up.

So how do we find such an answer? We start by working through the most influential arguments in our subject. This quest, like most quests in contemporary political philosophy, begins with Rawls, even if it does not stay with him for long. In fact, rather than dwelling too long on any one argument at this stage of our enquiry, the point at first will simply be to juxtapose a large number of well-known arguments in terms of their answers to OQ and FQ – including libertarian, egalitarian, and communitarian alternatives to Rawls' case – in order to see just what kind of argument is likely to be necessary to generate the sort of convincing and meaningful political principles we seek. Or, alternatively put, rather than pausing too long to examine the many details of each argument, together with the details of those arguments directed against them, the aim at this stage is rather to identify the type of argument deployed by each thinker in order to see just what prospect there is for producing an argument of that type capable of convincing all of these different thinkers.

This point about focusing on the 'kind' or 'type' of argument employed is difficult to fully capture in advance, although it should become at least a little clearer if I say that the gist of my conclusion at the end of this stage is that each of the thinkers considered tries to make convincing their particular set of political principles by grounding that set in some further set of values, the force of which is supposedly secured by yet a further case to the effect that these are values to which we are *already* committed. It should also become clearer if I say that, following this tentative conclusion, and also the conclusion that not one of these thinkers is likely to convince the others in terms of the particular set of values they put forward, my attention shifts to a set of arguments that at least *claims* to do something fundamentally different to the first group considered. These arguments tend to be arguments that begin by saying that they accept some or other form of 'value-pluralism', even if they do not always use that term. A wide number of thinkers and positions are examined here. As regards thinkers who appear to provide a way past such pluralism, special attention is paid to Isaiah Berlin, the later Rawls of *Political Liberalism*, Stuart Hampshire, Joseph Raz, Alasdair MacIntyre, and Richard Rorty. And, as regards some of the more collaborative efforts that claim to have transcended this deadlock, special attention is paid to arguments that attempt to unite us either with a particular ideal of democracy or with a particular ideal of tolerance. It turns out, however, that these arguments do little better than their forerunners. A brief sketch of the problems they encounter, starting with Berlin, runs as follows.

Berlin's case fails in the first instance because his argument that history shows both the truth of pluralism and the horrors of its political denial, and thus in turn the necessity of liberalism, is undone by the fact that pluralism itself, on account of its insistence on the incommensurability of different human values, undermines the absolute political prioritisation of avoiding human suffering. But this is just the initial problem. His case fails in the second instance because when he tries to bolster that position by claiming that there are historically proven universal evils to be avoided, it turns out that even if this is true, the avoidance of such things is only a very general political goal achievable by a wide range of regime types, which means that we are still a long way short of distinctive and thus meaningful political principles.

Rawls' argument in *Political Liberalism*, by contrast, has no such struggle in generating sufficiently precise principles. His problem is that those principles are unconvincing. They are unconvincing because, even if he is right that a particular ideal of reasonableness requires that we accept whatever answer to OQ is generated by his well-known impartial choice situation, the 'original position', he is wrong to think that at least modern Western societies share that ideal in the way that would be required in order for its entailments to be convincing. His particular conception of reasonableness, it turns out, differs considerably from conceptions that could be said to be shared in the required fashion, which means that it is hard to escape the conclusion that it would be perfectly reasonable to be convinced by a completely different set of political principles to the ones that he claims are generated by the 'original position'.

This takes us to the arguments concerning, respectively, democracy and tolerance. The democratic case is perhaps the stronger of the two. This case – as advanced or contributed to by the likes of Amy Gutmann and Dennis Thompson, Thomas Nagel, James Bohman, and Richard Bellamy – holds that rather than trying to decide on the right answer to OQ through philosophical argument, we should try to decide on at least some of its trickier parts through public debate. The primary problem with this case is that the values it draws on in order to set the necessary rules of this debate, together with the wider political system required by these rules, cannot be produced themselves, and thus justified, by that debate. The secondary problem is that the thinkers who advance these rules provide even less defence of them than can be found in the libertarian, egalitarian, and communitarian cases considered at the first stage of our enquiry, with not one part of those defences, even when combined with other arguments, appearing at all capable of convincing most people in the required manner.

The case for tolerance also relies on a set of values for which insufficient argument has been offered, despite beginning, just like the democratic case, with what appears to be a rather promising idea. This idea is that different people could be convinced by a single answer to OQ provided that that answer gave enough leeway to different cultural groups to ensure that everyone's way of life is supported, regardless of the different opinions each group holds about the lifestyles of the others. The problem with this position is that it elides much too readily between the interests of traditional cultural groups and the interests of the individuals who inhabit them. It is claimed by the proponents of this case that the well-being of all is well served by a system that protects the traditional cultural identities already found in a given political system, but that is just not true. What *is* true is that the well-being of those who prize such traditional cultural ways of life above all else is promoted at the expense of those who do not, including most obviously those who inhabit cultural groupings that stand at odds with their own personal ideals and ambitions. This means that the case for such a political order cannot be put in terms that would be rationally compelling to a large number of those who would have to live with it, and thus that that the order itself cannot be deemed a convincing answer to OQ.

This takes us to Stuart Hampshire, who echoes Berlin's second line of argument by saying that the idea of universal evils holds the key to our problems. He also echoes Berlin by saying that a proper understanding of history is crucial, although the particular historical story he tells is rather different. His story centres on an idea he calls 'adversarial reasoning', which is the kind of reasoning that occurs when a verdict is reached through a comparison of two or more rival positions. This is the kind of reasoning we find in law courts and parliamentary debates, but not just here. According to Hampshire, it has been the successful political model adopted through the ages, on account of its ability to solve fierce disputes whilst avoiding universal evils. And, of course, it is also the kind of reasoning that Hampshire thinks gives us our convincing answer to OQ, just insofar as it brings with it clear requirements for the kinds of political system required for such reasoning to occur. But just how clear are those requirements?

Hampshire admits that in different cultures the two questions of (1) what kinds of political claims are settled by such reasoning and (2) how those claims should be balanced have been answered very differently, which is why he thinks the particular institutions adopted in each society will differ significantly. But this is rather worrying. What happens politically when different sections of society disagree both about the current political framework and the decision it reaches? And, on a more philosophical level, who should be blamed if one side turns to violent conflict (thus perpetrating a universal evil) in order to change that framework? Is it the group who started the conflict or the establishment who denied that group whatever it was they were requesting? Unfortunately, Hampshire's argument is unable to avoid or solve this problem, which means that his answer to OQ will be convincing only for societies in which there is complete consensus on the right set of 'adversary' political institutions and practices. But then, given that such societies are almost entirely non-existent, this makes Hampshire's position almost entirely unconvincing.

Joseph Raz, by contrast, offers a rather more promising, and certainly more complicated, route from a particular model of reasoning to a purportedly convincing answer to OQ. His argument begins with the claim that good practical reasoning involves the rational assessment of objective yet incommensurable values. This means first that for an individual to live well, he or she must live autonomously, which means being both free and able to choose amongst a healthy array of objective yet incommensurable values. It means second that for a political order to be convincing to a given individual, it must ensure that individual's autonomy. And it means third that every citizen of a given system must enjoy such autonomy in order for that system to be convincing to all. This is a tricky thing to do, given that ensuring autonomy for all, on Raz's understanding of that concept, will mean promoting and protecting ways of life that many in society deplore. It is also a tricky thing to do given that on his pluralist account of practical reasoning, individuals who do deplore certain other ways of life are not necessarily unreasonable for doing so. This is a function of the fact that to embrace one value may well involve opposing another, a fact that Raz calls 'competitive pluralism'. So why should I be expected to promote the autonomy of others at the expense of my own values? Unfortunately Raz never manages to successfully answer this question, which is why, on the one hand, his prescribed political system, given that it is democratic, would never promote the policies he would want it to, and, on the other, his answer to OQ falls some way short of convincing us.

Alasdair MacIntyre provides yet a third attempt to move from a convincing account of practical rationality to a convincing answer to OQ, although he does not *begin* with that account. Instead he begins with a claim that in order to make the right choice amongst different plausible accounts of practical reasoning, we shall have to compare the merits of the different intellectual traditions that lie behind them. So what do we find when we make such a comparison? According to MacIntyre, when we compare the two most important such traditions, we find that 'Aristotelianism' has been able to defend itself against all manner of objections through the ages, whereas the more recent and dominant 'Enlightenment Project' has so far failed by its own standard, which MacIntyre takes to be the standard of providing a set of moral and political principles to which no reasonable person could object. Why, though, should this project be judged a failure simply because it has not succeeded so far? And indeed, why should I reject whatever set of Enlightenment-era principles I currently feel attracted to in favour of an Aristotelian set, simply because these have emerged out of what MacIntyre judges a more impressive history? A dubious criterion of models of rationality hardly seems a promising basis on which to convince me to change my mind as regards the right answer to OQ. MacIntyre bolsters this argument in his latest work by saying that in order for anyone to become a good (Aristotelian) practical reasoner, everyone must become one, but this only takes us back to Raz's problems. As already noted, I do not need everyone to be autonomous in order to be so myself, any more than I need every child to become autonomous in order for my children to become so.

Perhaps a more promising idea is to concentrate less on reason and more on rhetoric. This is the hope of Richard Rorty, who thinks that even if there is no rational argument as to why people should prefer a particular liberal answer to OQ over its alternatives, there is every reason to think that people could be emotionally persuaded into subscribing to things which make that answer a convincing one to them. In particular, Rorty thinks that if people are made aware of all the many instances of cruelty in the world, they will want to help those who suffer, and ultimately want to adopt a political system which minimises such suffering. There is, however, an inconsistency in Rorty's argument, given that in addition to believing people can be turned into liberals by being made aware of cruelty, he also believes that human nature is entirely plastic. How then can everybody be turned into liberals if not everybody comes from a culture where avoidance of suffering is highly prized? But then what if Rorty is wrong about his belief in this plasticity? Surely then the argument he offers could still get us a convincing answer to OQ? Unfortunately not. As it turns out, there is a deeper problem with his position, which is that even when people are made aware of suffering, they often choose not to prioritise its alleviation. Societies, in short, are often completely aware of the problems they opt not to fix. Rorty seems to assume that the only reason people avoid tackling these problems is that they have not had their consequences for particular individuals made clear and vivid enough to them – but this is not so. Human beings, both in the West and elsewhere, are often perfectly aware that certain political and economic arrangements cause many individuals to fall through the cracks, which is why simply stressing that fall, in as many places, and with as many metaphors as one likes, will always be insufficient to convince them of an answer to OQ that entirely avoids it.

So where do we go from here? Three options present themselves fairly readily. The first is to go right back to the start. This option holds that pluralism, or whatever other framework we might adopt to explain our problems so far, does not go nearly as deep as we might imagine. Instead, proponents of this option say, we should carry on in the manner of the libertarian, egalitarian, and communitarian arguments considered at the first stage, and continue to look for a shared value or set of values capable of entailing a set of political principles by which all should be convinced. The second option, by contrast, says we should have more faith in the power of human judgement. Proponents of this option hold that rather than looking for an answer to OQ that can be rationally deduced from a prior value or set of values, we should see that truly reasonable people, even when they have to make the trickiest of political choices, actually make the same choice as each other. So what about the third option? This option is even slimmer than the first two. It holds that even if we have not succeeded so far, that is no reason, contra MacIntyre, to believe that we never shall. Proponents of this position echo Derek Parfit's claim that secular, professional political philosophy is, despite certain assumptions we might make to the contrary (Ancient Greece? The Enlightenment?), a rather young subject, and should not, as such, be prematurely judged.

Not one of these three options – denial, judgement, or deferral – turns out to hold much promise. The problem with the first is simply that its proponents have had no more success than our earlier considered thinkers, and so have still not been able to provide us with the convincing and meaningful answer to OQ we require. The problem with the second, even more simply, is that it is hopeless to say that judgement can solve our problems when we know, from political philosophy as much as anywhere else, that even the most experienced and expert judges judge differently. And the third? Well, it is not entirely clear that this is even a proper option. To say that it is still 'early days' in our quest for a convincing and meaningful answer to OQ is at best an admission that what we have found is something they also accept – namely, that no one has cracked it yet – and at worst an admission that there is not even anything more promising on the horizon. Even if continued failure is no proof that we should abandon our search, it is hardly a reason for optimism.

This takes us to the key conclusion of the chapter, which is that contemporary political philosophy appears to be rationally interminable. That is, it seems to be impossible to provide a meaningful answer to

OQ capable of convincing at least the rational members of even one society, let alone all societies. But that is not the only impossibility in town. Alongside this problem, there is also the challenge that even if it is impossible to provide a convincing and meaningful answer to OQ, we are still unavoidably going to be living with one answer or another, whether we like it or not. This second impossibility is a function of the fact that human beings always and necessarily live alongside one another, which means that they cannot help but live in accordance with one or other set of political principles – even if those principles amount to nothing more than 'let the strongest survive', or even 'let the strongest dictate to everyone else'. All political environments obey one or other set of dynamics, and as a result one or other set of principles, which means that regardless of whether or not the inhabitants of that environment have ever been consulted on those principles, those are still the principles by which their collective existence is being governed.

A further though minor conclusion here is that arguments for a particular answer to OQ tend to fail either because they are meaningful but unconvincing or because they are convincing but indeterminate (I am loathe to say 'meaningless'). For example, whilst thinkers such as Raz and the later Rawls fit the first mould, thinkers such as Berlin and Hampshire readily fit the second. And these are not the only examples on offer. In response to those who might doubt whether enough arguments have been considered, given the severity of the conclusion offered, a number of further approaches to our problem, including approaches that could be called historical-contextualist, realist, and post-modern, are also examined in order to further strengthen the case.

This conclusion is also bolstered in a different way. Consider here that in response to the criticism that my argument so far has been unduly regressive – in the sense of digging too deep for foundations – and thus unduly demanding in terms of how overwhelmingly rationally compelling any answer has to be in order to count as convincing, it can be pointed out the required standard is a function, not of *my own preferences*, but rather of the very *scale of disagreement* in contemporary politics and political philosophy, at least when combined with the fact that we have always to live out one or other answer to that subject's defining question. And indeed, it can also be pointed out that each of our considered thinkers actually seems to agree with me, at least by implication, and at least for the most part, just insofar as they believe, either implicitly or explicitly, that almost every position bar their own is unconvincing.

This then takes us to what I call in this book the 'impossibility thesis' – the near-paradox that political philosophy seems both impossible and unavoidable. However much we might like things to be different, it just seems impossible to generate a convincing and meaningful answer to OQ, despite the fact that it is impossible to avoid adopting one, or, for want of a better phrase, living one out. Or have we *still* not been radical enough in the spread of arguments we have considered? This question continues to pull at us, which is why, before this chapter closes, four more positions, however unpopular they might be with contemporary philosophers, are given a chance to change our verdict. These four are relativism, subjectivism, cynicism, and scepticism.

As it turns out, there is good reason for their unpopularity. Relativism fails in the first instance because it cannot avoid being at least partly universalistic, and in the second because there are no internally homogenous cultures of the kind it requires in order to be convincing. Subjectivism fails because, even if helps to explain what many of our considered thinkers call pluralism, it is ultimately more of a problem than a solution, with absolutely no clue as to how people with different subjective preferences ought to live with each other, given that, as the second half of the impossibility thesis tells us, they cannot help but do so. Cynicism fails because it is both easily empirically falsified and, at the same time, and echoing subjectivism, completely silent regarding how a multitude of self-interested individuals can live together. Scepticism fails because, even in its most plausible form, it is paradoxical. That is, it is paradoxical when it claims that there *is* a right answer despite us *not* being able to know it, because showing this would require knowledge of what that right answer is. All of which means that we remain stuck, given that political philosophy remains, or at least appears to remain, impossible.

Synopsis of Chapter 2

To repeat: political philosophy appears impossible, and not just because it is impossible to avoid living out one or other answer to its organising question, but also because arguments about this answer are rationally interminable, or at least seem to be given the futility of the way in which those arguments are currently conducted. This last clause is important here, given that the aim of this chapter is to show why the *appearance* of rational interminability is also a *necessity*. Or, alternatively put, if we can say that the rational interminability of contemporary arguments about OQ is our *symptom*, what I now want to do is provide the appropriate *diagnosis*.

This diagnosis, which might also be called an explanation or proof of the described interminability, serves three ends. First, because the existence of any symptom becomes even more probable once the proper cause has been identified, our diagnosis helps to prove that this interminability really does exist, and is not, for example, some kind of an illusion brought about by as yet unidentified factors, such as the pig-headedness of rival political philosophers, or the shoddiness of my analysis of their arguments. Second, identifying this cause grants us a much better understanding of the nature of that symptom. Third, if we arm ourselves with the kind of understanding this diagnosis affords, then perhaps in time we will be well placed to offer some form of a cure. My aims are thus to prove the impossibility of contemporary political philosophy, to explain the existence of that impossibility, and perhaps also to offer some hope, even if that hope is not explored in this chapter, of a way past the challenge this condition represents.

The chapter begins with a description of what I take to be the real cause of this condition: the adherence of political philosophers to a method of argument I call *mentalism*. Mentalism is the hidden methodological orthodoxy of modern political philosophy, in part because nobody has realised why it cannot succeed, and in part because no one has imagined an alternative. According to this orthodoxy, political philosophers should proceed in their work by attempting to discover and then apply whatever set of political principles is already implicitly expressed within our normative thoughts. Do our deepest thoughts about what should and should not exist in the world, and about what should and should not be done within it, follow a utilitarian pattern? Do they express something like Kant's categorical imperative, or some alternative formulation of morality's so-called golden rule? Do they entail, politically, a system of deontological rights, or perhaps some rule about the centrality of a test of 'reasonableness' to all public, political arguments about the right answer to OQ? These are the kinds of questions that mentalism asks, and that contemporary political philosophers address either directly, by attempting to provide their own answers, or indirectly, by contributing to debates that address one or more of the smaller issues that any such answer must encounter.

What, then, is the problem with this method? It is that they can never provide true and thus agreed-upon answers to such questions because there are no patterns of the required kind to be found, even in our deepest normative thoughts. This is not to say that there are no thoughts supportive of one or other principle or set of principles. The difficulty is rather that different thoughts contradict each other, either directly or by supporting different and contradictory principles. The scatter-graph of our normative thoughts, we might say, is just too scattered.

How, though, can we be sure that this inconsistency exists, or that mentalism cannot succeed given its existence, or indeed that mentalism is the orthodoxy that I have taken it to be? In order to answer these questions, the first thing we need to do is find out more about how mentalism works in practice. That is, if we can explore with even greater detail than was on offer in Chapter 1 the ways in which different political philosophers argue, and thus the techniques that make up mentalism's arsenal, we will have enhanced both our grasp of mentalism's nature and our confidence that it is the described orthodoxy. We will, though, need to be sure that we are not confined even to the wide spread of arguments considered in the previous chapter, which is why, in setting out what I take to be mentalism's key techniques, an additional set of arguments is considered alongside those already examined. These are arguments drawn from a number of thinkers who were left out of that first spread, including Brian Barry, Thomas Christiano, G. A. Cohen, David Estlund, Phillip Pettit, and Phillipe Van Parijs.

The result of this analysis is that six distinct mentalist techniques can be identified. These are, in the order that I consider them, and also the order in which they would tend to be applied, grounding, falsifying, cohering, refining, eliminating, and reflecting. Taken together, they make up the toolkit contemporary political philosophers use in their quest for the buried political principles of our normative thought patterns. There is no need here, however, to explain and illustrate each of these techniques here – that can wait for the full chapter. What matters more is that we get some kind of advance understanding of the proof that these techniques, however elaborate and intuitively plausible they might turn out to be, are all doomed to failure.

There are two parts to this proof. The first part brings some much-needed focus to our picture of the normative thoughts mined by the described mentalist techniques by dividing those thoughts into three types, or, as I sometimes prefer to call them, levels. These three types I call 'impartial choices of ideal state', 'considered judgements', and 'intuitive choices of abstract principle'. The first of these labels applies to the decisions we think we would make when we are (1) asked to choose an ideal political system and (2) denied enough knowledge about ourselves and the world to consider our decision an impartial one. The second applies to judgements we already have about the worth of various past and present political institutions and processes. The third applies to decisions we think we would make either when given a direct choice between different abstract principles or when given a choice within a moral dilemma, the parameters of which are supposed to ensure that whatever choice is made, it functions as a choice between two or more abstract principles.

The second part of the proof explains why not one of these types of thought is capable of doing the job required of it by mentalist political philosophy. Put briefly, rather than providing the kind of clear patterns out of which political philosophers could plausibly extract meaningful and convincing political principles, each type turns out to be too internally inconsistent, in terms of revealing conflicts between thoughts, both within and between individuals – and without even considering conflicts between the different thought types.

More specifically, the problems encountered in each of group of thoughts can be distilled as follows. Impartial choices of ideal state, first, fail to deliver because either they generate different answers from different people when the conditions that define the situation are widely acceptable, or they generate one and the same answer from everyone when the conditions that define the situation require justification from elsewhere. As a result, they require justification from either considered judgments or intuitive choices of abstract principle. Yet neither can help us. Our second thought type, considered judgements, cannot help because, as it transpires, they are either widely shared, despite being politically indeterminate, or not remotely shared, despite being sufficiently precise. They generate, in other words, either convincing and imprecise political principles, or unconvincing and meaningful ones. So what about intuitive choices of abstract principle? The problem with our third thought type is, again, twofold. With much supporting evidence from moral psychology, including from 'experimental ethics', it turns out both that different people produce different intuitive responses to one and the same dilemma, *and* that one and the same person will give different responses to one and the same dilemma according to how that dilemma is framed.

These arguments bring 'normative dissonance' – this deep and unavoidable inconsistency between our various normative thoughts – into full view. But they also do something else. They pose a question that has been stalking this argument from the beginning, namely, if contemporary political philosophy is mentalist, and mentalism is impossible, why do so many clever people persist with it anyway? Naturally, that is a difficult question to answer. I am not 'many clever people' and arguably not even one clever person. There is, though, one way of shedding at least some light on the situation, which is that even if a strong majority of scholars did think that the vast majority of arguments are doomed, there could still be a strong majority who consider mentalism a viable enterprise. For example, even if 60 per cent of scholars thought impartial choices of ideal state unfit for purpose, 60 per cent thought considered judgements unfit, and 60 per cent thought intuitive choices of abstract principle unfit, it could still be the case that 100 per cent of scholars thought that at least one of these types of thought worked, and thus that mentalism as a whole was a viable enterprise.

Or there could be an entirely different reason for my finding this question difficult to answer, namely, that I am entirely wrong about the futility of mentalism. This possibility is at least one reason why it is so important, given a desire to avoid premature conclusions about either the nature or fate of mentalism, to consider whatever important objections might remain to my case, once the full detail of it has been spelled out. These objections come under three headings: 'radical pluralism', 'particularism', and, most importantly of all, 'reflective equilibrium'. Each of these three offers plausible hope of a pro-mentalist escape route, though not one of them, in my view, succeeds in overturning either the fact of normative dissonance or the necessity of the interminability described.

Radical pluralism, first of all – a position advanced most promisingly by G. A. Cohen – offers hope by attempting to ease back on the scale of ambition required by mentalism. He says that we should just accept that trade-offs between different key values are non-rational, and focus instead on working out a proper understanding of each of them, including, for example, justice. But this is misleading. Cohen, after all, still wants to make politics largely subordinate to justice, and still wants to study our normative thoughts in order to see both what true justice is and what it requires – and as noted, this is a job for which such thoughts are entirely unfit.

So what about particularism, which again offers hope by saying, following those believers in 'judgement' noted earlier in Chapter 1, that even though we have to make these difficult trade-offs between conflicting values, those trade-offs are a matter, not for rational argument, but rather for expert choice. Again, this is a claim that gets us nowhere, despite having some mileage in moral philosophy, given the nature and burdens of individual moral choices, as opposed to society-wide political ones. The problem, in short, is that different experts give different and conflicting verdicts regarding, not just different cases, but also differently framed instances of the same case.

All of which takes us to mentalism's final and most important redoubt: reflective equilibrium, and specifically wide reflective equilibrium. The hope here is that if we consider all of our relevant normative thoughts at once, together with all possible political principles, we will soon be able to eliminate both some of those thoughts and some of those principles, and will be able to carry on doing so until we are down to just one set of consistent thoughts and one set of clearly required and sufficiently determinate political principles. Some thinkers also try to strengthen this idea by saying that, in addition to our normative thoughts, we should put other things into the mix, such as 'meta-ethical theories', and even various political 'facts'. Yet even that cannot save us. Even reflective equilibrium's most keen interpreters, such as Norman Daniels and T. M. Scanlon, acknowledge that it is, fundamentally, a first-person exercise, which means that even if it were the case that one person could settle on just one set of coherent thoughts and one set of appropriate principles, this is still no solution, given the problems set out earlier, when it turns out that different people arrive at different sets.

There are, therefore, no harmonious patterns in our normative thoughts of the kind required by mentalism, even when we try as best we can to tidy our thinking up. This is why contemporary political philosophy is unable to rationally end its debates, and why the subject, at least as currently practised, is impossible in the manner described in Chapter 1.[2] So, is there any hope? Only one thing is clear at this juncture, which is that if there is hope, it must lie in an entirely new model of politico-philosophical argument, which is to say, an entirely new method for arriving at a convincing and meaningful answer to what I have called political philosophy's organising question – *how should we live?*

Synopsis of Chapter 3

The aim of Chapter 3 is to answer this hope by presenting, applying, and defending a new method of politico-philosophical argument that I call *normative behaviourism*. This method works as follows. Political philosophers, I say, should look for patterns in our behaviour, not our thoughts. They should do this because, if they look at the right kind of behaviour, they will soon see that the regular patterns it exhibits could readily be translated into a set of convincing and meaningful political principles. This kind of behaviour is the kind we engage in via (1) acts of insurrection, and (2) criminal acts. The 'beauty' of this behaviour, I believe, is twofold. First, it involves a level of risk, and so expresses a level of commitment, that cannot be reproduced with speculative, armchair-bound, mentalist reasoning. Second, it displays a level of convergence that is, as we have seen, entirely absent from such reasoning.

The broad hope of this approach to political philosophy is that we can successfully treat certain forms of human action as expressions of normative preferences ripe for conversion into political principles, in much the same way as certain forms of thought are currently treated. But there is also fear, alongside such optimism. The fear is that when we try to do so we will unacceptably violate what philosophers call the 'naturalistic fallacy'.

---

[2] This is not to say that it achieves nothing! The point is only that it fails in the specific aim discussed, of generating just one convincing and meaningful answer. For other ways in which the subject offers us various valuable contributions, see the final section of this book.

To that worry, however, normative behaviourists can say many things, the first of which is that that objection conveys itself something that we might easily refer to as the 'mentalistic fallacy'. This fallacy is the belief that when normative behaviourism moves from behavioural facts to political principles, it is doing something that mentalism does not. But that is not true. To move from the 'is' of an action to the 'ought' of a principle is no different to moving from the 'is' of a thought to the same endpoint. Both action and thought can be treated as expressions of normative preferences, just as both action and thought can be converted into principles. The only key difference between the two, as noted, is that actions display a degree of both commitment and convergence which, however much we wish otherwise, is simply not there in our thoughts.

So what happens when we put normative behaviourism to work? What happens is that it picks out what I call 'social-liberal-democracy' as the most convincing set of meaningful political principles available. It does this by drawing on a wide variety of behavioural facts, including the fact that numerous alternative systems, including totalitarianism, authoritarianism, theocracy, monarchy, and aristocracy, exhibit clear tendencies towards collapse; the fact that as prosperity rises so does the demand for democracy; the fact that minimally prosperous liberal democracies have lower levels of crime, rebellion, and collapse than other attempted regime types; and the fact that more egalitarian, and thus more social, liberal-democracies do better than less egalitarian ones.

These 'facts', however, taken just as they are, are still not enough for what we need to do here. In order to generate a convincing and meaningful answer to OQ, we need at least two more things, the first of which is an explanatory theory of why social-liberal-democracy does better than other political systems by the set criteria, and the second of which is a set of reasons for why its performance by these criteria amounts to a convincing case for accepting it as the best available answer to that question.

The explanatory theory is as follows. Social-liberal-democracy succeeds on one level, almost tautologically, because it is egalitarian, liberal, and democratic. By reflecting on, in particular, various debates in contemporary political philosophy, we can see that each of the three elements of this system provides strong incentives for individuals to co-operate with its rules. But we can also say more than this. We can also say that on a deeper level, by reflecting on the logic of 'open-access societies', as described by Douglass North, John Wallis, and Barry Weingast, there are a number of positive feedback loops running between the various constituent features of this system, and which further compound its political success. And that is still not all. We can also say, on the deepest level of all, that by setting out a choice matrix similar to the prisoners' dilemma for the decision of whether or not to be a 'good citizen' – which means the decision of whether or not to engage in crime, and insurrection – we can see how these various features of social-liberal-democracy succeed in both boosting the benefits of choosing to co-operate, and ramping up the costs of choosing not to do so.

Again, though, this is *still* not quite an argument as to why we should be convinced by this system as the best available answer to OQ. We might ask here, for example, just why we should prefer a system that appears to be found unpalatable by the least number of people over a system that does better by some other measure. Actually, that question is a misleading one, even if the worry it expresses is a valid one at this point in the argument. One key point in this context is that it does not matter if different people are convinced by this system for different combinations of reasons, just so long as they are all convinced, or at least would be given a certain level of rationality. Another key point is that although the explanation of the political success of social-liberal-democracy can be treated itself as a set of reasons to be convinced by it, there are also further reasons to be convinced which themselves add to that explanation. Four reasons in particular are important. First, this system does a better job of providing personal security to you and your loved ones than any other possible system. Second, this system, as Richard Rorty would have appreciated, minimises the amount of suffering both you and others are likely to encounter. Third, this system does an excellent job of helping both you and others to live what are, for you and those others, flourishing lives. Fourth, this system, because it convinces the maximum number of people, will also cater to your desire, should you possess it, to live in a state that is as reasonable as possible in the sense of being justifiable to as many people as possible.

Of course, some readers will still be unconvinced by this, which is why we now need to stress the difference between *would* and *should* be convinced. Even if some people would not be convinced by the reasons we have adumbrated so far, there are still reasons why they should be so convinced. Note, though, that this does not mean we fall back here into mentalist habits, and say that they should be convinced in terms of values and judgements that either we say they already have, or perhaps, and even more awkwardly, say that they should have. Instead, we simply say the following three things. First, if you care at all about living in accordance with the most convincing answer possible, then this is it. Second, if you come to harm under some alternative and less benevolent system, where that harm is caused by some downtrodden soul who, amongst other things, is entirely unhappy with the options given to him or her throughout his or her youth, adolescence, and early adulthood, then do bear in mind that you cannot claim that you would not have done the same had you been in their shoes. Third, do bear in mind that there is, at this point, no mentalist argument available to you against your aggressor of the form 'you are violating the rules of a just regime'.

This, then, is a sketch of how normative behaviourism is presented and applied in Chapter 3, though only of these two things. Perhaps even more important is the extent to which this form of political philosophy can be defended against the objections it will inevitably encounter. The five most important of these objections are as follows: (1) Isn't normative behaviourism just bad mentalism in disguise? (2) Given that normative behaviourism appears to imply that everything human beings do is fine, how on earth are we supposed to read off normativity from behaviour when there is so much crazy variety to that behaviour? (3) Isn't normative behaviourism a bit too conservative? After all, we would never have produced social-liberal-democracy without radical change and upheaval, so why stop now? (4) Why privilege as universals what appear to be parochial Western ideas? (5) How can you read off expressed preferences from what are in fact collective dynamics, especially given the twin difficulties of collective action problems and unintended consequences?

Unfortunately, in the context of a synopsis, there is not enough room to deal with even one of these objections properly. It will simply have to suffice to say that normative behaviourism is not mentalism in disguise; does not imply that everything human beings do is fine; is not overly conservative; does not unduly generalise Western ideals; and can deal with both collective action problems and unintended consequences. That assertion by itself, of course, is very unlikely to convince you, which is why, if you want to be truly convinced, or indeed truly convinced that I am wrong about all of this, you will have to read right up until the end of this last chapter.

Who Am I to Say This?

It might be wise to address one last point before embarking on the full version of this argument. This point is the fact that the argument described represents a rather grand topic for a relatively junior scholar. Or, alternatively put, you might say it's a rather pretentious book given the brevity of my own writing career to date. It would be hard to deny the fairness of that point, for it is true that I have written, taught, presented, and especially published relatively little compared to some of those with whom I engage in the pages that follow. It would also be hard given that I am not someone who can claim to have been thinking about this question of method for the past fifty years of a long and scholarly life, even if it has had my attention, one way or another, for the past fifteen. Sadly enough, and unlike several of the scholars whose work I admire the most, I have not been holed up in some oak-panelled room in All Souls College for decade upon decade, whittling and whittling away at the questions this book addresses.

So why the big topic? Why say to so many hard-working, brilliant, and above all intellectually experienced philosophers, whose work I continue to admire, that they should stop doing things their way and start doing things my way? One response here, I think, is simply to say what many philosophers have been right to say over the years, which is that of the many things we can choose in life, we cannot choose what to believe. We can, of course, change what we believe through reasoning about it, and exposing ourselves to new arguments, but if, having undertaken such reasoning and exposure, one happens to believe a certain proposition or set of propositions, then there is really not much more to be done. I could no more adopt the belief that I am wrong about my subject on the basis that I am in no position to hold forth on such things than I could adopt the belief that God exists on the basis that it would make me happy if I did. The thing is, if I am right about political philosophy – if I am right, for instance, that it would be pointless to try and systematise my various intuitions and considered judgements into one unimpeachable theory of justice (or legitimacy, or animal rights, etc.) – then there is little point in my trying to contribute to its endeavours in the way that those endeavours tend to be practised. If I believe, that is, that this activity is relatively futile (and what I mean by *relatively* will come out towards the end of the book) then really I have no option but to either say nothing, and leave the academy, or say what I have chosen to say (though not *chosen* to believe) in the chapters that follow this overview.

Do also consider here that it is hardly careerist ambition that drives one towards the topic and argument described. One is hardly likely to be published anytime soon in *Ethics* or *Philosophy and Public Affairs* when writing about how flawed the standard model of enquiry adopted in those journals really is. Clearly, things would be much easier for me, and perhaps everybody else, if I just *thought something different* about my subject. But again, the fact that things would go better for me if I believed something else is not a fact that can change those beliefs. It ultimately does not matter that I might be able to take out a bigger mortgage, buy a bigger house, drive a better car, take more holidays abroad, and perhaps even have more children if I believed something else. What matters is that I do believe something else, and also that that something matters, because, after all, if I did not, and if *it* did not, why on earth would I want to stick around in political philosophy?

What could you avoid reading?

I have always appreciated it when authors take the trouble to point out the bits of their book that you might *not* want to read. For example, I should have said earlier, had you wanted to speed things up, that you probably could have managed without reading the preceding synopses, given the duplication of their content in the chapters that follow. Sorry about that. Hopefully they helped all the same. Going forward, though, my advice is quite simple. If you already accept that political philosophy is unable to settle its central arguments, and would like to know why, please jump to Chapter 2. If you already accept this inability *and* have no interest in its causes, but would like to see an alternative way of doing things, please jump to Chapter 3. If, however, you have no interest in any of these three things, and also no interest in any of the many topics picked out by the extensive and, I hope, easy to navigate table of contents, then there is little I can do for you. Perhaps you were after a different Floyd?

1   Symptom: Interminability

1.1   Overview

This chapter moves through three stages. First, I argue that political philosophy should be defined in terms of what I call its organising question – *how should we live?* Second, I ask whether contemporary political philosophers have produced a *convincing* and *meaningful* answer to this question. Third, having concluded that they have not, I introduce what I call the *impossibility thesis*, which is the idea that political philosophy seems both impossible to do *and* impossible to avoid. In short, I argue that it is impossible to do because arguments over the right answer to our subject's organising question appear rationally interminable, and impossible to avoid because we are always living, whether we like it or not, one or other answer to that question.

1.2   Three Questions: OQ, FQ, GQ

As a starting point, consider the following two ways of defining political philosophy. First, we could define it in terms of an abstract *concept* such as justice, power, or authority. On this account, which begins in the world of ideas, the task for political philosophers would be to tell us what justice is and requires, or how power ought to be regulated, or what justifies one person or institution claiming authority over another. Second, we could define it in terms of a concrete *institution*, such as the state, government, or constitution. On this account, which begins in the world of contemporary politics, the task would be to draw a picture of an ideal state or government, or to tell us how existing constitutions ought to be amended, and so on.

Both approaches have their attractions and adherents. Rawls, for example, appears to adopt the first when he tells us that 'justice' is the first virtue of political institutions,[1] as does Berlin when he tells us both that political philosophy is about the 'ends of life'[2] and that it concerns 'men's relationships to each other and to their institutions'.[3] Blackburn, in a similar vein, writes of the centrality of 'relations between the collective and the individual',[4] whilst Williams, more specifically, writes that political philosophy centres on 'distinctively political concepts', such as 'power' and 'legitimation'.[5]

Some expressions of this approach, however, are rather more question-begging, just insofar as they define our subject in terms of something that seems to be just as ambiguous as the phrase 'political philosophy', namely, 'politics'. Strauss, for example, does this when he defines it in terms of 'the attempt truly to know both the nature of political things and the right, or the good, political order',[6] as does De-Shalit, who claims that political philosophy is philosophy about politics,[7] and Quinton, who holds that it involves conceptual analysis of *whatever* key terms (power, freedom, authority, equality, etc.) appear to be central to both past philosophy *and* contemporary political science.[8]

What, then, of the second approach? Examples of this are even easier to find. Consider, for instance, Swift's claim that:

Political philosophy asks how the state should act, what moral principles should govern the way it treats its citizens and what kind of social order it should seek to create. As those 'shoulds' suggest, it is a branch of moral philosophy, interested in justification, in what the state ought (and ought not) to do.[9]

This focus on the *state* is shared by all sorts of scholars, regardless of their normative bent. Nozick, for example – the arch-libertarian, in contrast to Swift's luck-egalitarianism – writes that moral philosophy sets limits for

---

[1] J. Rawls, *A Theory of Justice* (Cambridge, MA: Harvard University Press, 1971), 3.

[2] I. Berlin, 'The Pursuit of the Ideal', in *The Proper Study of the Mankind* (New York: Farrar, Straus, and Giroux, 1998), 1. Berlin uses this phrase again in R. Jahanbegloo, *Conversations with Isaiah Berlin* (London: Prentice Hall, 1992).

[3] I. Berlin, *Political Ideas in the Romantic Age: Their Rise and Influence on Modern Thought* (London: Chatto and Windus, 2006), 12.

[4] S. Blackburn, *Oxford Dictionary of Philosophy* (Oxford: Oxford University Press, 2005), 282.

[5] B. Williams, *In the Beginning Was the Deed: Realism and Moralism in Political Argument* (Princeton, NJ: Princeton University Press, 2005), 77.

[6] L. Strauss, *What Is Political Philosophy: And Other Studies* (Chicago, IL: University of Chicago Press, 1988), 12. Though note that in a separate essay he uses 'just' instead of 'good'. See L. Strauss, 'Political Philosophy and History', *Journal of the History of Ideas*, 10:1 (1949), 30.

[7] A. De-Shalit, *Power to the People: Teaching Political Philosophy in Skeptical Times* (Lanham, MD: Lexington Books, 2006).

[8] A. Quinton, *Political Philosophy* (Oxford: Oxford University Press, 1967), 1–18.

[9] A. Swift, *Political Philosophy: A Beginners' Guide for Students and Politicians* (Cambridge: Polity Press), 5.

its political sibling just insofar as it sets limits for the conduct and scope of the state, and also that the fundamental question for political philosophy is whether there should be any state at all.[10] Others, in turn, say that our focus should be the *government*. Plamenatz, for example, defines our subject as 'systematic thinking about the purposes of government',[11] whilst Miller calls it 'an investigation into the nature, causes, and effects of good and bad government'.[12] And consider Pettit: he adopts both routes when he says not just that he follows Plamenatz's definition, but also that the subject is about the evaluation of *both* government and state.[13]

In parallel to the conceptual approach, there are also institutional scholars who widen their definition of our subject by resting it, not on a distinct institution like the state or government, but rather on the more general notion of *politics* or *public affairs*. Scanlon, for example, takes this route when he claims that political philosophy is about the 'standards by which political, legal, and economic institutions should be assessed',[14] as does Matravers, who suggests that our central question is 'what political practices and institutions are justified and ought to be established?'.[15] Or consider, for still more open-endedness, Bevir's description of our subject as 'the more or less deliberate reflection on the nature of public affairs and collective decision making',[16] or even McAffee's claim that it is a 'field for developing new ideals, practices, and justifications for how political institutions and practices should be organized and reconstructed'.[17]

Notice something very interesting about these claims: the fact that our concept/institution distinction has become steadily more blurred, given that it seems difficult, with some of these authors, to know whether they have in mind a vague and potentially timeless concept, such as 'relationships of power between human beings', or a more particular, empirically sourced abstraction, such as 'the existing functions and behaviour of

---

[10] R. Nozick, *Anarchy, State, and Utopia* (New York: Basic Books, 1974), 3, 4, 6.

[11] J. Plamenatz, 'The Use of Political Theory', *Political Studies*, 8 (1960), 37.

[12] D. Miller, *A Very Short Introduction to Political Philosophy* (Oxford: Oxford University Press), 2.

[13] P. Pettit, *Contemporary Political Theory* (London: Prentice Hall, 1991), 1.

[14] T. M. Scanlon, *The Difficulty of Tolerance* (Cambridge: Cambridge University Press, 2003), 1. He has also said, in an interview given to Harry Kreisler in 2007, that 'It has to do with our relations with each other that are mediated through the institutions we share.' The transcript for this can be found at: http://globetrotter.berkeley.edu/people7/Scanlon/scanlon-con0.html.

[15] M. Matravers, 'Twentieth-Century Political Philosophy', in D. Moran (Ed.) *The Routledge Companion to Twentieth Century Philosophy* (London: Routledge), 901.

[16] M. Bevir, *Encyclopaedia of Political Theory* (London: Sage, 2010), xxxiii.

[17] N. McAffee, 'Feminist Political Philosophy', in the *Stanford Encyclopedia of Philosophy*, available at http://plato.stanford.edu/entries/feminism-political/political philosophy.

modern states'. As a result, we might start to wonder: is this *really* our definitional choice – between a concept or set of concepts and an institution or, presumably, set of institutions? Perhaps not, given that we might easily define the problem of how the state should act *as* the problem of justice, and thus re-describe what both Swift and Nozick are doing as the study of *that concept*. Or, in reverse, if we say that Berlin's and Quinton's concepts are in truth problems that have been *derived*, though *abstracted*, from real political life, in what way is that different from saying that they are ultimately concerned with how existing states should (1) be redesigned, and (2) act, following that redesign?

With this problem in mind, consider a further definition offered by Wolff. He writes that political philosophy is primarily about the distribution of goods (who gets what?) and the distribution of power (says who?).[18] On the face of it, this looks like a conceptual definition. We could, for example, say that the key concepts are 'goods' and 'power', or, more abstractly, that questions about the distribution of goods and power are really questions represented by the concepts of, respectively, justice (who gets what goods?) and legitimacy (who decides who gets what goods?). But this is not our only option. We could also take an institutional route, and say that Wolff is really starting with the question of how *existing* processes or institutions should operate – which means in this case the economy and the state. What, then, does that mean for our dichotomy? It might mean that there are grey areas on the edges of both approaches, which would be acceptable. Or it might mean that the dichotomy as a whole is confused. In that case we seem to be long on suggestions, but short on clarity.

Put differently, our problem so far is that both approaches, by blending the descriptive with the normative, appear to end up in much the same place. This becomes especially vivid if we imagine the following pair of scholars. The first says that she is beginning with an *existing institution or practice*, such as the state or politics, and then asking not how those things *do* work, but how they *should* work. The second says that he simply wants to know what justice *is*. But consider: if the first wants to know how politics *should* work, and the second defines justice as the value that *should* guide politics, what real difference is there between the two? Are they not *both* asking how politics should work? Are they not *both* asking what justice is?

Perhaps we can solve this problem by looking at definitions that list a number of 'problems' for our subject, and that combine both abstract concepts and concrete institutions. Cohen, for example, directs our attention to what he takes to be three distinct issues – what justice is,

---

[18] J. Wolff, *An Introduction to Political Philosophy* (Oxford: Oxford University Press, 2006).

what the state should do, and how social states rank normatively[19] –
whilst Waldron argues that to this list we should add the further question
of exactly which institutions we should adopt within whatever counts as
a generally just state (A bicameral legislature? An independent judiciary?
Devolution? Federalism? And so on).[20] Or consider Rawls, once again,
who, in one of his later works, agrees with Waldron that there are four
defining issues, whilst disagreeing about their nature. He writes that
political philosophy concerns: (1) agreement – finding a basis for, if not
philosophical, then at least political agreement between different sides in
a divisive moral dispute; (2) orientation – helping to place and direct us, in
terms of principles, within our own political environment; (3) reconciliation – calming our frustrations within the right political order by showing
us the rationality of our governing institutions; and (4) realistic utopia –
probing the limits of practical possibility, which means finding out what
a just society would be under unavoidable conditions, such as the 'fact of
reasonable pluralism'.[21]

Do these suggestions help us? Maybe, but if so, they also create at least
one new puzzle: How are we to decide what's *in* and what's *out*?
The solution to this puzzle might lie in a practice that is more normally
identified with the study of the *history* of political philosophy, namely,
interpretation. Pettit, for example – who earlier followed Plamenatz's
institutional definition – writes in a later work of the task of working
critically with the existing languages of political discussion and legitimation of our time,[22] whilst Walzer once wrote that 'another way of doing
philosophy is to interpret to one's fellow citizens the world of meanings we
share'.[23] Broadly speaking, we might say, the task for political philosophy,
at least as expressed here, and despite the differences between these two
thinkers, is the task of working with pre-existing and contemporary political concepts and values in order to repackage and then sell them back to
those to whom they are already somewhat familiar.

And not just for these two. Consider also Dworkin who, despite his own
deviations from both Walzer and Pettit, certainly shares their belief in the
centrality of interpretation. In his work, the fundamental task for political

---

[19] G. A. Cohen, *On the Currency of Egalitarian Justice? And Other Essays in Political Philosophy*
(Princeton, NJ: Princeton University Press, 2011), 228.
[20] J. Waldron, '*Political* Political Theory: An Inaugural Lecture', *The Journal of Political
Philosophy*, 21:1 (2013), 1–23.
[21] J. Rawls, *Justice as Fairness: A Restatement* (Cambridge, MA: Harvard University Press,
2001), 1–4.
[22] P. Pettit, *Republicanism: A Theory of Freedom and Government* (Oxford: Oxford University
Press, 1997), 2–3.
[23] M. Walzer, *Spheres of Justice: A Defense of Pluralism and Equality* (New York: Basic Books,
1983), xiv.

philosophers is to analyse, not just the existing political values of our time, but also our wider moral and even aesthetic values, in order to find interpretations of each of them that avoid conflicts with all of the rest.[24] So: in all three cases it seems that rather than starting from putatively timeless concepts, or particular concrete institutions, the defining task here for political philosophy is simply one of working with the whole spread of existing concepts and institutional understandings found in a particular context in order to see what tweaking and remoulding of that spread generates the best set of guiding principles given, presumably, whatever turns out to be the best interpretation of our local and contemporary political goals.

Or is it? The question to ask here is: how exactly are these authors identifying the relevant 'understandings', 'values', and so on? Ultimately, there are only two ways. Either we are interpreting views that invoke particular concepts – justice, legitimacy, politics, etc. – or we are interpreting views that invoke particular institutions – the state, government, law, etc. As a result, we are back where we started. Even if, for example, we say we are only interested in *local* understandings of politics, we still need some *prior* concept of politics to identify the relevant understandings. None of which, of course, is a problem for these authors, provided that they are happy with the concept(s) or institutions(s) they use to organise their material, but how about us? What concepts or institutions should *we* be happy with?

There might just be an interpretive way of answering even this question, given that, for some scholars, the way to define political philosophy is to define it as nothing more or less than whatever *other people* have studied in recent times under the rubric of either 'political philosophy' or – a subject that is generally though not always taken to be the same thing – 'political theory'.[25] Examples of this approach include Wolin's *Politics and Vision*, which identifies the subject with the topics of its great books,[26] textbooks by the likes of Held and Kymlicka, and edited collections by White and Moon, as well as Leopold and Stears.[27] In addition, it

---

[24] R. Dworkin, *Justice for Hedgehogs* (London: Harvard University Press, 2011).

[25] Consider, for example, how the journal *Political Theory* describes itself as 'an international journal of political *philosophy*'.

[26] S. Wolin, *Politics and Vision: Political Philosophy from the Classic Problems of the Greeks to the Contemporary Problems of the 'Organization Man'* (London: George Allen & Unwin Ltd, 1960), 1–27. Note that although Wolin picks out several patterns and recurring themes within what he calls a 'tradition of discourse', and even at one point something that could function as an extremely vague definition – 'reflection on matters that concern the community as a whole' – the key point remains that he both (1) defines the subject as the sum of what people have contributed under its remit and (2) lacks a precise idea of that remit.

[27] D. Held, *Political Theory Today* (Cambridge: Polity, 1991); W. Kymlicka, *Contemporary Political Philosophy: An Introduction* (Oxford: Oxford University Press, 2002); D. Leopold

also includes more rarefied treatments, some of which are more historical – such as Gunnell's *The Descent of Political Theory* – and some of which blend the historical and analytic – such as Vincent's *The Nature of Political Theory*.[28] For the authors of these books, the 'problem' of defining political philosophy, or even politics, is apparently avoided altogether, as they define the subject in terms of what other people have defined in those terms, even if *those* people, in turn, simply defined things as they saw fit.

Now, though, we have a new problem. Just as I had to make a choice about which books to include in this discussion, these authors have to decide which further texts are, for them, appropriately worthy or canonical. As a result, we have a worry about regression (where does the relying on others end?) that soon turns into a worry about power and privilege (who does it end with?). And it's not hard to guess what sort of power and privilege will be involved. Once we start defining political philosophy as whatever prominent and influential individuals have defined it as, we are very likely to be invoking people from just a small set of universities, who in turn are likely to fit a particular profile when it comes to gender, race, class, language, and so on – and especially so the more we work back through the history of such works. These are the confident individuals who, blessed with the right publishing platform, and enjoying an attentive audience, simply define the subject as they see fit, and without reliance on the further definitions of others.

But perhaps that is not a fatal worry. Perhaps, that is, it is enough to say there that people from particular universities are, somehow, people with the best expertise, or judgement, when it comes to such things – and we can say that whilst still wishing for, and working towards, a world where such expertise is more widely distributed, or at least where membership of such institutions is as meritocratic as possible. Nevertheless, there would still be a deeper worry that we have yet to consider. This deeper worry relates to the fact that, when browsing through these texts, we are soon reminded of Nietzsche's claim that only things with no history can be defined,[29] given that we soon find ourselves considering *no end* of concepts and institutions, whilst becoming ever more unsure regarding, not just what unites this variety of arguments, but also whether we should

---

and M. Stears, *Political Theory: Methods and Approaches* (Oxford: Oxford University Press, 2008); and S. K. White and J. D. Moon, *What Is Political Theory?* (London: Sage, 2004).

[28] J. G. Gunnell, *The Descent of Political Theory: The Genealogy of an American Vocation* (London: University of Chicago Press, 1993); D. Held, *Political Theory Today* (Cambridge: Polity, 1991); and A. Vincent, *The Nature of Political Theory* (Oxford: Oxford University Press, 2004).

[29] F. Nietzsche, *Genealogy of Morality* (Cambridge: Cambridge University Press, 2011), 53.

despair at or be cheered by (as is the view of most of these authors) the sheer scale of that variety.

This is where my own addition to this debate comes in. My view, as encouraged by the 'philosophy' half of our subject's title, is that we *should* despair at such variety. And indeed, we should despair not just at this latter, more descriptive and historical approach, with all the variety it brings, but also at all the conceptual, institutional, and hybrid multi-problem approaches considered so far. Why is this? Broadly speaking, because (1) single-concept and single-institution approaches seem *excessively narrow*, excluding what we want to include, whilst (2) multi-problem approaches, and especially interpretive multi-problem approaches, seem to *lack coherence*, including disparate items of no clear connection. We ask in the first case – is there not *more* to our subject? – and worry about how we are supposed to know what the best political principles are if we do not know what makes those principles *political*, given that a focus on, say, justice or the state might leave us with a worse set of principles (in various ways) than those produced by, say, a focus on legitimacy and global governance. We ask in the second – surely something has to unite these various problems, as well as the variety of approaches that study them, in order for them to all add up to just *one* subject? – and worry about how we are supposed to identify political philosophy with its canonical texts if we do not know what makes those books *count* as exemplars of that subject.

To compound these problems, consider further that many of the approaches that strike us as too *narrow* also smuggle particular values into the definitions themselves. In these cases it seems as though arguments *in* political philosophy are discretely corrupting arguments *about* it. Berlin is guilty of this when he claims that political theory's very existence is predicated on the truth of value-pluralism,[30] whilst Rawls writes not just of the centrality of agreement and justice to political philosophy, but also the so-called facts of 'reasonable disagreement' or 'reasonable pluralism', suggesting from the off that both people and their existing values are to be treated in what many would regard as an excessively *deferential* fashion.[31] And consider finally Larmore, who claims, with echoes of both of these two thinkers, that what distinguishes political philosophy from the apparently 'wider' discipline of moral philosophy *is* this very starting point of trying to find political agreement between people whose rival moral conceptions are judged in advance as incommensurable, and thus beyond the reach of rational argument.[32]

---

[30] I. Berlin, 'Does Political Theory Still Exist?', in *The Proper Study of Mankind*, 63–66.

[31] J. Rawls, *Political Liberalism* (New York: Columbia University Press, 2005).

[32] C. Larmore, 'What Is Political Philosophy?', *Journal of moral philosophy*, 10:3 (2013), 276–306.

So: what we need, I think, is a definition that includes what we want to include whilst excluding what we want to exclude. I therefore propose that we define our subject from now on, not in terms of a concept or institution, or even in terms of a set of problems, but rather in terms of a single question: *how should we live?*

This approach has several merits. First, it is sufficiently exclusive to be distinguished from similar definitions I would offer of both the moral philosopher's enquiry – 'how should *I* live?' – and the social scientist's (including the political scientist's) – 'how *do* we live?'. Second, it is sufficiently inclusive as an account of political philosophy to avoid being identified with any one approach to or problem within it. For example, unlike 'what sort of government ought we to have?', it avoids the anarchist's response, 'why have any *government* at all?'; unlike 'what is the ideal form of human organisation?', it avoids the communitarian response 'why just *one* ideal form for everyone?'; and, unlike 'what does morality require of politics?', it avoids the Hobbesian response, 'why not treat *rationality*, rather than morality, as our guide to normative political enquiry (and perhaps order or happiness, rather than justice, as the object of political design)?'.

This mixture of precision and inclusiveness becomes even clearer when we consider the flexibility of interpretation inherent to each of our question's parts. The 'how' and 'live' of 'how should we live?' are open to whatever form of collective regulation (or deregulation) political philosophers might come to recommend – state, global government, anarchist commune, and so on; the 'should', as noted, is open to being a 'should' of morality or rationality; whilst the 'we', finally, is open to being a 'we' of all human beings, or of the members of a single faith, community, locality, nation, and so on. As a result, we manage to maintain a strong degree of clarity (meaning that we can distinguish our subject from others) without as yet ruling out any of those approaches to political philosophy that we would not want to prematurely exclude (meaning that we have so far stayed faithful to the subject as it has been practised to date).

There is also a further merit to this question-as-definition, which is that when it is asked, it soon connects us to a *second* (and even more fundamental) enquiry. This second enquiry emerges as soon as one tries to address the first. Consider here that if we ask of a political philosopher 'how should we live?', the way she will normally respond, after protesting that she cannot tell you how to live every last aspect of your life, will be to say something of the form 'well, I do think your life ought to be lived in accordance with (or governed by, regulated by, constrained by, etc.) such and such principles' (say, liberal principles). And in turn, if we now ask 'why those principles and not another set?', she will then respond 'because these principles correspond to some further set of principles or values' (say, utilitarian principles). This sequence is crucial, though it does raise an important question: how exactly should we accommodate it within our 'definition', if it is true that the second question is always triggered by whatever answer one provides to the first?

The way to accommodate it is simple. All we need to do is say, yes, there are always two questions. First: *how should we live?* Second: *why should we live that way and not another?* This is hardly a problem. All it means is that, although it remains true that the *subject matter* of political philosophy is captured by the first question, it is also true, as a matter of necessity, that any answer to that question will require support from whatever answer we give to the second. As a result, whilst we can still, I think, understand everything written under the rubric of political philosophy (or theory) as either an *answer* or a *contribution to an answer* to the question 'how should we live?', we always have to remember that the real meat of that question lies in the still further question required of any answer provided to the first. I shall therefore call these two enquiries, from here on in, political philosophy's *organising* and *foundational* questions (or, for short, OQ and FQ): the first because it usefully organises the subject matter of political philosophy under one simple heading, and the second because it concerns those foundations required of any answer provided to the first.

One might object here, though, by saying that the question should not be 'how should we live?', but rather 'how should we live *together*?'. Barry, for example, comes close to proposing the latter question as a definition of political philosophy when he writes that 'justice as impartiality' is an answer to the problem of 'how to live together',[33] as does Gibbard when he writes, somewhat more confusingly (from our point of view), that moral thinking in general is 'thinking how to live with each other'[34] (and note: he also defines 'ethical theory' later on as 'planning how to live with each other'[35]). This choice, between these two questions, is admittedly a tricky one, but perhaps also an unimportant one. After all, most of the value of what I have said so far lies in the argument I have given for, potentially, *either* definition. Just as is the case when it comes to OQ and FQ, there is always a substantial difference between a conclusion and the case one makes for it. Consider, for example, how disappointing Plato's

---

[33] B. Barry, *Justice as Impartiality* (Oxford: Oxford University Press, 1995), 77.
[34] A. Gibbard, *Reconciling Our Aims: In Search of Bases for Ethics* (Oxford: Oxford University Press, 2008), 30. James Rachels follows a similar route for moral philosophy in the popular teaching text *The Elements of Moral Philosophy* (New York: McGraw-Hill, 2010), 1.
[35] A. Gibbard, *Reconciling Our Aims*, 59.

Republic would have been if he had done nothing more than write down the sentence 'justice *does* pay for the individual'.

Nevertheless, why *have* I stuck with the first question (i.e. the one without 'together')? The key reason is simply that, in response to the alternative question used by Barry – and following some of the problems of other approaches noted earlier – one might easily say 'why live *together* at all?' After all, what if it turns out that the best life for human beings involves them living apart, with perhaps only sporadic meetings for the purposes of mating? Now, that might *seem* crazy, given that it appears to identify our core political ambitions with the life of male grizzly bears, but that would only make it *bad* political philosophy, not something *other than* political philosophy.[36] It seems, then, that 'together' gives us one too many clauses, a point that becomes even clearer if we imagine substituting 'live' for phrases such as 'common existence' or 'collective regulation', both of which I use at various points later on in this book. Again, such phrases assume too much *about* political philosophy to be put into a definition, before arguments *within it* have even started.

Note, though, that I am still, and deliberately, not calling my question political philosophy's *defining* question, but rather its *organising* question, even if I have insisted, rather confusingly, that the subject should be defined *in terms of* that question (or at least primarily in terms of that question, given the further existence of the *foundational* question). So what does that mean? In simple terms, it means that the organising question is where the subject begins, though not where it ends. Nevertheless, it might also mean that we need to discuss, in depth, the differences between organising and defining questions. Or that I need to explain at length that whilst the former offers a useful starting point for a subject, it cannot achieve the level of comprehensiveness achievable with definitions of at least some, rather more easily defined academic subjects. Or that we need to discuss the relative merits of question-based and non-question-based definitions. Or even that we should just take one big step back and discuss the definition of 'definition', before then moving on to ask, presumably, what is a *good* definition of *good definition*.

---

[36] Later on I argue under the idea of the 'impossibility thesis' that political philosophy, as a subject, is impossible to avoid, given that it is impossible for human beings to avoid having some form of interaction with other, and thus adhering to some or other kind of political system. I leave it to readers to judge as to whether that counts as an argument *in* or *about* political philosophy, but either way, it does not affect what I say here. My point here is simply that, because we might want to minimise our interactions, the clause 'together' is too strong for an all-encompassing definition.

You can see the problem here. For one thing, it is simply not true that in the best of all possible worlds we would explore every last issue to its limits. After all, if in the best of all possible worlds, everything will be all right in the end – as Dr Pangloss tells us – it cannot be right to head off on every last tangent, as then we will never get to the end, and thus never make things alright. More to the point though, this regress illustrates something important about the challenge of defining our subject, and indeed any subject of similar nature and complexity, which is that solving the problem of *question-begging-ness* can only ever be a matter of *degree*, given that, although the problem can be made less severe, it cannot be avoided altogether. Of course, we don't want to define our subject in terms of something that tells us as little as the term *political philosophy* itself (e.g. politics), or identify it with a series of things that appear to lack any unity (e.g. an historical list of texts), but even so, we only aim with this question-as-definition to make things clearer and justifiably narrower than they would be if we had *only* the phrase 'political philosophy', without as yet trying to illustrate its fruitfulness by arguing for a particular answer to it, given that that would be doing, rather than defining, political philosophy. The key thing in all of this, then, is still that OQ marks out the point where our subject begins, without dictating where it goes from there. In doing so, it provides a common starting point for our arguments, as well as a common framework with which to organise the arguments of others. That, I think, should be more than enough for our purposes here.

So, rather than exploring further the question of definitions, or indeed the definition of a question, I now want to do something else, which is to introduce a third and *final* question. This question, which I call the *guiding* question, will lead us through both the rest of this chapter and, in a more general way, the second and third. It runs as follows: is it possible to provide a convincing and meaningful answer to OQ?

This means we have the following three questions to bear in mind:

The organising question (OQ):	*How should we live?*
The foundational question (FQ):	*Why should we live that way and not another?*
The guiding question (GQ):	*Is it possible to provide a convincing and meaningful answer to OQ?*

So, what I want to find out in this book, as stated earlier, is whether it is possible to provide a 'convincing and meaningful' answer to the question 'how should we live?', or, if one prefers a more dramatic phrasing, whether it is possible to achieve real success in political philosophy. For now, though, I trust I will be forgiven for sticking with the less dramatic version, particularly given what I take to be the important qualities described by, respectively, 'convincing' and 'meaningful'.

We begin with 'convincing'. By a 'convincing' answer to OQ, I mean something of the form 'most rationally compelling given the epistemological character of both question and subject matter'. What I should like to know is whether or not it is possible to provide an answer to OQ that is, if not demonstrably correct, then at least demonstrably more compelling than all other possible answers. Such an answer would contain not one but two arguments. Because, as explained previously, any convincing answer to OQ requires a convincing answer to FQ, what we need is a convincing argument in favour of one particular answer to FQ (which tells us that we ought to act in accordance with such and such principles) *and* a convincing argument to the effect that this entails one particular answer to OQ (which tells us that this one answer to OQ is exactly what is required by those principles). If an answer to OQ is to be convincing, it must meet both of these criteria.

For example, in order to defend a utilitarian answer to FQ and a liberal answer to OQ, we would need to show both (1) that utilitarianism offers the most convincing set of all available principles and (2) that liberal principles provide the most convincing application of utilitarianism for political life. If an answer to OQ is to be convincing, therefore, it must meet both of these general criteria. But note, by saying 'most convincing', we say only that an argument has to be the *best* of all possible arguments, given the relevant subject matter, and nothing of any more controversial ideas, such as its platonic truth, or correspondence with our considered judgements and intuitions, or legitimacy, or reasonableness, or stability under reflective equilibrium, or contextual justifiability and applicability, and so on. All of which is important given my concern here to separate questions regarding (1) the subject matter of political philosophy, and (2) the structure of arguments within it, from (3) questions regarding the particular merits of all the varying arguments that could and have been made within that structure.

By 'meaningful', in turn, I mean an answer that is (1) applicable in feasible circumstances, (2) correct for a significant number of co-existing people, and (3) selective amongst (at least) the various well-known templates for an ideal political constitution (anarchist commune, social democracy, cosmopolitan global government, etc.). A meaningful answer to OQ is thus an answer suitable for application to the world as we know it. Although we do not require of an answer that it could be implemented within the next few years – given existing political preferences, existing distributions of political membership, and existing distributions of power – we do require that it could be implemented in conceivable political circumstances. And note that by inserting this criterion, I do not mean to rule out timeless or universal principles of justice. All I ask is that principles of justice, if they are to be timeless or universal, be realisable in realistic political circumstances. Some readers will perhaps misread me here, particularly in light of the current wrangles over ideal versus non-ideal theory, and moralism versus realism,[37] yet all I mean to rule out from the beginning is political visions whose attraction relies, for instance, on human beings gaining the power of telepathy, or losing the capacity for speech, or becoming immortal, and so on and so forth. Political philosophers are human beings proposing political principles for other human beings, not human beings proposing principles for aliens, or indeed aliens proposing principles for human beings (despite it sometimes appearing that way – or would aliens proposing principles for aliens be yet more apt?).

So, although it would be *true* to say that what I want to establish is whether or not some particular answer to OQ can be judged *the right one*, it is important, in order to avoid misunderstandings, that I use, instead, the terms 'convincing' and 'meaningful'. But there is also a further reason for this, which is that an answer to OQ could be either (a) convincing and meaningless or (b) unconvincing and meaningful. We could, for instance, say that we ought to live in a feudal monarchy because then there would be more jousting tournaments. This is a meaningful but unconvincing argument. Alternatively, we could say that human beings ought to regulate their collective existence in such a way as to ensure that each and every subject of the political order is guaranteed a regular supply of oxygen. This would be a convincing answer but not a meaningful one. It would not be meaningful because it would not distinguish for us between any of the most influential and competing visions provided in the history of political argument. It would not, for example, tell us whether we should have our oxygen delivered by philosopher-guardians or liberal parliaments, in states or in empires, as free citizens or as royal subjects. And consider finally, we might say that the members of culture X – where X is comprised of twenty members, each of them living in a different part of the world – ought to regulate their collective political life in accordance with the established dictates of that culture (as understood, for instance, by a sacred text or long-standing conventions). Again, whilst this answer to OQ might, according to a number of plausible answers to FQ, be a convincing one, the number of co-existing people (people who

---

[37] See, for example, M. Sleat, 'Realism, Liberalism and Non-ideal Theory or, Are There Two Ways to Do Realistic Political Theory?', *Political Studies*, 64(1) (2016), 27–41.

actually *have* a collective political existence) to whom it applies would be too small (in this case 0) for it to provide us with a meaningful answer (in this instance because it would fail to tell those individuals what sort of a political regime they ought to construct and maintain with those who do live around them).

This, I think, is where my elaboration of 'convincing' and 'meaningful' has to stop, if only because it is impossible to provide any substantially better account of what I mean by either term in advance of an examination of such arguments as have already been given both for and against particular answers to OQ and FQ (just as it would be impossible to provide a complete account of what I mean by a 'substantially better account' in the absence of an example of what I take to be one ...). We can adapt a line from Rousseau here and say: only in the light of what has been argued, should we consider what can be argued.[38] That is, it is only when we have seen what can be said for and against various political arrangements that we shall know what is to count as a convincing case in any arrangement's favour, which is why my next task will be to examine what have been deemed in recent times the most convincing group of answers to political philosophy's organising and fundamental questions (and remember throughout: any convincing answer to OQ will require a convincing answer to FQ in order to be convincing itself).

My plan from now on, then, will be to examine some of the most prominent arguments in political philosophy in order to see just how convincing and meaningful are their answers to OQ. But let's be open-minded here. Consider in what follows (a) that a potentially convincing answer to OQ might come supplied with an unconvincing answer to FQ, and (b) that, generally speaking, normative arguments in political philo-sophy have been framed as matters of either rationality *or* morality (or both), as applicable to all human beings *or* some select group thereof, and as concerned with every single political topic *or* just a very basic constitu-tion. And, even more importantly, when examining these answers, we need to be alive to three possibilities: (1) that it is possible to give a compelling answer to OQ *and* that that answer has already been given; (2) that it is possible to give a compelling answer to this question *even though* that answer has not been given; (3) that it is *impossible* to give a compelling answer to OQ. That is, we might find when we come to look at these debates that a highly convincing and meaningful answer is already out there; or that although one is not already out there, there is good

---

[38] The 'original', in my English translation, reads 'in the light of what has been done, let us consider what can be done'. J. J. Rousseau, *The Social Contract* (London: Penguin, 1968), 136.

reason to think that one could be developed; or that there is neither an existing answer nor any apparent prospect of one being produced.

The only problem is where to begin. But if in doubt, says the conservative, go with convention, which is what I intend to do here. As is so often the case in books in our subject, and even more the case in university courses, I intend to start my search, not with *Jean-Jacques*, from whom I borrowed a moment ago, but *John 'Jack'* – that is, for those unmoved by my shaky pun, not Rousseau, but Rawls. By just about any measure, Rawls' *A Theory of Justice* is the most influential of all recent works in political philosophy, and it is by considering the well-known answers to OQ and FQ provided therein that I will begin to answer the guiding question introduced earlier. Nevertheless, although this is where I want to start, it is not where I intend to dwell. Veteran readers of political philosophy will be relieved to learn that I plan on only briefly exploring Rawls' celebrated treatise through the medium of my questions OQ and FQ, before then doing similar work as regards a number of his influential rivals. My goal at first is thus simply to juxtapose in one simple format as many recent and famous attempts at providing a convincing answer to OQ as possible, and with as much concision as the subject matter will bear. Breadth matters a great deal more than depth at this point in our enquiry, as should become clear over the course of what follows.

1.3   Rawls and a Few of His Rivals

Rawls' answer to OQ is called *Justice as Fairness*, and it is as simple as it is familiar:

[1] Each person is to have an equal right to the most extensive total system of equal basic liberties compatible with a similar system of liberty for all. [2] Social and economic inequalities are to be arranged so that they are both: (a) to the greatest benefit of the least advantaged ... and (b) attached to offices and positions open to all under conditions of fair equality of opportunity'.[39]

So, Rawls wants freedom for everyone, as much equal opportunity as possible, and only so much economic inequality as will work to improve the condition of society's worst off. He also wants us to prioritise freedom over equality of opportunity, and equality of opportunity over the improvement of the worst off, in the event that there is any conflict between the three ambitions. Clearly then there is a lot that can be said in favour of this vision, and thus a lot that can be said as part of an answer to FQ, including the obvious point that it promises such *prima facie* good

---

[39] J. Rawls, *A Theory of Justice*, 302.

things as freedom (for all), equality (for those of equal merit and application), and utility (for those who find themselves at the bottom of the economic pile), but what else? Crucially, Rawls claims that this set of principles for regulating our common existence is just that set which each of us would choose if we were truly impartial, and thus entirely free of prejudice and personal bias. He tells us that if we were in an imaginary situation he calls 'the original position', and had no knowledge of either our current social and economic standing or our current capabilities and ambitions, then his principles would be the ones that we would pick for how our world ought to be run. So, this is an answer to OQ which delivers freedom, equality, and utility, and which any truly impartial person would choose if given the chance – what more could we want?

Well, according to Robert Nozick, we might want both more and less than Rawls demands. Nozick objects in particular to the idea that wealth ought to be redistributed in order to guarantee the kinds of equality and utility just described, given that it *already belongs* to particular individuals.[40] As long as whatever anybody owns, they only own on account of freely made decisions to trade, invest, work, and give or receive, why on earth should political philosophers and politicians start interfering? If I work hard throughout my life in order to leave a generous inheritance to my children, why would it be just or fair to confiscate some part of that inheritance in order to reduce their chances and comfort in life to the level of the poorest child? And in turn, whilst I am earning that money, why should some part of it be taken away from me to fund greater comfort for those layabouts and the untalented who find themselves at the bottom of the economic heap? For Nozick, taxation from earnings is on a par with forced labour,[41] which is why his proposed answer to OQ is that we live in a 'minimal' or 'night-watchman' state, the only function of which is to ensure that whatever choices we make in life, we make freely – which is to say in the absence of coercion from either other individuals or groups, or from the state at large.[42] But still, why is it *so* important to ensure that nobody has anything taken away from them that they have not chosen to give, even at the cost of society being unable to provide help to those who desperately need it? For Nozick, the bottom line, and thus his central response to FQ, is that human beings have rights, which means that there are just some things which cannot be done to them in the absence of their consent, even in the cause of a greater good.[43] Sure, it would be a wonderful thing if people did freely decide to help each other out, either directly or through charities organised for that purpose, but is

---

[40] R. Nozick, *Anarchy, State, and Utopia*, esp. 198–219.   [41] Ibid., 169.
[42] Ibid., ix, 25–28.   [43] Ibid., ix, 30–32, 166.

it not up to them whether or not they do? After all, no one would force the lazy to work, so why the hard-working to give?[44]

But why *not* force the hard-working to give, says Ronald Dworkin, given that the market value of their work has almost nothing to do with their own endeavours? Without national security, an effective police force and judiciary, a developed infrastructure, and an educated and affluent workforce, just how rich would you be as a result of your particular talent for football, corporate law, banking, or accountancy? For example: if you were born in Sierra Leone, and had a particular talent for developing software or social networking websites, just how likely is it that you would earn the billions which, in Europe or America, you might consider 'naturally' and 'entirely' yours? Yet this is not to say that everything we earn automatically belongs to society, or that wealth should be perfectly equalised across the board.

In contrast to Rawls, Dworkin thinks it crucially important just *why* the worst off *are* the worst off. Is it because of laziness, or a freely chosen gamble, or just brute bad luck? This is why his answer to OQ is that we should live in a state in which inequality is attributable only to freely taken choices, with nobody at the same time allowed to drop below a level that they would have chosen to insure against in advance of knowing just how their life would turn out. But why exactly set things up this way? Clearly part of the appeal is that it marries, on the one hand, personal responsibility, freedom, and merit, and, on the other, impartiality (in the level of social insurance provided), equality (of exposure to risk) and utility (for the worst off). Yet this is not how Dworkin sees it. Being dismissive both of the power of 'impartiality' and of the idea of 'balancing' or 'trading off' different competing ideals, he insists instead that what makes his described state legitimate is that it expresses 'equal concern' for the fate of all its citizens, as shown by the fact that it does its best to ensure that nobody's life is wasted (what he calls the 'principle of equal importance'), whilst also respecting our own responsibility for just how successful we are (what he calls the 'principle of special responsibility').[45] These two aspects of 'equal concern' provide what Dworkin considers two overriding reasons to support it, and thus what seems to be a highly compelling response to FQ.

But it's not all about money in contemporary political theory, or indeed how free and equal we are in our chances of earning it. For the so-called communitarians ('so-called' because they rarely call themselves that – like

---

[44] Ibid., 170.
[45] Dworkin, *Sovereign Virtue: The Theory and Practice of Equality* (Cambridge, MA: Harvard University Press, 2000), 4–7.

most people in academia, they've been labelled by their enemies) what needs to be remembered in all this worrying about liberty and equality is both (a) that there are other political ambitions to be considered and (b) that how one balances even these two things should depend on what kind of society is doing the balancing. Michael Walzer, for instance, stresses that we are social creatures who identify with the wider groups of which we are a part (family, local community, nation, etc.) and who want to see those groups politically protected. We do not want to see a bland, bureaucratic world in which everyone and everywhere looks the same, but rather one in which the 'distinctiveness of cultures and groups' is preserved.[46] And for this to be the case, Walzer tells us, communities ought to distribute different goods, and manage things like equality and liberty, by reference to the local cultural understandings of the goods involved.[47]

And indeed, communities are not just to be preserved for their own sake – because the world is a more interesting place when it includes cultural variety, or because membership of a greater social collective gives meaning to our otherwise empty mortal lives – but also because it is only in stable communities that we can even dream of the kind of liberty and equality discussed by Rawls, Nozick, and Dworkin. As Charles Taylor stresses on the subject of liberty, 'the free individual of the West is only what he is by virtue of the whole society and civilization which brought him to be and which nourishes him'.[48] And as Michael Sandel argues, this time on egalitarian redistribution, '[t]he justification of my sacrifice . . . is not the abstract assurance that unknown others will gain more than I will lose, but the rather more compelling notion that by my efforts I contribute to the realisation of a way of life in which I will take pride and with which my identity is bound'.[49] All of which means that we can take the following positions on OQ and FQ as broadly representative of the communitarian case: We ought to be governed in accordance with the particular character of our community (OQ) because only that way will politics preserve an importance aspect of our identity, as well as ensure that various other goods (liberty, equality, etc.) remain achievable (FQ). And it's not just equality and liberty that have been harnessed in the cause of justifying communitarian government. According to Sandel, for whom 'loss of self-government and . . . erosion of community . . . define the anxiety of the

---

[46] M. Walzer, *Spheres of Justice: A Defense of Pluralism and Equality* (New York: Basic Books, 1983), esp. 39, 62.

[47] Ibid., 6.

[48] C. Taylor, *Philosophy and the Human Sciences: Philosophical Papers*, vol. 2 (Cambridge: Cambridge University Press, 1985), 206.

[49] M. Sandel, *Liberalism and the Limits of Justice* (Cambridge: Cambridge University Press, 1988), 143.

age', there can be no proper *democracy* without citizens who 'identify sufficiently with [their] communities to think and act with a view to the common good'.[50] Or, as Taylor writes, if one wants a society made up of 'autonomous' individuals, one requires the appropriate 'social matrix'.[51]

So, following Rawls' answers to OQ and FQ, we've now picked out a number of libertarian, egalitarian, and communitarian alternatives. What has become clear is that there's a rather long and competing list of things that people want delivered in politics, including liberty, equality, utility, impartiality, personal responsibility, community, democracy, and autonomy. Yet there is also something else going on here, which has so far been only implicit: the fact that our discussed thinkers believe not just that their prioritised value or values ought to be so highly prized, but also that their readers already share their views on this matter, or at least would do if only they would consult their own political consciences. Rawls is particularly explicit on this topic. In defence of his 'original position', he writes that:

it seems *reasonable and generally acceptable* that no one should be advantaged or disadvantaged by natural fortune or social circumstances in the choice of princi- ples. It also seems *widely agreed* that it should be impossible to tailor principles to the circumstances of one's case.[52]

Rawls' claim here is that we already subscribe to a certain ideal of impartiality regarding just *how* political principles ought to be chosen, with the task then being to work out just *which* principles would actually be chosen in such a situation. Or, more generally speaking, Rawls' argu- ment moves from a claim about what we do already believe to a claim about the political implications of that belief (i.e. given that you already believe x, you should believe y). Rawls says as much himself. Justice as fairness, he says, is 'a theory of our moral sentiments as manifested by our considered judgements in reflective equilibrium',[53] and 'a more dis- criminating interpretation of our moral sensibilities'[54] than any previous answer given to OQ (Aristotelianism, natural law, utilitarianism, etc.). But what if we do not all share these sentiments? Or, even if we do, what if those sentiments are compatible with a wide range of meaningful answers to OQ? Rawls acknowledges this problem. Although he hopes that 'the original position . . . unites in one conception a reasonably clear problem of choice with conditions that are widely recognised as fitting to impose on the adoption of moral principles',[55] he also acknowledges that 'the idea

[50] M. Sandel, *Democracy's Discontent: America in Search of a Public Philosophy* (Cambridge, MA: Harvard University Press, 1996), 3, 202, emphasis added.
[51] C. Taylor, *Philosophy and the Human Sciences*, 49.
[52] *Theory of Justice*, 18, emphasis added.   [53] Ibid., 120.   [54] Ibid., 587.   [55] Ibid., 584.

of the initial agreement can only succeed if its conditions are in fact widely recognised, or can become so'.[56] We are therefore only supposed to accept the answer Rawls gives to OQ if it is true that the 'conditions embodied in the description of the [initial] situation are ones that we do in fact accept'.[57] But do we accept them?

Perhaps a better question would be, 'do even other philosophers accept them?', to which the obvious answer is no. But then how are we to tell whether one meaningful answer to OQ is more convincing than all the rest? Do these thinkers simply hope that we will just *find* one answer more attractive than all the rest, without being able to give any further reasons for that special attraction? Well, yes and no. It's certainly true that, as illustrated with Rawls, each of them tries to move from moral judgements we are claimed to already share to political conclusions we are then supposed to adopt, but there is also a critical side to this work. Each of them also tries to show that their rivals have failed in just this task, either by showing that their arguments have implications that no ordinary person could stomach (self-destruction, totalitarianism, slavery, etc.) or that their political prescriptions don't actually deliver what they are intended to deliver (liberty, equality, and so on). An example of the first move would be Nozick's claim against Rawls that taxation, when properly understood, is forced labour (echoing and inverting Proudhon's famous claim that 'all property is theft'). An example of the second, by contrast, is provided by one of Nozick's most strident critics. For G. A. Cohen, rather than preserving or promoting liberty, the kind of libertarianism Nozick propounds would in fact undermine it.[58] So, in the first example we are supposed to reject Rawls' argument on the grounds that it leads to an obviously intolerable implication, whilst in the second we are supposed to reject Nozick's alternative to Rawls' answer to OQ on the grounds that it actually undermines the value (liberty) from which it draws its appeal. But can this kind of reasoning really reveal for us an answer to OQ that is clearly more compelling than all the rest?

1.4   A Reassessment of the Problem and a Switch in Literature

The problem is that for the kind of reasoning just described to produce the kind of answer we desire, there would have to be only one way of ranking the values discussed above (liberty, equality, community, etc.) that avoids both intolerable and self-defeating political consequences.

---

[56] Ibid., 585.   [57] Ibid., 587.

[58] G. A. Cohen, *Self-Ownership, Freedom, and Equality* (Cambridge: Cambridge University Press, 1995), 14–37.

This means we are right back where we were a moment ago. If one theorist tells us that we ought to have a particular political system on account of its being a system in which everyone is as free as possible, whilst another tells us that we ought to have a different system on account of its nurturing a stronger sense of community, how are we to choose? I could of course just choose according to my own preference, but what if you make a different choice? How are we then to argue about who's right? Another thought is to try and combine all of these things as best we can. Elizabeth Anderson, for instance, wants to reconcile liberty, equality, community, and democracy by way of a certain model of citizenship, whilst G. A. Cohen aims for both equality and community by way of a certain form of socialism.[59] But combinations, whatever else they might be, are still compromises, so without some argument as to what our priorities ought to be that does not rest, for its final appeal, on one or more of these values, how are we to know what to do?

Zooming out for a moment, our problem here is that it appears to be impossible to produce a convincing answer to OQ, if only because it appears impossible to show that one meaningful answer is truly more compelling than all the rest. Arguments in political philosophy therefore seem to be rationally interminable, by which I mean impossible to rationally resolve. So can we already adopt the third of those three possible conclusions noted earlier? That is, can we really already say that it is impossible to provide a convincing and meaningful answer to OQ? It is much too soon to make that claim. What we ought to do instead is change our focus. Rather than looking at arguments that proceed in the manner described previously, what we need to do now is look at arguments that appear to offer an alternative approach to the kind of value-conflict encountered. In what follows I try to consider as many of these alternatives as possible, beginning with what most commentators would take to be the two most influential: Isaiah Berlin's 'liberal pluralism' and John Rawls' 'political liberalism'.

1.5   Isaiah Berlin: From Value-Pluralism, to Universal Evils, to Liberalism

Isaiah Berlin would not be surprised by our stalemate. For him, these kinds of problems are just what you would expect of philosophers unwilling to accept the truth of *value-pluralism* – the idea that there are various incompatible and incommensurable values of the world, all of which are worthy of our attention. So, just as there is more than one right way to live

---

[59] See E. Anderson, 'What Is the Point of Equality?', *Ethics*, 109 (1999), 287–337.

an individual life, there is also more than one right way of organising politics. But does that mean that there is no such thing as a convincing answer to OQ, and thus no way in which we can say that some political systems are better than others? Not necessarily, says Berlin, for whom there is still one way of moving from an acceptance of pluralism to a justification of modern liberal democracy. The trick is to pay attention to history, because if we look at what people have valued and fought for in the past, two salient facts emerge. First, the fact that individuals and societies have striven for a great many different things – liberty, equality, community, self-determination, and so on. This fact supports value-pluralism, because it shows that reasonable people have been animated by a great many different and often incompatible things. Second, the fact that when people have denied this truth – that is, when they have believed that there is only one right way of doing things, both individually and politically – all manner of bloodshed and suffering is the result. This fact supports what Berlin often calls political pluralism, because it encourages us to practice a politics that is as tolerant and flexible (and thus as liberal and democratic) as possible.[60]

Surely, though, there is a tension here between pluralism and liberalism. After all, if we are to take history as our measure of value, and thus the long list of everything that people *have* valued as a measure of what *is* valuable, have we not made it impossible for ourselves to prioritise the avoidance of suffering over everything else, even assuming that liberal democracy is the one political system able to achieve this, given the bloody realities of human history? Berlin would reply that the objection is misplaced. Bloodshed and suffering, he might claim, are not themselves *genuine* values, only by-products of them. So let's reformulate the objection: why should a rational person prioritise political principles that do not include even a little suffering amongst their by-products over principles that do, given that vast numbers of rational people in the past have also done just that? For instance, why not prioritise liberty over equality? Sure, this could make life harder than is strictly necessary for the poor, but it might also be crucial for human progress. And in turn, why not prioritise community over compassion, because even if this does sometimes mean turning away desperate refugees, might it not also be vital for social cohesion? It seems, then, that there is a contradiction in Berlin's argument regarding his use of history, because although the variety of ideals it

---

[60] Berlin's repeated claims to this effect can be found scattered throughout his many essays. For his best-known and most clear-cut statement, see 'Two Concepts of Liberty', in I. Berlin, *Four Essays on Liberty* (Oxford: Oxford University Press, 1969), 118–172.

presents to us appears to support his value-pluralism, it also makes it harder to justify any one political system, liberal democracy included.

But perhaps we are being too hasty here. Although the described historical argument seems to fail, it is not the only line of reasoning Berlin employs. Consider the following statement:

> May it not be true ... that there are no human values. ... Men simply commit themselves as they commit themselves, for no reason. ... We choose as we choose, that is all that can be said; and if this leads to conflict and destruction, that is a fact about the world which must be accepted as gravitation is accepted, something which is inherent in the dissimilar natures of dissimilar men, or nations, or cultures. That this is not a valid diagnosis has been made clear if only by the great and widespread horror which the excesses of totalitarianism have caused. For *the fact of shock reveals that there does exist a scale of values* by which the majority of mankind ... live.[61]

Here Berlin suggests that we should not be *too* struck by history's variety, and instead recognise the universality of our revulsion at certain historical events. Even if we cannot agree on what is perfect, we should recognise our agreement on what is abominable. Or, to put the point more classically, even if there is no *summum bonum* to be achieved, there is at least a *summum malum* to be avoided. This point again, according to Berlin, moves us towards liberal democracy. Yet how easy is it to make that move? Let's grant here that Berlin is right about the existence of universal evils: torture, starvation, genocide, famine, disease, and so on. If we grant this, and also make the list as extensive as possible, does this then produce for us a watertight defence of liberal democracy, and thus in turn a convincing and meaningful answer to OQ?

I think not. If the problem before was contradiction, the problem now is indeterminacy. Although Berlin might be right that our reaction to all sorts of historical events – including the French, Russian, and Chinese Revolutions, as well as Nazi Germany – does reveal a very widespread recognition of certain universal evils, the problem here is that ruling out regime types capable of producing such evils hardly leaves us with one single, uniquely compassionate political system. Berlin's answer is thus potentially convincing but without being meaningful, if only because it fails to select for us between even those main rival answers to OQ contemplated by contemporary political philosophers. That is, even if we were to grant that liberal political systems, *very* generally understood, do produce less suffering than the alternatives, there would still be no way of selecting between the different models of, say, Rawls and Nozick. This is

---

[61] I. Berlin, *The Crooked Timber of Humanity* (London: Pimlico, 2003), 203, emphasis added.

why so often in Berlin's work he tells us that we need to find a balance between competing political ideals without giving us any clue as to how that balance should be struck.[62] None of which helps us here. Saying that we *need* to end an argument is not the same as telling us *how* to do so, so we shall have to look elsewhere for the answer we need.

1.6   Rawls' Second Set of Answers: From Reasonableness to Liberalism

Rawls, like Berlin, describes the problem he is trying to solve in his second major treatise, *Political Liberalism* (PL), as the problem of pluralism. Rejecting several of his earlier arguments, he now claims that the state set-up in *A Theory of Justice* (TOJ) could never be stable on account of the free exercise of reason under liberal democratic institutions. This is because, given what he calls the 'burdens of judgement', reasonable people, once granted the freedoms of thought and speech, soon come to disagree with each other about all sorts of fundamental moral and political decisions (just as our egalitarian, libertarian, and communitarian philosophers were doing throughout **1.3**). Rawls had assumed in TOJ that people growing up in his ideal state would come to affirm Justice as Fairness as what he calls a 'comprehensive moral doctrine', yet now realises that even if this state *is* the perfect political system, it will not run perfectly, or even retain its perfect structure, if the society living under it does not also believe in its perfection.

So, if liberal freedoms breed reasonable pluralism, which in turn breeds instability, what options does he have? Part of the solution, it seems, is to narrow down the 'we' in 'how should we live?'. Rawls thinks that he can provide a meaningful answer to OQ which, even if it is not convincing to everyone, should at least be convincing to those in living in modern liberal democracies (I'll call them 'moderns'). His general method, however, remains the same as before. Once again he wants to identify one or more deep-set moral beliefs on which at least moderns agree and then work upwards from that agreement towards binding political principles.[63] There are several possibilities here. For instance, he claims that we

---

[62] See, for example, 'The Pursuit of the Ideal', or 'From Hope and Fear Set Free', in I. Berlin, *The Proper Study of Mankind* (London: Farrar, Straus, and Giroux, 2000), 16 and 117–118, respectively; or I. Berlin, *Three Critics of the Enlightenment* (London: Pimlico, 2000), 237–238; or 'My Intellectual Path', in I. Berlin, *The Power of Ideas* (Princeton, NJ: Princeton University Press, 2000), 22; or 'Political Ideas in the Twentieth Century', in I. Berlin, *Four Essays on Liberty* (Oxford: Oxford University Press, 1969), 39–40.

[63] J. Rawls, *Political Liberalism* (New York: Columbia University Press, 2005), 8, 9, 14, 28, 94, 101, 149.

share an ideal of individuals as free and equal persons, an ideal of society as a system of fair cooperation over time, and an implicit ideal, partly expressive of the first two, of a well-ordered society as one governed by a single agreed-on political conception of justice.[64] He also claims, just as he did in TOJ, that we share a number of important beliefs regarding justice. These include 'slavery is wrong', 'exploitation is wrong', and 'religious persecution is wrong'.[65] He even claims, most importantly of all, that we share, implicitly, and as expressed by all of the above, a particular ideal of 'reasonableness'.[66] This ideal is as follows:

Citizens are reasonable when . . . they are prepared to offer one another fair terms of social cooperation [and] agree to act on those terms . . . provided that others act on those terms. For these terms to be fair terms, citizens offering them must reasonably think that those citizens to whom such terms are offered might also reasonably accept them.[67]

According to Rawls, reasonableness means that we moderns should only propose rules for social and political cooperation which (a) it would be reasonable for others to accept and (b) we would be prepared to live by even if they adversely affect our particular interests. This idea has four key entailments. First, its 'criterion of reciprocity' – that we should only propose principles which it would be reasonable for others to accept – entails that we could not propose any of those principles which would be permissive of slavery, exploitation, or oppression.[68] Second, it entails what Rawls calls the 'principle of liberal legitimacy'. This principle states that political power is legitimate only when exercised in accordance with principles which it would be reasonable to accept (thus meeting the criterion of reciprocity).[69] Third, being reasonable requires respecting the 'burdens of judgement'. This means, with echoes of Berlin, that one needs to recognise the impossibility of providing final and demonstrative arguments in favour of either certain supposed moral truths or certain comprehensive moral doctrines as a whole. And because it is reasonable to differ on these things, it is then *unreasonable*, according to the criterion of reciprocity, to enforce those principles which *rely* upon their being true. Fourth, reasonableness entails an ideal of public reason. This ideal holds that, when deliberating in the public political forum about constitutional essentials and matters of basic justice, we must argue only on the basis of principles which it would be reasonable for others to accept (which means again that they are meeting the criterion of reciprocity).[70]

---

[64] Ibid., 14, 15, 19.   [65] Ibid., 8, 124.
[66] Ibid., xlii, 49, 50, 52, 54, 60, 61, 124, 127, 446.   [67] Ibid., xlii.
[68] Ibid., xliv, xlix, 16–17, 446, 483, 488–489.   [69] Ibid., xliv, 137–140, 157, 447.
[70] Ibid., xlviii–xlvix, li, 440–444.

The most important entailment of reasonableness, however, is the fact that it is supposed to provide a new justification for using the original position as a means of generating a convincing answer to OQ.[71] Note the parallel here with TOJ, wherein the original position functioned as an expression of our supposedly shared ideal that social and natural inheritance ought not to affect the choice of political order. Now the procedure is treated as an expression of reasonableness, although in both cases the design of the position is the same. What is not always clear is whether the answer to OQ generated is still the same. Consider here that in early contributions to PL (a book written in several stages), Rawls writes that moderns would choose Justice as Fairness,[72] whereas in later contributions he says that we would select a rather more general set of liberal rules which, although they do permit the earlier ideal, would also permit certain political variations along a clearly liberal theme.[73] But we should not be misled by that shift. In both cases the answer given is that moderns ought to inhabit a state governed by a fixed liberal-democratic constitution and respectful of the norms of public reason.[74] This state would guarantee certain fixed basic liberties as well as provide effective opportunities for their exercise. It would also, on account of its need to protect the full and free exercise of public reason, ensure decent education for all (including civic education), full state funding for political parties, substantial equality of opportunity to positions of political office and candidature, and equality of access to deliberative-democratic forums.[75] So, whatever else we might say of this answer to OQ, there is certainly no political indeterminacy here as there was in Berlin.

Now, the argument thus far holds that because we moderns want to be reasonable, we should accept the design of the original position, which means in turn accepting its verdict that we should support a highly specific liberal constitutional order. Yet this is not quite the final stage in Rawls' case. A separate clause in PL holds that we should now only adhere to these emergent principles if it is also true that they could be the basis of an 'overlapping consensus'. Because we are only reasonable if they adhere to the liberal standard of political legitimacy, we are also only reasonable if it is the case that these principles could be adhered to by the holders of the various reasonable comprehensive moral doctrines found in liberal-democratic societies. But again, we should not be misled, given that this clause is really something of a red herring. Consider here that both secular and religious viewpoints are only reasonable for Rawls if (1) they accept his ideal of reasonableness and (2) they accept the decisions of the original

---

[71] Ibid, 23–25, 79, 90, 96–97.   [72] Ibid., xlvi, 154.   [73] Ibid., 439.
[74] Ibid., xlvii–xlviii, lvi–lvii, 44, 48.   [75] Ibid, lvi–lvii.

position. This means that because comprehensive doctrines opposed to these claims are deemed *un*reasonable, they do not have to be part of the relevant consensus. Although they might not consent to the proposed political order, their opposition is judged neither a failure of the order itself nor the argument which issues in its prescription.

There are, however, at least three problems with this argument, each of which relates to the proposed ideal of reasonableness, and each of which gives us good cause to regard his answer to OQ as unconvincing. These three I now want to address by way of what I call the mild critique, the strong critique, and the internal critique. The mild critique distinguishes between two kinds of reasonableness: Rawlsian and normal. One is normally said to be reasonable if one (a) proposes political principles, (b) sticks by them even when they adversely affect your own particular interests, and (c) proposes nothing ridiculous (e.g. that we construct a state in which everything is dyed purple) or unacceptable (e.g. that we construct a state in which all but one of us functions as absolute slaves to a randomly selected king). By contrast, Rawlsian reasonableness, in addition to agreeing with (a) through (c), adds one further clause. That clause is (d) that one ought only to propose principles which an abstract, disembodied self would choose when deprived of knowledge of both his or her ideals and his or her place in society.

Clause (d) is *in effect* what Rawls ultimately means when he says 'only propose principles which it would be reasonable for others to accept'. According to Rawls, for a principle to be acceptable, it would have to be the case that it could be chosen in the original position. This is the clause, remember, which takes us by entailment to Rawls' answer to OQ, and which is supposed to replace the parallel move made in TOJ, which held that we should agree to those principles which would be chosen in an impartial choice situation designed to reflect the norm that natural and social fortune ought not to affect the choice of political order. The problem, however, is that this clause is not itself contained within ordinary and thus widely accepted (even within the West) notions of reasonableness. Normally we would say that someone is reasonable if they are cooperative, rational, and honourable. For example, we would say that a libertarian is reasonable if she (a) proposes libertarian government and (b) is prepared to accept whatever changes to her status and fortune result from free exchanges, just as we would say that an egalitarian is reasonable if he (a) proposes egalitarian redistribution and (b) is prepared to accept substantial taxation of his earnings, should he come to draw a particularly high salary. So, if Rawls hopes to move from premises moderns *already share* to political ideals they are then supposed to adopt, it seems that he has already come undone.

Consider now a stronger critique. Imagine a third conception of reasonableness which, as well as removing (d) from the list of criteria, also removes (c). Proponents of this argument distinguish between things that are *truly* ridiculous or *completely* beyond the pale and things that are reprehensible only to moderate liberal minds. According to this understanding of the term, a woman would be reasonable if she proposes Sharia law and is prepared to live with the consequences, whilst a man would be reasonable if he proposes a martial state and is prepared to lose his life in its campaigns. On this account of reasonableness, it is enough (1) that we propose principles for cooperation and (2) that we are prepared to live with the consequences. So, again, given that even this form of reasonableness seems more recognisable than Rawls' model, why should we moderns be bound to the rest of his argument?

There is more to these critiques than just semantics. What both of them highlight is that if one wants to convert even modern, Western individuals into egalitarian liberals – and in particular constitutional egalitarian liberals desiring to fix the terms of social cooperation once and for all – then one needs to give a reason to those of them who hold the more ordinary notions of reasonableness for why they should give that creed their support. That reason could potentially, of course, be a number of things. It could be that there will be civil strife if they do not, or that not all will flourish and realise their potential if they do not, or that many will suffer if they do not. It could be that the country will be less productive if they do not, or that it will lose power relative to other countries, or that it will be less creative, or perhaps that it will grow morally degenerate or culturally stagnant. It could even be all of these in combination. But that is hardly the point. What matters is that if one wants to recommend a particular liberal state, it is not enough simply to call those who possess other ideals unreasonable, particularly if your intention is to put that state's constitution out of easy reach of democratic forces.

Some readers, however, will remain sympathetic to Rawls' argument as a whole, which is why a third and 'internal' critique now needs to come into play. There are two parts to this. First, because it would be reasonable for many people to reject Rawls' concept of reasonableness, it would also be reasonable for them to reject his liberal ideals. Second, because it would be reasonable for them to reject these ideals, the liberal standard of legitimacy cannot be met. Remember here that a state is only legitimate for Rawls if its power is exercised in accordance with principles which one ought to accept if one is reasonable. Given then that many people will want to reasonably reject those principles, even those who *are* convinced by them would be unreasonable if they enforced them on the rest regardless of that fact.

The bottom line, therefore, is that although Rawls often describes his ideal of reasonableness as something *innate* to human beings as such (and not even just moderns), and also as bound up with both their basic desire to be moral and their specific capacity *for* and inclination *to* act on a sense of justice,[76] it is fairly clear that to the extent that many of us *do* want to be reasonable, we only want to be morally honourable and logically consistent. We only want, that is, to propose non-contradictory principles which we are fully prepared to abide by, whatever consequences they might bring. Reasonableness, at least in its more universal forms, is simply not powerful enough an idea to isolate the kind of narrow (and thus meaningful) answer to OQ we are after. And indeed, it is not even clear that it is any more determinate, in these forms, than Berlin's idea of universal evils. For now then, given that it is perfectly reasonable to reject Rawls' standard of reasonableness, it is also reasonable to start looking elsewhere for inspiration.

1.7 United by an Ideal of Democracy?

In trying to find a convincing answer to OQ, and surmount what seemed to be intractable conflicts of value in **1.3.**, we have so far considered the ideas of universal evils and reasonableness. But perhaps we have been after entirely the wrong sort of answer. Perhaps, instead of trying to find some deeper and politically determinate value on which even staunchly opposed libertarians and egalitarians could agree, what we need is to identify a real-world political procedure capable of practically arbitrating between the various values and principles they hold dear. Perhaps, that is, we should take these problems away from the philosophers, and hand them over to the people.

This ambition, a common one for thinkers working in the wake of Berlin and Rawls, is sometimes described as the attempt to make political philosophy more *political*. What exactly this means varies from author to author, but some common themes are as follows. First, they want politics to be more open to democratic forces than has often been the case in liberal theory. For example, they want the constitution, if there is one, to be more open to amendment, and public debate to be more open to radically different viewpoints than was the case in, say, Rawls' political liberalism. Second, they want politics, thus expanded, to be less guided by any one particular conception of justice, and more guided by ideals of fair compromise and respectful negotiation.[77] As a general label, we can call

---

[76] Ibid., 19, 52, 81–86.
[77] C. Audard, 'Political Liberalism, Secular Republicanism: Two Answers to the Challenges of Pluralism', in D. Archard, *Philosophy and Pluralism* (Cambridge:

these thinkers the deliberative democrats, which is a term they often employ themselves, though I am using it here to include more advocates and contributors than would often be covered by the term. The label, however, is not what matters. What does matter is that this group is democratic insofar as they want value conflicts resolved by way of a democratic decision, and deliberative insofar as they want that decision to be reached by way of an appropriately conducted prior discussion.

In order to assess this approach, we need to consider a number of its proponents, beginning with Thomas Nagel. He claimed early on in the debate about pluralism that we need to adopt a 'a kind of epistemological restraint . . . a higher standard of objectivity, which is ethically based [and] a highest-order framework of moral reasoning . . . which takes us outside ourselves to a standpoint that is independent of who we are'.[78] Agreeing with the critique advanced in **1.6.** (that the reasonable/unreasonable distinction in unworkable on account of the fact that genuinely reasonable people disagree about a great deal), he thinks instead that we need to adhere to a common, 'objective method of reasoning', the key aspect of which is that we only reason with each other, at least where political coercion is concerned, in terms of what he calls 'impersonal values'.[79] Impersonal values include many of the things we have already discussed in this chapter – such as liberty, equality, or alleviation of suffering – whilst

Cambridge University Press, 1996), 163–176; A. Baumeister, 'Cultural Diversity and Education: The Dilemma of Political Stability', *Political Studies*, 46 (1998), 919–936; R. Bellamy, *Liberalism and Pluralism: Towards a Politics of Compromise* (London: Routledge, 1999); R. Bellamy and M. Hollis, 'Consensus, Neutrality and Compromise', in R. Bellamy and M. Hollis, *Pluralism and Liberal Neutrality* (London: Routledge, 1999), 54–78; 'Back to the Future: Pluralism and the Republican Alternative to Liberalism', in M. Evans, *The Edinburgh Companion to Contemporary Liberalism* (Edinburgh: Edinburgh University Press, 2001), 175–187; J. Bohman, 'Public Reason and Cultural Pluralism: Political Liberalism and the Problem of Moral Conflict', *Political Theory*, 23:2, 253–279; S. Caney, 'Liberal Legitimacy, Reasonable Disagreement and Justice', in R. Bellamy and M. Hollis, *Pluralism and Liberal Neutrality*, 19–36; I. Chowchat, 'Moral Pluralism, Political Justification and Deliberative Democracy', *Political Studies*, 48 (2000), 745–758; M. Deveaux, 'A Deliberative Approach to Conflicts of Culture', *Political Theory*, 31 (2003), 780–807; J. S. Dryzek, 'Deliberative Democracy in Divided Societies', *Political Theory*, 33 (2005), 218–242; A. E. Galeotti, 'Neutrality and Recognition', in *Pluralism and Liberal Neutrality*, 37–53; A. Gutmann and D. Thompson, 'Moral Conflict and Political Consensus', *Ethics*, 101:1 (1990), 64–88; M. R. James, 'Communicative Action, Strategic Action, and Inter-group Dialogue', *European Journal of Political Theory*, 2 (2003), 157–182; S. Mendus, 'Pluralism and Scepticism in a Disenchanted World', in M. Baghramian and A. Ingram, *Pluralism: The Philosophy and Politics of Diversity* (London: Routledge, 2000), 103–120; T. Nagel, 'Moral Conflict and Political Legitimacy', *Philosophy and Public Affairs*, 16:3 (1987), 215–240; G. Newey, 'Metaphysics Postponed: Liberalism, Pluralism, and Neutrality', *Political Studies*, 45 (1997), 296–311; B. Parekh, 'Moral Philosophy and Its Anti-pluralist Bias', in *Philosophy and Pluralism*, 117–134.

[78] 'Moral Conflict and Political Legitimacy', 229.   [79] Ibid., 226, 231, 235.

excluding things like salvation or racial purity. The idea is to debate and negotiate with others only on the basis of things that would be of value to anyone, regardless of their particular comprehensive moral doctrine.[80]

Consider second the arguments of Amy Gutmann and Dennis Thompson, who think that instead of adopting Rawls' restrictive ideal of reasonableness, we ought to follow an ideal of 'mutual respect' which, according to them, is a 'prerequisite of democratic deliberation'.[81] Mutual respect, they say, 'requires a favourable attitude towards, and constructive interaction with, the persons with whom one disagrees', and manifests itself in 'a distinctively democratic kind of character – the character of individuals who are morally committed, self-reflective about their commitments, discerning of the differences between responsible and merely tolerable differences of opinion, and open to the possibility of changing their minds or modifying their positions at some time in the future if they confront unanswerable objections to their present point of view'.[82] It requires citizens and officials to 'enter ... discussion in the political forum with the purpose of discovering principles on which the society as a whole can act, rather than with the aim of devising agendas by which they can advance only their own interests'.[83] Amongst other things, it 'makes possible, at the level of political decision, the deliberate choice of substantive moral values for the society as a whole'.[84] So, just as was the case with Nagel, the key idea here is for disagreeing parties to look for common ground with each other, whilst being open-minded as to what that common ground might be.

Third, consider James Bohman, who thinks that we can achieve 'fair, moral compromises' just so long as we adopt, in our deliberations, a norm of 'dynamic reason'.[85] This norm requires that we are prepared to adapt our moral ideals and political demands in the light of arguments concerning both. Provided, then, that we possess 'a minimal commitment to ongoing cooperation and public reason-giving', it should be possible to deliver compromises that enough people find acceptable.[86] This will be the case *partly* for different moral reasons – according to their own comprehensive doctrines – and *partly* as a result of 'how common deliberation and dialogue with the conflicting moral view has changed the original moral beliefs'.[87] What this means is not only that two different supporters of a given compromise might hold different reasons for their support, but also that those reasons might well be reasons that would not

---

[80] Ibid., 237.   [81] 'Moral Conflict and Political Consensus', 64–65.   [82] Ibid., 76.
[83] Ibid., 77.   [84] Ibid., 77.
[85] 'Public Reason and Cultural Pluralism: Political Liberalism and the Problem of Moral Conflict', 267.
[86] Ibid., 270.   [87] Ibid., 270.

have appealed to them prior to the public debate which occurred on the issue. Dynamic reason, Bohman tells us, is necessary 'for working out the reasonable moral compromises needed to resolve deep conflicts in pluralist democracies',[88] and can 'transform the cultural framework of each culture through mutual criticism and interpretation'.[89] A further claim for him is that overly restrictive sets of rules for political deliberation – amongst which he includes, not only Rawls' ideal of public reason, but also Nagel's requirement of sticking to impersonal values – fail to take seriously enough the problems set for contemporary liberal political theory by pluralism. As he puts the point, 'only by going beyond the restrictions of impartiality, unanimity, and singularity can public reason be made a workable norm for resolving conflicts of principle in pluralist democracies'.[90]

Fourth, consider Richard Bellamy, who writes that 'to accommodate plurality requires ... democratic liberalism'.[91] Of republican inspiration, this response to pluralism 'eschews a pre-political consensus on basic liberties for political negotiation aimed at a fair compromise [and instead] of relegating [differences] gives them public recognition'.[92] We now need to 'reconstruct the liberal constitutional consensus in terms of a fair compromise achieved through new forms of democratic politics'.[93] Value-pluralism, he tells us, is liberalism's greatest challenge and requires that we adopt a 'democratic politics of compromise', including a form of political deliberation which 'clarifies a broader context of reasons and negotiates a path through them'.[94] By contrast, he claims, Rawls' restrictions on democratic power and public deliberation 'prevent politics from performing its crucial function of reconciling difference through negotiation and debate'.[95] Instead of restricting themselves to a singular conception of political justice, political actors should aim to 'negotiate' reasonable compromises with each other.[96] As negotiators, these actors 'practice reciprocal accommodation as part of a search for conditions of mutual acceptability that reach towards a compromise that consists of a shareable good ... They seek a mutually satisfying solution rather than one that simply satisfies their own concerns'.[97]

There are clearly several important suggestions here. From Nagel we can take the idea that political debate should be conducted by reference to impersonal values. From Gutmann and Thompson we can take the idea that we should always look to find new common ground and not only rely

---

[88] Ibid., 256.   [89] Ibid., 272.   [90] Ibid., 274.
[91] 'Back to the Future: Pluralism and the Republican Alternative to Liberalism', 176.
[92] Ibid., 176.   [93] *Liberalism and Pluralism: Towards a Politics of Compromise*, ix.
[94] Ibid., 1, 3, 12.   [95] Ibid., 60.   [96] Ibid., 101.   [97] Ibid.

on things we already know people share. From Bohman we can take the idea that different people can happily support the same thing for different reasons, and need not all adhere to the same conception of justice. And from Bellamy we can take the idea that compromise and negotiation are more important to good political conduct than perfect unanimity. We can also say that what all of these arguments share is a desire (1) to provide an alternative discussion-shaping ideal to Rawls' 'reasonableness', and (2) to set out an alternative, though not radically different, political system to that proposed in *Political Liberalism*. This second point is important. Just as the idea in each approach is to identify a set of standards capable of guiding negotiations between all genuinely reasonable individuals, however diverse those individuals might be, the upshot in each approach is that those standards can only be achieved within a liberal-democratic system. So, just as was the case in the two previous sections, what we see here is again a liberal answer to OQ in need of justification. But these theorists have so far told us only how citizens and politicians should approach politics, and not yet why they should adopt that approach. In order to work out whether or not they can convince us, we need to look carefully at their answers to FQ.

Consider the various justificatory arguments provided in the four approaches. Nagel's prescriptions of impartiality and epistemological restraint are underpinned by Kantian ideals. As he writes, 'when we force people to serve an end that they cannot share, and that we cannot justify to them in objective terms, it is a particularly serious violation of the Kantian requirement that we treat others not only as a means, but also as an end'.[98] He then adds, 'of course liberal impartiality claims for itself an authority that will not in fact be universally accepted. ... But since it is a substantial moral position, that is not surprising'.[99] Gutmann and Thompson, in turn, ground their deliberative agenda in an ideal of 'mutual respect', which itself appears to be underpinned as follows: '[the] underlying assumption is that we should value reaching conclusions through reason rather than force, and more specifically through moral reasoning rather than self-interested bargaining'.[100] This assumption we might describe as the ideal of consensual politics, or perhaps, following Nagel, as an ideal of Kantian-cum-Rawlsian liberal legitimacy – that one should try as hard as one can to avoid authoritarianism by providing reasons capable of eliciting genuine political consensus. Bohman's approach, by contrast, is relatively simple. He defends his political measures as (1) requirements of 'equality' and (2) necessary to

---

[98] 'Moral Conflict and Political Legitimacy', 238.   [99] Ibid., 240.
[100] 'Moral Conflict and Political Consensus', 65, 77.

achieve 'fair' moral compromises.[101] So what about Bellamy? In his case there seem to be several things grounding his particular democratic response to pluralism. Sometimes he describes democratic liberalism's animating value as 'reciprocity',[102] sometimes as 'equal concern',[103] sometimes as 'accommodation',[104] sometimes as 'mutual recognition',[105] sometimes as 'mutual respect and the common good',[106] and sometimes as 'mutual acceptance and accommodation'.[107] He also claims that it 'incorporates the liberal concern with freedom and justice into the democrat's desire to ensure that citizens have an equal say in influencing and holding to account the rules and rulers governing them'.[108] And indeed, he *also* defends it on the grounds that it can promote empowerment, community, and a sense of identification with the adopted policies.[109]

We should not, though, be distracted either by interpretive challenges focused on particular thinkers, or by minor variations between them, given that what really matters is the way in which all of these arguments, once boiled down, are worryingly question-begging. Unlike Rawls, for example, none of these scholars provides anything approaching a substantial answer to FQ. Consider here that rather than arguing at length that there *is* some shared political ideal common to all of us, these thinkers simply assert whatever value they feel most attracted to – mutual respect, reciprocity, consent, etc. – and then go on to show how this value can be used to underpin a particular solution to what they call the problem of pluralism. They do this, perhaps, because they are so convinced of the wisdom of their own answer to OQ that they think its merits speak for themselves, but what about everybody else? Why should the libertarians, egalitarians, and communitarians discussed in **1.6.** abandon their own political programmes in favour of this new politics of compromise?

The problem, remember, is that we have already encountered too many conflicting political values in this chapter, each of which tempts us into giving it political priority. Earlier we saw that Berlin and Rawls were unable to find some basic determining ideal on which we all agree and of a sort that would overcome the problems of pluralism. Now we see that the deliberative democrats fare no better, regardless of whether or not their political programmes could turn out to be the right ones for pluralist

---

[101] 'Public Reason and Cultural Pluralism: Political Liberalism and the Problem of Moral Conflict', 267, 274.
[102] *Liberalism and Pluralism: Towards a Politics of Compromise*, 105, 110.
[103] Ibid., 107, 111.   [104] Ibid., 101.   [105] Ibid., 105, 111.
[106] Ibid., 114; 'Consensus, Neutrality and Compromise', 176.
[107] 'Back to the Future: Pluralism and the Republican Alternative to Liberalism', 185.
[108] Ibid., 185.
[109] *Liberalism and Pluralism: Towards a Politics of Compromise*, 107–109.

societies. The key point is that the ideals these thinkers have applied in order to design value-conflict-solving political systems have not themselves been adequately grounded. If we ask what justifies liberal freedoms, then they can say that they are required for full and fair deliberation. If we ask what justifies this deliberation, then they can say that it is required by some or other further value, such as mutual respect. But what then? If we now ask what justifies mutual respect, we hear silence. And consider, as a further problem: would deliberative democracy even function as it is supposed to function without at least *some* degree of consensus regarding its supposedly superior merits? This point, clearly, parallels the tension Rawls encountered in the previous section between reasonableness and liberal legitimacy.

That latter point, however, is hardly the main challenge. The fundamental difficulty, to repeat, is this: even if deliberative democracy *does* turn out to be the best response to pluralism at the political level, it cannot function as a *convincing* answer to OQ until it solves the problems of pluralism plaguing FQ; that is, until it provides a solution to pluralism at the level of justification. The deliberative dilemma, as we might call it, is that deliberation cannot go all the way down. At some point, this political model for resolving value conflict has to be justified in just the same way that the original position had to be justified. Yet whilst Rawls at least gave us something worth analysing – first the idea of avoiding the effects of natural or social circumstance and second the idea of reasonableness – here we have nothing to work with.

1.8   United by an Ideal of Tolerance?

Many scholars agree that the deliberative democrats, like Berlin and Rawls, fail to solve the problem of pluralism. Of these, a significant number think that the best way to provide a convincing and meaningful answer to OQ is to draw on an ideal of tolerance. By easing up even more on liberal-democratic strictures, they say, we can find a way to accommodate all in a mutually satisfying manner. Consider the following arguments.

Tariq Modood claims that whilst we should do our best to encourage inter-community deliberation, we would also do well, given the current political climate, to grant legal and political protection to both different cultures and different religions.[110] Although this will often require abandoning certain liberal aims – fostering individual autonomy, for

---

[110] T. Modood, '"Race" in Britain and the Politics of Difference', in D. Archard, *Philosophy and Pluralism*, 190.

instance – it will also serve the greater cause of social cohesion.[111] Jonathan Seglow agrees, adding that the abrogation of liberal rules is often justified on the grounds that such protection is required if individuals are to have a strong sense of identity – a condition which is itself vital if individuals are to be effective agents in what is still, broadly conceived, a liberal state.[112] Andrew Mason is sympathetic to both demands. He claims that instead of obsessing about liberal absolutes involving non-interference and facilitated autonomy, we should simply look to see what brings about the greatest amount of well-being for the greatest number of people. In practice, he claims, this will involve giving different communities a great deal of legal and political leeway.[113]

John Kekes provides a more substantial argument along similar lines. He claims that 'in all but the most extreme situations, the value of our conceptions of a good life or the value of the traditional system of values to which we adhere will be greater than that of either of the two values whose conflict we are facing'.[114] Although we will always have initial preferences regarding any particular moral or political conflict, it is nearly always the case that the fundamentals of our own way of life take priority over them. So, given a choice between prioritising liberty or equality, the assumption here is that I will choose whatever best fits with my current way of life. But what exactly does this mean for politics in general? For Kekes, it means that the state should hold no overriding commitment to one value or conception of the good life.[115] It also means that if we want as many people as possible to live worthwhile lives, then what the state needs to do is ensure access to as many different ways of life as possible.[116] It should, as Kekes puts it, 'guarantee the conditions in which its citizens can make for themselves whatever they regard as good lives'.[117] This means that the state is going to have to be more tolerant of illiberal ways of life than was imagined by, for example, the deliberative democrats. Yet for Kekes, this is just what follows when one recognises both (1) the truth of pluralism and (2) the connection between individual flourishing and participation in a collective way of life.[118]

Kekes' argument is essentially that if everyone is to have a chance of a good life, we will need to make available as many different values and

---

[111] T. Modood, 'Multiculturalism, Secularism and the State', in R. Bellamy and M. Hollis, *Pluralism and Liberal Neutrality*, 95.

[112] J. Seglow, 'Liberalism and the Politics of Recognition', in M. Evans, *The Edinburgh Companion to Contemporary Liberalism*, 89.

[113] A. Mason, 'Imposing Liberal Principles', in R. Bellamy and M. Hollis, *Pluralism and Liberal Neutrality*, 113.

[114] J. Kekes, *The Morality of Pluralism* (Princeton, NJ: Princeton University Press, 1993), 25.

[115] Ibid., 211.   [116] Ibid., 213, 216.   [117] Ibid., 214–215.   [118] Ibid., 199.

ways of life as possible, and as a result should be tolerant of those values and lives. Or, even more simply put, he is claiming that a maximisation of human well-being requires tolerance. This is the heart of, not just Kekes' argument, but also Modood's, Seglow's, and Mason's. With echoes of the communitarians considered in **1.3.**, each of these scholars thinks that, for various reasons, participation in a shared way of life is a key ingredient of any meaningful existence. Whether that existence is religious and traditional or secular and modern, local and territorial or on-line and virtual, what matters is that each individual's way of life is tolerated by society at large because, if it is not, he or she will not be able to live what is, for him or her, the only sort of life worth living.

It appears to be a virtue of this argument that it works its way up in utilitarian fashion from well-being to tolerance, rather than from some more particular, culturally contingent moral ideal to an equivalent political agenda.[119] It also appears to be a virtue that because it is more permissive of political variety and social diversity, it requires less in the way of justification than any of the approaches we have considered so far. Both appearances are misleading. Like all political arrangements, those suggested by our tolerant theorists result in winners and losers, the only question being whether the particular balance achieved is more or less justifiable than its alternatives. Consider the winners and losers in this tolerant state – a state in which different ways of life are permitted to flourish with little or no regulation and interference. The winners, clearly, are those who want above all else to live in accordance with their own traditional values. These will include community and religious leaders as well as their faithful adherents. They will also include parents who want to inculcate in their children the virtues and aspirations proper to their own way of life. But what about the losers? They will be those unwilling to conform to the traditions into which they have been born, or to which they once signed up as adults. Women will commonly receive fewer life chances than men, deviant or unorthodox members of traditional communities fewer than conservative ones, rebellious or progressive children fewer than their faithful cultural or religious fellows, and so on and so forth.

So how are we to assess this trade-off? In order to do so, it might be helpful to differentiate here between (1) ideological victories and defeats and (2) changes to personal circumstance. We can say, for instance, that one gains ideologically if one's political doctrine is luck-egalitarianism and one's political system is an egalitarian state. We can also say that if

---

[119] For an example of such an argument, see D. Wong, 'Coping with Moral Conflict and Ambiguity', *Ethics*, 102:4 (1992), 763–784.

one is both an egalitarian and rich, then that state might well reduce your disposable income and thus, at least potentially, the quality of your material existence. Here an egalitarian state would be ideologically beneficial, though detrimental to personal circumstances. Now consider a second example. Imagine an academically ambitious daughter, living in a state tolerant of cultural variations in education policy, and born into a religious family which, according to tradition, educates its daughters only to become homemakers, and which will not permit or support anyone to go to university besides their eldest son. In this case, we can say that the daughter's personal circumstances suffer, despite her family's ideological triumph. A tolerant state is then ideologically beneficial to her family, or at least to her father, whilst being personally detrimental to her.

These trade-offs bring to the fore two well-known problems in political philosophy: the problem of whether or not a state could and should be neutral (in some suitably defined sense) and the problem of whether or not utility (interpreted here as 'well-being') could and should be a coherent measure for political maximisation. We see the first when we see how a family's gain can be a daughter's loss. We see the second when we see how political promotion of one's ideology can be accompanied by a downturn in personal fortunes. There is, of course, nothing very radical about these distinctions and illustrations, so I am not going to labour the point. What matters for our assessment is that if a state practices tolerance towards the various cultural and religious groups found within it, it in effect does two things: (1) It increases substantially the well-being (as understood by the gainers) of those whose ideals and personal life plans coincide with the traditional dictates of those groups, whilst simultaneously reducing the well-being (as understood by the losers) of those whose ideals and life plans do not; (2) it *therefore* prioritises a conception of well-being which includes participation in the traditional culture of one's parents or ancestors over a conception of well-being which includes engagement with one's own autonomously chosen and non-traditional ideals.

This second entailment of the tolerant answer to OQ highlights the fact that, for the tolerant answer to FQ to be convincing, there must be good reason to support its adopted conception of well-being. That is, if we are to be convinced that our politics should be shaped by the described ideal of tolerance, then we shall also have to be convinced that human well-being is best served by preserving traditional ways of life. Yet this claim seems dubious. For one thing, it only even *potentially* commands the support of anyone whose conception of well-being includes participation in a flourishing traditional way of life. It might not, for instance, command the support of those whose personal circumstances and ideological ideals come into conflict as a result of the adopted policies. But this is hardly a fatal objection. After all, any move from one political order to another is going to affect the distribution of material wealth, so it can hardly be the case that this makes the proposed answer to OQ beyond hope.

I do want to argue, though, that just as it was untenable to say that because (1) we agree on a norm of reasonableness we should (2) support a liberal-democratic constitution, it is untenable to say that because (a) we care about well-being, we should (b) support such a tolerant state. The problem is that the notion of 'well-being' employed here is just as contentious as the notion of 'reasonableness' employed by Rawls. There are two reasons for this. First, it is contentious because it is not clear that adhering to the cultural norms of your parents is more important than following your own chosen life plan. Second, it is contentious because it is not clear why individuals, and especially children, should not have full and continued access to a variety of ideals and ways of life in order that they could, at least potentially, form and reform such plans. Is the level of well-being achieved by faithful adherents to a protected illiberal culture really so high that it outweighs the loss borne by those who would opt for an alternative way of life? And, if so, is it obvious that we should prefer a higher *aggregate* of well-being to a guaranteed *minimum* level for all – a minimum which would be above the level likely to be experienced by those denied the conditions of autonomy found in a liberal political order?

This is where the real contradiction for this approach comes to light. Although the argument we have been considering holds that tolerating illiberal ways of life is good for human well-being, the reality is that it is only good for the well-being of those who are happy with the choices offered to them from within those inherited lives. Individuals who want to leave their allotted community without suffering undue penalties, or who want to remain whilst enjoying opportunities not supported by those who decide what the community stands for, are left out in the cold. Remember here that we are after an answer to OQ that would be convincing to *all* those who have to live with it. If we are to allow the lives of certain individuals to be restricted in the name of preserving established commu-nal ways of life, then we shall have to be able to give a good reason to them for that restriction – we cannot simply say that it promotes human well-being, when their own well-being is being curtailed. Nor can we fine-tune our answer and say to them that *overall* well-being is being *maximised*, even at the cost of their own happiness. It is no consolation to a Christian that the Coliseum is amused by his torment. For some people, of course, it will not matter if a few suffer in the cause of the greater good, but that is not our concern here. Our concern is to see if there is a meaningful answer to OQ which would be convincing to *all* those who have to thrive and suffer in its name. Although we are often happy to accept the results of elections or games on the grounds that we accept the rules by which they were reached, there is no parallel to that acceptance here. In this instance we have been told to prioritise one conception of well-being over another, without being given a reason for that prioritisation. Those who do not subscribe to traditional values are being told to suffer in the name of traditional values, and that claim, whatever else we might call it, is certainly an unconvincing argument.

1.9   Stuart Hampshire and a Second Argument from Universal Evils

> Whatever the divergences in conceptions of the good, these primary evils stay constant and undeniable as evils to be at all costs averted, or almost all costs. One matching constant on the positive side is common everyday rationality, the power of argument – a weak protection, you may say, and that is why I am a pessimist.[120]

Stuart Hampshire, a largely neglected figure in recent political philosophy, shares with Isaiah Berlin a belief that we need to focus more on our agreements regarding what is awful than our disagreements regarding what is ideal. He also shares with the deliberative democrats a belief that we need to solve conflicts of value through political procedures rather than philosophical trickery. Where he differs from both is in the political system he ends up prescribing. Consider the following argument.

Hampshire begins by telling us that 'humanity is united in the recognition of the great evils which render life scarcely bearable, and which undermine any specific way of life and any specific conception of the good and of the associated virtues'.[121] As a result, 'the proper business of politics, as Hobbes perceived, is protection against the perennial evils of human life [such as] physical suffering, the destructions and mutilations of war, poverty and starvation, enslavement and humiliation'.[122] But it is not enough merely to want to avoid such things – we also need to recognise their causes, and in particular the fact that they often come about as a result of unavoidable conflicts between conceptions of the good. The only hope is thus to peacefully manage such conflict by means of an appropriate political procedure.[123] This procedure will be a 'means of facilitating co-existence and survival',[124] and *should* be desired by *all*, at least if the details can be agreed on, given that every

---

[120] S. Hampshire, *Justice Is Conflict* (London: Duckworth, 1999), 47.
[121] S. Hampshire, *Innocence and Experience* (London: Allen Lane, 1989), 107.
[122] *Justice Is Conflict*, 8–9.   [123] Ibid., 18.   [124] *Innocence and Experience*, 109.

society, regardless of its own cultural distinctiveness, will somehow have to balance the claims of rival ways of life.[125]

So, Hampshire's argument holds that because (1) there are universal evils which everyone wants to avoid as a matter of priority, and (2) such evils are triggered by violent conflict, it follows that (3) all societies will require some kind of procedure for peacefully adjudicating between the claims of the various ways of life they contain. But what kind of procedure? He writes at one point that the only 'universal and positive moral requirement' in politics is the 'application of procedural justice and fairness' in the handling of conflicts between rival ways of life.[126] What this means is that politics everywhere should be conducted in accordance with what he considers the universal model of fair argument.[127] This model, which is less prescriptive than those proposed by the deliberative democrats considered earlier, centres on the practice of 'adversary reasoning and compromise'.[128] It also involves adhering to the norms of listening to the other side, of working methodically through a process of claim and counter-claim, and of dealing in what Hampshire calls 'balanced adversary thinking'.[129] The key idea, however, is that of adversary reasoning and compromise. What Hampshire envisages is a political world in which even our most fundamental value conflicts are handled by way of a negotiating forum in which (1) all rival points of view are heard and (2) everyone is prepared to strike compromises with everyone else.

Above and beyond any initial appeal this idea might have, Hampshire also seeks to draw support for it from both history and practical reasoning. On the first front he says that this model has emerged through time in almost every society, however imperfectly it has been adopted, as a result of the inevitable conflict of moral ideals conducted against a background of universal evils.[130] Although particular institutions have come and gone over time, this way of managing conflict has always been preserved and recognised as a necessary requirement of any political system that aspires to be fair.[131] We ought then to be reassured in our belief that what Hampshire calls the 'universal principle of adversary argument' *is* universal precisely because it has always been universally recognised, if not always properly adhered to by the powers that be.[132] But we can also reassure ourselves of this universality by consulting our own minds. As Hampshire writes at one point, his thesis 'is a kind of transcendental argument', according to which everyone can recognise the wisdom of utilising the 'balancing of pros and cons in politics by recognising that

---

[125] *Justice Is Conflict*, 9, 20, 92.   [126] *Innocence and Experience*, 107.   [127] Ibid., 108.
[128] *Justice Is Conflict*, 8–9.   [129] Ibid., 21–22.   [130] Ibid., 25.   [131] Ibid., 27.
[132] Ibid., 37.

that is what he or she already does in his or her own mind'.[133] Because we already employ adversarial reasoning in our mind, it is then perfectly natural that it should form the basis for universal procedures of conflict resolution.

There is, however, a real worry here about how politically determinate and thus meaningful this model is, despite its apparent historical and mental familiarity. Hampshire concedes this point himself, admitting that there is no rational necessity regarding its particular institutional implications.[134] But if this is true, how are we to know whether any given assembly, or set of judges, or entire population is properly acting in accordance with its ideals? Hampshire's answer is that particular institutional expressions of the general idea will be justified, not by rational argument, but rather by the 'loyalties and . . . deep-seated habits of living together and arguing together' we already find in any given existing context.[135] The basic idea seems to be consistency. As long as whatever manifestation of the idea of adversarial arbitration we encounter has been practised steadily over time in any given location, it will be justifiable to those who are subject to it precisely because they have grown up to trust it, whilst also building their expectations around it. All that is required, he claims, is that 'the institutions involved in the resolution of conflicts must have earned, or be earning, respect and recognition from their history in a particular state or society'.[136] These steadily maintained procedures 'constitute the cement that holds the state together, and supply a common ground of loyalty'.[137]

Surely, though, there is something rather worrying about an argument which holds that because a particular practice is already in existence, we ought to continue to support it. After all, slavery was around for a rather long time before being abolished, whilst universal suffrage has only just emerged, historically speaking. As Brian Barry once wrote, the fact that something has been going on for a very long time is not itself much of a reason to continue with it – you could just as well say: 'well, it's high time you stopped'.[138] This matters even more when we consider that most political contexts are characterised, not by unwavering loyalty to local institutions, but rather by substantial disagreement about their nature. Normally, that is, there is deep disagreement about what kinds of claims are considered and by whom, and even if it were to be universally acknowledged that politics ought to involve principles of adversarial reasoning, the questions of what comes under its remit, and also of who

---

[133] Ibid., 46.   [134] Ibid., 28.   [135] Ibid., 89.   [136] Ibid., 58.   [137] Ibid., 77.
[138] B. Barry, *Culture and Equality: An Egalitarian Critique of Multiculturalism* (Cambridge, MA: Harvard University Press, 2001).

gets to decide once all sides have been heard, would continue to be answered in many different ways. Just consider: if the majority in a society considers a certain authority, a certain social structure, a certain economic model, and a certain familial hierarchy to be beyond question – that is, to be natural – then none of those things shall come under the remit of justice according to Hampshire. And even if they were up for debate, in any society riven by a permanent division of majority and minority, what reason has the minority got to accept the majority's verdict? Surely we would need to say more to them than just, 'well, this is how it's been for a very long time, and it's always worked just fine for us'.

Hampshire might well respond to this problem by reminding us of the existence of universal evils. He might say that although it is true that we face deep pluralism and severe indeterminacy as regards his supposedly universal concept of justice, it is also true that we acknowledge the need to avoid universal evils. And because we acknowledge this need, he might continue, we must also acknowledge the need to run with his proposed principles of conflict resolution, however indeterminate they might be. But this is where the argument really crunches. Consider the following abstract conflict. Group (a) and group (b) are trying to resolve a disagreement about how to distribute goods (x) and (y). Group (a) cares most about good (y) whilst group (b) cares most about good (x). Now, in adversarial negotiations it emerges that, although group (a) is prepared to let group (b) have its way with good (x), group (b) is not prepared to let group (a) have its way with good (y). As a result, group (a) goes to war with a view to getting its own way on both. But consider: if that happens, who is responsible for that war, together with all the disease, torture, and starvation it brings? Is it (a) for starting the war or (b) for obstructing (a)'s demands? The problem here is that, if both parties adhered to the minimal requirements of putting forward and listening to opposing arguments, there is nothing we can do to gauge responsibility. We cannot decide who was responsible for producing these universal evils unless we turn to some independent set of values against which to assess (a)'s demands – but then the existence of such values is just what Hampshire denies!

Indeterminacy, it seems, is Hampshire's vice, just as it was Berlin's. Because his proposed model of justice-as-adversarial-reasoning is too weak to provide determinate answers to OQ, it cannot help but fall short as either a meaningful or a convincing answer to that question. Very simply put, we cannot be expected or expect other people to be loyal to a particular set of procedures and institutions just because those procedures and institutions either have been around for a long time or are now here to stay. Nor can we be expected to avoid perpetrating the universal evil of violent conflict – bar the existence of some other universal ideal – if the only alternative to that perpetration is to live without something we consider fundamental to our own existence.

1.10   Joseph Raz: Practical Reason as a Guide to Political Morality

It is time to consider another possibility. What if, in contrast to Hampshire, we had a theory of practical reasoning that was both more detailed and more determinate? And what if, in contrast to Rawls, we had a theory of reasonableness that was universal enough to function as a shared basis for precise political prescriptions? This is the hope offered by Joseph Raz. His argument is that if we look carefully enough at how human beings think, then we shall soon come to an understanding of how they ought to act, and in turn an understanding of what sort of political system would be most supportive of those actions. Or, alternatively put, the idea here is that we can go from an answer to 'how do I *think?*' to an answer to 'how should I *live?*', and from there to an answer to 'how should *we* live?'.

This argument begins with a general claim about theories of practical reasoning, which is that their truth depends on how well they map on to ordinary, everyday thinking. For example, if concepts such as 'intention' or 'the will' play an important role in a particular theory, then for that theory to be true, it must also be true that humans do think in ways that can recognisably be described in those terms. It might, for instance, make more sense to say that Sarah intends to go to the shops on Saturday than it would to say that she wants to go the shops despite having not yet gone. It might also make more sense to say that John wants to do his homework but is suffering from weakness of the will than it would to say that he wants to do his homework but wants even more to stay in bed. Here, then, we could say that a theory which contains these two concepts chimes better with ordinary thought patterns than one which only contains the concept of a want, and is for that reason a truer theory.

Raz's own theory contains a multitude of concepts of this sort, including most importantly 'value' and 'reason'. As he writes on one occasion:

People pursue goals and have desires for *reasons*. They believe that the objects of their desires or their pursuits are *valuable* (and sometimes that the pursuit itself is valuable not merely as a means to achieve its object). This reason-dependent character of goals and desires entails that any person who has a goal or a desire believes, if he has a minimal understanding of their nature, that if he came to believe that there were no reasons to pursue the good or the desire, he would no longer have them.[139]

The key idea here is that, cases of addiction aside, I only want something when I believe it to be valuable. For example, if I take political philosophy to be a subject organised around the question 'how should we live?', then I should only want to pursue that subject as long as I believe both that that question can be answered (thus making my subject valuable) and that I am capable of answering it (thus making my engagement with it rational). Were my *belief* that either of these things holds to change, it would be *unreasonable* of me to continue, just as it would be unreasonable of me to *want* to continue. Or consider a simpler example. Imagine that I want to open a box because I believe it contains my birthday present. I long for this box and often have to be restrained from pulling it apart. So what would happen if I were to discover that the box is empty – surely now my desire to open it would be gone? What we see in both cases is that desires normally do and always should track beliefs, which means that I should only pursue things that I not only want but also believe to be valuable. This is how Raz moves from the 'is' of how we do think to an 'ought' of how we should think. By showing us that normal, healthy practical reasoning makes desires subordinate to reasons and values, he is also showing us that this is how we must always try and operate.

This bedrock of values and reasons is accompanied in Raz's theory by three separate theses: incommensurability, value-pluralism, and social dependence.[140] Incommensurability is the idea that different options in life, and thus the values that they represent, are often rationally incomparable. Consider fox-hunting and chess. No matter how exciting the hunt or how complex the chess, the two activities lack a common measure. This then leads to value-pluralism, according to which different values are not just incomparable, but also irreconcilable. For example, being a monk is a valuable way of life, just as is being a father, but there is no way that I can be both. And consider finally social dependence. This is a three-part idea according to which (1) most values are the creations of cultures; (2) most values depend for their accessibility on the existence of a supporting

---

[139] J. Raz, *The Morality of Freedom* (Oxford: Oxford University Press, 1986), 140, emphasis added. For further exposition of the same point, see J. Raz, *Engaging Reason: On the Theory of Value and Action* (Oxford: Oxford University Press, 1999), 47ff.

[140] The best discussions of value-pluralism and incommensurability can be found in *The Morality of Freedom* and *Engaging Reason*; the best discussion of social dependence can be found in *The Practice of Value* (Oxford: Oxford University Press, 2003). For useful discussion of some of the groundwork of the latter, see also J. Raz, *Value, Respect, and Attachment* (Cambridge: Cambridge University Press, 2001).

culture; and (3) individual well-being normally requires membership in a flourishing culture. Here the most important point is that it will be impossible for me to engage in objectively valuable ways of life unless (a) I have been socialised in those ways and (b) those ways are supported by the society in which I live. For example, I am unlikely to become a concert pianist if friends and family have no knowledge of classical music, and even more unlikely if no one in my society has ever been to or put on a show of such music.

The ground is now laid for Raz's political argument. His answer to OQ is that governments ought to provide what he calls the 'facilitating conditions' of autonomy. This means that individuals must (1) not be prevented from accessing a wide range of valuable pursuits and ways of life, (2) be educated so as to be able to make an informed choice amongst that range, and (3) must have the means to do so, which means having not just economic resources, but also the appropriate societal support for all those various culturally grounded options with which they want to engage. These three conditions can be further clarified by spelling out their implications. Echoing the theorists of tolerance in **1.8**, the freedom described by (1) implies that societies need to tolerate all sorts of ways of life, whatever the majority might think of them. Echoing the egalitarians of **1.3**, the mental abilities described by (2) imply that substantial taxation and economic redistribution should occur in order to ensure that everyone is capable of autonomous choices. And echoing the communitarians of **1.3**, the resources and support described in (3) imply both public provision of certain cultural resources (e.g. community centres, leisure facilities, tennis courts, art galleries, university scholarships) and, as a result, further economic redistribution.

We have, then, an answer to OQ which holds that the role of political systems and the governments they produce is to ensure that each and every individual is fully able to pursue whatever valuable form of life he or she chooses. So what is Raz's answer to FQ? Here he tells us that politics ought to be shaped by what he calls the 'humanistic principle', according to which 'the explanation and justification of the goodness or badness of anything derives ultimately from its contribution, actual or possible, to human life and its quality'.[141] Or, as he writes on another occasion, 'political morality is concerned primarily with protecting and promoting the well-being of people'.[142] The idea, then, to connect these answers to OQ and FQ with the theory of practical reasoning set out earlier, is that if it is the case that human life is lived well when it is lived in the rational pursuit of objective values, and if it is the case that those values are plural

---

[141] *Morality of Freedom*, 194.   [142] *Ethics in the Public Domain*, v.

and culturally embedded, then what governments need to do, if they are
to discharge the requirements of political morality, is ensure that everyone, regardless of cultural background, can pursue whatever set of values
it is that he or she has rationally chosen.

So what are we to make of this argument? Its essential problem, it
seems, is that there is a tension between the requirements of living well
described by Raz's theory of practical reasoning and the requirements of
autonomy's facilitating conditions entailed by his humanistic principle.
This tension concerns in particular the third of his three facilitating
conditions of autonomy, so it is worth reproducing two of his clearest
statements on the subject. First, consider the general idea of the
condition:

The principle we should uphold is simply that every person should have access to
an adequate range of options to enable him to have a successful life. . . . Ours is
a moral concern with the well-being of others. . . . The main cause for social
reform, and for moral action based on concern for others' well-being, is to secure
adequate access.[143]

Second, consider the condition's cultural implications:

Liberal multiculturalism [is] a normative principle [which] affirms that . . .
a political attitude of fostering and encouraging the prosperity, cultural and
material, of cultural groups within a society, and respecting their identity, is
justified. . . . These considerations call on governments to take action which
goes beyond that required by policies of toleration and non-discrimination.[144]

So, the argument we are dealing with is that political morality involves the
promotion of everyone's well-being, which in turn requires the promotion
of everyone's autonomy, which in turn requires serious redistribution in
order to support every valuable cultural form of which there are members
in the society in question. But there are theoretical and practical difficulties here. The theoretical difficulty is that there is actually no necessary
connection between my ability to live well and everybody else's ability to
do the same. Although I may well need help from the state in order to live
autonomously, there is no requirement, as far as my own needs are
concerned, for the state to do the same thing for other people. So long
as I possess the right mental abilities and economic resources, and so long
as the state supports those cultural forms required for my own chosen way
of life, my own ability to live well will not be impaired if other people lack
those things. The practical difficulty is that three features of Raz's theory
of practical reasoning make it, not just possible for the requirements of
individual rationality and political morality to diverge, but also very likely.

[143] Ibid., 23–24.   [144] Ibid., 189.

These three features are (1) taste, (2) culture, and (3) competitive pluralism. The problem of taste is that, when faced with plural and incommensurable options in life, I will just naturally feel attracted to some options rather than others, which within the parameters of Raz's theory of practical reasoning is perfectly reasonable. As he puts it at one point, 'our chemistry, rather than our rationality, explains why some like it hot'.[145] And this is just what we should expect given value-pluralism and incommensurability. If we cannot have all good things in life, and if there is no common measure of all good things, then how else are we to decide between those things approved of by reason if not by reference to whatever desires we already happen to have? So, if I simply prefer tennis to football, I do no crime against reason by joining a tennis club rather than a football club. But now consider, if I also choose to support political parties supportive of my own preferences in life rather than political parties supportive of the autonomy of all, I also do no crime against reason. So long as I am acting in the rational pursuit of objectively valuable things, there is nothing to be said against my supporting, either privately or politically, only those things which cater to my own autonomy.

This, then, takes us to culture, because where preferences driven by taste end, preferences driven by socialisation begin. Wherever we draw the line between nature and nurture, the problem now is that if I have been acculturated in such a way as to make me prefer mosque to church, medicine to banking, and libertarian political principles over their egalitarian alternatives, then there is no rational requirement for me to change my mind. Again, remember that Raz tells us that we live well when we engage in the rational pursuit of objective values. So long as what I pursue is valuable, and so long as it is rational given my current situation for me to pursue it, then there is nothing unreasonable about my behaviour. But, then, if that is true, there is also nothing unreasonable about my choosing to support my own cultural institutions over those of other cultures. And, in turn, if there is nothing unreasonable about that, then there is also nothing unreasonable about supporting political parties who share that view.

Consider, third, competitive pluralism, which again is a concept already found in Raz's work.[146] Raz intends the concept to capture the fact that, in pluralistic societies, most of the ways of life to which individuals are committed will involve, as part and parcel of their outlook on the world, strongly disapproving views of many of the alternatives. For example, if I am an atheist and a hedonist, those ideals may well lead to my

---

[145] *Engaging Reason*, 66.   [146] *Morality of Freedom*, 404–407.

being repulsed by the Christian ethic of asceticism. Or, if I am an animal rights activist, then I may well denounce and wish to restrict kosher butchery. The idea here is that because each of us really values what we value, we will also often condemn and oppose its opposite. Competitive pluralism is, then, an ineluctable fact about the world, insofar as it is just what we should expect to see when people think and act in natural and perfectly reasonable ways. Just as Rawls recognised that perfectly reasonable people operating under liberal conditions will naturally come to disagree about the right answer to OQ, Raz recognises that perfectly reasonable people will, as a function of the content of their values, come to dislike and compete with those who subscribe to alternative – though reasonable – ways of life. But if this is just what we should expect, how are we supposed to prevent it happening? Or, more precisely, if people are going to naturally want to prioritise their own way of life over the ways of others, what reason can we give them to do otherwise?

Raz's work contains several possible solutions to these problems, none of which is adequate to the task. First is his suggestion that serving my own values will often mean serving the values of others.[147] This is sometimes true. If I am a nurse who heals the sick, then I will often be helping those who subscribe to ways of life to which I do not subscribe myself. Or, if I am a police officer, then presumably I will be helping to bring law and order to all, which again will presumably serve the cause of everybody's autonomy, and not just my own. And consider finally, as a result of the general requirements of the state, and as a result of the democratic need to compromise, I will often be happy to agree to governments which support both my values and those of other people, provided that the alternative is a government that would support neither. Yet this solution, as far as it goes, only helps in situations where the balance of preferences would lend itself to the kind of policies that Raz prescribes. Where there is a recognisable majority interest in society, as there usually is, there will be no need for the minority's interest to be catered to, at least above and beyond doing things that fall far short of Raz's own demands. Although law and order and general infrastructure might be available to all, this would still be a good deal less than the kind of universal provision of autonomy's facilitating conditions Raz envisages.

Raz's second solution turns on the point that there is nothing *irrational* about acting morally. If the statement 'it is an excellent painting' is enough to explain the purchase of a work of art, then surely the statement 'she needed help' functions as sufficient explanation for the granting of aid. Promoting another's well-being is really no more unreasonable than

---

[147] *Morality of Freedom*, 319. See also *Value, Respect, and Attachment*, 158–159.

the purchase of a car, which should make us wonder: what more do we need for an answer to OQ to be convincing above and beyond the fact that instantiating it would serve everybody's well-being?[148] The problem here is that if we say that a convincing answer to OQ is an answer that would convince all rational people to whom it is applied, then we face a challenge, given that, according to Raz's own theory, rational people are highly likely to want different and incompatible political settlements. And indeed, even if someone does value the well-being of all, and by extension the autonomy of all, there is still no reason for them to prioritise this over the maximisation of their own well-being and autonomy. And again, this prioritisation is just what we should expect given what are, within Raz's theory, predictable deviations in preference driven by taste, culture, and the oppositional nature of many values.

We are now left, then, with Raz' third solution, as captured by the claim that 'An autonomy-sustaining common culture is a presupposition of the freedom of one and all.'[149] Yet this is simply untrue. Although Raz is right to stress that each of us requires the co-operation of others in order to achieve our own autonomy, he is wrong to claim that the autonomy of anyone requires the autonomy of everyone. My own autonomy no more necessarily requires the autonomy of others with whom I have no shared values than it requires the autonomy of those living on the other side of the planet. If my own parents support me, and my own culture and personal preferences are supported, then there is really nothing more I need. Of course, I may still be prepared to water down this support in order to help others, but there is no requirement of reason for me to do so. And indeed, even if I did wish to do this, the chances are, according to Raz's theory, that most of my peers would disagree with me.

It seems, then, that even as we live well by the lights of Raz's theory of practical reasoning, we are likely to live selfishly by the lights of his theory of political morality. This renders Raz's answer to OQ an unconvincing one, if only because there is no way of reconciling the two opposed parts of his argument. Although his theory of practical reasoning is intended as a partial grounding for his political philosophy, it actually undermines it.[150] However, although this aspect of Raz's own answer to FQ under-mines his answer to OQ, it does at least appear to leave open the

---

[148] The claim that it is rational, though not a requirement of rationality, to place moral values above non-moral values is one Raz makes repeatedly throughout his many works. See, for example, the last three chapters of *Engaging Reason*. See also the discussion of reasons for respect in *Value, Respect, and Attachment*, esp. 166–167.

[149] *Ethics in the Public Domain*, 122.

[150] For an extended version of this argument, see J. Floyd, 'Raz on Practical Reason and Political Morality', *Jurisprudence* (2016).

possibility of a different argument bridging the gap. Perhaps, we might think, there is a way of altering his theory of practical reasoning so as to render the provision of autonomy-for-all a convincing answer to OQ for all. And yet, at the same time, we do now seem further away from establishing any convincing answer to OQ than we were before we looked at Raz's argument, because to the extent that his theory of practical reasoning is a convincing one – and everything he says about how it chimes with ordinary thought appears seems to support that – it also seems to make even more chimerical that ambition. Or, alternatively put, if rationality is at odds with political morality, what hope have we got?

1.11   Alasdair MacIntyre: Competing Traditions as a Guide to Morality

Perhaps our best hope will be to see if we can identify an approach to practical rationality that is both more convincing than Raz's and more successful in terms of an answer to OQ. This is why Alasdair MacIntyre's work is so interesting, because although he agrees with Raz that any convincing answer to OQ has to be grounded in a convincing theory of practical reason, he disagrees with him about how that theory ought to be developed. Rather than study what appear to be transparent and pre-theoretical patterns of ordinary thinking, MacIntyre claims that we should conduct a comparative study of the different intellectual traditions out of which rival theories are developed.[151] Whether or not he is right about this will depend in large part on how his argument concludes at the normative level. Consider the following steps in his reasoning.

MacIntyre begins by telling us that the two traditions we need to compare are Aristotelianism and what he calls the Enlightenment Project. By Aristotelianism, we would expect to encounter a theory that makes great play of the idea of a 'virtue', and that is just what he delivers, but this is by no means his central idea. Instead, MacIntyre presents an approach to practical rationality that centres on the idea of a narrative. As he puts it at one point, we are 'co-authors' of our own lives; persons who enter on a stage they did not design. This means that although we get to choose what form of life we adopt, we do not get to choose exactly what those forms entail. It may be up to me whether to become a father, or a priest, or a barrister, or a teacher, but if I do decide on any of these things, then what counts as excellence in each case, and what the 'telos' of my endeavours should be, will already be long established. The idea of

---

[151] The key arguments to this effect can all be found in A. MacIntyre, *Whose Justice? Which Rationality?* (Notre Dame, IN: University of Notre Dame Press, 1988).

human life being shaped by narrative is then the idea that what each of us ought to do will depend, most fundamentally, on what the established virtues and goals are of the ways of life we have adopted. MacIntyre also makes the further point that we should aim for a unity across our narratives, but that is not the most important claim here. What matters more is what he sees as the key political implication of this view of human nature – that if human beings are to live flourishing lives, they will have to live in political communities that actively support the ways of life they have adopted. And indeed, not just any political communities, but communities united by a shared view regarding just what sorts of life ought to be encouraged. MacIntyre therefore agrees with Raz that individuals need to have their culturally embedded ways of life supported by the state, whilst also agreeing with the communitarians that political systems ought to map on to and represent particular cultural groups.

This, then, takes us to an alternative view of human life which MacIntyre claims has philosophically and politically supplanted Aristotelianism, despite being inferior to it on both counts. This alternative, which he calls the Enlightenment Project, rejects the idea that practical rationality hinges on cultural context, and instead aspires towards principles for right action which any rational person would have to accept, regardless of background and circumstance. We can think of Thomas Scanlon's well-known criteria for a universal moral rule as a particularly clear expression of the general idea: 'Judgements of right and wrong ... are judgements about what would be permitted by principles that could not reasonably be rejected, by people who were moved to find principles for the general regulation of behaviour that others, similarly motivated, could not reasonably reject.'[152] In this case, although the notion of 'reasonable' is particular to the theory proposed, the aspiration is typical of the project as a whole. Provided that they are rational, two people should be able to agree on moral and political principles, and thus a meaningful answer to OQ, regardless of their different cultural standpoints.

How, though, are we to compare these rival approaches? MacIntyre gives two plausible answers to this question. The first answer is that we need to see which tradition holds the superior dialectical record over time. This approach asks us to investigate just which tradition has done best in its interactions with other traditions throughout history. For example, if Aristotelianism has managed to respond well to a wide range of objections over centuries of intellectual endeavour, then that is to be regarded as a point in its favour. Or, by contrast, if the Enlightenment Project has

---

[152] T. M. Scanlon, *What We Owe to Each Other* (Cambridge, MA: Harvard University Press, 1998), 4.

failed to respond to numerous strong objections over the course of its own history, then that ought to lower its comparative standing in relation to its rivals. This failure is just what MacIntyre thinks has happened. At its simplest, the problem for the Enlightenment Project, at least as far as MacIntyre is concerned, is that it has proven unable to formulate principles of practical rationality to which no reasonable person could object. Each rival tradition, including Aristotelianism, will have its own explanation for why this ambition has not yet been realised, but that is not the point. What matters, from the point of view of tradition-centred enquiry, is that if one tradition has proven itself incapable of responding to those who claim that its central ambition is impossible, then that tradition is, *for that reason*, to be deemed a failure. We are supposed to take our criteria of practical rationality, together with their entailed political principles, from traditions that have managed to stay the course of intellectual combat, not from those that have proven incapable of realising their defining ambitions.

The problem with this approach, however, is that it fails to account for what Karl Popper called radical conceptual innovation. Popper's argument is that we cannot predict the future because we cannot even imagine many of the inventions and developments that will determine its course. Consider, for example, the invention of the computer, a device which just like the wheel, steam engine, telephone, or assault rifle, has had dramatic consequences for the way contemporary humans live their lives. Who could have predicted the invention of the computer in 1900, let alone in 1600? Nobody could have had even the vaguest notion of such a device, let alone the many innovative uses to which it might be put. Of course, people could have imagined what the world might look like if humans could fly, or communicate across the globe, or send down great big firestorms on one another, but that is just what it is – imagination. It is idle speculation, or the stuff of science fiction, not predictive social science. From the point of view of tradition-centred enquiry, it is a fitting irony that the credibility of futurology is so undone by its own history, but that is hardly a boon to MacIntyre. The crucial problem with writing off the Enlightenment Project on the grounds that it has not yet delivered after, say, 300 years of endeavour, is that we have no way of knowing just what new innovations it might be capable of in the future. We also have no more reason to regard it as futile than we would have had to regard modern science as futile during the many centuries that preceded Newton's breakthroughs.

This means that we need to turn to MacIntyre's alternative approach to the comparison of rival traditions. Sometimes, instead of telling us that we need to compare the dialectical record of each tradition with its rivals, he tells us that we need to see just which tradition is most logically consistent. Consider, for instance, genealogy as an intellectual tradition. MacIntyre argues that genealogy is logically flawed because it both assumes and denies the existence of an inner, ahistorical self.[153] Claiming on the one hand that even our deepest values and presuppositions are the product of history and on the other that we can both identify that history and emancipate ourselves from it, the genealogist appears to be in an unavoidable logical bind. If there is some inner 'me' to which genealogical history can be revealed, and if that 'me' is also capable of independently appraising that history, then the claim that my identity and values have been formed by history becomes a nonsense. But now consider two further examples, this time borrowed from the Enlightenment Project. Regarding utilitarianism, MacIntyre tells us that it is doomed to failure because regardless of whether it tries to ground universal moral and political principles in pleasures, desires, or conceptions of well-being, the inescapable difficulty is that different people prefer different varieties of each. And, in turn, regarding intuitionist approaches to moral and political justification – including approaches which seek to ground various universalisability tests in particular intuitions – he tells us that they have never succeeded for the simple reason that different people have different intuitions. So, the argument now, in short, is that we ought to reject the Enlightenment Project for the simple reason that each of its manifestations can be revealed as unavoidably flawed. It is for that reason an inconsistent tradition, and ought as such to be rejected.

The problem with this approach, however, is that even if we accept that intuitionist and utilitarian approaches cannot succeed, this would still be no reason by itself to reject any of the other manifestations of the Enlightenment Project. For example, we would not on this basis have had reason to reject out of hand several of the arguments we have already considered in this chapter, including those which centred on the ideas of reasonableness, tolerance, deliberation, or universal evils. Paralleling the problem with MacIntyre's first approach to comparing traditions, the difficulty here is that showing that one particular manifestation of the Enlightenment Project does not work, or even that all existing manifestations do not work, still does not rule out for us the possibility that a new, successful manifestation might be developed. But there is also an even bigger problem. MacIntyre, remember, is telling us not only that we ought to reject the Enlightenment Project on the grounds of its apparent inconsistency, but also that we ought to reject it *for* Aristotelianism. But

---

[153] See A. MacIntyre, *Three Versions of Moral Enquiry: Encyclopaedia, Genealogy, and Tradition* (Notre Dame, IN: University of Notre Dame Press, 1990).

why should we do that? If I currently subscribe to one set of political principles, and it turns out that the tradition out of which those principles have been developed is currently unable to respond to one or more serious challenges, does that then give me good reason to adopt a completely different set? For example, even if I agreed that the ultimate aspiration behind libertarian principles is to find principles that no reasonable person could reject, surely whatever values those principles represent will continue to attract me, even if I discover that there are reasonable people who do not feel as I do. Presumably, unless I am shown some further set of principles which absolutely no reasonable person could reject, I will just carry on as I did before. MacIntyre often seems to think that we should prefer consistent systems we find distasteful over inconsistent systems we do not, but this is surely just philosophical bias.[154] For most people, there are more important things in life than theoretical consistency.

MacIntyre does, however, offer us one further line of argument, as presented in his more recent work, *Dependent Rational Animals*.[155] Here he attempts to provide a brand new argument in favour of an Aristotelian approach to politics that has apparently nothing to do with the comparison of rival intellectual traditions. In this book, he describes his problem to date as a failure to show why the virtues are needed for *any* flourishing life, and insofar as he has not managed to convince us that the difficulties so far encountered by the Enlightenment Project *automatically* render his approach to politics a convincing one, that admission is certainly an encouraging one. The key idea now, by contrast, is that every human being, if he or she is to flourish, needs to become what MacIntyre calls an 'independent practical reasoner'. Again there are echoes of Raz here, because what MacIntyre means by this is that, if everyone is to live a worthwhile life, everyone will have to develop a certain kind of mental capacity. Drawing once more on his Aristotelian model of practical reasoning, MacIntyre seeks to show that it is in the interest of anyone, regardless of cultural background, to cultivate this capacity, and as a result have the state support him or her in that cultivation.

We do not, though, have to revisit MacIntyre's theory of practical reason, or indeed his earlier claims regarding how that theory is vindicated by the history of the tradition out of which it has been developed, in order to see just where this new argument goes wrong. The basic problem

---

[154] This preference is at its clearest in his later essays, including in particular 'Moral Dilemmas', as found in A. MacIntyre, *Ethics and Politics: Selected Essays, Volume 2* (Cambridge: Cambridge University Press, 2006), 85–100.

[155] A. MacIntyre, *Dependent Rational Animals: Why Human Beings Need the Virtues* (London: Duckworth, 1999).

now is the basic problem Raz faced in the previous section. Even if we grant that everybody needs to become an independent practical reasoner in order to flourish, and also that no one can become an independent practical reasoner without the help of others, it does not follow that everyone needs to become one in order for anyone to become one. Just as we saw with Raz, it does not follow from the fact that I need others in order to become autonomous that I need everyone to become autonomous. If I am already an independent practical reasoner, then I do not need anyone else to become one in order to stay as I am. Or, in turn: if I am a parent, and my wife and I are independent practical reasoners, then it will be enough for us if our child's teachers are also such reasoners, for that will surely be enough for him to also acquire that status. And indeed, judging from the way in which private schooling is purchased throughout the world, it seems standard practice for many parents to want a certain quality of education for their children precisely *because* it is not available to all. However much they might like to dress it up as the desire to achieve a 'decent education' for their children, what they are really after is a comparative advantage – a way of increasing their children's opportunities relative to those whose parents are unable to afford the premiums involved.

MacIntyre tries to bolster this argument at one point by drawing on a certain idea of human vulnerability. He writes:

It matters also and correspondingly that those who are no longer children recognise in children what they once were, that those who are not yet disabled by age recognise in the old what they are moving towards becoming, and that those who are not ill or injured recognise in the ill and injured what they often have been and will be and always may be.[156]

His point here is not just that those of us who are currently autonomous adults were once children, but also that each of us will one day become old and infirm, with some of us even becoming disabled along the way. We shall all grow weak at one point, with many of us quickly becoming dependent upon the goodwill of others. So might we not then want, on the basis of this vulnerability, to facilitate the development of those virtuous, supportive communities prescribed by MacIntyre? The problem with this is that too many people will be unwilling to make the sacrifices required in order to create these communities because they fail to believe that such a condition of vulnerability will happen to them. By this I do not mean the age-old problem of our being 'in denial' regarding the ageing process, but rather the problem of optimism regarding how each of us will be placed to

---

[156] Ibid., 146.

deal with it. It is often remarked of American voters, for instance, that they continue to give their support for tax cuts for the rich on the basis that they expect to be wealthy one day themselves. Pensions are not invested in and property assumed to offer sufficient security, whilst the assumption that a lottery win, spectacular investment, lucrative job opportunity, or radical improvement in business fortune is just around the corner continues to loom large. Though each accepts that such good fortune will probably *not* come to the majority, and though each accepts that extreme infirmity *will* come to a significant minority, people tend to believe that they will, in both instances, be on the lucky side of the division. That such optimism is often irrational, and that such irrationality ought to be criticised, is perhaps true, but that fact is no good to us here. Consider here that in our search for a convincing answer to OQ, we are trying to find arguments which, even if most people have never encountered them, could potentially generate a political consensus, which is to say a consensus on the principles that ought to regulate politics. The problem with MacIntyre's vulnerability argument here is that it adds nothing to what people either already know, or already know and do not want to hear.

We can conclude, then, by saying that MacIntyre ultimately shares with Raz a failure to prove that the autonomy of anyone depends on the autonomy of everyone. If he had managed to show that, or if he had managed to show that the historically revealed difficulties of one tradition gave us good reason to switch our own political allegiances in favour of those entailed by another, then we might have got close to a convincing answer to OQ, but he did not. We turned to MacIntyre, in part, because he offered us a way of answering OQ that seemed radically different to any of the failed approaches we have already considered. Perhaps what we need to do now is find something that makes his methodology look as conservative as his politics.

1.12   Rorty's Liberalism by Redescription

Our next hope, Richard Rorty, can certainly be described as less politically conservative than MacIntyre, though whether he is more radical in his methodology is unclear. What is clear is that Rorty agrees with the communitarians that our answers to OQ have to vary according to cultural context, whilst disagreeing with them that there currently exist communities harmonious and homogenous enough to be described as having one or other coherent set of values. He claims that rather than trying to find something upon which either all human beings or even a small community already agrees, the trick instead will be to try and *create* that agreement. And in particular, rather than trying to show that people are already egalitarian liberals at heart – by trying to show, for instance, that they already subscribe to certain ideals of reasonableness, or deliberation, or autonomy, etc. – he thinks that they can be made into liberals by way of the right kind of emotive rhetoric. So, rather than trying to demonstrate that a particular answer to OQ is convincing on account of the fact that we already agree with its premises, Rorty thinks that he can completely transform our entire moral outlook by using the right kind of persuasive language. Consider the following claims.

According to Rorty, the best way to make people liberals is to make them aware of all the various forms of cruelty going on in the world. Making people aware of cruelties, he tells us, makes them sympathetic to the plight of those involved, which in turn makes them more liberal as regards appropriate political behaviour. He elaborates on this point by telling us (1) that liberal regimes are the least cruel of all possible regimes, and (2) that news articles, novels, films, and so on are the most powerful means for the raising of awareness regarding such cruelties.[157] This means that whatever our current moral and political beliefs might be, we can have our sympathies manipulated in such a way as to ensure a liberal outcome. It is striking that Rorty accepts that he is only a liberal because he was raised a liberal. He also accepts that in the grand scheme of things there is nothing more to be said for this political position than any other, at least as far as rational philosophical argument is concerned – a point which certainly chimes with our difficulties so far. What he does not accept, however, is that there is nothing we can do to affect other people's positions, given this contingency. If you do just happen to be a liberal, there is still a great deal that can be done to persuade other people of your point of view.

The problem with these claims is that it is not at all clear just how these lists of cruelties are supposed to weave their magic. Rorty's assumption is that to be *made aware* of the performance of cruelty is also to be *motivated to end* it, an assumption which implicitly has to rely on the existence of some deep, pre-social, Humean quality of sympathy in human nature. This is surprising given that in most of Rorty's work he is concerned to deny that there is any such quality – that there is any *pre*-social, *pre*-linguistic human nature. According to him, people only possess particular attitudes – including liberal, sympathetic attitudes – because 'people in the past spoke a certain way'.[158] Liberals in the West, he claims, are

---

[157] R. Rorty, *Contingency, Irony, and Solidarity* (Cambridge: Cambridge University Press, 1989), esp. xvi, 9, 192; *Philosophy and Social Hope* (London: Penguin, 1999), esp. 14, 82.

[158] Ibid., 61.

merely the product of the liberal universalism of their ancestors.[159] As he writes at one point, he subscribes to a picture of 'human beings as children of their time and place, without any significant metaphysical or biological limits on their plasticity', the upshot of which is that 'a sense of moral obligation is a matter of conditioning rather than of insight'.[160]

That problem of contradiction, however, is only an internal one in Rorty's theory. Although it seems true that he cannot subscribe both to this view of human nature and to this rhetorical approach to convincing people of the merits of a liberal answer to OQ, we might still want to abandon here the first view whilst sticking with the second. Yet that is easier said than done. The problem is that, although the kind of rhetoric he describes might possess the power to convert liberals into moral cosmopolitans, it could not possibly convert non-liberals into liberals. It could not do this because it relies upon a view of human nature which holds that to be apprised of a given instance of suffering is also to be motivated to make ending it a *priority*. And was this true in the Mayan or Aztec empires? Was it true in Sparta, or at the Roman Coliseum? Is it true today in modern China, or even the liberal West? Both history and anthropology seem to undermine Rorty's case here.

Rorty might reply to this, of course, by saying that the reason these societies are insufficiently obsessed with cruelty, and thus in turn insufficiently liberal, is simply that they have not yet been subjected to enough of the right sort of rhetoric. The point of good political philosophy, he might say, is to show us how to change people's minds, not simply interpret them as they are or have been. That would all be well and good, were it not the case that in most of these examples, it is not denied that the people suffering *do* suffer, only that that is not the most normatively relevant concern. For example, it would not have been denied in ancient Rome that screaming Christians, torn limb from limb by the lions, *suffered* for the entertainment of others. Nor would it be denied in modern China that some of the people who lose their homes in order to make way for grand new industrial projects experience trauma as a result of that fate. Nor would it be denied by many in twenty-first-century America that homeless people get cold, and suffer hardship and misery, as a result of their homelessness. All that is denied in each case is that suffering should be avoided at *any* cost.

We do not need to push these examples too far. Even if it were the case, in each of these scenarios, that cruelty was in some sense obscured by propaganda peddled in defence of private, material interests, there is still

---

[159] Ibid., 44. For a rather worried expression of the same point, see C. Larmore, *The Morals of Modernity* (Cambridge: Cambridge University Press, 1996), 63–64.
[160] *Contingency, Irony, and Solidarity*, 14.

no easy leap from suffering to liberalism. Note also the elisions between cruelty and suffering. Even if I were to accept that the poor within a capitalist economy suffer, I still need not accept that this is a result of anybody, or even society as a whole, treating them cruelly. I may well accept that their fate is the result of bad luck, and not at all a result of their own laziness or carelessness, but still, I need not necessarily move from this belief to an overwhelming desire to improve their circumstances. Recall here a problem noted of Berlin's theory, according to which it seemed perfectly reasonable for someone to support a dynamic, progressive society that enjoyed little equality over one which was as fair as it was stagnant. Recall also a problem encountered within Hampshire's theory, whereby even if one accepted the existence of universal evils, there would still be ample room to disagree about whose responsibility they are. Putting these two problems together, we can now readily imagine someone who (1) accepts that the poor suffer in a libertarian society, whilst still supporting that society for the benefits it brings, and (2) accepts that extreme poverty is a universal evil, whilst disagreeing that the rich are in some way responsible for its existence.

To be clear, my purpose here is not to support the view described by these two positions. The point is simply that if such people are to have their minds changed, we need to do more than merely point out to them that there are people in their society who suffer.[161] And note, in making that point – in saying that we need to do more than simply tug at people's consciences in order to turn them into liberals – we do not need to claim, as Rorty sometimes does, that our conscience, just as much as our tastes, is a completely non-natural and utterly malleable feature of our selves. We can therefore conclude by saying that although Rorty was brave enough to declare pluralism an insurmountable philosophical problem, he has failed to show us a rhetorical route around it, and thus failed to show an alternative way in which we could get some significant number of people to agree to a single answer to OQ. It seems, then, that persuasion, given the scale of contemporary disagreement, is no easier to effect than justification.

1.13   A Variety of Further Responses: Denial, Judgement, Deferral

We have now considered a variety of attempts to provide a convincing and meaningful answer to OQ, yet appear to have got nowhere. All of the arguments we have examined since **1.4** seemed initially promising on account of their recognition of the problem of plural, conflicting values,

---

[161] Ibid., 177.

yet not one of them succeeded. But perhaps their fundamental problem *is* that recognition. It is a strange notion, but perhaps we need to return to arguments which actually pay less heed to pluralism, or at least which put the emphasis less on finding radically new ways of working up an answer to OQ, and more on finding better ways of doing the kind of thing already discussed in **1.3**. Consider the following positions.

First, consider a group of thinkers who think that, although we do face a pluralism *of sorts*, that pluralism is not nearly so *deep*, nor nearly so *fractious*, as many thinkers have assumed it to be. Jonathan Riley, for instance, thinks that liberalism emerges out of a 'common moral horizon [which] all decent cultures share'.[162] He thinks that all reasonable agents have to accept that there are things – liberal things – which all people have an interest in, regardless of social context.[163] Donald Moon argues along similar lines, claiming that although 'autonomy' might be too strong an ideal to recommend universally, we can prescribe a value of 'agency' – a sort of autonomy-light – for all. He believes that because all agents have an interest in protecting their capacity to direct their own activity, distinguishing agency from autonomy alleviates the tensions in liberalism.[164] This claim to the effect that autonomy is too strong an ideal to prescribe for all is echoed by William Galston, although he thinks that, rather than 'agency', we should recommend what he calls 'expressive liberty' to all.[165] He argues that because free association yields vital human goods, no state can be legitimate which denies it as much free reign as possible. Echoing Riley and Moon, Galston explains that, although expressive liberty is not strictly speaking a value, it is a 'fact about human agency, and gains value from the goals it allows agents to fulfil'.[166] And consider finally George Crowder, who thinks that although it is true, as all pluralists stress, that there exist a vast number of important values, it is also true that we are better off if there are more rather than fewer of these values available.[167] He also claims that we are better able to engage with these values if we are autonomous than if we are not.[168] Taken together, then, each of these

---

[162] J. Riley, 'Defending Cultural Pluralism: Within Liberal Limits', *Political Theory*, 30 (2002), 78.

[163] Ibid., 89–90.

[164] J. D. Moon, 'Liberalism, Autonomy, and Moral Pluralism', *Political Theory*, 31 (2003), 134.

[165] W. A. Galston, *Liberal Pluralism: The Implications of Value Pluralism for Political Theory and Practice* (Cambridge: Cambridge University Press, 2002), 3.

[166] W. A. Galston, 'Liberal Pluralism: A Reply to Talisse', *Contemporary Political Theory*, 3 (2004), 145.

[167] G. Crowder, 'From Value Pluralism to Liberalism', in R. Bellamy and M. Hollis, *Pluralism and Liberal Neutrality*, 3.

[168] Ibid., 16.

arguments takes us from a moderate position on pluralism to an argument in favour of autonomy-centric liberalism – however much some of these theorists might want to shy away from using that particular term.

A second group of thinkers believes that, although it is true that we possess no knock-down arguments in favour of one particular answer, it is also true that we possess a capacity for *judging* one answer better than another – even if we cannot always spell out the reasons which support those judgements. Seung and Bonevac, for example, argue that although we lack a universal common measure in these sorts of argument, that fact does not by itself preclude verdicts of 'better' or 'worse'.[169] In this claim they draw heavily on the work of James Griffin, and also echo Nagel, who we considered earlier, and who claims at one point both (a) 'there can be good judgement without total justification' and (b) 'in most cases a reasonable decision can be reached only by sound judgement, informed as well as possible by the best arguments that any relevant disciplines have to offer'.[170] The argument now, therefore, is both (1) that even if we do not always know what is best, we do know what is *better*, and (2) that even if we do not always know *why* something is best or better, we do still know somehow that it *is*, for we are able, somehow, to *judge* it as such.

A third set of thinkers believes that although it is true we have not yet worked out the final answers in political philosophy, that by itself is no reason to abandon hope. These thinkers echo Derek Parfit, who once wrote that 'Non-Religious Ethics is at a very early stage. We cannot yet predict whether, as in Mathematics, we will all reach agreement. Since we cannot know how Ethics will develop, it is not irrational to have high hopes.'[171] Isaac Levi, for instance, writes that he fails to see why 'we should do anything other than what we would do were there to be a hope of successful inquiry'.[172] He thinks that we should continue to try and avoid inconsistency in value judgement, and encourage any and all attempts to systematise the blooming, buzzing confusion of moral judgement.[173] Lawrence Becker echoes this call, stressing that there is no reason for us to rule out, amongst other things, the possibilities of our developing mildly pluralist versions of consequentialism, deontology, and virtue ethics.[174] Writing in support of these hopes, Peter Railton claims that the drive to systematise our moral thought comes, not from a fetish for coherence and purity, but rather from the problematic existence of

---

[169] T. K. Seung and D. Bonevac, 'Plural Values and Indeterminate Rankings"', *Ethics*, 102:4, 800.

[170] T. Nagel, *Mortal Questions* (Cambridge: Cambridge University Press, 1979), 134, 141.

[171] D. Parfit, *Reasons and Persons* (Oxford: Oxford University Press, 1984), 454.

[172] I. Levi, 'Conflict and Inquiry', *Ethics*, 102:4 (1992), 830.   [173] Ibid., 833–834.

[174] L. C. Becker, 'Places for Pluralism', *Ethics*, 102:4 (1992), 707–718.

moral conflict.[175] One of his most interesting suggestions is that, in addition to continuing to work on our existing grand moral theories, we should try to develop alongside them what he calls a set of 'mid-level theories'.[176] The thought here is that we might be able to work out matters of wrong and right in particular ethical domains without necessarily being able to see, at least at first, just how those truths might be derived from more abstract moral foundations. And consider finally Thomas Hurka, who thinks that we ought to opt for 'moderate' rather than 'extreme' pluralism. He thinks that if we would just go back to the early twentieth-century intuitionist theories of Moore, Rashdall, and Ross, we might well find a way of resolving many of the dilemmas which confront us.[177]

Now, although one could easily fill a book with further examples of each of these three responses to our difficulties, there would be little point in doing so, given that each approach faces its own insurmountable problems. Consider the first group. Their problem is that they are in denial. Denying that pluralism runs as deep as our earlier considered thinkers have taken it to run, they believe that fairly high-level moral universals are still an open and relatively accessible option. These thinkers do not even try, as Rawls and Hampshire tried, to find some deep-lying norm or procedure upon which we could all agree, choosing instead to declare moral universals from the start, and only pausing to discuss what those universals might entail for our political existence. Recall that most of the thinkers we have considered so far both (1) worked their way up from a deep-set universal ideal towards determinate political prescriptions and (2) tried to make a case for why that ideal *was* deep-set and universal. By contrast, thinkers such as Riley and Galston do not even attempt (2), opting instead to simply declare *their* universal as 'the choice of any reasonable individual'. Such work fails to seriously address the breadth and depth of disagreement found both in existing political societies and in contemporary political philosophy. It neither (a) explains the existence of that disagreement, nor (b) attempts to construct any new and alternative means by which we might transcend it. And so, because they simply add to the long list of moral ideals invoked in contemporary normative argument, we should consider these arguments, not a part of the solution, but a part of the problem.

Our second group fares little better. It is actually quite astounding to say that we can judge either right from wrong or better from worse when it is precisely the disagreements we have about those judgements – as given by

---

[175] P. Railton, 'Pluralism, Determinacy, and Dilemma', *Ethics*, 102:4 (1992), 721.
[176] Ibid., 742.
[177] T. Hurka, 'Monism, Pluralism, and Rational Regret', *Ethics*, 106:3 (1996), 575.

different and esteemed political philosophers – that are the problem. How can it be the case that more experienced judges judge better when even our most experienced philosophical judges judge differently? Libertarians, egalitarians, communitarians, deliberative democrats – all of them disagree both with each other and with that group of more comprehensive liberals considered in the previous paragraph. Saying that an exercise in judgement is the solution to a problem of *differences* in judgement is like saying that an exercise in choice is the solution to a problem of differences in choice, or an exercise in taste the solution to a problem of differences in taste. What we are trying to find, remember, is an answer to OQ capable of drawing support from very different groups of people, each of whom is currently possessed of a variety of different moral judgements.

The third group defers the problem. Rather than trying to look for some alternative means by which we could provide a meaningful and convincing answer to OQ, they believe that we should just continue to try and find, roughly speaking, some moral norm or ideal upon which all reasonable people can be shown to agree. Following our first group, these thinkers fails to take seriously the problem of why political philosophers – so *many* political philosophers, and for so *many* years – differ so wildly in their answers to OQ and FQ. Not only do they lack a convincing and meaningful answer to OQ, they also lack any explanation for why we have not yet found one. This does not by itself, of course, rule out the possibility of their finding an answer – that is not my argument. All I argue is that these thinkers offer us nothing in the way of assistance with solving that problem. They neither solve the problem nor explain its scale and longevity. And even if they were to try and explain the problem by saying, haughtily, that the only reason we have not solved it is that we have not yet found the right universal norm, we would still not be any better off, for we would still not be any closer to finding that solution. Heartfelt encouragement aside, these thinkers leave us no better off, having read their pleas for patience, than we were before we came to consider them.

1.14   Interminability Described: The Impossibility Thesis Introduced

It's time to step back and note, for the first time, the central trend that has emerged from all of the above. This trend is that our considered answers to OQ have fallen down for one or another of two reasons: either they have appealed to only some of those who would have to live with them, and have thus been unconvincing, or they have been politically indeterminate, despite being appealing to all, and have thus not been meaningful.

The Rawls of *Political Liberalism*, the MacIntyre of *Dependent Rational Animals*, the deliberative democrats, the tolerance theorists, and Richard Rorty are all examples of the first failure. Berlin, Hampshire, and Raz are all examples of the second. The first group grounded its arguments in values that many people, and certainly many other thinkers, find either less than universal or less than a matter of priority. The second group grounded its arguments in ideas of more universal appeal, and yet were unable to use those ideas to substantially narrow down our political options.

It is worth illustrating these two types of failure with a few further examples, even if these examples were not ones worth discussing at length in the preceding sections. Consider first of all a position that I have described elsewhere as historical contextualism.[178] Historical contextualists, such as Charles Larmore and Bernard Williams, follow a similar line of argument to the Rawls of *Political Liberalism* just insofar as they begin by trying to identify a value or set of values which, even if they are not universal, are still held consistently enough throughout a particular political community. Larmore claims that people in the modern West share two norms that he calls 'rational dialogue' and 'mutual respect', the political entailment of which is that they should support, again following Rawls, an answer to OQ that he calls political liberalism.[179] Williams, in turn, claims (1) that all political orders need to be able to publicly legitimate themselves in order to properly function; and (2) that in the modern West only liberal legitimations are, as a matter of fact, acceptable.[180] But guess what? The problems with these two arguments are exactly the problems we have encountered already. In Larmore's case, for example, it takes only the briefest examination of the existing moral and political culture of the modern West to discover that there is no more social consensus on his two norms than there is philosophical consensus on the proper senses and relative priorities of liberty, equality, justice, and so on. So what about Williams? His argument runs in parallel with Berlin's insofar as it only succeeds in ruling out

---

[178] See J. Floyd, 'Is Political Philosophy Too Ahistorical?', *Critical Review of International Social and Political Philosophy*, 12:4 (2009); J. Floyd, 'Historical Facts and Political Principles', *Critical Review of International Social and Political Philosophy*, 14:1, 89–90 (2011); and J. Floyd, 'From Historical Contextualism, to Mentalism, to Behaviourism', in J. Floyd and M. Stears (Eds.), *Political Philosophy versus History? Contextualism and Real Politics in Contemporary Political Thought* (Cambridge: Cambridge University Press, 2011).

[179] See in particular C.Larmore, *The Morals of Modernity*; but also C. Larmore, *The Autonomy of Morality* (Cambridge: Cambridge University Press, 2008).

[180] B. Williams, *In the Beginning Was the Deed: Realism and Moralism in Political Argument* (Princeton, NJ: Princeton University Press, 2005).

severely illiberal regimes without being able to differentiate between any of the leading positions in contemporary political discourse. Larmore's answer is thus meaningful without being convincing, whilst Williams' case is (at least potentially) convincing without being meaningful.

Consider second a position often labelled as realism. Realists agree with the historical contextualists that moral and political ideals tend to vary from place to place, according to different histories, and often agree with the likes of Berlin and Hampshire that the key focus in political theory and practice ought to be on universal evils.[181] Given the way in which political decisions occur under conditions of uncertainty, the way in which aspiringly just policies are restricted by economic constraints, the way in which domestic politics is hemmed in by international affairs, and the way in which, as Williams stressed, we have always to ensure order over and above any more lofty ideals, realists say that there is normally little scope for the kinds of ambitious answers to OQ that are generally bandied around in academic discussion. So what *should* we be aiming at? On this point realists are rather unclear, although a general theme, as noted, is that we need to focus on avoiding universal evils. If we can stay clear of war, famine, severe poverty, disease, and the like, then presumably we are doing well. Yet this is surely a rather meagre argument. After all, in the historical context of the modern West, as discussed by the likes of Rawls and Larmore, there is clearly a lot more that can be achieved than just holding back the four horseman of the apocalypse. All of which means that, once again, and following Berlin, Hampshire, and Williams, we have an argument that can tell us what to avoid without as yet being able to select between any of a vast range of possible political possibilities. Realism is thus another argument that is (at least potentially) convincing without being meaningful.

Consider third a position we could label either post-modern or post-structural.[182] A first example of this is Chantal Mouffe, who begins her argument with a critique of the deliberative democrats. Their mistake, she says, was to think that deliberation could completely overcome those inter-group hostilities which occur, inevitably, in any political environment. Instead, she tells us, we need to *reconstitute* rather than ignore or

---

[181] The most influential recent statement of this kind of realism is R. Geuss, *Philosophy and Real Politics* (Princeton, NJ: Princeton University Press, 2008). For more recent discussion of the topic, see the chapters gathered in J. Floyd and M. Stears (Eds.), *Political Philosophy versus History?*. For my own early appraisal of the literature, see J. Floyd, 'Should Political Philosophy Be More Realistic?', *Res Publica*, 16 (2010), 337–347.

[182] For more extensive analysis of post-modern political theory, as well as the broader 'continental' oeuvre in inhabits, see J. Floyd, 'Analytics and Continentals: Divided by Nature but United by Praxis?', *European Journal of Political Theory*, 15:2, 155–171.

attempt to replace these identities.[183] This would mean making these groups more receptive to democratic values, which in turn would produce a 'pluralistic' politics that is open to a 'multiplicity of voices'.[184] A second example is William Connolly, who shares with Mouffe the idea of reforming rather than side-lining the range of pre-existing political identities found in modern societies. For him, the way in which we transform antagonism into 'agonism' is to nourish a 'pluralist ethos'[185] that expresses 'care' and 'hospitality', whilst also honouring faith and facilitating peace.[186] The nature of the problem shared by both these arguments depends on exactly what kind of 'pluralist' politics it is that they envisage. If, on the one hand, they say that they support the kind of liberal and egalitarian deliberative democracy supported by many deliberative democrats, on the grounds that it opens up politics to a 'multiplicity of voices', whilst also expressing 'care' and 'hospitality', then what we have is an argument that is meaningful but unconvincing. Egalitarians, after all, will say that their arguments already express care and hospitality by treating people as equals, whilst libertarians will say that there are more important things to be considered. Yet on the other hand, if they envisage only the thinnest of procedural understandings of democracy, with echoes now of Hampshire, then what we have is an argument that is neither meaningful nor convincing. In short, if all we are going to demand is that voices are heard and votes counted, then we cannot know whether neo-liberalism or Nazism will be the result.

We do not, I think, need any more examples at this stage. Instead I should like to point out something simple but important about the way in which both these and the earlier positions considered in this chapter have been treated. Consider here that, although one could always have pressed these positions harder on points of theoretical consistency, or perhaps basic issues of political feasibility, it has not been necessary to do so, if only because, as we have gone along, it has become abundantly clear that whatever value or values each thinker has put forward as grounds for their own answer to OQ, there are always rival candidates available. This means two things. It means (1) that it is easy to be unpersuaded by each argument, given the many temptations of the long list of alternative values it has ignored, as highlighted by rival scholars, and (2) that it is even easier to be unpersuaded once one realises that each of

---

[183] C. Mouffe, 'Deliberative Democracy or Agonistic Pluralism?', *Social Research*, 66:3 (1999), 753.

[184] Ibid., 752.

[185] W. E. Connolly, *Pluralism* (Durham, NC, and London: Duke University Press, 2005), 42–47.

[186] Ibid., 65.

these clever scholars also deems the arguments of their rivals unpersua-
sive, regardless of whether or not they make that judgement explicit.
The incompatibility of all these arguments, it seems, only adds to the
evidence of the weakness of each, by which I mean, the fact that so many
wise political philosophers disagree so radically with each other only adds
to our faith that the negative judgement reached in each of the cases so far
is the right one.

But on the other hand, some will say that rather than being too soft on
these positions, I have been too demanding, and that when I look for some
reason or justification beyond or below the reasons and justifications
already given, I am looking for something that could never be provided.
Perhaps the roots of these kinds of arguments are akin to matters of taste.
Consider that, if I like tomato ketchup on my chips, there is not much
more I can say to justify that preference beyond the fact that I like it.
Perhaps I could go a little further and say, by way of supporting reasons,
that I *particularly* like it on account of the *particular* combination of
vinegar and tomatoes found therein, but this would not really solve the
problem, for I could not say anything in support of *that* combination
beyond 'I like it'. Perhaps the same thing could be said for many of my
preferences, from music to architecture, clothes to paintings, and sporting
pursuits to sexual predilections. That is, we really might have little more
to say in each instance beyond the circular pairing of 'I like it because it's
nice' and 'it's nice because I like it'.

Our problems in political philosophy, however, have little in common
with these things. First of all, it does not matter a great deal to my
neighbours if, whilst they dine on caviar, I munch away on my chips
and sauce. Nor does it matter if, as regards art, I prefer Klimt to
Rembrandt and they the reverse. In politics, by contrast, there is no
such luxury. We simply do not get to diverge so happily from each other
in this way. Consider here that the rules governing our collective existence
are, in an important sense, the same for both of us, even if (1) those rules
give you one status and me another, and (2) those rules result in a political
order – anarchical, hierarchical, liberal, or otherwise – that you are better
placed than I am to navigate. Whether we like it or not, we are ruled by
one and the same system, and so cannot, in political life, just agree to
disagree, at least all the way down. Because both of us are governed by
one and the same set of rules, both of us have our life structured in one
and the same way. And these are not minor disagreements. Decisions
about whether we live in a Christian theocracy, deliberative democracy,
Hobbesian state of nature, or anarchist commune are decisions with huge
implications for both of us. Both of our lives will be deeply affected, for
better or worse, by the chosen or imposed political order, which means

that neither of us can simply ignore or privatise the question of what that order should be.

A second difference is that we just do not agree about matters of political normativity the way we agree about, say, the unpleasantness of the sound of nails being dragged down a chalkboard. Although we might well agree that all human beings require oxygen, food, water, and accommodation capable of ensuring a temperature range compatible with the demands of homeostasis, we do not agree, at least at present, about whether we should live in, for example, a libertarian minimal state or a socialist deliberative democracy. And indeed, even if we do all agree that the basic needs listed are biologically required, it does not follow that we think it our duty to ensure that others are either protected from or supplied with such things. It is often claimed that we will not be able to agree on what is right unless we can agree on a conception of what any good life requires, yet even if that were necessary, it would still be a long way short of sufficient.

Taken together, these two problems leave us with the following quandary: people *permanently* disagree about something for which they *have* to provide a collective answer. Although it is true that we have been unable to find an answer to OQ capable of garnering universal approval from citizens and political philosophers alike, it is also true that we are unable to avoid, every day, living our life in accordance with one or other such answer. Or, to put the second part of that point slightly differently, because we have always to live by some or other set of rules – and remember, even anarchy counts as such a set – we have always to live by the dictates of one or other answer to the described question. This means that political philosophy appears both impossible to do – just insofar as we are unable to find a convincing answer to OQ – and impossible to avoid – just insofar as we have no choice but to live by the demands of one or other answer. Taken together, these two challenges make up what I am going to call, from now on, the impossibility thesis.

1.15   The Impossibility Thesis Sustained

To repeat: political philosophy seems impossible to do and impossible to avoid. It *seems* impossible to do because every answer given so far by political philosophers to OQ has been unconvincing and, as a result, rejected in perfectly rational fashion by a majority of his or her fellows. It *is* impossible to avoid because we have all the time to live by the rules of one or other such answer, regardless of whether that answer be anarchist or authoritarian, socialist or libertarian, or liberal or communitarian in content.

Now, some would object to this claim that I have so far neglected what are in fact the most compelling possible responses available to OQ and FQ. That objection is true up to a point: I have certainly ignored these answers up until now, if only because they have also been widely dismissed or ignored by contemporary political philosophers, despite their being routinely expressed, however inarticulately, by many ordinary people on a daily basis. That dismissal, however, particularly in light of the problems just described, is not by itself enough of a reason for me to ignore them completely, which is why I now want to give proper consideration to the following four positions.

The first of these is *relativism*. Relativists claim that what is right is right *relative* to some particular culture (or group, or state, or religion, or civilisation, etc.) at a particular time in its history. This thesis, which is really just a less reflective form of historical contextualism, fails for two reasons. It fails first because it is *itself* a universalistic normative answer requiring further universalistic justification. Even if one answers OQ with some variation on the theme 'when in Rome, do as Romans do', one still has to answer FQ with some further claim, such as 'cultural stability is required for minimally sufficient human well-being. It fails second for the same reason that the historical contextualism mentioned earlier failed, namely, that cultures are internally, as well as externally, contested. If we are ever to provide compelling answers to OQ and FQ, we shall have to try and find normative arguments capable of appealing to people possessed of a variety of cultural influences.

A second response found outside of regular politico-philosophical inquiry (though not meta-ethics) is *subjectivism*. Subjectivists tend to be emotivists. They believe that when I say something is right, all I really mean is that I have a basic, reason-less preference for that 'something' being done or protected. This claim, even if it is true, at least on some level, is not a solution to our problem. Just as we have to try and find an answer capable of bringing together people influenced by different cultural backgrounds, so do we have to try and find an answer capable of bringing together different people possessed of different subjective preferences. Saying that we *do* have different preferences is no answer to the question of what we *should* agree to in political life. For example, if subjectivism were to provide some sort of a plausible explanation for the existence of pluralism, it does nothing to help us transcend it. This does not, of course, rule out the possibility that some radical form of subjectivism is true; it might well be the case that some of us *are* just too different in preference to others to make talk of better or worse political orders possible. I do not deny that. All I claim is that these theories themselves offer no aid in our attempt to try and distinguish better from worse political orders. Although it is true that if we want to refute radical subjectivism, we will have to try and prove that some answer to OQ *is* capable of being better than all others, it is also true that so long as we are looking for that answer we can ignore this thesis.

A third response is *cynicism*, understood in the modern rather than the classical sense of the term. Modern cynics hold that, whatever they choose to say about themselves, all other human beings are motivated only by self-interest. By 'self-interest', cynics tend to have in mind something like power, status, or glory. But in any case, it does not really matter what precise aim they propose as the sole motivation of human action, for whatever it is, such reductivism stands completely at odds with everything we know of human nature. Although it is true that many human beings *do* enjoy the sensations of power, glory and status, it is also true that they enjoy the things which come with them. These include, not just self-regarding goods, such as material comforts and sexual favours, but also the chance to instantiate one's own moral and artistic goals. Rich and powerful individuals are not, at least as a rule, lecherous dictators; they are often also philanthropists, antique collectors, football club owners, and commissioners and patrons of art and architecture. Power and money are for them, as for most of us, instrumental – catering to all the various goals and values by which human beings are capable of being motivated. It is a truth at the heart of much pluralist thinking that human beings get motivated by many things, most of which are incompatible, at least when maximally or perfectly realised, with the others. Yet given that we *are* motivated by so many things, our problem thus continues to be: how can some significant number of different people, possessed of different ideals (as well as different cultural influences, and different subjective preferences) come to agree on one single answer to OQ?

A fourth possibility is *scepticism*. Sceptics claim that we can never know if one answer is better than another. That claim is either insignificant or paradoxical. It is paradoxical if it is intended as the claim that there is a right answer, even though we could never *know* it. Any proof to the effect that there is an unreachable right answer requires some proof that there is such an answer. And, in turn, any proof that there is an answer requires some knowledge of that answer. Imagine that we claim, for instance, (1) that aliens created humanity and (2) that only they know how we ought to live (and one can exchange aliens for God if preferred). To *prove* that claim, you would have to prove not just that aliens did create us, but also that we should live in accordance with their secret code. Yet to prove *that* you would have to be able to show that *that* code is the right code *for us* and, to show *that*, you would have to know both that code *and* what is best for human beings. In short, knowledge of political right is required for justifiable scepticism about it – a paradox. Scepticism is insignificant, on the other hand, when it takes the form: there is no right answer because some theory x (where x could be radical subjectivism) shows that no right answer is possible. In this instance we are not really encountering scepticism, because it is not really true that we cannot know what the right answer would be. Instead, it is *demonstrably* the case here that there *is* no right answer. This answer is insignificant for all the same reasons that subjectivism was insignificant. So long as we *are* still looking for a convincing answer to OQ, scepticism cannot help us.[187]

1.16   Summary of Arguments and a Sketch of What Follows

I have argued three key things in this chapter: (1) that political philosophy should be defined in terms of what I call its organising question – *how should we live?*; (2) that political philosophers have failed to provide a *convincing* and *meaningful* answer to this question; and (3) that political philosophy is both impossible to avoid and, apparently, impossible to do. This last point I call the *impossibility thesis*, the extended meaning of which is that, although we cannot help but live by the dictates of one or other answer to our organising question, we also cannot manage to agree, even at the highest, rational, and philosophical levels, on what the right answer to that question would be. In the course of making these arguments, it further transpired that the best arguments we could find tended to be either meaningful and unconvincing, or convincing and politically inde-terminate, and thus insufficiently meaningful in the intended sense – a point I then further illustrated by way of a brief trio of previously unconsidered examples that went by the names of historical contextual-ism, realism, and post-modernism. It also transpired that our faith in the impossibility thesis is further bolstered by reflection on perhaps the last remaining alternative – though not necessarily productive or normative – arguments left to us, namely, relativism, subjectivism, cynicism, and scepticism. But this is not the point to dwell on here. More important by some way is my use of the term 'apparently' when I say that political philosophy is both impossible to avoid and, apparently, impossible to do. The problem here, to which the following chapter responds, is whether we can be *sure* of this second impossibility. It asks, in particular, two related questions: (1) is political philosophy *really* impossible? and (2) if so, *why?*

---

[187] For more sophisticated thoughts on scepticism and its discontents, compare R. Dworkin, *Justice for Hedgehogs*, 23–98, with S. Street, 'Objectivity and Truth: You'd Better Rethink It', *Oxford Studies in Meta-ethics*, 11 (2016).

2 Diagnosis: Mentalism

A reminder:

By 'OQ', I mean political philosophy's organising question, 'how should we live?'.

By 'FQ', I mean political philosophy's foundational question, 'why should we live in accordance with one set of principles and not another?'.

By 'a convincing and meaningful answer to OQ', I mean an answer that is both (1) compelling to all rational individuals who would have to live with it and (2) determinate amongst, at the least, the most popular political options, as supported by either political philosophers or citizens and politicians.

2.1 Introduction

My central claim in this chapter is that rational interminability in political philosophy is explained by that subject's adherence to a paradigm I call *mentalism*. In what follows, I begin by explaining what mentalism is, continue by explaining why it fails, and then prove, step by step, the necessity of that failure. The essence of the argument is that political philosophy fails because, when it attempts to work up from deep-lying normative thoughts we are already supposed to share to determinate political principles we are then supposed to adopt, it always runs up against the fact that those thoughts are just too *inconsistent*, both within and between individuals, to generate just one set of principles. This means, for example, that my thoughts about equality are likely to clash with my thoughts about liberty, which in turn are likely to clash with your thoughts about the same thing, not to mention your thoughts about utility, and so on and so forth.

2.2 What Mentalism Is

The problem with political philosophy, as we have seen, is that its arguments are rationally interminable, but why? The answer offered in this chapter is that the subject adheres to a model of enquiry I call mentalism. According to this model, political philosophers proceed in their work by trying to identify something that they are convinced already exists: *the* principle or set of principles systematically underpinning our normative thoughts. More precisely, we can say that they are committed to finding either a single master-principle or set of foundational principles which, when correctly formulated, will be capable of generating most, if not all, of our established moral judgements and intuitions; principles which chime with and, in a sense, are capable of *explaining* the majority of our existing normative beliefs. And in turn, once they have discovered this principle or set of principles, their task is then to apply it to the political domain in order to produce either determinate institutional prescriptions or, more probably, determinate political principles (such as principles of distributive justice) which would themselves be capable of providing us with a reasonably determinate institutional template (for an ideal state, or anarchist utopia, or global empire, etc.), and thus would themselves already constitute a convincing and meaningful answer to OQ.

Political philosophy's self-set task then, as I see it, has been to discover whatever set of normative political principles is *already* and *implicitly* expressed in the blooming, buzzing confusion of our existing normative thoughts. That is almost a definition of what I call the mentalist approach, but not quite. The best definition for the purposes of our discussion is as follows:

Mentalist political philosophers attempt to discover and then apply whatever set of normative political principles is already implicitly expressed within our existing normative thoughts.

So why call this approach *mentalist*? The key idea is that political philosophy's building blocks, its data, its working material – call it what you will – are *thoughts*, and in particular what I call *normative thoughts*. These thoughts are thoughts about what should and should not be the case in the world and about what individuals and groups ought and ought not to do. So why not call them *moral* thoughts? The reason is simple: many people, due to their separation of morality from the aims of prudence, interest, and utility, exclude much of what political philosophers have in mind when they do their work, and thus much of what I have in mind when describing it.

The crucial point here, however, is that political philosophers are fundamentally interested in a sub-group of *mental* phenomena, and *not*, for instance, physical, observable, and empirical objects, states of affairs, and actions. This contrast will become important in what follows, in part because I think this exclusive attention to thoughts has been the undoing of political philosophy, and in part because I think there is a better alternative of my own creation which lacks this exclusivity. But let's not get ahead of ourselves. For now it is enough to note that, whereas philosophy is often characterised as thinking about thinking, I am characterising political philosophy as something like political thinking about normative thoughts, and at the same time claiming that this aspect to political philosophy's work is also the reason for its stalemate. And indeed, when I say 'aspect', what I really mean is 'fundamental nature', but then, given how deep-set this nature is, and given that it is as unnoticed as it is shared, the term 'aspect', with its connotations of viewing the same thing from a different viewpoint, seems more appropriate, at least for the time being.

The basic dynamic of this approach is easily illustrated by noting a few of the general suggestions made as to what the sought-for principle or set of principles might be. For example, some thinkers claim that at least all politically relevant normative judgements correspond to the rule 'maximise social utility', whilst others hold that they fit a test of universalisability, according to which one ought only to undertake and approve such actions as one would want to be permitted by a universal law. Others still suggest that these judgements derive from a basic set of non-conflicting deontological rules, whilst a further group holds that they fit a test of reasonableness, according to which one is only reasonable when one proposes and lives by such principles as it would not be reasonable for others to reject (with 'reasonable' then given some further and suitable content of its own).

Note that I use the term 'politically relevant' in these examples. I do this because there are at least two important and general possibilities regarding what mentalist political philosophy might discover. A first possibility is that, when we delve into the heart of our normative thoughts, we find that there is one single principle (or set of principles) applicable to all domains of life, with the task for political philosophers then being to work out just what that principle (or set of principles) entails for the political domain. The second possibility is that our normative thoughts regarding politics differ significantly from those regarding, say, personal relationships, or the relationship between humanity and the animal kingdom. In this instance, rather than discovering a single master-principle capable of regulating every aspect of our lives, we would discover either different basic principles or different sets of basic principles applicable to each ethical domain (domains which would, in time, be understood by reference to those very principles).

That distinction, however, is not nearly as significant as it might initially appear to be, because ultimately whether or not the first or second possibility holds is a matter of what we actually discover when we come to examine our thoughts. I mention it only in order to avoid confusion as to the exact *ambition* of the mentalist programme. What matters fundamentally is that the method described here is the same in all instances, regardless of the particular normative structures it yields once applied – which is to say, mentalists of all colours burrow into the turmoil of our normative thoughts in order to establish that principle or set of principles to which those thoughts can be reduced, regardless of whether those principles are few or many, and regardless of whether they differ according to the sphere of life to which they apply.

In early discussions of this argument, the question of the difference between what Bernard Williams calls 'moralism' and what I call 'mentalism' has sometimes arisen, and I have been encouraged by some to connect, or even equate, the former with the latter. This is unsurprising, given popular trends, but also unnecessary, given the nature of the concepts involved. Apart from phonetic similarity, there is no real relationship between the two. Nevertheless, given that contrasts sometimes prove the best means of clarification, I will briefly juxtapose them as a pair. So: whereas for Williams, moralism is the practice of applying abstract moral principles to political practice regardless of constraints of popular opinion and, more generally, political feasibility,[1] for me, mentalist political philosophy tends to comprise both this task *and* the prior exercise of trying to isolate that set of politically relevant principles already latent in our normative thoughts. I do stress 'tends', though, given that there is no essential need for mentalism to be moralist. If political philosophy's only methodological mistake was to engage excessively in moralism, or indeed what many call 'ideal theory', then matters would be considerably more salvageable than I believe them to be.[2] Or, alternatively put, if our only problem was that we spend too much time demanding abstract ideals of political practice and too little time working out how best to deploy and rank those ideals in existing political contexts, then things would not be, I believe, nearly as bad as they have become. By contrast, the much bigger problem, or so I shall argue, is not that political philosophy is too utopian; it is that we disagree too radically about what utopia would be. We disagree too much about what *are* the right normative principles, and thus about what *is* the best form of government.

---

[1] B. Williams, *In the Beginning Was the Deed*, esp. 1–17.
[2] For a particularly clear treatment of the ideal/non-ideal theory distinction, see A. Swift, 'The Value of Philosophy in Nonideal Circumstances', *Social Theory and Practice*, 34:3 (2008). See also A. Swift and Z. Stemplowska, 'Ideal and Nonideal Theory', in D. Estlund (Ed.), *The Oxford Handbook of Political Philosophy* (Oxford: Oxford University Press, 2012), 373–392.

Before that argument can be considered, however, we need to better clarify what mentalism is, which for now, I believe, requires a detailed example of mentalist political philosophy in practice. This example would ideally be a programme of mentalist thought both highly familiar and highly methodologically explicit, which is why Rawls' work, as is so often the case, provides the perfect case study. From early talk of 'explication' to later talk of 'reflective equilibrium', he suggests throughout his many writings that, if we could but find a set of principles capable of generating as many as possible of our considered politically relevant moral judgements, then that would be the set of principles (1) which captures our underlying conception of justice and (2) which we should adopt both when attempting to design particular political institutions and when attempting to decide between two or more rival positions in a given political conflict or dilemma.[3] Consider first, then, as early expressions of this thought, the following two statements from 'Outline of a Decision Procedure for Ethics':

Consider a group of competent judges making considered judgments in review of a set of cases which would be likely to arise in ordinary life. Then an explication of these judgments is defined to be a set of principles, such that, if any competent man were to apply them intelligently and consistently to the same cases under review, his judgments ... would be ... identical, case by case, with the considered judgments of the group of competent judges.[4]

And:

The attempt to discover a comprehensive explication may be thought of as the attempt to express the invariant in the considered judgments of competent judges.[5]

Consider second, this time from 'The Sense of Justice', the following description of foundational normative political principles:

the principles [of justice] are those which account for the considered judgments of competent persons concerning the justice of political and social institutions.[6]

Consider third, from 'The Independence of Moral Theory', a later description of the task, now refined by the qualifier that we want only those principles capable of fitting our considered judgements in reflective equilibrium:

one tries to find a scheme of principles that match people's considered judgments and general convictions in reflective equilibrium. This scheme of principles

---

[3] For sustained attention to Rawls' method, see J. Floyd, 'Rawls' Methodological Blueprint', *European Journal of Political Theory*, 16 (2016).
[4] J. Rawls, *Collected Papers* (Cambridge, MA: Harvard University Press, 1999), 7.
[5] Ibid., 9.   [6] Ibid., 97.

represents their moral conception and characterises their moral sensibility. One thinks of the moral theorist as an observer, so to speak, who seeks to set out the structure of other people's moral conceptions and attitudes.[7]

And consider finally, again from the same article:

adopting the role of observing moral theorists, we investigate what principles people would acknowledge and accept the consequences of when they have had an opportunity to consider other plausible conceptions and to assess their supporting grounds. Taking this process to the limit, one seeks the conception, or plurality of conceptions, that would survive the rational consideration of all feasible conceptions and all reasonable arguments for them.[8]

Rawls' objective throughout these works was to find that rule or set of rules which, when applied to particular circumstances, produces just that set of normative beliefs to which we continue to cling, *even* after sustained reflection, argument, and the consideration of alternative principles. Just as we attempt, in the natural sciences, to uncover such laws and principles as are capable of fitting the great and growing mass of relevant experimental data, so, in mentalist political philosophy, we are supposed to find such principles as are capable of fitting our existing spread of normative thoughts. We think, apparently, that slavery is wrong, that inequality between the sexes is wrong, and that torture is wrong, so we ask: what underpins all these different beliefs? Is it a particular ideal of autonomy? Is it a rule to maximise the greater good? Is it a principle that no policy is permissible which could not be reasonably justified to all those to whom it will apply? We think that money ought not to be allowed to buy political office, that children ought not to be put to work in factories, and that theft and murder ought to be prohibited and punished. So again: what principle or set of principles fits all of these supposed 'moral facts'? What common element might be identified in each and every one of them? What underlying rule or set of rules can we find such as would bring greater clarity and consensus to our contemporary deliberations?

Another way of illuminating mentalism's nature is to consider its canonical pedigree. Consider here that, whatever predisposition already exists in human nature (1) to assume the existence of this sort of underlying normative coherence and (2) to produce this sort of scholarship, its intellectual roots tangle down to, in particular, the works of David Hume. He gave modern mentalism perhaps its most candid expression when he wrote:

a philosopher . . . needs only enter into his own breast for a moment, and consider whether or not he should desire to have this or that quality ascribed to him, and

---

[7] Ibid., 286.   [8] Ibid., 289.

whether such or such an imputation would proceed from a friend or an enemy ... to observe that particular in which the estimable qualities agree on the one hand, and the blameable on the other; and thence to reach the foundations of ethics, and find those universal principles from which all censure or approbation is ultimately derived ... we can only expect success, by ... deducing general maxims from a comparison of particular instances.[9]

And indeed, his conclusion having conducted such a study was that:

It appears to be a matter of fact, that the circumstance of utility, in all subjects, is a source of praise and approbation: That it is constantly appealed to in all moral decisions concerning the merit and demerit of actions: That it is the *sole* source of that high regard paid to justice, fidelity, honour, allegiance, and chastity ... in a word, that it is a foundation of the chief part of morals, which has a reference to mankind and our fellow creatures.[10]

Note, though, something which Hume does not make explicit: the basic assumption that there is, somewhere deep down, a unity and pattern to our normative thoughts just waiting to be formulaically expressed by whichever philosopher is clever enough to discover it. This is one of the common threads uniting all mentalist enquirers, however much their claims regarding what they have discovered might differentiate them. Consider, for instance, modern moral and political philosophy's second great forefather after Hume, Immanuel Kant, who once wrote that:

an impartial rational spectator can take no delight in seeing the uninterrupted prosperity of a being graced with no feature of a pure and good will, so that a good will seems to constitute the indispensable condition even of worthiness to be happy.[11]

And also:

There is no one – not even the most hardened scoundrel, if only he is otherwise accustomed to use reason – who, when one sets before him examples of honesty of purpose, of steadfastness in following good maxims, of sympathy and general benevolence (even combined with great sacrifices of advantage and comfort), does not wish that he might also be so disposed.[12]

This is not to deny something which many objectors would stress here: that Kant spent a much greater part of his work attempting to show that *only* people who acted morally were free and rational, and that *only* those who acted on the basis of his categorical imperative lived as autonomous,

---

[9] D. Hume, *An Enquiry concerning the Principles of Morals* (Oxford: Oxford University Press, 1998), 7.

[10] Ibid., 45.

[11] I. Kant, *Groundwork of the Metaphysics of Morals* (Cambridge: Cambridge University Press, 1998), 7.

[12] Ibid., 59.

free, rational, creatures, exercising that unique capacity – freedom of will – granted to them by God. That truth, however, does not change the fact that, for Kant, it remained important to show that this rule did not contradict what he took to be shared (Christian) moral judgements and, in any case, it was Hume's inductive, introspective, and almost scientific approach, not Kant's ambition to derive morality from metaphysics, that became the orthodoxy. Consider, for instance, that the chief ambition of modern-day Kantians has been, not to show that morality is a require-ment of rationality, but rather that Kantian principles fit our existing judgements and intuitions. As Charles Taylor once wrote of Rawls' ambitions: 'his aim was to re-edit something of the Kantian theory, with-out the metaphysics'.[13]

We have then, in mentalism, not just a method which has at its heart the belief that all human beings share a core of normative thoughts, but also a movement defined by the shared faith of its members in both the existence of the described core and the virtues of the described method. Mentalist political philosophers, in other words, and despite their differ-ences of opinion regarding the proper answers to FQ and OQ, all agree both that there is this core of normative thoughts common to all human beings, and that it can be laid out and examined in order to see what principles unite them, and thus in turn what principles should be used to answer OQ (subject perhaps to mediation via various facts about local circumstances, including local beliefs and ideologies, the importance of which would itself already have been defined by whatever principles mentalism had already delivered, including, for example, a principle of consent or legitimacy).

So, is this all that we need to know of mentalism prior to explaining its failure? Not by a long shot. One caveat and two elaborations are still required. The caveat, first, regards a claim that has so far only been implied – that all political philosophers past and present either are or were mentalists. In fact, all I really need to claim here in order to be able to show that contemporary political philosophy fails on account of its adher-ence to mentalism is that mentalism is adopted by the vast *majority* of *contemporary* scholars; that it is, to all intents and purposes, the dominant orthodoxy. I cannot, of course, know of every existing political philoso-pher's work, both published and unpublished, and so could never be in a position to make the more extreme claim – but clearly I do not need to be. Nevertheless, I do happen to believe that political philosophers are even more united in their adherence to mentalism than they are in their

---

[13] C. Taylor, 'Leading a Life', in R. Chang, *Incommensurability, Incomparability and Practical Reason* (Cambridge, MA: Harvard University Press, 1997), 174.

use of a move which often denotes it, namely, the indiscriminate use of the pronoun 'we' (as in, 'we believe that rape is wrong', or 'if we saw a child drowning in a pond whom we could easily help, we would certainly try to save them'). Naturally, this still does not alter the fact that there might be thinkers out there for whom the label 'mentalist' is unfair, just as there will be some who no doubt feel discriminated against by my own indiscriminate use of the pronoun 'they' in the previous sentence, but that is by the by. All that matters here is how hegemonic and apparently universal the method is – as I hope to show in the next section.

What, though, of past thinkers? Here I am on shakier ground. My own belief is that mentalism underpins Rawls' reflective equilibrium just as much as it does Plato's dialogues. We might loosely say here that philosophers, because they are lovers of knowledge, are also lovers of reason, which means that they – at least in general – want to convince all of their readers, whoever they might be, of the truth of their arguments. As a result – and again, in general – they will be working with the assumption that there are thoughts to which they can refer – whether those thoughts be beliefs, values, intuitions, or principles – that will shared by reader and author alike. I judge it then both a part of their nature and a part of their heritage that they only ever tell us how to think on the basis of things which, in their judgement, we already think. Nevertheless, I again have to concede here that rather than divert attention into a question that is neither necessary nor best answered by me, I think it best to stick to what is really required here, namely, a completed explanation of what mentalism *is* followed by a proof of the *necessity* of its failure. The proof, assuming that I am right, will come in good time, so what of the explanation? I mentioned a moment ago that, in addition to one caveat, two elaborations are also required, and it is these, when taken together, that round off the explanation. The first of these will be an elaboration of the techniques mentalist political philosophers actually employ, with the second devoted to categorising the types of thought those techniques utilise. There is, however, more to this elaboration than mere explanation, for what I am hoping to achieve at the same time, by way of as many examples of contemporary political philosophy as possible, is to illustrate as best one can the extent of mentalism's sway.

2.3   Mentalism's Techniques

In order to fully understand what mentalism is, we need to understand both its techniques and its materials. In this section we deal with techniques. There are six of these, all of which, apart from the last, are used *ad infinitum* in contemporary politico-philosophical argument. They are, in the order in which I deal with them, *grounding, falsifying, cohering, refining, eliminating,* and *reflecting*. With each of them I try to provide as much illustration from contemporary political philosophy as possible, and deliberately provide as much material as can be garnered from texts which, for various reasons, were not considered either in full or at all in Chapter 1. This way, we clarify mentalism's nature, but also further convey its pervasiveness. A few of these texts I will use repeatedly, given both their status within the subject and the number of clear examples they contain. These few are David Estlund's *Democratic Authority*, Philip Pettit's *Republicanism*, Brian Barry's *Justice as Impartiality*, Thomas Christiano's *The Constitution of Equality*, and Philippe Van Parijs' *Real Freedom for All*.[14]

We start, then, with *grounding*. Consider the following arguments by Estlund, Pettit, Barry, and Christiano:

Estlund
The idea that even unjust law is sometimes legitimate and authoritative is, first of all, consistent with many ordinary convictions. [Consider] the jury context: the legitimacy and authority of the verdict are not cancelled just whenever the jury is mistaken.[15]

Pettit
[Examples of domination are] the husband who can beat his wife for disobeying his instructions ... the employer who can fire his employees as whim inclines him ... the teacher who can chastise her pupils on the slightest excuse ... the prison warder who can make life hell for inmates.[16] And: the intuition from which republicans begin [is] that domination is a salient evil, and that removing it or reducing it is a more or less unambiguous enterprise.[17]

Barry
[M]y argument presupposes a certain desire: the desire to live in a society whose members all freely accept its rules of justice and its major institutions. ... The desire ... is, fortunately, widespread.[18]

Christiano
[My argument] relies on the intuitive strength of the starting premises concerning the dignity of persons and the importance of well-being in the argument for equality.[19]

---

[14] The full titles and citations are: D. Estlund, *Democratic Authority: A Philosophical Framework* (Princeton, NJ: Princeton University Press, 2008); P. Pettit, *Republicanism: A Theory of Freedom and Government* (Oxford: Oxford University Press, 1997); B. Barry, *Justice as Impartiality: A Treatise on Social Justice*, Volume II (Oxford: Oxford University Press, 1995; T. Christiano, *The Constitution of Equality: Democratic Authority and Its Limits* (Oxford: Oxford University Press, 2008); and P. Van Parijs, *Real Freedom for All: What (if Anything) Can Justify Capitalism?* (Oxford: Oxford University Press, 1995).
[15] D. Estlund, *Democratic Authority*, 110.   [16] P. Pettit, *Republicanism*, 57.
[17] Ibid., 103.   [18] B. Barry, *Justice as Impartiality*, 164–168.
[19] T. Christiano, *The Constitution of Equality*, 5.

In these four examples, we can say that Estlund is grounding his argument about legitimacy and authority in our opinion of juries; Pettit is grounding his argument about republicanism in our aversion to domination; Barry is grounding his argument about justice in our desire to live in a society to which people can freely consent; and Christiano is grounding his argument in our attachment to the ideals of dignity and well-being. Each of them is grounding a normative argument X in a normative thought or set of normative thoughts Y. So, to *ground* a principle or set of principles is to show that it or they can be derived from normative thoughts we already have. For example, when Peter Singer says that because we would help a drowning child whom we could easily save, we should also provide aid to the world's poorest, he is attempting to use the former as grounds for the latter.[20] That is, he is using our thought that we would save the child as a reason for us to think that we should provide that aid. And consider again John Rawls' 'original position'. When he says that the design of the position is supported by our belief that natural and social fortune should not influence our choice of political principles, he is using this belief as grounds for that design.

There are, however, limits to this one-step manoeuvre, the most important of which concerns the extent to which a particular grounding thought is compatible with multiple derivations. We have to be careful about the analogical fit between hypothetical situations and those political situations targeted by our principles, just as we have to be careful about the number of principles deducible from a given thought. In Singer's case, for instance, we need to be wary of the differences between the situation with the child and the situation with the aid, whilst in Rawls' case we need to be wary of the fact that the belief he draws on might also be used to support rival positions to his own. But there is also a second problem. In addition to these challenges of analogy and indeterminacy, we have also to be wary of the fact that any grounding thought might easily get overruled by alternative and conflicting thoughts that are either more applicable or more dearly held.

In order to make our political principles truly convincing, therefore, mentalists need to do more than just show that their particular principles are supported by one or more of our pre-existing normative thoughts. This is where *falsification* comes in. Consider the following examples of this technique in action.

Estlund
It can sometimes seem as if everything should be fair. . . . But there seems to be a legitimate question about this. . . . For example, to defend my choice to save my

---

[20] P. Singer, 'Famine, Affluence, and Morality', *Philosophy and Public Affairs*, 1:3 (1972).

son from drowning rather than saving the stranger next to him, it is not obvious that I should need to show that doing so conforms to some appropriate standard of fairness.[21]

Christiano
Justice does not obey the 'ought implies can' principle entirely. In part it serves as an ideal to be approximate. We can see this in a variety of contexts. We know that even the best penal system is likely to convict some innocent persons and let some guilty persons go free and we are inclined to think that these are injustices even though we cannot improve the system that makes these errors beyond a certain point. I think we can see it in the distributive case as well. If we have two persons who have contributed equally to the production of a pair of unequal but indivisible substantial goods, we may think that there is some injustice in giving the better good to one and the lesser good to the other.[22]

Van Parijs
[T]he suggestion that a free ... society is to be conceived as a maximally democratic society ... cannot be adequate. To understand why, it suffices to reflect on the following two situations. In situation A, each of us can decide for herself whether to scratch her nose. In situation B, we decide together, in perfectly democratic fashion, whether nose-scratching is permissible.[23]

Amy Gutmann and Dennis Thompson
Fish seems to suggest that there is no way to distinguish between justified and unjustified exercises of political power. Does he really think that the best reasons for extending equal rights to all human beings regardless of skin colour are no better than those offered for slavery and racial discrimination? ... He seems to have put democracy on the same moral footing as apartheid, authoritarianism, and fascism.[24]

In these four examples, Estlund falsifies the idea that fairness is a universally applicable ideal by reference to our intuitions regarding the drowning son; Christiano falsifies the idea that justice should obey the dictum 'ought implies can' by reference to our understandings of legal justice and distributive injustice; Van Parijs falsifies the idea that a free society would be maximally democratic by reference to our revulsion at the idea of society deciding whether or not we get to scratch our nose; and Gutmann and Thompson falsify the idea that we cannot distinguish justified from unjustified exercises of political power by reference to our conviction that such things as slavery and fascism are categorically unjustified. So, in contrast to grounding, to *falsify* a principle or set of principles is to show that it or they are wrong because they violate one or more of our dearly held normative

---

[21] D. Estlund, *Democratic Authority*, 67.
[22] T. Christiano, *The Constitution of Equality*, 36.
[23] P. Van Parijs, *Real Freedom for All*, 8.
[24] A. Gutmann and D. Thompson, *Why Deliberative Democracy?* (Princeton, NJ: Princeton University Press, 2004, 47.

thoughts. Robert Nozick, for example, attempts this when he says that coercive taxation is morally equivalent to forced labour, with his conclusion then being that no principles offered as an answer to OQ could be truly convincing which, either directly or indirectly, required such taxation (or, at least, taxation of a kind not required in order to stop still greater coercion). And consider G. A. Cohen's summary of the anti-contractarian objection to Rawls' 'original position':

> If I would have agreed (but did not) on Monday to pay you £1000 for the painting you were to paint on Tuesday, it does not follow that I have made a kind of agreement with you to pay you that money and that I am therefore now obliged to pay £1000 for the painting. Accordingly a hypothetical contract is not worth the paper it isn't written on, and, the objection concludes, the original position is therefore an unsound device.[25]

This example is interesting in part because it shows yet again the way in which pre-existing thoughts can be used to falsify proposed political principles, but also because it shows the way in which political philosophers summarise each other's arguments. Cohen is distilling, without reflecting on, the logic of falsification. But there is at least one problem with this technique: what if, despite being able to ground my proposed answer to OQ in one or two appealing thoughts, and despite also being able to falsify a few rival arguments with further thoughts, I am still not able to produce a principle or set of principles that accounts for further political positions that are also widely held, despite being untouched by the logic of my principles? The worry now is that I have a position which, at best, is convincing without being meaningful, given its silence on many important choices, but which at worst might also turn out to be unconvincing, were it to be too readily compatible with positions we find deeply unpalatable.

This is where *cohering* comes in. Consider the following two examples.

Estlund
Procedural fairness alone cannot explain most of the features of democratic institutions that we are likely to feel are crucial.[26]

Van Parijs
Real-libertarianism [is] an attempt to articulate the importance we ascribe to liberty, equality, and efficiency. [But I also need to show that it is] consistent with our well-considered judgements.[27]

In these two examples, Estlund is claiming that the principle of procedural fairness does not cohere with other strongly held beliefs we have

---

[25] G. A. Cohen, *Rescuing Justice and Equality* (Cambridge, MA: Harvard University Press, 2008), 341.
[26] D. Estlund, *Democratic Authority*, 66.   [27] P. Van Parijs, *Real Freedom for All*, 28–29.

about democracy, whilst Van Parijs is acknowledging that, for his principles to be convincing, they must cohere with all sorts of beliefs to which we already cling. To check for coherence is thus to check for two things: first, that our initially supported principles are compatible with *other* beliefs we already hold dear, and second, that our principles are capable of generating, when applied, as many as possible of those same beliefs. The more compatible our considered principles are with pre-existing convictions, and the more capable they are of producing and, in a way, explaining those convictions, the more convinced by them we should be as the essence of an answer to OQ.

There is, though, a real theoretical difficulty with cohering, which is to cleanly distinguish it from both grounding and falsifying. If in the one case we say that a principle is convincing because it is derivable from an idea we already support, and in the other that it is convincing because it entails ideas we already support, what is the real difference? Consider further the distinction between cohering and falsifying. If with cohering we seek to show that an answer to OQ implies positions we already find attractive, even if those positions are not already set out in the principles that make up that answer, and with falsifying we seek to show that an answer is wrong because it implies positions we find unattractive, then again, what is the real difference?

The differences here have ultimately to do with where we are in the process of argument construction, as well as the verdict of the theorist, whilst the similarities have ultimately to do with the simple fact that all three techniques are instances of mentalism. As regards the question of stage of argument construction, we can say that grounding is a natural first step. We might begin our answer to OQ, that is, by saying that an argument X is implied by an apparently attractive thought Y. And in turn, as a next step, we might then check to see whether this argument X also entails further thoughts, Z, which, again, we also find attractive. Even if, therefore, the thoughts in X and Z are of a similar kind, and even if we might begin with either of them, there is a difference of technique which stems from the use we make of a given thought. And note further that the general tendency – though it is certainly not a rule – is to use concrete political judgements, such as 'democracy is the best system of government' or 'juries are a fair system of trial', as tests of coherence, with more abstract thoughts, such as 'people should not be held responsible for things they cannot control', used as grounds.

As regards the verdict of the theorist, the difference between falsifying and cohering is simply a matter of whether or not the thought in question is seen to falsify or support the principle under consideration. The thought 'slavery is wrong', for instance, could be used to both falsify a utilitarian principle *and* support a principle of autonomy. An example from outside political philosophy might also help here. Consider the theory of evolution. One might begin by *grounding* a particular version of this theory in various facts we know about the fossil record on Earth, before then showing that the theory *coheres* with everything we already know about climate history and plate tectonics, only to have all of this *falsified* by certain facts we know about genetics. Here again, then, just as with the slavery example, although the roles given to each body of evidence are different, it would certainly have been possible to, say, ground and develop a theory out of genetics, only to have it falsified by climate history, despite it cohering with the fossil record.

And remember, the idea is not only to check a given principle for its compatibility with other normative ideas to which we are already loyal, but also – as noted with the limits of falsification – to check that the principle we are considering is itself capable of generating those ideas. In the example from Estlund cited earlier, for instance, his complaint is not that fairness is in conflict with some of our important convictions (and would thus be falsified by them), but rather that fairness *alone* could not produce them, and thus that fairness cannot be the central value when it comes to justifying democratic authority. Cohering is therefore an important and distinct application of thought to principle, even if some readers might now be wondering whether it should instead be called confirmation or verification. Cohering, however, is a less bold and, as a result, more accurate label than either of those two possibilities. Although if we can say that a principle coheres with a variety of thoughts we can be more confident in it, we cannot yet go so far as to say that we have verified or confirmed the truth of that principle.

We have, then, three moves so far that are available to the mentalist political philosopher, to which we now need to add a fourth. Consider the following statements.

Van Parijs
[On negative liberty] no refining of the definition could make nonsense of the following intuitions: if I am penniless, I am not really free to join the cruise; if I have no option but to starve or to accept a lousy job, I am not really free to turn the latter down.[28]

Pettit
Freedom as non-domination does better [than freedom as non-interference] in three other aspects, all of them of intuitively great importance. It promises to do better in delivering a person from uncertainty ... from the need to exercise strategy with the powerful ... and from the subordination that goes with

---

[28] Ibid., 22.

a common awareness that the person is exposed to the possibility of arbitrary interference by another.[29]

Barry

[J]ustice as mutual advantage fails egregiously to do one thing that we would normally expect a conception of justice to do, and that is provide some moral basis for the claims of the relatively powerless.[30]

Each of these three statements is an example of *refining*. When we refine, we try to home in on the essence of an attractive normative idea by steadily ruling out candidates for that essence that hold unattractive implications. Or, alternatively put, to refine a value or principle is to work out the best version or interpretation of it by falsifying every other such version or interpretation bar one. In these examples, both Van Parijs and Pettit attempt to refine our understanding of an already attractive idea – liberty – by ruling out its interpretation as non-interference, whilst Barry seeks to show that another attractive idea – justice – could not possibly be interpreted as mutual advantage given that that interpretation has deeply unattractive implications.

Refining is thus a species of conceptual analysis, although it is important to be clear about just what it is that we are analysing. The aim, as already touched on a moment ago, is to try and capture the essence of an attractive idea – such as freedom or justice – in order to generate a similarly attractive partial or complete answer to OQ. But note that ideas are being investigated and refined in order to establish their best, not their conventional meaning. This is not to say that mentalist philosophers are trying to do something here other than discern patterns in the way we already think. The point is rather that they are trying to work out the proper essence of normative ideas by seeing which candidates for that essence best fit with other related judgements we already hold. For example, if we were sure that a slave was unfree, then even if a particular interpretation of freedom appeared to hold true to most of our conventional uses of that term, it could not be deemed a plausible interpretation of that idea if it were possible, according to the logic of that interpretation, to be a free slave.

As with cohering, it is important to get the relationship between refining, grounding, and falsifying as clear as possible. As regards grounding, we should note that we have returned with refining to the problem raised earlier that a given grounding thought might be compatible with more than one principle or set of principles. So, although the idea of freedom might easily lend itself to supporting one particular answer to OQ, the fact

---

[29] P. Pettit, *Republicanism*, 89.   [30] B. Barry, *Justice as Impartiality*, 46.

that it could also lend itself to alternative answers calls into question that answer's credentials. As a result, we might simply reduce our options by ruling out that answer to OQ and, with it, the idea that grounded it. But that is not the only option we have. We could instead, as discussed, only falsify the *particular* principle or set of principles that has been derived from that grounding, by managing at the same time to produce a derivation of our grounding idea that avoids the critique mounted by the falsification. So, to return to the idea of freedom, although we might be tempted to falsify this general idea as a grounding ideal for any answer to OQ on the basis that freedom for the sheep also means freedom for the wolves, we could instead refine and save that idea by offering an interpretation of freedom – say, 'freedom as the ability to make an informed choice amongst genuinely valuable options' – which avoids that falsification. Refining is thus an aid to grounding, whilst being more mild than falsifying, because whilst falsifying rules out an idea from consideration, refining falsifies only one interpretation of it, which then in turn gives more credence to interpretations of it that avoid this falsification, and also more attraction to the idea as a guide to politics – provided of course that the idea is itself already vaguely attractive.

For some readers, it will be helpful to note here that when contemporary political philosophers utilise the technique I am calling refining, they often use one or more of the following terms: 'capturing', 'interpreting', and 'reflecting'. For example, Barry is drawing on this technique when he claims that Rawls' 'original position' 'fails to capture' the idea of not aggregating the interests of different people that it is intended to capture.[31] Or consider the following two examples, this time taken from articles by Joseph Carens and Kasper Lippert-Rasmussen:

In what follows, I implicitly presuppose the legitimacy of liberal democratic principles, but not any particular interpretation of them. Providing such an interpretation is one of the tasks of the article. In pursuing this interpretive task, I will often start with intuitive responses to actual policies (or hypothetical variations on these policies). If we can articulate why some arrangements seem intuitively acceptable while others do not, we may succeed in identifying the underlying principles more fully and adequately.[32]

Some libertarians think that 'full self-ownership is the most appropriate reflection' of our status as 'self-directing beings with full moral standing'. They assert that self-ownership explains or grounds 'the intuitive wrongness of various forms of nonconsensual interference with bodily integrity'.[33]

---

[31] Ibid., 53.

[32] J. H. Carens, 'Live-In Domestics, Seasonal Workers, and Others Hard to Locate on the Map of Democracy', *Journal of Political Philosophy*, 16:4 (2008), 421.

[33] K. Lippert-Rasmussen, 'Against Self-Ownership: There Are No Fact-Insensitive Ownership Rights over One's Body', *Philosophy and Public Affairs*, 36:1, 114–115.

In the first of these two statements, in which Carens adopts the term 'interpretation', the task is to see just which versions of an idea we already like – in this case liberal democracy – stand up to scrutiny, in order to then home in on a version of that idea that could be used as a convincing answer to OQ. His aim is thus to refine our understanding of liberal democracy by successfully falsifying several possible versions of it. This, he hopes, will result in the isolation of just one set of principles as a plausible candidate for our understanding of that idea, and in turn a principled answer to OQ which would be attractive precisely because of that isolation. In the second statement, by contrast, Rasmussen is simply lining up for attack the idea of self-ownership as a 'reflection' (and we could of course say version, or interpretation, or essence) of the idea that human beings are 'self-directing beings with full moral standing'. He is thus questioning the popular interpretation of full moral beings as self-owning persons without as yet offering a more refined understanding of that idea.

There is, though, something missing in our discussion here. Why exactly should we want to give our political adherence to a particular interpretation of an attractive idea – whether it be a more concrete idea like 'liberal democracy' or a more abstract ideal like 'non-aggregation of the interests of separate persons' – just because that interpretation is the *most refined* one that political philosophy has so far managed to produce? Or indeed, to consider the more general problem, why should I be truly convinced by an answer to OQ, even if (1) it has been grounded in an attractive idea, (2) it is entailed by the most refined version of that idea, (3) it coheres with many of our pre-existing moral and political judgements, and (4) several alternatives to that answer have been falsified? For example, if deliberative democracy were the most refined version of an idea I already vaguely like – in this case democracy – and if I am already convinced that, say, communism and fascism are unattractive, does it automatically follow that I should give my political support to that idea?

It is in response to this problem that the fifth and perhaps most important mentalist technique, *elimination*, comes into play. Political philosophers engage in elimination when they try to show that *all* principles apart from their own refined offering fail on grounds of falsification, coherence, or even just self-contradiction, and thus that their principles offer the most convincing basis for an answer to OQ. Again, though: why should we be convinced by a given set of principles just because it has avoided the problems encountered by other sets? The absolutely crucial assumption political philosophers make is that to falsify what they take to be the main rival positions to their own in contemporary scholarship is to have *singled out* their own position, by effectively eliminating all other plausible alternatives. This is a very deep and very important belief which, although it is almost impossible to find arguments that make it explicit, takes us right to the heart of the mentalist programme. Political philosophers just take it as a given, almost a matter of faith, that our normative thoughts do have an inner system to them just waiting to be figured out. They accept, of course, that a few thoughts will be too far outside of the patterns they perceive, and should thus be treated as outliers on an otherwise consistent scatter graph of beliefs, but they assume that these can be filtered out by way of the right kind of reflective equilibrium – which means, in effect, that they can be filtered out by seeing just which principles can cohere with the maximum number of firmly held pre-existing convictions.

Reflective equilibrium, however, is a separate issue to which we will return later in this chapter. For now, we need to focus on the technique of elimination and, in particular, the assumption that underwrites it. I said a moment ago that it is almost impossible to find arguments that make this assumption explicit. This is true, although for illustration of the assumption in action, just think of how almost every work of modern political philosophy, from the shortest article to the longest book, devotes almost all of its attention to the task of arguing *against* alternative positions to the one it is actually intended to advance. Or consider Mill's claim that, in such matters, 'three-fourths of the arguments for every disputed opinion consist in dispelling the appearances which favour some opinion different from it'.[34] Of course, there will always be a fair amount of grounding going on, but in order to make that grounding really appealing, the crucial thing is to make it seem like the only kind of grounding we could achieve. For example, books such as Estlund's *Democratic Authority* or Philippe Van Parijs' *Real Freedom for All* spend such a large majority of their time arguing *against* rival accounts of democracy and liberty, it is difficult to see how they could function *without* the assumption in question.

Consider further, for an at least slightly more explicit use of this logic of elimination, the following statement by Hillel Steiner:

[W]hat my argument more generally sought to do was to offer a coherent integration of many of our common justice-related intuitions concerning such issues as the nature of rights themselves, exploitation, genetic disadvantage, and rights and duties with respect to minors. If exploitation is, as is widely believed, a form of injustice, and if the demands of justice are presumed to be mutually consistent and to enjoy priority over competing moral demands of other types, then it's difficult to see how there could *be* 'mightier considerations' that trump the entitlement of all individuals to the fruits of their labour.[35]

---

[34] J. S. Mill, *On Liberty* (London: Penguin, [1859] 1974), 98.
[35] H. Steiner, 'Universal Self-Ownership and the Fruits of One's Labour: A Reply to Curchin', *Journal of Political Philosophy*, 16:3 (2008), 350.

Here we can see not just how Steiner wants to work up from our intuitions to political principles, and not just how he grounds part of his argument in the widely held assumption that justice trumps other moral considerations, but also how he assumes that the various demands we place under the umbrella concept of justice are already (at least mostly) consistent, and thus perfectly open to being worked up into a system which, in turn, could form the essence of an answer to OQ (which would be something of the form: because we already accept that justice is a trump value in political life, and because I have shown that my theory of justice offers the best interpretation of our normative thoughts, rational individuals would be convinced by an answer to OQ which tells us to realise this theory).

Consider, though, a contrast between this line of reasoning and a line from the natural sciences. If I am confident that the Earth revolves around the Sun, and also confident about what the best existing theory is for that revolution, then I can see that I have good reason to adopt that theory, but does anything like that reason hold in the case of political philosophy? This contrast highlights the questionable parallel between our belief that the physical universe is ordered and regular, and thus entirely open to being theoretically modelled, and our belief that normative mental phenomena possess an inner order and regularity, and are thus similarly open to systematisation in the form of principles. I can see that if I apply the theory of gravity, then it will accurately predict all sorts of easily verified planetary movements – but what about my normative thoughts? Could there be a theory of justice or obligation or liberty that accurately predicted all, or at least almost all, of my pre-existing normative beliefs?

My answer, as noted at the start of this chapter, will be that there could not be, though we have yet to reach the point where I try to prove that impossibility. For now we need only note how universal the assumption is that our thoughts could be so systematised, and also how widely adopted the practice is of trying to home in on this system by way of the logic of elimination. By utilising the discussed techniques of grounding, falsifying, cohering, and refining, mentalist political philosophers hope that they are eliminating *all but one* argument from the field of battle. Nevertheless, there is still a sixth and final mentalist technique which could, perhaps, be used to buttress their position. This technique revolves around a defence of all of the above that claims that the assumption of an inner system is *itself shared* – that it is itself implicit in human morality *along with all those other beliefs* to which we are trying to find the connecting thread. This meta-mentalism, if you will, is a kind of mentalism about mentalism, though I will call it, for want of a more precise term, *reflecting*.

Unfortunately, finding examples of reflecting is almost as difficult as finding examples of elimination. This is not because it is hard to find statements that display an adherence to the logic of mentalism, or at least one of its techniques. Estlund, for example, shows this when he writes, 'We could never arrive at a general principle of this kind without resting much of our case for it on its matching a number of less general plausible convictions'.[36] Norman Daniels shows this when he writes of the widely held view that 'a moral theory consists of a set of moral judgements plus a set of principles that account for or generate them'.[37] T. M. Scanlon shows this when he writes of his reasonable rejection principle that it is 'intended as a characterisation of the common element implicit in our judgements of wrongness, an element that explains the motivating power of these judgements and guides our interpretation of their content'.[38] Yet these are all just statements communicating, more or less explicitly, a commitment to the mentalist quest. What of arguments that utilise mentalist reflection, which is to say, apply mentalism to itself? Consider the following statement by Pettit:

This is a deeply counterintuitive position. For in ordinary ethical discussions we question the rightness of what we or others do, we invite judgements as to whether we did the right thing in this or that case. ... [This is] how we ordinary people think of ethical discussions.[39]

This statement is interesting precisely because Pettit asks us to reflect on how we normally think of normative enquiry, though it is *still* not a claim to the effect that such reflection reveals something like mentalism. Perhaps a better example is found in Cohen's work, when he complains of how 'people seek in moral matters a level of precision and certainty that they would not expect to find in matters that fall within personal preference'.[40] He goes on to illustrate how we often wriggle out of donating to charity by citing a kind of incommensurability between different causes that would never trouble us when, say, choosing a restaurant, but that is not the key point here. The key point is that Cohen is asking us to think about how we often *think* about both moral and self-interested choices with a view to convincing us of the merits of what he calls 'intuitive balancing'.[41] If, then, he falls short of asking us to reflect on how we are all, deep down, mentalists, he is at least asking us to think of how we do already think about moral versus self-interested matters, with a view to guiding our choices in the former.

---

[36] D. Estlund, *Democratic Authority*, 64.
[37] N. Daniels, 'Wide Reflective Equilibrium and Theory Acceptance in Ethics', *The Journal of Philosophy*, 76: 5, 256.
[38] T. M. Scanlon, 'The Aims and Authority of Moral Theory', *Oxford Journal of Legal Studies*, 12:1 (1992), 21.
[39] P. Pettit, *Republicanism*, 146.   [40] G. A. Cohen, *Rescuing Justice and Equality*, 5.
[41] Ibid., 5.

Beyond such examples, it is difficult to provide more concrete evidence of reflecting in contemporary scholarship, which is a shame, but also not that surprising given how rare I believe the practice to be. What matters more in this context is what I take to be its potential as a way of buttressing applications of grounding, falsification, cohering, refining, and elimination – which might otherwise fall down. In order to do justice to mentalism, we might say, we need to consider all of its options.

It is at this point that we leave our discussion of its techniques. Now that it is clear just what they are and how they are applied, we can see much more clearly just what mentalism *is* in both theory and practice. What I want to do now, by contrast, is look a little closer at the kinds of thoughts invoked by all of the six techniques. Note in the examples used that some thinkers have invoked beliefs, others intuitions, and others convictions. What are we to make of such things? Are they all much of a muchness, or is each term used to denote a different concept? The truth, I would suggest, is that there are really three distinct types of thought involved. Despite highly varied uses of such terms as 'principle', 'value', 'judgement', 'belief', 'conviction', 'desire', 'commitment', and 'intuition', there are in fact three basic concepts to which those things can be reduced when it comes to the 'data' of mentalism. It is to these that we now turn.

2.4   Three Types of Mentalist Evidence and a Synopsis of Why Mentalism Fails

The three distinct types of thought utilised by mentalist political philosophy are as follows: impartial choices of ideal state, considered judgements, and intuitive responses to abstract dilemmas. These are the three types of normative thought drawn on by mentalist enquiry, of which at least one has to be fit for purpose if the enquiry is to succeed. Except of course that I do not think it can succeed. This is why, before I describe in detail each of these three types, I want to give a very short account of why that is. I do this partly in order to give a little context to the arguments that follows, but also to give a greater sense of why these three types of thought matter, and thus what we have to consider when evaluating their worth to the mentalist enterprise.

Broadly speaking, my argument is that mentalist political philosophy, and thus all the techniques and thought types that constitute it, is doomed to failure because different *reasonable* people disagree about the *fundamentals* of political normativity. Our problem is not, for example, that grumpy old men in pubs disagree with each other about the latest fiscal policies of the government of the day. Nor is it that well-heeled ladies, halfway through their merry morning's mah-jong, disagree about the proper place of private education in a just society. Nor is it even that political philosophers disagree about, say, the particular foundations and requirements of a just and liberal state (although that is an important part of the problem, as discussed in **2.6**). After all, it might well be possible to explain away every last one of these disagreements by means of various and compelling lines of argument. No doubt many of the positions taken up involve various degrees of logical inconsistency. No doubt most of them involve a number of factual errors – sociological, historical, economic, mathematical, or otherwise. Our problem is bigger than this. Our problem is that even when all these mistakes have been boiled away, educated, reflective, honest individuals still find themselves in a state of conflict regarding the fundamentals. They disagree both *with each other* and even *within themselves* about the very basics of political 'right'.

A more exact way of expressing this objection would be to say that our normative thoughts are *dissonant*. Note that I say *thoughts* rather than *actions* and *normative* thought rather than, say, *scientific* beliefs. I do not claim in this chapter that all that we *do* is confused, nor even that all that we *think* is a mess. I claim only that our various *normative thoughts* shoot off in different directions both within and between persons. At this point we can zoom out to the context of this book as a whole. Bearing in mind all of the problems encountered in the first chapter, my argument now is (1) that debates in contemporary political philosophy are rationally interminable because the mentalist methodology to which political philosophers cling is unworkable and (2) that mentalism is unworkable because our normative thoughts are dissonant – that is, because there are no determinate patterns and, in turn, principles to discover in the depths of human normative thought, where 'discovery' involves the techniques just described in the previous section.

What, though, do I mean by 'dissonant' and 'determinate patterns'? Simply put, my claim – and it is only a claim until I can prove it – is that the normative thoughts mentalist political philosophers utilise are too much in conflict, both within individuals and between different people, to admit of systematisation. For example, my various thoughts about liberty are inconsistent, just as my thoughts about liberty and equality are inconsistent, just as my thoughts about liberty and equality on the one hand and good and bad existing political institutions on the other are inconsistent, and just as all of these thoughts and the thoughts I have about abstract moral dilemmas about when to save strangers are inconsistent. There are, therefore, no clear and determinate patterns in my normative mind because there is too much dissonance between the thoughts that constitute it. And indeed, not only are *my* existing thoughts deeply inconsistent – they are also different from the inconsistent thoughts held by other people. As a result, our problem is not that *almost all* of my normative thoughts could be rendered consistent *if* we could only find the right principles, with those principles then also being capable of rendering consistent almost all of your thoughts, even if those left over are different in each case. Our problem is that my thoughts are *too* different – too dissonant – to be systematised in this way. Perhaps, if I work at it, I can find a way to render consistent and coherent my thoughts on liberty or democracy separately, but both of these things together? And with the same result as similar exercises performed by everyone else? No chance.

As I say though, this is nothing more than a controversial claim for now. It is not a proof, and not even an argument, until I can provide the evidence for it. This is where the three types of normative thought come in. My reasoning is that if I can prove that each of these types is unfit for purpose – that each of these types is too prone to internal conflict to be used, by way of the various techniques described earlier, to generate convincing political principles – then human normative thought *as a whole* is unfit for the project mentalist political philosophy makes it. Clearly, this is tantamount to saying that mentalism cannot *ever* succeed, which in turn provides a very plausible explanation of the interminability discussed in the previous chapter. As a result, my task from now on will be to mount this proof; to show that human normative thought at each of these levels is just too incoherent for the uses made of it by political philosophy; to show that there is no stable pattern or set of patterns within our thoughts out of which political philosophers could plausibly extract convincing and meaningful political principles.

So, this task is the task within which my threefold categorisation of normative thoughts gains its relevance, and in what remains of this section I want to briefly introduce these three types, before then explaining, in the next three sections, just why each of them fails to meet the standard mentalist political philosophy requires of it.

The first type is *impartial choices of ideal state*. These are hypothetical situations of political choice in which the choosers, whoever they might be, are subject to various constraints of both (a) knowledge (what they know of themselves and the world) and (b) consequence (what that choice will mean for them and the world). These constraints are further supposed to be both (c) independently morally acceptable to everybody and (d) restrictive enough to ensure that anybody who inhabits the position of the hypothetical chooser would make exactly the same political choice. The guiding hope of such situations is this: that whoever is placed in them, it is always the same answer to OQ that is given, either in the form of a concrete political vision or in the form of reasonably determinate normative political principles.

Our second type is *considered judgements*. These thoughts are the thoughts that all reasonably informed and intelligent people are supposed to have about (a) particular abstract political procedures (e.g. majority voting), (b) particular concrete social and economic practices (e.g. wife-beating, slavery, racial segregation, discrimination against homosexuals), (c) particular concrete legal and political procedures (e.g. *habeas corpus*, national referenda, executive prerogative, proportional representation), and (d) particular concrete states of affairs (e.g. high levels of economic inequality, high levels of poverty, high levels of environmental degradation).

Our third type is *intuitive choices of abstract principle*. These choices are the choices we are assumed to make under conditions of abstract choice in which either (a) we have to choose directly some or other abstract normative principle, or (b) we have to make a decision regarding some abstract moral dilemma, the content of which (that is, the content of that decision) is supposed to tie us to some or other abstract principle (such as 'always save the greatest number' or 'never deliberately take a life').

Now, exactly how and why I divide up these categories the way I do is not as important as one might think here. In part, this is because each of the three bodies of normative thought found under these headings is already highly familiar to contemporary moral and political philosophers. As will soon be clear from the material discussed, there is nothing particularly controversial about the various arguments I canvass under any of these headings. More significantly, though, it is not particularly important because, as I intend to show, there is fundamental dissonance at *every one* of the three levels. It does not matter very much, for instance, (1) whether or not certain normative thoughts ought to be placed under choices of abstract principle rather than considered judgements, or (2) whether or not we should think of choices of ideal state as composites of particular considered judgements and intuitions – what matters is that there is dissonance at *every* level; that there is conflict *within* each class of normative thoughts. Similarly, it does not matter whether or not there is *also* conflict *between* the different sets of thoughts we find at each of the three levels – and there certainly is, as will be shown – just so long as it is understood that there is conflict *within* each domain.

So, if we can show that each level of normative thought is unfit for purpose, it does not matter whether there are *also* numerous conflicts between the different normative thoughts found at different levels, for we will already have shown that human normative thought as a whole is incapable of delivering what the mentalist hopes of it. Consider that, if every fundamental aspect of a house is unfit for human habitation, it does not matter whether one organises its failings by room – when all the rooms are beyond the pale – or by floor – when everything on each and every one of those floors is long overdue condemnation. My claim is that human normative thought is analogous to this house, at least for all relevant politico-philosophical purposes (for I do not deny that there might be a variety of minor, politically indeterminate principles upon which our thoughts *do* converge, e.g. 'do not kill family members for sport').

2.5   The Evidence for Failure, Part 1: Impartial Choices

> The Lawes of Nature therefore need not any publishing, nor Proclamation; as being contained in this one Sentence, approved by all the world, Do not that to another, which thou thinkest unreasonable to be done by another to thy selfe.[42]

> [T]he legislative power is put into the hands of divers persons who duly assembled, have by themselves, or jointly with others, a power to make laws, which when they have done, being separated again, they are themselves subject to the laws they have made; which is a new and near tie upon them, to take care, that they make them for the public good.[43]

> [T]he man within the breast, the supposed impartial spectator, the great judge and arbiter of our conduct. If we place ourselves completely in his situation, if we really view ourselves with his eyes, and as he views us, and listen with diligent and reverential attention to what he suggests to us, his voice shall never deceive us.[44]

> The basic idea of justice as impartiality can be expressed in a variety of ways. One is the notion of an impartial observer: justice is seen as what someone with no stake in the outcome would approve of as a distribution of benefits and burdens. Another is to ask each of the parties, 'How would you like to be treated in the way you are proposing to treat the other?'[45]

Each of these statements is an expression of the dream of impartiality – the dream that when we completely remove all sources of partiality from an individual's mind, that individual will give his or her support for just the same set of principles as any other equally impartial individual. Our precise subject here, though, is narrower than that dream. We are concerned with a particular part of it I call *impartial choices of ideal state*. These choices are a species of what are often called *universalisability* or *impartiality* tests. They are a type of thought experiment, the point of which is to tease out those political ideals that all of us are revealed to share once self-interest,

---

[42] T. Hobbes, *Leviathan* (Cambridge: Cambridge University Press, 1996), 188.
[43] J. Locke, *Two Treatises of Government* (London: Everyman, 1993), 189.
[44] A. Smith, *The Theory of Moral Sentiments* (Indianapolis, IN: Liberty Fund, 1984), 233.
[45] B. Barry, *A Treatise on Social Justice, Vol. 1: Theories of Justice* (Berkeley: University of California Press, 1989), 362.

ignorance, and prejudice have been removed from the picture. In these experiments we have to imagine a chooser placed in a hypothetical situation designed to guarantee his or her impartiality, and who would provide, more or less directly, just the same answer to OQ as any other person would when placed in the same situation. These choices thus embody the specific hope that if we ask everybody the right impartial question regarding what *would* be an ideal state, everybody will reply with exactly the same answer, but also, and by extension, the more general hope that, at least at the level of impartial choices of ideal state, our normative thoughts exhibit a politically determinate degree of consensus.

Why, though, do I say impartial choices of *ideal state*, as opposed to impartiality tests in general, or impartial choices of something else? Consider here that there are three kinds of impartiality test of relevance to our enquiry. First, I might be interested in impartial choice situations designed to elicit detailed political principles, understood here as principles that actually pick out the particular institutions and processes we ought to adopt. Second, I might be interested in situations designed to generate more abstract political principles which, despite being abstract, are still determinate enough that they could be applied, in conjunction with local facts and preferences, to generate such institutions and processes. Third, I might be interested in situations designed to generate abstract normative principles (or what many would call moral principles) which could themselves be applied in order to generate political principles of the kind described under the second variant. In this section, I am only interested in the first and second variants, both of which, in effect, are asking the chooser to select between different political orders, described here as *ideal states*, and understood either in terms of institutions and processes or in terms of principles. I am not interested in the third variant because it will be considered, in effect if not in name, in the third section.

Remember here that mentalism is after patterns in thoughts that could be turned into principles. If patterns could be found at the level of impartial choices of ideal state, then that would be enough for mentalism to deliver. If, however, they could be found in considered judgements or intuitive responses to abstract dilemmas, then it would not matter whether those patterns translate into principles which generate political principles by entailment, or principles which generate impartial choice situations for the selection of political principles, or principles which generate impartial choice situations for the selection of principles which themselves generate political principles – all that would matter would be that there *were* patterns of the right kind. For instance, we might say with the Rawls of *Political Liberalism* that our considered judgements point towards an ideal of reasonableness, which itself leads to things like the liberal principle of legitimacy and the ideal of public reason, which themselves lead to a particular conception of liberal democracy. But we will get to that. For now I just want to consider the first of our three levels.

In order to do so, however, and in order to be able to explain just why it is that this level of normative thought is unable to deliver the goods, we need to know more than this brief description provides about the wider role of impartiality tests in contemporary moral and political philosophy, and also the relationship between this role and what I am calling impartial choices of ideal state. Three things are worth noting in this vein. First, we should note that a faith in the problem-solving capacity of impartiality tests lies at the heart of three overlapping movements in moral and political philosophy: contractualism, contractarianism, and constructivism. In contractualist political philosophy, for example, one is trying to find out just what kind of political order an impartial chooser or congregation of choosers would select, whilst in contractarian moral philosophy one is trying to establish whether or not certain aspects of our normative thought (including its foundations) *are* contractual in character, and, if so, just *what* those contractual features entail further up the justificatory line.

In both cases, then, and also that of constructivism, one is hoping that some or other acceptable interpretation of impartiality might hold the power to transform the dissonance of everyday moral and political opinion into a consensus on workable principles for moral and political deliberation. Or, alternatively put, in all three schools of thought there exists the belief that convincing principles only emerge by way of a particular impartial choice situation. Yet at the same time, whether those principles be deep moral principles or detailed political principles, whether the parties to the procedure are selfish or not, and whether they are allowed to be aware of their individual differences or not – none of these sources of disagreement in contemporary scholarship really concerns us here. Nor should we be concerned by, amongst other things, the differences between what Estlund calls primary and subsidiary questions in contractualist procedures.[46] All that matters in this context is what all of the rival positions share – at least when they are concerned with political philosophy – which is the conviction that at least a part, and probably the whole part, of the process of generating convincing political principles will be centred upon some kind of impartial choice situation.

Second, we should note that impartiality tests are often understood as expressions of an imperative generally referred to as morality's 'Golden Rule', a rule that is normally taken to mean something like 'only treat others as you would yourself like to be treated'. This understanding is

[46] D. Estlund, *Democratic Authority*, 246.

both accurate and misleading. It is accurate, up to a point, because it is true that most situations of impartial moral and political choice are understood as expressive, in some way, of the implied ideal of reciprocity. Where it misleads is in its obscuring of the two more fundamental assumptions in play when the situations are designed and deployed, both of which are relevant to our enquiry. These assumptions are as follows: (1) proponents of impartial choice situations assume that there is some or other abstract rule of reciprocal treatment to which all human beings *already* subscribe (at least in particular situations, such as the drawing up of political constitutions); (2) they assume that there exists *at least one* uncontroversial interpretation of this rule capable of delivering reasonably determinate moral and political principles.

Third, we should note not just how popular, but also how varied the application and form of these tests have been over the course of their history in the canons of moral and political thought. From Plato's law-giver to Rousseau's lawmaker, and from Kant's categorical imperative to Adam Smith's impartial spectator, right up to the various universalisability theorems constructed by Hare, Rawls, Scanlon, Gauthier, and Barry, impartiality tests have been applied to all manner of different conflicts and disagreements in the hope that they will elicit for us some significant degree of moral and/or political consensus.[47] And, as I say, not just variation in subject, but also in form. Consider for example the following two injunctions, both put forth in Hobbes's *Leviathan*:

(1) 'Whatsoever you require that others should do to you, that do ye to them.'[48]

(2) 'Do not that to another, which thou wouldest not have done to thy selfe.'[49]

---

[47] For explorations of this idea both classic and contemporary, see R. M. Hare, *Freedom and Reason* (Oxford: Oxford University Press, 1963); J. Rawls, *A Theory of Justice*; J. Rawls, *Political Liberalism*; D. Gauthier, *Morals by Agreement* (Oxford: Oxford University Press, 1986); B. Barry, *A Treatise on Social Justice, Vol. 2: Justice as Impartiality* (Oxford: Oxford University Press, 1995); T. M. Scanlon, *What We Owe to Each Other* (Cambridge, MA: Harvard University Press, 2000). For an insightful discussion and defence of impartiality-centred moral and political theory, see S. Mendus, *Impartiality in Moral and Political Philosophy* (Oxford: Oxford University Press, 2002). For an illustration of why this sort of mentalist inquiry has always to go astray, see my earlier discussion of Rawls' *Political Liberalism* (**1.9**). For insightful pieces on the general trials and tribulations of impartiality and universalisability tests, see P. Bamford, 'The Ambiguity of the Categorical Imperative', *Journal of the History of Philosophy*, 17:2 (1979), 135–141; B. Gert, 'Moral Impartiality', *Midwest Studies in Philosophy*, XX (1995), 102–128; P. Mongin, 'The Impartial Observer Theorem of Social Ethics', *Economics and Philosophy*, 17 (2001), 147–179; C. Stark, 'Decision Procedures, Standards of Rightness and Impartiality', *Nous*, 31:4 (2002); and J. Reinikainen, 'The Golden Rule and the Requirement of Universalizability', *The Journal of Value Inquiry*, 39 (2005), 155–168.

[48] T. Hobbes, *Leviathan*, 92.   [49] Ibid., 109.

Note here that whereas the first requires that you actively *do* to others what it is your duty to do to them, the second orders only that you *do not do* anything to them that you would not like to be done to yourself. Again, though, this distinction is as irrelevant to our enquiry as the distinctions mentioned a moment ago between different kinds of contractarian and contractualist hypothetical procedures, and I mention it only in order to be as clear as possible regarding what I have in mind in this section. All that really matters to our analysis of mentalism is the underlying hope at play in *each and every* injunction or question of this sort when applied to politics. This hope is the hope that there is at least one test or question, positive or negative, comprehensive or minimal, and derived from or representing at least one universally accepted notion of impartiality or universalisability which, when formulated, will lead to a minimally determinate consensus regarding what would be *the* ideal political order.

Or, put differently, what matters in this section is the possibility that there is at least *one* reasonably uncontroversial question which, when asked, will elicit a univocal answer from a whole host of different people. It does not matter whether that engineered political consensus comes in the form of a few simple and abstract principles or in the form of a comprehensive picture of an ideal political order – all that matters is the possibility that a genuine and reasonably determinate consensus could be achieved. Consider here that we are evaluating the viability, not of one particular question, but of a general form of normative inquiry. We want to know whether or not it is possible to establish *any* sort of politically determinate, uncontroversial consensus by means of this sort of test because, if it is, it would show that there is at least one branch of our normative thoughts (or one level, as I have called it) capable of saving mentalism.

That, I think, is more than enough discussion of the place of impartiality in moral and political philosophy, and also of what we do and do not need to bear in mind when analysing impartial choices of ideal state as a species of impartiality test. As a result, we can now return to the crux of the matter, which is that this described level of inquiry fails to do justice to the pedigree of its proponents. Whether taking up the role of Plato and Rousseau's drafter of constitutions, or something akin to Rawls's denizen of the 'original position', the basic problem for this type of normative thought is quite straightforward: real, reasonable people opt for different ideal orders when asked to provide a universal or impartial political choice.

Different people would, for example, even if told by Plato or Rousseau that they will *never* live in the state that is being chosen, come to choose different sorts of political order for one and the same group of people.

Some will demand a state in which every citizen is guaranteed a minimal standard of welfare; others that no great inequalities are permitted between different citizens, regardless of choices of lifestyle or the varying market value of different careers. Some will demand of an ideal state that it maximises aggregate happiness; others that it guarantees the core freedoms of exchange and contract, come what may. Still others, even when instructed by Rawls that they could end up as *any one* of the different citizens set to occupy this chosen state, would select, again, different combinations of values to be realised and different sets of principles to be applied. And, just to be clear, this claim is not the claim that they would make such choices given the confines of Rawls's theory – which is to say, given the conditions of the 'original position' – only that, when asked, as fully fledged adults, what sort of a state they would like to inhabit, they will still disagree *even when told* that they could end up as any one of the new state's citizens. Some will choose states conforming to the difference principle and others a state matching Nozick's ideal of justice in holdings. Some will go the way of Walzer, aligning distributions of goods with those principles regarding their distribution to which the majority of each society subscribes; others the way of Cohen or Dworkin, and so on and so forth.

Why, though, *must* there be this disagreement? The simple answer is this: because impartiality tests of any sort, when they are uncontroversial, require only consistency in the chooser – understood as a genuine ability to accept whatever outcome results from the choice – different people, animated as they are by different combinations of ethical beliefs and different conceptions of the good life, inevitably select different political orders.[50] This much, I think, is perfectly clear to most political philosophers, which is why they inevitably find it necessary to place rather restrictive and, as such, awkwardly controversial conditions of knowledge and choice upon their situated choosers. But then as soon as they *do* find it necessary to place these restrictions on their choosers, they also instantly have to find a way of justifying those restrictions. And why is that a problem? Because that justification, by necessity, has to be extracted

---

[50] R. M. Hare considered what is *in effect* this problem under the rubric of the problem of the 'fanatic', as a result of his worry that some people are genuinely capable of both prescribing and living with the consequences of things like slavery and genocide. The real problem, by contrast, is both less and more troubling than that. On the one hand, I do not think we have to worry too much about that hard-core minority of people, the defining feature of which is that they deny, as universal evils, what the vast bulk of humanity takes to be just that. On the other, we do have to worry a great deal about the fact that all sorts of non-monstrous people disagree with each other about what would constitute the correct or best decision in a given impartial choice situation. See R. M. Hare, *Freedom and Reason*, 171ff.

from our normative thoughts *elsewhere*. My point is thus as simple as it is significant for mentalism: impartial choices of ideal state are incapable of providing mentalists with a convincing answer to OQ, at least by themselves, on account of the fact that they inevitably require justification from one or both of the other two levels of normative thought.

So: because impartial choices of ideal state need to constrain their choosers in highly controversial ways in order to generate reasonably determinate injunctions, they end up requiring justification of a sort unobtainable from within the impartiality test itself, which means of a sort unobtainable at the level of impartial choices of ideal state. Whether our subject is Rawls' 'original position', Harsanyi's equiprobability measure of political principles, Dworkin's hypothetical insurance market, or Nagel's impartiality criterion for arguments deployed in political deliberation, the basic problem is the same.[51] If, for example, we inform an individual that when choosing political principles they will not be allowed to know their own conception of the good, or that they will not be allowed to know the probabilities of occupying various social positions, we will also have to give them some rather good reasons – reasons that will have to be taken from outside this level of normative thought – for why they subsequently *have to adhere* to those principles, for why those principles are still, in an important sense, *theirs*.

Mentalist hopes at this juncture, therefore, rely on the possibility that there *is something else* about which we agree; some other domain of normative thought within which there is a consensus of a sort that would justify the sort of restrictions necessary to produce determinate normative political principles out of impartial situations of political choice. Or, more precisely, we can say that they hope, either at the level of considered judgements or at the level of intuitive choices of abstract principle, that there is some agreement to be found of a sort that would justify one or other constrained situation of choice regarding our selection of *the* ideal political order. Perhaps, though, instead of ending this section with that conclusion, we would do better to end it with an example of the justificatory move in question – a move designed to take us from level 2 to level 1 to a convincing answer to OQ; that is, from considered judgements, to an impartial choice situation, to determinate normative political principles. Consider once more the following defence given by Rawls for the constraints of the 'original position'.

[51] J. Rawls, *A Theory of Justice*; J. C. Harsanyi, 'Morality and the Theory of Rational Behaviour', in A. K. Sen and B. Williams, *Utilitarianism and Beyond* (Cambridge: Cambridge University Press, 1982), 39–62; T. Nagel, 'Moral Conflict and Political Legitimacy', *Philosophy and Public Affairs*, 16:3 (1987), 215–240; R. Dworkin, *Sovereign Virtue*.

[I]t seems *reasonable and generally acceptable* that no one should be advantaged or disadvantaged by natural fortune or social circumstances in the choice of principles. It also seems *widely agreed* that it should be impossible to tailor principles to the circumstances of one's case.[52]

Is it generally acceptable? Is it widely agreed? Rawls is trying here to justify his use of a hypothetical social contract to select principles of justice by reference to a number of what he considers 'fixed points' in our moral thought. These points he generally refers to as considered judgements, and it is to them that we now turn.

2.6   The Evidence for Failure, Part 2: Considered Judgements

> [T]he moral convictions of thoughtful and well-educated people are the data of ethics just as sense-perceptions are the data of a natural science. ... The existing body of moral convictions of the best people is the cumulative product of the moral reflection of many generations, which has developed an extremely delicate power of appreciation of moral distinctions.[53]

Mental dissonance occurs second at the level of *considered judgements*. Considered judgements are those normative judgements regarding particular practices or states of affairs in which fully informed and reflective individuals have the greatest confidence.[54] For mentalists working at this level of inquiry, the hope is that the vast majority of the considered judgements held by the vast majority of the various educated and reflective people in the world point in the same political direction. Or, more precisely, their hope is that these judgements exhibit some sort of clear pattern or tendency out of which we will be able to extract determinate political principles, just as natural scientists are able to extract physical laws from observable regularities. And, as noted previously, these principles could well turn out to be such principles as would justify, in turn, some or other constrained situation of choice of ideal state, though it is not necessary that they do so – it might well be the case that they already directly justify some or other particular political order themselves.

It is this second use of considered judgements – considered judgements as directly requiring one or other set of principles – that I want to

---

[52] *A Theory of Justice*, 18, emphasis added.
[53] W. D. Ross, *The Right and The Good* (Oxford: Oxford University Press, 2002), 41.
[54] For further treatment both of the nature of considered judgements and of the relationship between considered judgements and normative principles in Rawls' work, see P. Singer, 'Sidgwick and Reflective Equilibrium', *Monist*, 55 (1974), and T. M. Scanlon, 'Rawls on Justification', in S. Freeman, *The Cambridge Companion to Rawls* (Cambridge: Cambridge University Press, 2003), 139–167.

concentrate on from here on in, partly because I have already paid enough attention to the mechanics of impartial choice situations, but also, and more importantly, because the objections I want to make to this latter usage apply just as much to the former. Consider that, if considered judgements turn out to be deeply inconsistent, then they will be unfit for justifications not just of a particular set of normative principles, but also of any particular procedure for their selection.

Our first step, however, is to explain the basic dynamics of using considered judgements to provide, pretty much directly, a convincing answer to OQ. Consider Rawls once again. As noted, he placed great stock in this type of thought. For him, because considered judgements are those judgements 'given under conditions favourable for deliberation and judgment in general', they are also 'those judgments in which our moral capacities are most likely to be displayed without distortion'.[55] There is also good reason to think that these judgements are more fundamental to his theory than the contractarian dynamic of the 'original position'. Just bear in mind here that, for Rawls, *no* procedure for the selection of principles could be acceptable which violated a majority of our considered judgements. He does, of course, also believe that, by themselves, they are unable to determine just one set, but even so, we have to make sure *first* that the sets of normative principles we propose *do* match up to at least the vast majority of our considered judgements *before* we try to establish just which of these sets is the one we should adopt – just as, according to his political principles, we are to satisfy the condition of equal liberty before we attempt to satisfy the condition of equal opportunity (and, in turn, the difference principle).

We can describe this acid test of considered judgements as a test of *correspondence*. That is, if a set of political principles is to be convincing, it must correspond, both in content and implications, to our existing considered judgements (where 'correspond' is understood here as an umbrella term for the appropriate uses of 'ground', 'falsify', 'cohere', 'refine', and 'eliminate' – the point being that these are all ways of establishing whether considered judgements fit with a given set of principles). We know, then, when we have arrived at the right principles because, when we apply them, they lead to the judgements we *already have* about which we are *already sure*. Principles which pass this test are principles in which we can have confidence when we come to apply them to those problems about which we are, as individuals, uncertain, and, as groups, in disagreement. Rawls effectively describes this requirement when he writes:

[55] *A Theory of Justice*, 48.

[W]hat is required is a formulation of a set of principles which, when conjoined to our beliefs and knowledge of the circumstances, would lead us to make these judgments with their supporting reasons were we to apply these principles conscientiously and intelligently. A conception of justice characterizes our moral sensibility when the everyday judgments we do make are in accordance with its principles.[56]

In and of itself, however, correspondence as a measure of principles is indeterminate between two different approaches. The first of these, as implied earlier by Hume (see **2.2**), is to try to look for those elements common to all our considered judgements in order to then produce, directly, universal political principles. In this case, we proceed first by collecting as many judgements as we can, and second by studying those judgements in order to try and find the common element within them, which means the common ideal or ideals they implicitly express. As Adam Smith – Hume's contemporary – put the point:

It is thus that the general rules of morality are formed. They are ultimately founded upon experience of what, in particular instances, our moral faculties, our natural sense of merit and propriety, approve, or disapprove of. We do not originally approve or condemn particular actions; because, upon examination, they appear to be agreeable or inconsistent with a certain general rule. The general rule, on the contrary, is formed, by finding from experience, that all actions of a certain kind, or circumstanced in a certain manner, are approved or disapproved of.[57]

The second approach, however, which at the present time is considerably more fashionable, is to repeatedly hypothetically propose different principles until you find one which fails to violate – and thus fails to be falsified by – any of our considered judgements (or at least so few as to make us doubt *them*, rather than the theory). In this case, one attempts to find such principles as do not contradict, either directly or by implication, any of our deeply held normative convictions; principles which, both at first sight and in their necessary consequences, we do not find unpalatable. Here, given a simple choice between two sets of principles, the first of which violates certain considered judgements and the second of which does not, we ought in all cases to prefer the first. As Russ Shafer-Landau puts the point:

If all of our considered judgments are on one side of an argument, then, absent a very compelling argument to the contrary, we are probably right to favour that side in constructing principles of governance.[58]

For ease of discussion, I shall call the first of these approaches *extractive* and the second *eliminative*. According to the extractive approach, our task

---

[56] Ibid., 46.   [57] A. Smith, *The Theory of Moral Sentiments*, 159.
[58] R. Shafer-Landau, 'Liberalism and Paternalism', *Legal Theory*, 11 (2005), 184.

is to induce determinate principles from a collection of considered judgements by searching for the common ideal or ideals that underpin them, whereas according to the eliminative, it is to rule out such principles as go against those judgements. Note that whereas the first approach puts the emphasis on what I called earlier the technique of grounding, the second puts the emphasis on falsifying. This emphasis, however, is more of a hope than a rule. Consider here that whereas the first could determine for us a single principle or set of principles, the second might leave us with several competing principles (or sets thereof), none of which violates any of our considered judgements. If so, we might well have to apply not one but both approaches in order to get our principles – the eliminative first, perhaps, in order to narrow down the field, followed by the real interpretive labours of the extractive. In this case the eliminative would be a sort of first-step shortcut, taken in advance of the rather tricky task of trying to interpret all our various different considered judgements as a singular expression of a single principle or set of principles. So, although one might *hope* to be able to isolate just one set of principles by way of the eliminative method, one cannot *rule out* a turn to the extractive method if this proves impossible.

Ultimately, however, just as was the case with distinctions between different types of ideal-state tests, these differences are not nearly as significant as they initially appear to be.[59] In the context of the present evaluation, as is perhaps already clear, the two approaches are simply two sides of a single methodological coin. They share the same basic idea – that if our principles are to be correct, they have to predict and thus correspond to our considered judgements – and the same basic hope – that these judgements (or nearly all of them, at any rate) exist in a state of near-perfect consistency. And indeed, given the amount of common ground they share, we should not be particularly surprised to learn that Hume was prepared to use, not just the first, but also the second in the course of his own mentalist endeavours. As he writes in *Of the Original Contract*:

[N]othing is a clearer proof that a theory of this kind is erroneous, than to find that it leads to paradoxes repugnant to the common sentiments of mankind.[60]

---

[59] For further discussion of the use of considered judgements, see N. Daniels, 'Wide Reflective Equilibrium and Theory Acceptance in Ethics', *The Journal of Philosophy*, 76:5 (1979), 256–282; O. O'Neill, 'The Power of Example', *Philosophy*, 61 (1986), 5–29; M. Timmons, 'Foundationalism and the Structure of Ethical Justification', *Ethics*, 97 (1987), 595–609; S. Sencerz, 'Moral Facts and the Problem of Justification in Ethics', *Australasian Journal of Philosophy*, 73:3 (1995), 368–388; S. Kagan, 'Thinking about Cases', *Social Philosophy and Policy*, 18:2 (2001); G. Harman, 'Three Trends in Moral and Political Philosophy', *The Journal of Value Inquiry*, 37 (2004), 415–425; P. Singer, 'Ethics and Intuitions', *The Journal of Ethics*, 9 (2005), 331–352.
[60] D. Hume, *Selected Essays* (Oxford: Oxford University Press, 1993), 292.

It does not matter, then, in the context of the present argument (a) which variant of this method for using considered judgements one chooses, or even (b) whether or not one then goes on to use those derived principles in the construction of some or other contractarian procedure – what matters is whether or not our considered judgements exhibit the sort of *harmony* required of them by all such variations. This, to reiterate, is our central question.

So what is our answer? It is that there is nothing like the required harmony. Contra Hume and Rawls, considered judgements are not the consistent body of data so many mentalists have taken them to be. This inconsistency can be proved by dividing disagreements between considered judgements into two types: (1) those which occur within one and the same person and (2) those which occur between two or more different people. Disagreements of type (1) can be thought of as contradictions. They are the contradictions produced when (a) one person produces a number of considered verdicts on different normative matters, and (b) those verdicts, either directly or by implication, conflict with each other. Disagreements of type (2) are disagreements brought about by the fact that different reasonable people produce different considered judgements regarding one and the same normative matter.

Consider the first of these two. We can imagine quite easily someone who issues the following statements in a more or less precise form: that no one should engage in any exchange to which he or she has not consented; that every individual is entitled to the product of his or her labour; that we should leave our natural environment either as we found it or in an even better state for future generations; that we should be able to direct our own lives without interference; that all children should be given a full spread of opportunities in life; and that parents should not have their parenting meddled with provided that they do no harm to their children. These judgements, although each of them appears individually reasonable, are also deeply contradictory, especially once their political implications are taken into account. We have, then, a perfectly recognisable case of someone who unwittingly contradicts themselves; of someone who suffers from dissonance between their own considered judgements.

Such examples, however, along with the type of dissonance they illustrate, are *not* the kind of thing that particularly bothers contemporary political philosophers, who tend to respond to their existence with something like the following: although it is true that human beings issue more demands than are compatible with each other, it is also true that, once they have such conflicts revealed to them, they soon begin to make reasonable, balanced choices as regards what the *proper* hierarchy of priorities *ought* to be. This reply amounts to the claim that, once apprised of the various conflicts found both in hypothetical normative reflection and real political practice, individuals soon begin (or at least, could soon begin, had they the right motivation) to generate internally consistent sets of politically relevant considered judgements. And indeed, some would no doubt add, converting such familiar confusion into rational hierarchy is part of the very *raison d'être* of our subject!

I shall allow, for now, that this reply holds true. Perhaps each of us would, or could, once given the time and resources, achieve a perfectly coherent set of considered judgements, with some being removed and others trimmed at the edges over the course of a comprehensive programme of reflective equilibrium. But then, even if this were possible, it would still not be enough to save the mentalist, because even if we were to produce a world of fully reflective and fully informed individuals, we would still be left with the second type of disagreement. This is because, when we ask people to provide their newly established and fully coherent set of judgements, we soon find that different reasonable people produce different rankings of political priorities.[61]

Consider, for example, that familiar conflict which occurs between (1) market freedoms, (2) education policy, and (3) the flourishing of every child in a state. Some will say that, because (a) we deserve the profit from our labour, (b) no constraint should be put on trade in the absence of negative externalities, and (c) parents should be able to raise their children as they see fit, so long as they do not harm them, we should, as a result, (d) keep taxes low, (e) permit private education, and (f) abandon a vast number of children to less empowering, lower-quality education. Others declare that, because (a) every child deserves an equal chance in life, regardless of social or economic background, we should, as a result, (b) prohibit private education, and (c) pay for excellent education for all by means of significant and income-proportionate taxation. And this is just one simple case. In other domains we find that whilst some choose human rights over national security, others permit torture in the name of the greater good. Some choose economic growth over environmental protection; some environmental protection over poverty relief; some poverty relief over investment in education; and some investment in education over economic growth. It is thus perfectly possible for even consistent, reasonable, reflective people to produce different and conflicting hierarchies of different political ideals.

---

[61] For some related thoughts on the problem of 'ranking', see: J. Floyd, 'Relative Value and Assorted Historical Lessons', in J. Floyd and M. Stears (Eds.), *Political Philosophy versus History? Contextualism and Real Politics in Contemporary Political Thought* (Cambridge: Cambridge University Press, 2011), 206–225.

I only say 'seems' at this point. In order to be more confident of the reality of this conflict, we still need to make a further distinction. Consider an alternative way of analysing the dissonance found at this level of normative thought. Instead of distinguishing between (a) dissonance within one person and (b) dissonance between two or more different people, we should now distinguish between (1) *determinate and contentious* considered judgements, and (2) *indeterminate and universal* considered judgements. Cases of the first are judgements which, *if* they were universal, *would* determine for us specific political orders. Cases of the second are judgements which, although they *are* universal, fail to significantly *narrow down* our political options. An example of the first is the thought that every child deserves an equal chance in life, perhaps understood as an equal spread of opportunities. Yet as we have already seen, given the conflict between (a) this goal and (b) both parental autonomy *and* independent ideals regarding market regulation and fiscal policy, it seems unlikely that the value *is* universal. A second example is the thought that there should be no inequality between the sexes. But what exactly would this judgement entail? Would it entail that parents ought not to encourage any distinction in ambition or behaviour between their sons and daughters? Would it entail that companies and government offices ought to ensure an equal representation of men and women at every level of their various hierarchies? Would it entail that no division of labour is permitted at home, and that men and women must be coerced into doing equal amounts of every task, from childcare to gardening? The point now is that whatever it entails, and there are certainly more and less popular interpretations of the judgement, there are again going to be some who disagree with it, by which I mean, always some who reject the policy or principle proposed.

Compare this situation to that of those judgements which are universal but indeterminate. An example of one of these would be something like 'never permit slavery'. Certainly, there are very few people left in the world prepared to tolerate (at least as slaves) or justify (as uninvolved observers) any conventional form of slavery. But that is not the problem. The problem is that, rather like Isaiah Berlin's rule regarding a guaranteed minimal amount of negative liberty (and it is, *almost*, Berlin's rule), this judgement is incredibly indeterminate between different answers to OQ. That is, it leaves open to us every single form of slavery-prohibiting government: libertarian *and* egalitarian *and* communitarian; democratic *and* undemocratic; fascist *and* communist; anarchic *and* aristocratic alike. Of course, it is perfectly possible that we would be able to eliminate several more of these systems by bringing in further universal considered judgements. We could perhaps eliminate fascism by way of some suitably phrased rule prohibiting states that are likely to perform acts of genocide, just so long as genocide is, as seems highly plausible, a widely condemned political practice. And, in turn, we could perhaps eliminate certain kinds of aristocracy by reference to the following judgement proposed by Rawls:

> [O]ne of our considered convictions, I assume, is this: the fact that we occupy a particular social position is not a good reason for us to propose, or to expect others to propose, or to expect others to accept, a conception of justice that favours those in this position.[62]

Given that an aristocrat might say, 'because I am Lord such and such, you ought to tend to my garden' or 'because I am your Baron, you shall have to grant me sexual favours every Tuesday evening, or not, as I see fit', we might remove such systems from the field on the basis that no educated person would accept them. But even if we do accept these two judgements as universal, that still leaves open to us a vast array of options. There are simply not enough universally agreed-upon building blocks out of which we could construct a workable normative political theory. Or, alternatively put, considered judgements are unfit for politico-philosophical purposes because, even if we allow that there are some which are universal, there are certainly not nearly enough to determine a meaningful answer to OQ. We disagree both too often and too deeply at this level to make any of the possible routes from considered judgements to normative principles a viable philosophical enterprise.

But then, for many political philosophers, even this argument will seem perfectly acceptable, which is why they think it obvious that we should reorganise and redirect such judgements by reference to principles worked up from either our impartial choices of ideal state or our intuitive preferences regarding abstract principles. Yet we have already seen that the first is a philosophical cul-de-sac. What, then, of the second?

2.7   The Evidence for Failure, Part 3: Intuitive Choices of Abstract Principle

Dissonance occurs third at the level of intuitive choices of abstract principle. This type of thought is different in both subject and form to considered judgements. It is different in subject just insofar as it involves verdicts on highly abstract scenarios, rather than on actual or possible states of affairs. It is different in form just insofar as it involves uninformed intuitions rather than informed judgements. Both of these differences will need clarifying, but it is worth dwelling on the second one first, given how

---

[62] J. Rawls, *Political Liberalism*, 24.

loosely the term 'intuition' is now used in political philosophy. Consider, for example, the following usages:

I plan to live with others, if I can, in mutual respect, on a basis that no one could reasonably reject on his own behalf. This plan constitutes an intuition on how to live with others, and as a plan, it can be couched as an imperative.[63]

[O]ur intuition that moral actions are voluntary.[64]

The retributive intuition that wrongdoers deserve punishment because of what they culpably do.[65]

Discourse ethics rests on the intuition that the application of the principle of universalization, properly understood, calls for a joint process of 'ideal role taking' ... everyone is required to take the perspective of everyone else, and thus project herself into the understandings of self and world of all others; from this interlocking of perspectives there emerges an ideally extended we-perspective from which all can test in common whether they wish to make a controversial norm the basis of their shared practice.[66]

[V]irtue ethics aims to reflect the basic moral intuition that the judgments of virtuous agents have no less consequences for them than for those affected by their judgments. From this viewpoint, it is not enough that an agent's judgment seems 'correct' according to some abstract calculation of human benefit (were this possible), for it should also be the sort of decision that a virtuous judge would make.[67]

The intuition that grounds this meta-constitutional principle ... is both simple and robust: some political changes are so momentous that the ordinary processes for making political decisions are inadequate, and in such cases the decision ought to be made by the ultimate source of political authority, the people.[68]

These uses of the term 'intuition' cover such diverse meanings as our intuitive understanding of abstract concepts and principles, our deeply held convictions regarding particular political decisions, and our gut feelings about the fundamental ingredients of morality and well-being. This variation in usage is rather regrettable, and tends to obscure rather than reveal the key element of the type of thought in question. This element, as Walter Sinnott-Armstrong has repeatedly stressed, is its *non-inferentiality* – a simple enough idea which holds that for a belief to be intuited, it cannot be inferred from another belief or set of beliefs (with sets of beliefs

---

[63] A. Gibbard, *Reconciling Our Aims: In Search of Bases for Ethics* (Oxford: Oxford University Press, 2008), 51.

[64] D. Colburn, 'The Concept of Voluntariness', *Journal of Political Philosophy*, 16:1 (2008), 107.

[65] L. Allais, 'Wiping the Slate Clean: The Heart of Forgiveness', *Philosophy and Public Affairs*, 36:1 (2008), 65.

[66] J. Habermas, 'Reconciliation through the Public Use of Reason: Remarks on John Rawls's Political Liberalism', *The Journal of Philosophy*, 92:3 (1995), 109–131.

[67] D. Carr, 'Character and Moral Choice in the Cultivation of Virtue', *Philosophy* 78 (2003), 219–232.

[68] A. Buchanan and R. Powell, 'Constitutional Democracy and the Rule of International Law: Are They Compatible?', *Journal of Political Philosophy*, 16:3 (2008), 326–349.

understood here to include theories).[69] So, for me to have reached an intuitive verdict about something, I must not have inferred that verdict from some other verdict I take to be analogous, or indeed some general theory for reaching such verdicts. I cannot, for example, intuit a verdict about saving a monkey by thinking about the verdict I made last week about saving a gorilla, any more than I can intuit that verdict by asking what utilitarianism would have me decide.

This takes us up to the particular kind of intuitions with which we are concerned here, and thus the way in which intuitive choices of abstract principle differ from considered judgements in terms of subject. The key idea here is that instead of capturing an individual's thoughts by asking for his or her considered judgements on particular social, economic, and political states of affairs, we capture them by asking for the decision they would make in an abstract moral dilemma. Note also that these decisions differ from the decisions we considered earlier regarding a person's conception of an ideal state. In those situations, we wanted to know the answers people would give precisely because those answers were *already* answers to OQ. Here we do not particularly care about what we should actually *do* in the highly hypothetical, and indeed often highly ridiculous, imaginary situations we are about to consider. Instead, what we care about is what those situations imply, by extension and analogy, for the kinds of political questions which, when answered together, combine into a meaningful answer to OQ.

Another way of putting this point would be to say that for political philosophers working at this level of normative thought, these decisions are thought of as expressions of our intuitive preferences for some or other abstract normative principle. If, for example, I say that I would rather save twenty sailors on one boat than ten sailors on another boat if I cannot save the crew of both boats, then it seems as though I am committed, intuitively, to the principle 'always save the greatest number'. Or, if I say that I would not return a gun that I have borrowed from a neighbour who is now deranged, even though I had promised to return it by the time he or she has come to ask for it back, then it seems as though my intuitive preference is for the principle 'always prevent serious harm' over the principle 'always keep a promise'.

Once again, though, my concern with this approach to capturing our underlying normative principles is more with its futility than its ambitions. This futility can be illustrated by way of a well-known pair of 'trolley

---

[69] See, for example, W. Sinnott-Armstrong, L. Young, and F. Cushman, 'Moral Intuitions', in J. M. Doris, *The Moral Psychology Handbook* (Oxford: Oxford University Press, 2010), 246–272.

dilemmas'. The first of these is as follows. You are sitting on a runaway trolley (the classic description of the dilemma says 'trolley'. Just imagine a train if it helps) which, if you do not hit a certain switch, will kill five people strapped to the track ahead, and, if you do, will redirect your trolley and kill one person currently working on the other track. So what ought you to do? Most people, when asked, say 'hit the switch'. Now consider the second dilemma. In this case you confront a choice over whether or not to push a 300-pound man onto the tracks. You know here that if you push the man, although he *will* die, his weight *will also* stop the trolley and save five people. You also know again that, if you do not, all of those five will die. In this case, most people tend to say, 'don't push the man'.[70] So what's the problem for the mentalist? The problem is that there is no good reason for the discrepancy. In both cases, we have to kill one person in order to save five, and in both cases, if you do not kill that one person, those other five will die. It seems, therefore, that this third and last kind of normative thought is just as riven by internal contradictions as the previous two.

The specific contradiction encountered here involves a normative instance of what is known in other subjects as the problem of 'framing'.[71] That is, the awkwardness for mentalists in such cases is that when trying to capture our normative thoughts, and to show where our intuitive preferences lie regarding the saving and ending of lives, and by extension hopefully our preferences regarding utilitarian and deontological principles, it seems as though our thoughts on a single choice come out differently according to how that choice is framed. As a result, it seems as though our intuitions could be dissonant in much the same way that our considered judgements and impartial choices of ideal state were dissonant. Yet to this the obvious objection would be that I have so far only cited one contradictory pair of dilemmas, and not just any pair, but one that has seen many worthy attempts at reconciliation, most of which claim that there is some important normative distinction to be made between 'doing' and 'allowing'.[72] As a result, my use of these dilemmas

---

[70] These findings are well summarised in K. A. Appiah, *Experiments in Ethics* (Cambridge, MA: Harvard University Press, 2008), esp. 89–120. See also J. M. Doris and A. Plakias, 'How to Argue about Disagreement: Evaluative Diversity and Moral Realism', in W. Sinnott-Armstrong, *Moral Psychology, Vol. 2: The Cognitive Science of Morality: Intuition and Diversity* (Cambridge, MA: MIT Press). Fittingly enough, these percentages are also the percentages produced, year after year, by Shelly Kagan's graduate students; see S. Kagan, 'Thinking about Cases', 50.

[71] See Appiah, *Experiments in Ethics*, 89ff.

[72] See J. Jarvis-Thompson, 'Killing, Letting Die, and the Trolley Problem', *The Monist*, 59:2 (1976), 204–217. For the most striking attempt at reconciliation, see J. Jarvis-Thompson, 'Turning the Trolley', *Philosophy and Public Affairs*, 36:4 (2008), 359–374. For the most recent attempts, see F. M. Kamm, *The Trolley Problem Mysteries* (Oxford: Oxford University Press, 2015).

is illustrative at best, misleading at worst, and certainly a long way short of evidence.

Two responses to this objection are possible. The first, which sorely tempts me, would be to argue against those attempted reconciliations by pointing out that the doing/allowing distinction – a distinction that takes its only support from the fact that it is taken to be implicit in our intuitive responses to such dilemmas – is itself intuitively unappealing once made explicit. That is, most people would say that the distinction, once revealed, is intuitively irrelevant, and perhaps not just irrelevant, but also commonly employed as a fudge in order to get people off the hook for things for which they would rather not take full or 'intentional' responsibility. Yet this response is too weak. Not only would it involve an unnecessary digression through the relevant arguments, but also, even if I *could* prove my case, the mentalist would still be able to say that this is still *only one* dilemma, and *perhaps* the rest of our intuitions of this kind are much more coherent.

This is where the second response kicks in. This response, rather than wasting time quibbling over just one contradiction between intuitions, simply accepts the objection. Fine, we can say, it's just one pair of dilemmas. As a result, what we need to do is consider, alongside that pair, the collective import of a whole range of similar contradictions – contradictions, in other words, between the different verdicts given in equivalent yet alternatively framed dilemmas. This means considering the import of something that contemporary political philosophy has so far completely failed to address, namely, the burgeoning field of moral psychology. In this field, and in particular in that part of it which most obviously traverses philosophy and psychology – the world of so-called experimental ethics – dissonance of the kind we are considering here has become an extensively studied phenomenon. We can now be very confident, I believe, on the basis of this field's findings, both (1) that the way in which we frame a single normative problem is likely to alter the intuitive responses one person gives to it, and (2) that different people give different verdicts even to the same framing of the same problem.[73] These are

---

[73] For the most recent discussion, see J. M. Weinberg and J. Alexander, 'Intuitions through Thick and Thin', *Intuitions*, 187; and S. Stich and K. P. Tobia, 'Experimental Philosophy's Challenge to the "Great Tradition"'. *Analytica: Revista de Filosofia* (forthcoming). Some of the crucial earlier pieces of work are as follows. For illuminating discussion of the various studies involving incoherent moral intuitions, see J. Knobe and J. M. Doris, 'Strawsonian Variations: Folk Morality and the Search for a Unified Theory', in J. M. Doris (Ed.), *The Handbook of Moral Psychology* (Oxford: Oxford University Press, 2010); W. Sinnott-Armstrong, 'Moral Intuitionism Meets Empirical Psychology', in T. Horgan and M. Timmons (Eds.), *Metaethics after Moore* (New York: Oxford University Press, 2006), 339–365; and W. Sinnott-Armstrong, 'Framing Moral

the core claims here, centred on framing, though other claims only add to the problem. For example, if the order in which we are presented with dilemmas, our mood at the time, or our blood-sugar level, all affect our verdicts, then these are just more reasons to be mistrustful of our intuitions.

Let's start off by noting just some of the specific findings produced by this literature, which when taken together provide a 'body of empirical research demonstrating that intuitions vary according to factors irrelevant to the [philosophical] issues'.[74] We know, for example, from Walter Sinnott-Armstrong, a key figure in all of this, that our intuitions about abstract cases clash with our intuitions about concrete cases on all manner of subjects, and that different intuitions can be elicited from one and the same person according to how we frame a problem in terms of wording and context.[75] We know that intuitions depend on cultural and

Intuitions', in W. Sinnott-Armstrong, *Moral Psychology, Volume 2: The Cognitive Science of Morality* (Cambridge, MA: MIT Press, 2008), 47–76. A vast number of different moral issues have been subjected to substantial testing and analysis in this growing subject. For insightful treatment of our conflicting intuitions regarding morality and responsibility, see R. L. Woolfolk, J. M. Doris, and J. M. Darley, 'Identification, Situational Constraint, and Social Cognition: Studies in the Attribution of Moral Responsibility', in J. Knobe and S. Nichols (Eds.), *Experimental Philosophy* (Oxford: Oxford University Press, 2008), 61–80; S. Nichols and J. Knobe, 'Moral Responsibility and Determinism: The Cognitive Science of Folk Intuitions', in J. Knobe and S. Nichols (Eds.), *Experimental Philosophy* (Oxford: Oxford University Press, 2008), 105–128; and E. A. Nahmias, S. Morris, T. Nadelhoffer, and J. Turner, 'Surveying Freedom: Folk Intuitions about Free Will and Moral Responsibility', *Philosophical Psychology*, 18:5 (2005), 561–584. For variation according to blood-alcohol level, see A. A. Duke and L. Bègue, 'The Drunk Utilitarian: Blood Alcohol Concentration Predicts Utilitarian Responses in Moral Dilemma', *Cognition*, 134, 121–127. For an interesting study of how mood can affect our intuitive verdicts, see P. Valdesolo and D. DeSteno, 'Manipulations of Emotional Context Shape Moral Judgment', *Psychological Science*, 17:6 (2006). See also, for a much older but now classic study on how different choices regarding how we frame the numbers involved in a given political choice situation (say, of people, of lives lost, of money gained, etc.) produce different intuitions, and, in particular, different *consequentialist* intuitions on the part of the chooser (and note that, in the sense of framing involved here, we will always *have* to frame the numbers, one way or another), A. Tversky and D. Kahneman, 'The Framing of Decisions and the Psychology of Choice', *Science*, 221 (1981), 453–458. For various attempts to map out this sort of dissonance, see J. D. Greene, 'From Neural "Is" to Moral "Ought": What Are the Moral Implications of Neuroscientific Moral Psychology?', *Nature Reviews Neuroscience*, 4 (2003), 847–850; J. D. Greene, R. B. Sommerville, L. E. Nystrom, J. M. Darley, and J. D. Cohen, 'An fMRI Investigation of Emotional Engagement in Moral Judgment', *Science*, 293 (2001), 2105–2108; and W. Sinnott-Armstrong, J. S. Borg, C. Hynes, J. Van Horn, and S. Grafton, 'Consequences, Action, and Intention as Factors in Moral Judgments: An fMRI Investigation', *Journal of Cognitive Neuroscience*, 18:5 (2006), 803–817.

[74] Weinberg and Smith, 'The Instability of Philosophical Intuitions: Running Hot and Cold on Truetemp', *Philosophy and Phenomenological Research*, 76:1 (2008), 138–155.

[75] W. Sinnott-Armstrong, 'Abstract + Concrete = Paradox', in J. Knobe and S. Nichols (Eds.), *Experimental Philosophy*, 209–230. See also 'Framing Moral Intuitions', in W. Sinnott-Armstrong (Ed.), *Moral Psychology: Volume 2*, 47–76.

socio-economic backgrounds,[76] as well as educational background.[77] We know that they vary according to gender[78] and, as noted, the order in which thought experiments are presented.[79] And what does all this tell us? Already it seems we should echo Alexander and Weinberg, who write that 'experimental evidence seems to point to the unsuitability of intuitions to serve as evidence at all'.[80]

Widening the picture, we also know from Joshua Knobe and Shaun Nichols that people give incompatibilist verdicts on the subject of moral responsibility and determinism when asked more abstract questions and compatibilist verdicts when asked questions that trigger their emotions.[81] We know from Fiery Cushman and Alfred Mele that people become progressively more likely to regard certain forms of immoral behaviour as unintentional the more cases of a given type they consider.[82] We know from Geoffrey Miller that studies of the evolutionary and sexual selection origins of our intuitions show that they are highly domain-specific; that they naturally apply to particular situations that have little similarity with modern ethical dilemmas; and that they are, partly as a result of this, highly likely to clash not just with each other, but also with requirements of logic and consistency.[83]

Continuing this theme, we know from Jesse Prinz that, even amongst moral nativists, those scholars concerned with trying to show the existence and nature of something approximating to a moral or normative 'sense', there is agreement that the actual content of 'innate morality' varies considerably according to various mechanisms and environmental factors.[84]

---

[76] J. M. Weinberg, C. Gonnerman, and J. Alexander, 'Are Philosophers Expert Intuiters?', *Philosophical Psychology*, 23 (2010), 331–355; E. Machery, R. Mallon, S. Nichols, and S. Stich, 'Semantics, Cross-Cultural Style', *Cognition*, 92 (2004), B1–B12.

[77] S. Nichols, S. Stich, and J. M. Weinberg, 'Metaskepticism: Meditations in Ethnoepistemology, in S. Luper (Ed.), *The Skeptics* (Aldershot: Ashgate, 2003), 227–248.

[78] W. Buckwalter and S. Stich, 'Gender and the Philosophy Club', *The Philosophers' Magazine*, 52 (2011), 60–65.

[79] A. Swain and J. Weinberg, 'The Instability of Philosophical Intuitions', 2008. See also, again, W. Sinnott-Armstrong's 'Framing Moral Intuitions'.

[80] J. Alexander and J. Weinberg, 'Analytic Epistemology and Experimental Philosophy', *Philosophy Compass*, 2 (2007), 63. See also J. M. Weinberg, 'How to Challenge Intuitions Empirically without Risking Skepticism', *Midwest Studies in Philosophy*, 31 (2007), 318–343; and J. S. Weinberg, S. Nichols, and S. Stich, 'Normativity and Epistemic Intuitions', *Philosophical Topics*, 29:1 (2001), 429–460.

[81] S. Nichols and J. Knobe, 'Moral Responsibility and Determinism: The Cognitive Science of Folk Intuitions', in J. Knobe and S. Nichols, *Experimental Philosophy*, 105–126.

[82] F. Cushman and A. Mele, 'Intentional Action: Two-and-a-Half Folk Concepts?', in J. Knobe and S. Nichols (Eds.), *Experimental Philosophy*, 171–188.

[83] G. Miller, 'Kindness, Fidelity, and Other Sexually Selected Virtues', in W. Sinnott-Armstrong (Ed.), *Moral Psychology: Volume 1*, 209–244.

[84] J. Prinz, 'Is Morality Innate?', in W. Sinnott-Armstrong (Ed.), *Moral Psychology: Volume 1*, 367–406.

We know from Gerd Gigerenzer that normative intuitions often seem to have been produced by heuristics the brain adopts which, although highly conducive to quick decisions, are both open to distortion by framing variations, as discussed earlier, and prone to getting us to exclude many of the possible actions and consequences that at least some moral and political philosophers would like us to take into account.[85] We know from Jonathan Haidt and Fredrik Bjorklund that there is evidence to suggest that the true relationship between reason and intuition in human normative thought is that *different* human beings have *different* intuitions, with reason only coming in *post*-intuition to try and find appealing justifications.[86] We know from Joshua Greene that deontological judgements tend to be driven, in the brain, by emotional responses, with consequentialist judgements being delivered in situations designed to encourage more theoretical, cognitive reasoning. This is why Greene concludes that it is 'exceedingly unlikely that there is any rationally coherent normative moral theory that can accommodate our moral intuitions',[87] a point only reinforced by the extensive studies of John Doris and Alexandra Plakias, all of which show that there is extensive 'evaluative disagreement' around the world, even regarding abstract dilemmas on which most Westerners agree.[88]

So, more and more evidence, with all of it pointing in the same direction. Nevertheless, I know what many readers make of these last paragraphs. They will balk at my use of the term 'know', and worry that my acceptance of these findings has been altogether too uncritical. As a result, what we need to do next is look carefully at the three broad lines of objection this kind of research has encountered. Remember, though, in all of this, my key claim here: it is that this body of research, when taken as a whole, reveals a degree of inconsistency amongst our normative intuitions that fatally undermines their suitability for mentalist political philosophy. Keep this in mind in what follows.

The first of these objections is methodological, and comes from a range of scholars who take issue, not just with the conclusions or relevance of

---

[85] G. Gigerenzer, 'Moral Intuition = Fast and Frugal Heuristics?', in W. Sinnott-Armstrong (Ed.), *Moral Psychology: Volume 2*, 1–26.

[86] J. Haidt and F. Bjorklund, 'Social Intuitionists Answer Six Questions about Moral Psychology', in W. Sinnott-Armstrong (Ed.), *Moral Psychology: Volume 2*, 181–218.

[87] J. Greene, 'The Secret Joke of Kant's Soul', in W. Sinnott-Armstrong (Ed.), *Moral Psychology: Volume 3*, 72. More recently, Greene has argued that those of us likely to use the first of these systems are akin to a different 'moral tribe' to those of us more likely to use the other – a description unlikely to encourage mentalism: J. Greene, *Moral Tribes: Emotion, Reason and the Gap between Us and Them* (London: Atlantic Books Ltd., 2014).

[88] J. Doris and A. Plakias, 'How to Argue about Disagreement: Evaluative Diversity and Moral Realism', in W. Sinnott-Armstrong (Ed.), *Moral Psychology: Volume 2*, 303–332.

this research, but also with some of its core assumptions and techniques. Several suggestions have been made on this front. One is that what appear to be clashes between intuitions are really just the product of ambiguities over the meaning of certain English words, such as 'responsible' and 'intentional'.[89] A second is that the people studied or tested in this research tend to be college students, and so are unrepresentative of the population as a whole.[90] A third is that our intuitions might actually be more distorted and thus more dissonant in thought experiments than they are in real-life, non-verbal situations.[91] A fourth is that apparent clashes between intuitions might actually be more to do with disagreements over relevant facts and background theories than the normative thoughts they are supposed to capture.[92]

These are all, on the face of it, promising objections, yet not one of them hits its mark. First of all, if key normative terms are too ambiguous for such thought experiments, then that is just as much a problem for moral and political philosophy as it is for moral psychology. This difficulty is a common one with arguments which, like this one, dabble in scepticism. Consider here that if we say that language is too ambiguous for us to capture our intuitions, and that as a result intuitions are unknowable, then they are unavoidably just as unfit for purpose for mentalist moral and political philosophy as they are for moral psychology. Or consider more generally, as Doris and Plakias have, the claim that it is impossible to prove conclusively the existence of real, deep intuitive disagreement in the world.[93] The implication of this is that it must be equally impossible to show agreement of the same kind, and thus perfectly impossible to use intuitions as grounds for a convincing answer to OQ. In other words, the claim doesn't just miss its mark – it backfires.

Second, if we say that college students are unrepresentative of the population at large, then that is already a fatal admission that there is deep disagreement on intuitions within the population as a whole. And indeed, given the common stress on reasonable as opposed to unreasonable disagreement in moral and political philosophy, should we not be particularly worried here if there is deep disagreement between college

[89] E. Sosa, 'Experimental Philosophy and Philosophical Intuition', in J. Knobe and S. Nichols (Eds.), *Experimental Philosophy*, 231–240.

[90] W. Tolhurst, 'Moral Intuitions Framed', in W. Sinnott-Armstrong (Ed.), *Moral Psychology: Volume 2*, 77–82; and R. Shafer-Landau, 'Defending Ethical Intuitionism', in W. Sinnott-Armstrong (Ed.), *Moral Psychology: Volume 2*, 83–96.

[91] R. Shafer-Landau, 'Defending Ethical Intuitionism'.

[92] J. Doris and A. Plakias, 'How to Argue about Disagreement', 320. See also N. Daniels, 'Wide Reflective Equilibrium and Theory Acceptance in Ethics'.

[93] N. Daniels, 'Wide Reflective Equilibrium and Theory Acceptance in Ethics', 315.

students, given that college students are surely more reasonable than the average citizen? Again then – backfire.

Third, as regards the contrast between hypothetical and real-life situations, surely the problem is that in real-life situations, on those rare occasions when we are given something approaching a free choice as to whether to be, say, utilitarian or deontological in our verdicts, then in addition to being partial, partially informed, and pressured, we also tend to be in deep disagreement – which is why people run these thought experiments in the first place! Although it is easily forgotten, and must seem like a fetish from the outside, we have to remember that the reason moral psychologists and moral and political philosophers turn to the world of abstract and hypothetical thought experiments is precisely because they encounter too much disagreement *outside of this world*. Again then – backfire.

Fourth, and finally, as regards the significance of facts and background theories, surely the truth here is that neither plays any significant part in most well-designed dilemmas. Or, if the objection has in mind the kinds of background theories Norman Daniels once discussed in a defence of reflective equilibrium to which we will return at the close of this chapter,[94] which means theories pertaining to such things as the nature of morality and the concept of a person, then the problem instead becomes that these theories are themselves composites of normative beliefs, which themselves are differently held and weighted by different individuals, as shown by the very experiments and studies we have been discussing (in addition to being weighted differently by one and the same individual in different though unfortunately related situations!). One last time then – backfire.

Now let's consider a second broad line of objection, and leave these methodological worries behind. This line queries the conclusions, rather than the methods, of this research, and two versions of it in particular stand out, both of which would appeal to many philosophers. The first of these holds that, even if we have been shown that *many* of our intuitions are unreliable, we still cannot say that *most* of our intuitions are unreliable, given that we might have an awful lot of intuitions about all sorts of choices, the details of which we have yet to examine.[95] This argument is both weak and irrelevant. It is weak because, if most of the intuitions we have studied turn out to be flawed, including intuitive preferences regarding many of our most fundamental normative principles, then the only verdict we can draw, at this point in time, is that they are unreliable. It is

[94] N. Daniels, 'Wide Reflective Equilibrium and Theory Acceptance in Ethics'.
[95] See W. Tolhurst, 'Moral Intuitions Framed'.

irrelevant because, even if only a significant minority of intuitions turns out to be unreliable, that would still be more than enough to undermine any use of them as grounds for an answer to OQ capable of convincing all those to whom it would apply.

Or would it? According to Russ Shafer-Landau, for example, even if most intuitions *do* turn out to need serious alteration, we only need a few *key* intuitions to be reliable, with an example of such an intuition being the following: 'The deliberate humiliation, rape, and torture of a child, for no purpose other than securing the rapist's pleasure, is immoral.'[96] This claim, however, only takes us back to the problem we encountered with considered judgements, namely, that although there may well be widespread agreement on a few key instances of immorality, this is still much too meagre material on which to build a convincing political argument. That is, although we might quite easily get a cohabiting population of hundreds, thousands, or even millions to agree on this verdict, as well as others like it, that is still no reason to expect them to agree on egalitarian rather than libertarian political principles, any more than it is reason to expect them to agree on hypothetical contractarian rather than concrete democratic procedures for the selection of such principles. Remember here the scale of mentalist ambition, and the need to find a convincing and meaningful answer to OQ. It is not enough to find just one small clearing of coherence and agreement, deep in the jungle of our normative thoughts.

We come, then, finally to a third broad line of objection, which questions whether this research, however good it might be, has any real relevance to normative philosophical endeavours. This line takes many forms. Sometimes it takes the form of a claim that we are not really interested in moral and political philosophy in what partial and irrational people believe, but only in what ideal people in ideal conditions believe.[97] Sometimes it takes the form of a claim that we are not really interested in how people do think, but only in what they should think.[98] And sometimes, though I can find no written discussion to reflect what I am sure, from conversations, many scholars believe, it takes the form of a claim that because we have nothing but intuitions to rely upon, we have no choice but to ignore their flaws. What, then, is the problem with all these claims?

The problem with the first is that in situations designed to capture ideal conditions, with all partiality and distortion from facts and background

---

[96] R. Shafer-Landau, 'Defending Ethical Intuitionism', 83.

[97] J. Doris and A. Plakias, 'How to Argue about Disagreement', 305, 320.

[98] J. Knobe and S. Nichols, 'An Experimental Philosophy Manifesto', in J. Knobe and S. Nichols (Eds.), *Experimental Philosophy*, 12.

theories removed from the picture, we still find that different people have different intuitions, and indeed, not just different intuitions, but intuitions supportive of different contradictory principles. This much is clear from the recent debate surrounding philosophers' 'expert' intuitions, which sprang up precisely as an attempted defence of the orthodoxy surrounding intuitions against the implications of experimental evidence.[99] Predictably, it did not take long for this claim to be empirically shot down.[100] What, then, has the philosopher of intuitions ultimately left to say, apart from 'believe what I say because I say it'? Once she or he has lost the ability to show that it is what any ideal person in an ideal situation would believe, there is nothing left to the argument but bald assertion. And consider, as Knobe and Nichols have pointed out, we could just as easily believe that they are much *more* likely to have distorted intuitions than an average individual, given their training, affiliations, and career interests. It was perhaps this combination of conviction and assertion that John Finnis had in mind when he wrote that:

[T]he staple of academic discussion of individual and political morality is now the appeal to 'my' or 'our' *intuitions* about specific types of conduct. The term 'intuition' claims respectability for positions which are defended not by reasons but by the more or less tacit appeal to consensus. But as a response to questions and objections, appeal to consensus is fallacious and rationally futile. Against objectors it merely insinuates that *we*, not they, are in charge around here.[101]

The problem with the second claim, by contrast, is more subtle. Certainly the claim that it does not matter what we do think, but only what we should think, will chime with many moral and political philosophers. But it is deeply misleading. It is misleading because philosophers have no choice but to base their claims on how we should think on claims about how we do think in related situations. They say, for example, that 'because you wouldn't take organs from a healthy person to save five

---

[99] J. Bengson, 'Experimental Attacks on Intuitions and Answers', *Philosophy and Phenomenological Research*, 86:3 (2013), 495–532; J. Demaree-Cotton, 'Do Framing Effects Make Moral Intuitions Unreliable?', *Philosophical Psychology* (2014), 1–22; M. E. Deutsch, *The Myth of the Intuitive: Experimental Philosophy and Philosophical Method* (Cambridge, MA: MIT Press, 2015); T. Williamson, 'Philosophical "Intuitions" and Scepticism about Judgement', *Dialectica*, 58:1 (2004), 109–153; T. Williamson, *The Philosophy of Philosophy* (Oxford: Wiley-Blackwell, 2008).

[100] K. Vaesen, M. Peterson, and B. Van Bezooijen, 'The Reliability of Armchair Intuitions', *Metaphilosophy*, 44:5 (2013), 559–578; K. Tobia, W. Buckwalter, and S. Stich, 'Moral Intuitions: Are Philosophers Experts?', *Philosophical Psychology*, 26:5 (2013), 629–638; and J. M. C. Gonnerman, C. Buckner, and J. Alexander, 'Are Philosophers Expert Intuiters?', *Philosophical Psychology*, 23 (2010), 331–355.

[101] J. M. Finnis, 'Commensuration and Public Reason', in R. Chang (Ed.), *Incommensurability, Incomparability, and Practical Reason* (Cambridge, MA: Harvard University Press, 1997), 218.

others, you shouldn't take money for redistributive justice'. Put bluntly, the truth is that every 'ought' they have ever issued has been grounded somewhere in an 'is' of how they think we already think, so claiming that we only care about what we ought to think just will not do.

So what about the third version of this objection? This version asks whether we should just rely on intuitions *anyway*, given that we have *no other choice*, and there is certainly some truth in that. Clearly, if what is meant is that individuals in the real world, acting individually, often have no choice but to trust their intuitions when faced with a dilemma, then it is difficult to see how they *could* do anything but act on those intuitions. But consider: private moral dilemmas are rather different from public political philosophy. Surely any political philosopher would accept that the epistemological standards a private individual has to meet in making his or her private decisions are considerably lower than the standards a political authority has to meet in not just choosing but also enforcing political principles. Or, if that claim sounds too much like a normative commitment masquerading as theoretical good sense, whilst relying on my own discreet mentalism, then remember here that what we are after in this book is an answer to OQ that would be convincing to all those individuals who have to live with its contents. Even if, therefore, we worry about the normativity of the claim that moral philosophy and political philosophy have different epistemological standards, we should at least see that their different organising questions have very different implications for the role intuitions can play within them.

All of which returns us to the central claim argued for in this chapter, namely, that human intuitions are too dissonant to reveal the kind of reliable principle preferences needed for grounding a convincing answer to OQ. Perhaps we should not be surprised that this claim has been sustained during our discussion of the findings of contemporary moral psychology given that we could already see, simply from the initial pair of trolley dilemmas, just how readily the principles we select in these dilemmas are going to come into conflict with each other. Now, though, we can really appreciate just how wide and deep our disagreements run. As this research makes clear, our intuitions clash, not just *between individuals*, but also within and between different dilemmas, and thus *within individuals*. As a result, we do not need now to work our way through still further dilemmas involving, say, ticking bombs or starving sailors in rowing boats, for it is already clear that whatever intuitions those dilemmas might reveal, they would be unfit for the purposes of mentalist political philosophy. Either different individuals would have different intuitions, or particular individuals would subscribe to different principles according to different dilemmas, or they would subscribe to different principles according to different framings of the same dilemma, or, finally, we would find agreement, but only on something too weak on which to build political principles, such as 'don't eat the sailor on your right when there's a full picnic hamper on your left'.

There are, however, still a few stones left unturned here. For example, we might think that we could try and dissolve these conflicts by arguing that, in some way, each apparently contradictory choice *only* applies to the specific scenario in which it was made – perhaps in some kind of extreme, Rossian, pluralistic manner. Once again, though, this option is unavailable to us given that the very point of such scenarios *is* to get a handle on what are assumed to be generalisable, deep-lying, coherent, harmonious and politically determinate principles in our normative thought. If the second trolley dilemma *only* tells us not to push fat men in front of trains, and *nothing* outside of that particular situation, then it is not of much use to moral or political philosophers. We simply cannot turn around and say, 'oh, these dilemmas have nothing to do with normative theory-building', given that *their very purpose* is to capture and prove the existence of one or other of our philosophical accounts of normative evaluation.[102]

Nevertheless, as with considered judgements, perhaps it still remains open to the mentalist political philosopher to say something like the following: whilst it is true that our various abstract choices come into conflict, it is also true that, once apprised of that fact, we soon begin to replace our confused, common-sense normative inclinations with a more seamless, coherent set of harmonious verdicts. This echoes a point made earlier in the discussion of considered judgements, and again the problem the mentalist faces is the same: *different* reasonable people, when asked, provide *different* coherent sets of verdicts, each of which expresses different priorities and different fundamental preferences regarding different political principles. Psychological research once more weighs in with supporting evidence here. Consider, as a simple example, the following experiment. When asked about whether a magistrate should kill one

---

[102] One exception to this might appear to be J. Dancy, *Ethics without Principles* (Oxford: Oxford University Press, 2008). Appearances can be deceptive. First off, Dancy is more properly understood as being interested in concrete considered judgements rather than intuitive choices given in situations of abstract choice. Second, he is not averse to us applying at least some intuitions and considered judgements to political life (certain caveats allowing). Third, and most important of all, his work still assumes that there is consistency across intuitions and judgements (or at least judgements) so, crucially, even if his model of morality were radically different to those discussed, he would still be wrong in the relevant sense, given that he would still be relying on a non-existent degree of coherence in our normative thought patterns. I say more about the particularism Dancy advances in **2.9**.

innocent murder suspect in order to prevent riots which would kill hundreds of innocent civilians, young American and Chinese subjects gave very different responses. In this case (apparently) deontological Americans disagreed with their (apparently) consequentialist Chinese counterparts.[103]

Of course, we know what many in political philosophy will say to *that*. They will simply say that many – if not most – of the people involved in these studies were *unreasonable*. They will say that, although it is true that under-educated, unreasonable groups of people provide such responses, it is simply not the case that *fully* informed, *properly* educated, *genuinely* reasonable people disagree about these kinds of choices amongst abstract principles.[104] But guess what? With this objection we have now come full circle. We are returned, in effect, right back to the travails of contemporary debates in moral and political philosophy explored in Chapter 1, given that there is surely no better evidence of deep disagreement between exceptionally reasonable people than the kinds of conflict we see in contemporary academic discourse, as illustrated by the discussions of Chapter 1. Rawls thinks that, because we do not *earn* our talents, we do not enjoy an *overriding* claim to what we gain from their possession; Nozick thinks that, whatever resources we acquire through labour and exchange, those resources are *ours* to decide what to do with. And note that it does not matter here whether we choose to frame this conflict as a conflict between two conceptions of fairness or as a conflict between fairness and freedom; what matters is that, when presented with different conceivable normative political principles, different political philosophers choose differently. Rawls disagrees with Nozick, who disagrees with Cohen, who disagrees with Dworkin, who disagrees with Walzer, who disagrees with the deliberative democrats, who disagree with theorists of tolerance, who disagree with Rorty, who disagrees with Hampshire, and so on and so forth.[105]

---

[103] See again J. M. Doris and A. Plakias, 'How to Argue about Disagreement'. See also an interesting survey conducted by the BBC, this time involving a scenario in which a group of people is trapped in a cave. One rather large member of this party has got himself stuck in the only exit from the cave, which is rapidly filling up with water. Another member of the party possesses a stick of dynamite which would blow up this man, and free the rest of the group. If they do not blow up the man, the whole party will perish, though if they do blow up the man, then, needless to say, he will perish. When asked, 74.12 per cent of people said that the group should blow up the man, with the remainder claiming they should not. See http://News.bbc.co.uk/2/hi/uk_news/magazine/4954856.stm.

[104] For an attempt to defend this practice in the face of such evidence, see S. M. Liao, 'A Defense of Intuitions', *Philosophical Studies*, 140:2 (2008), 247–262.

[105] This point finds some support, I would suggest, in Brian Leiter's response to the moral psychology literature. Although he agrees with much of its findings, he also points out that what it tries to prove can also be proven by simply studying the extent of

More abstractly still, we might add, contractarians disagree with constructivists, who disagree with utilitarians, who disagree amongst themselves as to whether acts or rules lie at the heart of our moral evaluations, and so on and so forth. And just to be clear: although it is true that some of these philosophers affirm *roughly the same* political order on the basis of *different* political principles (we're generally a lefty, middle-class lot), it is also true that many of us affirm both rival orders *and* rival principles, which means the unavoidable problem remains: different people – different, educated, reasonable, reflective, and even expert people – possess different intuitive preferences regarding the choice of abstract, normative, political principles. Or, to return to the terminology set out at the start of this section, they possess different *intuitive principle preferences*.

2.8 Normative Dissonance in Full View

> Strawson describes two kinds of philosophy, descriptive and revisionary. Descriptive philosophy gives reasons for what we instinctively assume, and explains and justifies the unchanging central core in our beliefs about ourselves, and the world we inhabit. But, by temperament, I am a revisionist. . . . I try to challenge what we assume. Philosophers should not only interpret our beliefs; when they are false, they should change them.[106]

My argument so far has been that normative mental dissonance occurs (1) at the level of impartial choices of ideal state, (2) at the level of considered judgements, and (3) at the level of intuitive choices of abstract principle. Yet to this many scholars would still respond as follows – and the tenor of the reply should be familiar by now: of course we know that there are conflicting claims made at each level; the point is to work out who is *right*. As I have already pointed out, though, that response would be all well and good, if not for the fact that it is *only* on the basis of a consensus putatively established at one of these three levels that philosophers have ever been able to claim an ability to solve those disagreements which occur elsewhere and, in particular, further up the normative line at the level of both political principles and concrete policy proposals.

There is a funny twist here, however, which is that although political philosophers do accept, by and large, that we disagree about all sorts of things, concrete and abstract alike, they also still believe that there is agreement to be had in *at least one* of these three domains. For instance,

disagreement in twentieth-century moral and political philosophy, and in particular the views of figures such as Nietzsche.

[106] D. Parfit, *Reasons and Persons* (Oxford: Oxford University Press, 1984), x.

some will say that, regardless of whether or not there is consensus to be found at the other two levels, when different people are asked to design a state in which either they will *never* live or in which they will take up a *random* position, they somehow speak with one voice. Others insist that although we might disagree when it comes to the choice of ideal state, if we are asked to provide intuitive responses to significant moral dilemmas (dilemmas of a sort analogous to normative political dilemmas), or considered judgements regarding various practical choices, people who are otherwise entirely opposed soon come to find themselves part of a consensus.

Contemporary scholars, in other words, have not been particularly troubled by these sorts of difficulties to date because, even when they accept that there is dissonance to be found at one or even two of these levels, they still think that there is coherence to be found in whatever set of thoughts remains. For example, even if there is a group of them who think that MacIntyre is right when he says that we disagree, at present, about substantive moral and political principles, that same group still holds firm in the belief that we agree elsewhere – if not about considered judgements, then perhaps about intuitive responses to choices of abstract principle. Much the same thing is true as regards contemporary attitudes towards theories of moral and value pluralism. Even those who accept that there are real problems of incommensurability in various spheres of human existence still believe that there is some ideal, found at one or other normative level, on which we do agree. They might agree that we *disagree* about conceptions of the good, about conceptions of happiness or desert, or about principles of retributive or redistributive justice, yet still claim that there is *something else*, some Kantian principle of right, or some rounded conception of well-being, or some abstract notion of democratic procedure, upon which we do or at least would agree, and by recourse to which we could solve the political dilemmas these various pluralisms generate.[107]

This optimism is not as surprising as it might seem. Consider here that, even if as many as two-thirds of philosophers were to agree that there is no consensus to be had at the level of impartial choices of an ideal state, two-thirds that there is no consensus available at the level of considered judgements, and two-thirds that there is no consensus to be found at the level of choices of abstract principle, it could still be the case that all of them, if asked, say that mentalist political philosophy was a viable philosophical enterprise. It is also not surprising when one considers that there may well be *some* normative matters – most probably particular

---

[107] See Chapter 1 for numerous illustrations of this assumption in practice.

considered judgements – upon which we *do* agree. The rule 'don't torture', for instance, might well be one such universal – though it's noticeable how easily we can chip away at it. What if, for example, an act of torture was necessary to stop a bomb exploding which would kill 1,000 lives? What if it were necessary to save your country? We might try instead: 'don't torture children'. Yet what if a child knew the code to that bomb? What if he or she knew the whereabouts of the plans for the invasion of your good, compassionate, innocent country? So we try instead: 'don't torture children purely for fun'. But now imagine, if you can, that you are the torturer, and that if you do not do carry out your wickedness for the sake of another's fun, that person will remember that she has to press the button that explodes the bomb.

We agree, I hope, that I should certainly not do it for my *own* fun. We also agree, perhaps, that I should not *support*, all else being equal, another's torture, and also maybe (although I am not convinced, given the existence of sadists and masochists) that one should not torture at all *unless* there exists some or other set of dire circumstances. Alternatively, perhaps we could agree that we should not take *pleasure* at the torture of children or, from a different perspective, that we should not be the *sort of person* who would, even if we were currently, just such a person. Nevertheless, whatever the precise detail of these rules, the key problem remains that, even if we concede minimal judgements of this sort, we still are not led to one particular normative theory – outside of a very minimal, very unenlightening deontology – let alone one particular, and meaningful, answer to OQ. Whatever rules we *do* or perhaps *could* agree upon, those rules just will not sufficiently narrow down our political options. Even if, for example, we could rule out states whose very purpose is to practise torture on 95 per cent of the population, or whose very purpose is to perform genocide or perpetuate slavery, we would still continue to face a huge array of underdetermined choices.

I would like to cautiously suggest here that this long-standing hope – that there still remains some corner of our normative thought into which no one has yet peered, and out of which we could derive determinate political principles – is unlikely to last forever. Outside of the ephemeral forces of convention, it is surely only personal obsessions with system and particular cognitive biases in favour of assuming an underlying order that can sustain mentalist political philosophy now. Certainly there will always be some, such as MacIntyre and, on occasion, Rawls, who place such a high value on possessing a coherent, systematic normative theory that, for them, it does not matter if one has to override a number of judgements held dear by a particular individual just so long as one achieves a theory that is both comprehensive over its domain (whether that domain be

political philosophy or all of morality) and incapable of producing indeterminacy and normative dilemmas.[108]

Sidgwick expressed this obsession with ethical systems well when he
wrote: 'If we are not to systematise human activities by taking Universal
Happiness as their common end, on what other principles are we to
systematise them?'.[109] It is easy to understand that, for individuals of
either a religious or, for that matter, a particular kind of scientific mind-
set, the notion that our normative thinking is a mess is a hard one to
accept. If one is used to seeing the world as a place of order or, indeed, if
one is raised to think that there is someone who has ordered it, then one is
naturally going to assume that our normative thoughts possess, at root,
just that degree of stable coherence to which we have become accustomed
in our investigation of the physical world.

And admittedly, with all that being said, nothing I have argued so far
need distract those philosophers from that particular enterprise, just so
long as it is recognised that the preference for producing and adopting
coherent normative theories rather than accepting complexity and conflict is *just that* – a preference, inculcated, genetic, or otherwise. And note,
even if it were true that *everybody* would prefer there to be a normative
system which fits everybody's considered judgements and solves every
last moral and political dilemma, it still would not follow that any particular individual should abandon even one cherished judgement for the
sake of systematisation. Nor, in turn, would it follow that everybody
should adopt the same system.

Contemporary political philosophers, we might say, reproduce their
very own, and very strange, version of the fable of the blind men and the
elephant. In the original version of this fable, we are asked to imagine
a number of blind men carefully examining the body of an elephant, the
upshot of which is that because each of them examines a different part of
that body, each of them reaches a different conclusion regarding the
identity of the creature they are examining. Political philosophers, by
contrast, agree that they are examining *some* kind of elephant, which
means in this case *some* sort of clear, clean, and systematic theory. What
they disagree about is the kind of elephant it is. In short, because of each of
them only focuses on one part of the creature in question – its intuitive tail
perhaps, or its considered head, or its impartial legs – they also all come
up with different conclusions as to just what kind of elephant it is that
they've encountered. Some, examining part of the tail, and disagreeing

---

[108] For illustration of this point, see Rawls' *A Theory of Justice*, 577–587, and MacIntyre's
Ethics and Politics, 85–100.
[109] H. Sidgwick, *The Methods of Ethics, 7th edition* (Indianapolis, IN: Hackett), 406.

with others who have looked at a different part, say that this is a deonto-logical elephant of libertarian breed. Others, examining part of the head, say that the beast is a thoroughbred utilitarian. Others still say that the best characterisation of the movement of at least the front legs identifies it as some kind of cross-breed: contractarian at the bottom and deliberative-democrat at the top. And so it goes on, *ad infinitum*, or, as we might say, following the conclusions of Chapter 1, *without rational termination*.

2.9   Objections and Clarifications

Although I am confident that the argument I have deployed so far can stand as presented, it will not be as comprehensive as it could be until full attention has been given to two final lines of objection. The first of these lines focuses on 'radical pluralism' and 'particularism'. The second focuses on something we have so far only touched on, and which indeed it has been hard to avoid – namely, 'reflective equilibrium'. We can say in general that whilst proponents of the first line appear to do less than I have claimed on behalf of mentalism, and thus evade the challenge that way, the second group appears to do more. We can also say that for most of those still unconvinced by the conclusions of this chapter, what optimism they still have for mentalist endeavours is likely to be grounded in some or other conception of reflective equilibrium. I therefore want to focus on the radical pluralist and particularist line of argument first, before giving rather more sustained attention to the ways in which reflective equili-brium could still, as many would hope or assume, save the day.

     G. A. Cohen both coined the term 'radical pluralism' and provided the clearest case in its favour. He wrote in his last major work that what he and other 'Oxford' people of his generation do, as opposed to what Rawls and other 'Harvard men and women' do, is look to uncover the precise shape and implications of our deep normative judgements *without* then trying to systematise all such judgements in such a way as would avoid conflicts between them. Is he not therefore aiming lower than mentalist political philosophy as I have described it?

     He is certainly aiming lower than many mentalists, though not so low as to make the label unsuitable, or the problems discussed inapplicable. Consider first of all that Cohen does *still* want to tell us what justice is and requires – an issue on which he disagrees with most other philoso-phers. As a result, although he might well think that there is more to life and politics than just justice, he still hopes to be able to tell us what all of us, deep down, *really think* about justice, and thus what all of us *should think* about the actual justice or injustice of particular concrete decisions and situations. Both his method and his conclusions, therefore, assume a degree of coherence amongst our deepest thoughts on justice that this chapter has denied. Or, alternatively put, the problem is that just as there is radical pluralism between values and principles, so is there radical pluralism, as we have repeatedly seen, in terms of what people really think on the question of justice. And just to be clear: if Cohen's position were to change, and he were to say that there is nothing to be done about the fact that he and Rawls and Nozick all just have different intuitions, and thus cannot ever agree about justice, then that is tantamount to abandoning the challenge set by this book, which is to find an answer to OQ that should convince all three of them.[110]

So what about particularism and its related positions? Jonathan Dancy, for example, writes that 'moral judgement can get along perfectly well without any appeal to principles',[111] whilst Albert Jonsen and Stephen Toulmin complain that people often 'talk as though "ethical principles" or "moral rules" were exhaustive of ethics.'[112] The hope here, we can say, which applies just as much to Dancy's particularism as it does to the 'new casuistry' of Jonsen and Toulmin, is that there is more normative agreement on *cases* than there is on *principles*. There is, I think, some truth to that hope, just insofar as it is certainly true for each individual that he or she will be more of one mind as regards particular cases than any of the principles we might hope to extract from them, even though there will often be no way in which we could describe the verdicts reached about those cases as compatible with each other.

That, however, is not the key problem. The key problem is the problem we already encountered in our discussion of considered judgements. Even ignoring intra-personal disagreement, and also the problem often raised by this argument that the line between principles and judgements can quickly become too blurred (if a judgement is reached in a general case, such as one concerned with a general choice between democratic and non-democratic institutions, in what sense is that judgement not also, and already, an expression of principle?), there is still the fundamental and intractable difficulty that inter-personal disagreement on cases goes

---

[110] Cohen does come quite close to this position early on in *Rescuing Justice and Equality* (4–5), but even so, I do not think he would want to accept the main implication of the view under discussion here, which is that the conclusions of the central arguments of his book, however internally consistent those arguments might be, are really only a matter of opinion. In person, interestingly enough, he would sometimes say things such as 'well, maybe Nozick and I just have different intuitions', but those remarks are hardly fair material for comment, and in any case could not affect the argument under consideration here.

[111] J. Dancy, *Ethics without Principles* (Oxford: Oxford University Press, 2004), 1.

[112] A. R. Jonsen and S. Toulmin, *The Abuse of Casuistry* (Berkeley: University of California Press, 1988), 6.

too far and too deep, at least for political philosophy's purposes. And this problem, note, applies regardless of whether Dancy and Jonsen and Toulmin have normative thoughts more like considered judgements or more like intuitions in mind at different points in their arguments, because as we have already seen, both types of case-specific verdict are incapable of providing a basis for political principles capable of winning the assent of all those who would have to live with them. I could stress this point further, but there is little point, given that I would simply be rehashing what has already been said in the earlier discussion.

We come, then, to the last great hope of mentalism – reflective equilibrium. What, precisely, does this idea involve? Although the term is rather loosely thrown around in contemporary political philosophy, and is invoked sometimes as a process, and sometimes as the desired product of a process, the key idea is simple: we are to find the principle or set of principles which best fits at least the majority of the normative thoughts we already have. In Rawls' case, those thoughts are confined to our considered judgements, but for most scholars the net can be cast wider, and would include the further two categories of thought discussed.

Note also that when I say principles, these principles might be political principles themselves, and thus a direct answer to OQ, or deep-lying principles of a kind that lead us towards such principles. So, generally understood, reflective equilibrium, initially, is a method by which we try to systematise the normative thoughts we already have, by identifying those principles towards which they point. I only say 'initially', though. The idea then is to check those principles against our thoughts, including the thoughts they are incompatible with, and subsequently decide whether we want to either revisit the principles or abandon those thoughts. For example, I might find a principle which fits almost all my existing normative thinking, yet which somehow rules out the judgement 'slavery is wrong', in which case I will want to try a different set of principles, which will presumably then fit a different set of thoughts. In this way, I carry on until I am happy with the fit between principles and thoughts, at which point I abandon those few that do not fit, and emerge with fully coherent and systematised normative thinking.

There is, though, a further tweak here. What I have described so far is properly understood as *narrow* reflective equilibrium, when really what philosophers are most interested in, though they rarely use the term, is *wide* reflective equilibrium.[113] This latter concept is almost

---

[113] For discussion of these differences, together with extended discussion of reflective equilibrium, which I take to the methodological beating heart of Rawls' work, see J. Floyd, 'Rawls' Methodological Blueprint', *European Journal of Political Theory*, 16 (2016).

identical to the process described so far, but there is one key difference: in addition to consulting our own normative thoughts, and trying to come up with principles that fit them, we are also to consider as many as possible of the best arguments philosophers have come up with, both for and against various candidate principles. In that way, it is hoped, we have a better chance of getting principles that are, not just a better fit, but also more likely to align with those adopted by others. Indeed, there is also a wider Rawlsian dream here of *general* and even *full* reflective equilibrium – a condition in which society not only agrees on the same political principles (even if it cannot agree on all principles), and agrees on them as a result of everyone having achieved, not just narrow, but also wide reflective equilibrium. That, however, is not an idea that need concern us here, and not simply because it seems a rather infeasible ideal (after all, it could still be a guiding ideal, despite feasibility problems). The key point for our discussion is simply the potential for people to agree in a reasonable manner, via the process of each of us achieving wide reflective equilibrium. That people might be too lazy to undergo that process is not the kind of problem I am interested in here. For mentalism to be impossible, it has to be impossible for people to achieve consensus on political principles via wide reflective equilibrium, and not simply unlikely due to, say, busyness or laziness.

So, is it impossible? Everything I have said so far in this chapter says that it is, for the simple reason that different people, when working with different impartial choices of ideal state, considered judgements, and intuitive choices of abstract principle, will naturally end up with different principles, even under wide reflective equilibrium – as illustrated by, most clearly, the disagreements canvassed in Chapter 1. Similarly, we might say that people could end up with all manner of different equilibriums, according to, say, the different framings of dilemmas they consider, or their varying judgements about which thoughts seem easier to 'leave out' in the process of systematisation. As a result, confronted once more with contradictions both within and between people, maybe we should abandon this idea already, given that it seems to add nothing to what we have already discussed.

That, however, would be too cheap an argument. Instead, what we need to do, in order to do justice to reflective equilibrium, is to consider suggestions made by those who do think the idea needs some modification in order to deliver the goods wanted by mentalist political philosophy. For example, Cohen, as discussed, mostly adheres happily to the process described so far, whilst also thinking that the problem with the Rawlsian version of it is that considered judgements should be less up for revision at the hands of general principles.[114] But as we just saw, that simply gets us into more trouble. As a result, and to repeat the point, what we need now is a new set of arguments regarding the defence and modification of this approach.

In order to do this, we can start with the following four suggestions. Philip Pettit proposes that we add meta-ethical theories, along with our intuitive assessments of them, into the mix of beliefs for consideration.[115] Brian Barry, advocating a more 'empirical method', proposes that we try to equilibrate our considered judgements with the political principles and policies actually adopted in countries which, in their government and policy selection processes, approximate to Scanlonian contractualism.[116] Thomas Christiano proposes that we include as many of our existing political judgements as possible, even beyond the remit of what otherwise count as 'considered moral judgements'.[117] Philippe Van Parijs, speaking more generally, proposes that in a move away from mere internal consistency, we simply try to seek out every bit of information we can, including further beliefs and principles to consider, but also presumably further factual information about the consequences of different practices and institutions.[118]

Unfortunately, none of these suggestions takes us as far as we would like. Weighing up the intuitive attractiveness of meta-ethical theories is simply double counting of what are, as we have already seen, unreliable normative intuitions. Looking to see what kinds of politics emerges from Scanlonian procedures simply relies upon us already agreeing – as we do not – on the appeal of contractualism. Adding in further information, including both more judgements and more political information, simply makes it more and not less likely that we will be in conflict both within ourselves and with each other. And so it goes on.

All of these problems run in recognisable parallel to the problem of regress that foundationalists always press against coherentists in ethical theory (although the fact that foundationalists themselves also lack the requisite foundations does rather soften the blow). At some point, you need to satisfactorily ground one thought in another, or we are just spinning round in an unsupported circle. We cannot say that d justifies c which justifies b which justifies a which justifies d, or we are little better than religious devotees. Or is that unfair? In line with, no doubt, many readers of this book, Pettit stresses that reflective equilibrium does more

---

[114] *Rescuing Justice and Equality*, 4.
[115] P. Pettit, 'The Consequentialist Perspective', in M. W. Baron, P. Pettit, and M. Slote (Eds.), *Three Methods of Ethics: A Debate* (London: Blackwell, 1997), 113.
[116] B. Barry, *Justice as Impartiality*.   [117] T. Christiano, *The Constitution of Equality*.
[118] P. Van Parijs, *Real Freedom for All*.

than simply reflect our existing normative thoughts – it also *redirects* them (and we could happily add replaces, advances, refines).[119] But again: redirection requires resources. Remember here: (1) that one thought or set of thoughts can only be redirected by some or other further thought or set of thoughts; (2) that different individuals will want to privilege different thoughts; and (3) that as a result, redirection will produce different conclusions in the minds of different individuals.

Nevertheless, perhaps if we move further away from the debates of political philosophy, and closer towards the world of more abstract ethical theory, we might find another set of suggestions that appears to offer hope to the mentalist. One of the best known of these is Norman Daniels' claim that we should focus on, not just intuitions and considered judgements in reflective equilibrium, but also so-called background theories, which he thinks are behind the bulk of our interminable disagreements. We mentioned this suggestion in passing earlier, but even so, it is worth briefly considering once again. Note here that by background theories Daniels includes such things as the 'reasonable moral psychology' set out by Rawls in a *Theory of Justice*, an inclusion that, I would imagine, already makes the fatal problem apparent. This problem is that such theories, given that they are no more than composites of pre-existing beliefs about the normative inclinations of all human beings, are also composites of normative thoughts which, as we have already seen, are dissonant at all three levels of our thought. And indeed, we might further stress here that if we were to actually look more empirically at the idea of a 'reasonable moral psychology' as a key for unlocking interminable normative arguments, what we would quickly discover, as discussed at length earlier, is that the field of moral psychology itself has nothing but bad news for us.

Consider, then, a second line of argument from ethical theory. According to scholars such as Geoffrey Sayre-McCord and T. M. Scanlon, we just need to *accept* that reflective equilibrium is, ultimately, a first-person exercise. This means, inevitably, that in many cases different people will just reach different equilibriums. Nevertheless, we can still hope that, over time, the kind of convergence of equilibriums we require will somehow emerge, as more and more information is added into the mix, and as each individual considers and reconsiders as much of that information as possible. Yet this is, as I say, just a *hope*, and not just any hope, but also the kind of hope we already saw in Chapter 1 under the heading of 'deferral'. Back then it was a response to rational interminability at the level of political philosophy, whereas now it's a response to conflict at a deeper level. Either way, it's not

---

[119] P. Pettit, 'Reply to Baron and Slote', in M. W. Baron, P. Pettit, and M. Slote (Eds.), *Three Methods of Ethics: A Debate*, 252.

the kind of optimism we should cling to. Just consider that saying 'I hope you eventually become an egalitarian' is not much of a way to convince a libertarian.

Perhaps both Sayre-McCord and Scanlon, along with many other thinkers, would respond here by saying that my argument, and indeed my entire discussion in this chapter, has so far treated human normative thoughts as being much too similar to the data points and perceptual data of science. Of course, they might say, if you consider our thoughts as points on a scatter graph, or crosses to be found in various places on a Venn diagram, then you may well be disappointed by both the number of outliers and the differences between outliers on the charts generated by different people, but normative thinking is not like that. And indeed, nor is political philosophy, given that it is only when we encounter such conflicts, and also the conflicts found by moral psychologists, that moral and political philosophers come into the picture! Yet this *again* is a reiteration of ideas we have already considered. For coherentism in general and reflective equilibrium in particular to take us anywhere in political philosophy, it has to be true that the vast majority of the normative thoughts people have are the same, because only then would we have a set of thoughts capable of 'redirecting' the remaining few without controversy. And that is *not* what we find. From the abstract intuitions illuminated by moral psychology to the complex wrangling of contemporary political philosophy, our hopes are simply drowned out by dissonance.

There is though one final rejoinder here, which takes issue with this idea that the 'vast majority' of our normative thoughts have to be in line both with each other and with the thoughts of other people. This rejoinder emerges from a position that I have called elsewhere 'revisionist mentalism'.[120] In my earlier discussion of this position the two key examples I gave of thinkers who subscribe to this position were Peter Singer and Derek Parfit, although I think in this context Allan Gibbard would be more useful. He writes at one point that:

Moral inquiry in philosophy often comes in either of two broad styles. One is humanistic and pragmatic, thinking what's in morality for us, for us human beings, and asking what version of morality best serves us. The other broad style is intuitionist, in one important sense of that term: Consult our moral intuitions, revise them as need be to achieve consistency, and embrace what emerges.[121]

---

[120] J. Floyd, 'From Historical Contextualism, to Mentalism, to Behaviourism', in J. Floyd and M. Stears (Eds.), *Political Philosophy versus History: Contextualism and Real Politics in Contemporary Political Thought* (Cambridge: Cambridge University Press, 2011), 38–65.
[121] A. Gibbard, *Reconciling Our Aims*, 34.

This statement seems to suggest both that reflective equilibrium always involves intuitions and that what he calls the 'humanistic and pragmatic' approach is somehow non-mentalist. Both appearances are misleading. The first is misleading because, like many philosophers, he is using the term 'intuition' rather loosely, and thus without any intention of ruling out the other two kinds of normative thought I have in mind. The second appearance, by contrast, is rather more important, though also rather misleading, as becomes clear as soon as he gives utilitarianism as an example of the first approach described. He writes here that:

If morality is for humanity, then we might expect utilitarianism to be right. Moral rules, we might expect, will tell us each to act for the benefit of all humanity.[122]

The problem here is clear enough. Following Singer and Parfit, who also work within the utilitarian tradition, and who also hold a low opinion of many of our intuitions, what Gibbard really wants to do under the auspices of this 'pragmatic and humanistic' approach is simply to use just one sub-set of our normative thoughts in order to overrule the rest. That is the key idea here. In the example he gives, just as in most cases where thinkers are prepared to ride roughshod over people's pre-existing inclinations in this fashion, the thoughts in question are pleasure-maximising or, more standardly today, well-being maximising ones. And, admittedly, if one clings particularly strongly to the idea that not just our institutions, but also our *feelings* ought to adhere to whatever most satisfies human needs and desires (without wanting to get into the issue of whether everyone or most people get satisfied, or what counts as needs and desires), then I suppose it would seem natural to treat much of what other people believe as simply misplaced sentimentality.

Yet this is still, remember, a mentalist enterprise, just insofar as it uses one or more pre-existing normative thoughts in order to redirect the rest. The only difference is that it is less convincing than the average enterprise, given that whereas the conventional mentalist at least tries to identify a *majority* of *shared* thoughts in order to reshape the remainder, and thus tries to find a way of convincing all those who would have to live with the resultant principles, the revisionist mentalist just boldly asks for a more severe transformation, without being able to give grounds for that transformation of a kind that might already be shared by those concerned. This is not, of course, to say that no reason can be offered: as noted earlier, for Sidgwick, Rawls, and MacIntyre, and also I think Singer and Parfit, it often seems as though system itself is a value capable of motivating such transformation – but that it hardly a value for everyone. Admittedly, it

---

[122] Ibid., 35.

remains possible that people *would* be happier if they could have their minds artificially altered to better serve this cause, but all the same, unless and until they prize that kind of happiness above all other normative inclinations, it would be impossible to rationally convince them of the desirability of that alteration.

2.10   The Problem Restated

The problem exposed by this chapter has been that there are no harmonious patterns in normative thought of the kind required by mentalist political philosophers. Apart from, perhaps, a few isolated pockets of limited political relevance, we disagree from top to bottom, and from the abstract to the concrete, on all the normative fundamentals. This makes mentalist political philosophy *impossible*. Yet note that my point here is not MacIntyre's, as discussed earlier. I am not simply saying that because Hume's quest has *yet* to be fulfilled after 300 years of trying, it could *never* be fulfilled. I do not claim that mentalism is a failure because it has failed so far. I claim that mentalism is *demonstrably* doomed to failure – that it is *demonstrably* futile. It is demonstrably futile because, at every single level of normative thought there is fundamental dissonance, which means that every single avenue potentially open to it has, upon examination, turned out to be a justificatory cul-de-sac. That is the proof I have attempted to mount.

Clearly, this futility has consequences for political philosophy as we know it. If the subject is ever to succeed – that is, if it is ever to provide a convincing and meaningful answer to OQ, and not just confine itself to the highlighting and distillation of theoretical conflicts and alternatives – it will need, not just a new set of suggested answers to OQ – each of which would have to be tirelessly tested against, our various intuitions, considered judgements, and impartial choices of ideal state – but an entirely new method for distinguishing good principles from bad or, at least, better principles from worse. My task in the next chapter, as I see it, is to deliver this method. Or, put differently, I hope to be able to provide an entirely new means of generating normative political principles. This would amount, I suppose, to a blueprint for a paradigm shift in political philosophy. Except of course this blueprint might itself turn out to be a *complete* failure. As a result, it is important to note here that regardless of whether or not I succeed in this ambition, everything said so far about mentalism continues to stand. That is, whether or not some viable alternative method exists by which we might try to provide a compelling answer to OQ, mentalism is still what I have shown it to be: an impossibility.

3   Cure: Normative Behaviourism

A Second Reminder

OQ = political philosophy's organising question = how should we live?

A convincing and meaningful answer to OQ = an answer that is both politically determinate and rationally compelling to all those who would have to live with it.

3.1   Introduction

The central argument of this chapter is that, instead of looking for patterns in our thoughts, political philosophers should look for them in our behaviour. If they did this, they would find that whilst human beings disagree about a great deal in the world of philosophical introspection, they converge upon a number of significant things in political practice. This argument proceeds through four stages. First, I provide the briefest sketch of this new model of political philosophy, which I call *normative behaviourism*. Second, I work through some preliminary points regarding its nature and possibility, in order to lay the groundwork for the arguments that follow. Third, I explain why it produces *social-liberal-democracy* as a convincing and meaningful answer to OQ – a political system and set of policies that roughly equates to what political philosophers call egalitarian liberal democracy, what Europeans calls social democracy, and what Americans call liberalism. Fourth, I defend it against the various objections it is likely to encounter.

3.2   Normative Behaviourism: A Brief Sketch

The shortest possible description of Rawls' *A Theory of Justice*, the most important work of political philosophy of at least the past 100 years, goes something like this. If you study our normative thoughts, as they connect to politics, either directly or by implication, then you'll discover that they are best expressed by way of a particular hypothetical choice situation in which

166

the role of the chooser is to select the political principles by which the political system they are to live in ought to be organised. This then gives us three arguments to get our teeth into, as explored over the course of the book. First, the argument that our normative thoughts, and in particular our considered judgements, do dictate for us just one kind of choice situation – the 'original position' – in which particular rules and options apply. Second, the argument that, from this situation, we would choose the political principles that Rawls organises under the heading 'Justice as Fairness'. Third, the argument that these principles require particular duties of individuals, as well as a particular kind of political system. There is of course more going on in the book than these brief remarks capture, but that is enough to be going on with for my purposes here.

By contrast, the briefest possible description of normative behaviourism goes something like this. If you study our behaviour, in response to variations in our political environment, then you learn that there are some systems we have little time for, some we have more time for, and perhaps one that suits us best of all. As a result, we learn that there is at least one way of justifying political principles – in this case the principles expressed by that last system – that has nothing to do with mentalism, because it has nothing to do with our normative thoughts. As with Rawls, this then gives us various arguments to get our teeth into, as explored over the rest of this chapter. We can argue about which kinds of behaviour 'matter', and why, when it comes to choosing political principles. We can argue about whether it is possible to move from 'facts' about our behaviour to 'principles' intended to govern our politics, given the relationship that is generally thought to apply to these things. We can argue about what kind of 'data' there is out there, such as might be thought to reveal a set of principles that 'suits us' more than others. We can argue about what 'reasons' we have for 'caring' about such data. We can argue about whether any part of this inevitably has us sliding back into mentalism. And so on and so forth. All of these and more will be discussed in what follows. We start, though, with some preliminaries concerning, amongst other things, the kind of behaviour we're interested in, and the way that 'facts' about such behaviour might connect us to 'principles' regarding politics.

3.3   Preliminaries, Part 1: Facts, Principles, Thoughts, and Behaviour

> [T]he worth of different modes of life should be proved practically, when anyone thinks fit to try them.[1]

---

[1] J. S. Mill, *On Liberty* (London: Penguin, 1974), 120.

> If the present be compared with the remote past, it is easily seen that in all cities and in all peoples there are the same desires and the same passions as there always were. So that, if one examines with diligence the past, it is easy to foresee the future of any commonwealth, and to apply those remedies which were used of old; or, if one does not find that remedies were used, to devise new ones owing to the similarity between events. But since such studies are neglected and what is read is not understood, or, if it be understood, is not applied in practice by those who rule, the consequence is that similar troubles occur at all times.[2]

My claim, again, is that political philosophers should look for patterns in our behaviour, not in our normative thoughts. Why? Partly because there is strong convergence in the former but not the latter; partly because this convergence points towards a political system to which many of them are already attracted; and partly because certain actions reflect a stronger normative commitment than most armchair reflections, though none of these is the fundamental reason. The fundamental reason is that doing so would provide a convincing and meaningful answer to OQ. In the new form of political philosophy proposed here, political principles are justified by what I call *expressed political preferences*. These preferences are normative preferences that get revealed by certain patterns of behaviour, as opposed to normative preferences that get revealed through certain patterns of thought, such as those captured by impartial choice situations like the 'original position' or abstract dilemmas like the trolley problem.

When it comes to capturing these preferences, what kind of behaviour do I have in mind? Migration? Investment? Voting? These are all interesting possibilities. For example, under which political system are people most likely to emigrate, and into which system are they most likely to immigrate? Or, under what political conditions are people most likely to spend, or save, or invest? Or, under what political circumstances are people most likely to vote for extremist parties, or even vote at all? Such questions are fascinating, and not just in terms of the political preferences they might capture, but also the political principles those preferences might convey. But they are not my focus here. Instead, the patterns of behaviour utilised by normative behaviourism, as I construct that idea in this book, are those involving two particular phenomena: (1) *insurrection*, and (2) *crime*. I focus on these for various reasons, though there is one that stands out above all else, as will become clear in what follows: amongst other things, these two behaviours are united by both the level of personal risk they tend to involve, and the fact that people tend only to partake of

---

[2] N. Machiavelli, *The Discourses* (London: Penguin, 2003), 208.

them when they find their current lives, which lack goods x, y, and z, unbearable.

Two things need noting here straightaway. First, I do not use the term 'goods' here in some strict, private, and materialistic sense. Although the relevant set of such things might include a minimal income and access to gainful employment, it could also include certain civil rights, as well as, more directly, a certain kind of political regime. Second, 'might' and 'could' are more than just statements of caution, given that the goods in question are not specified in advance by prior mentalist principles, but rather by empirical analysis of insurrection and crime in past and present political systems. Normative behaviourism looks for causal regularities surrounding the two types of behaviour in order to see just *which* things, when either present or absent, precipitate them. It is thus the behaviour that defines the goods, not the goods that define the behaviour.

For readers familiar with the relevant literatures, it is easy to guess the sorts of patterns that emerge involving these two kinds of behaviour. As will be shown later on in this chapter, the two most important from the perspective of OQ are (1) that the presence of liberal democracy minimises insurrection, and (2) that minimising inequality, by way of a more social or egalitarian set of policies, minimises crime. What is harder to guess is the relationship between these two things and the *justification of political principles* (and thus a convincing answer to OQ), not to mention the relationship between the two types of behaviour.

We can start to clarify that second relationship, and in particular what I see as the *hierarchical* relationship between the two types of behaviour, by saying something very general about the first. This something is that, when looking at past and present politics from a normative behaviourist perspective, a rough rule of thumb to be going on with is that principle justification = political commitment X numbers, with numbers meaning the percentage of people who commit a certain type of action under a certain type of political system, and political commitment defined as a combination of the personal risk involved and the extent to which it is intended as an act of insurrection. One implication of this rule is that political systems that produce less of this behaviour are more justifiable than those that produce more, with the one that produces the least, clearly, more justified than any other – but we will get to that argument in a moment. For now the more important implication is that, according to this logic, insurrection matters more than crime, partly because of the greater risks involved, and partly because of its political intentionality.

More methodological detail is, of course, desirable here, but also premature. In order to make those details relevant, we need to first address the two fundamental questions that have so far gone begging: (1) how on earth are we supposed to successfully move from an 'is' of behaviour to an 'ought' of principles? And (2) how exactly does that 'ought' become a convincing and meaningful answer to OQ?

My response to these questions has two parts. The first is defensive and points to the unnoticed similarity between what I am proposing and what conventional and thus mentalist political philosophy already does. Consider here that mentalism assumes that we can perfectly easily move from *thoughts* to principles – whether those thoughts be impartial choices, judgements, or intuitions – and so assumes that there is no implied violation of that concept which has overshadowed so much of twentieth- and now twenty-first-century philosophy – the 'naturalistic fallacy'. Why, though, should this fallacy apply to actions if it does not apply to thoughts? If, after all, a hypothetical political decision made in an imaginary situation can justify political principles, then why not a real political decision made in concrete circumstances? And, if contemplative considered judgements regarding what should and should not be the case can ground such principles, then why not judgements that show, not only consideration, but also considerable commitment, such as those expressed by a decision to engage in acts of insurrection? If there is a fallacy here, then it is what I will call the 'mentalistic fallacy', which is that thoughts are somehow non-factual, non-empirical – almost non-existent.

The real question, therefore, is this: can any type of fact, including both mental and behavioural facts, be used to ground political principles?[3]

---

[3] Or is it? Consider here that some readers will be wondering whether political philosophers have been wrong *all along* about this aspect of the way in which they use thoughts, just as I am saying they have been wrong all along about their assumption of a certain level of consistency between them. We might therefore want to pause our main argument in order to consider at length *all* of the various arguments that have been made both for and against the naturalistic fallacy in recent decades, in order to see as best we can whether or not either thoughts *or* actions are capable of avoiding defeat at the hands of this fallacy. Yet there is no real need for such a detour, and for several reasons. One is that the bulk of the 'debate' about the naturalistic fallacy has been carried out by those unpersuaded either by its relevance or by its very existence, despite the very contrary fact that most philosophers *do* apply it regularly as a critical tool against rival arguments, and assume that something like it applies to at least certain forms of naturalism. Another is that the best aspects of this debate render prolonged scrutiny of its subject excessive, just insofar as they point out just how much inappropriate conflation goes on of what are in fact several distinct though closely related problems – namely, the naturalistic fallacy, the fact/value distinction, the descriptive/normative distinction, and the is/ought distinction. And indeed, it is not just these problems that get confused, to the effect that each is readily misunderstood, but also a number of distinctions on which they may well depend – such as the analytic/synthetic distinction – as well as a further set of *further* distinctions that might depend on them, such as Williams' internal/external reasons distinction and Habermas' norms/values distinction. In this section, by contrast, although I address issues that bear on all of these problems, I only pay direct attention to what is both the most relevant case to normative behaviourism and the strongest case against it, i.e. Cohen's argument regarding the

This is where the second part of my response kicks in. This part claims (1) that facts can ground political principles, and also (2) that behavioural facts do a better job of this than mental facts – without saying anything about whether mental facts are *fundamentally* incapable of doing so.[4]

To see why these two claims hold, consider G. A. Cohen's recent argument to the effect that no fact *of any kind* can ground a principle in the absence of a deeper principle capable of explaining the relevance of that fact.[5] For example, if the *fact* that animals are capable of feeling pain is to ground the *principle* that one should not hurt them unnecessarily, there must be some prior principle of the form 'do not unnecessarily hurt creatures capable of feeling pain'. My argument so far, as regards this position, and as expressed just a moment ago, can be distilled into the following syllogism: If (1) political principles, for mentalism, are only justified for an individual in virtue of the thoughts in that individual's head, and (2) it is a matter of fact whether or not I hold a particular set of thoughts, then (3) it is also a matter of fact whether or not I am bound to such principles. As such, the principles we are bound to depend upon facts about us – which means in this case facts about the thoughts in our head. For example, if I intuitively think that I should rescue a group of twenty people rather than a group of ten, if I can rescue either but not both, then it is a fact that I have that intuition.

Now, one might respond to this claim by saying that, even if it holds at one level, it only holds in virtue of a hidden principle that I have not

---

impossibility of grounding principles in facts without recourse to further principles. For an old but still highly illuminating critical discussion of the naturalistic fallacy, see W. K. Frankena, 'The Naturalistic Fallacy', *Mind*, 48 (1939), 464–477. For a more recent case regarding both that fallacy and the way in which it diverges from other related problems, see J. Dodd and S. Stern-Gillet, 'The Is/Ought Gap, the Fact/Value Distinction and the Naturalistic Fallacy', *Dialogue*, 34 (1995), 727–745. Unfortunately, much of the 'debate' in this area concerns issues surrounding how these problems play out in fields of applied ethics, with the result that the core issues regarding the meaning and force of the relevant problems are often ignored. Examples of this kind of treatment include S. Schleidgen, M. C. Jungert, and R. H. Bauer, 'Mission Impossible? On Empirical-Normative Collaboration in Ethical Reasoning', *Ethical Theory and Moral Practice*, 13 (2010), 59–71; R. De Vries and B. Gordijn, 'Empirical Ethics and Its Alleged Meta-ethical Fallacies', *Bioethics*, 23:4 (2009), 193–201; and S. Brinkmann, 'Facts, Values, and the Naturalistic Fallacy in Psychology', *New Ideas in Psychology*, 27 (2009), 1–17. For a treatment of several of these issues that is both historical and analytical, see H. Putnam, *The Collapse of the Fact/Value Dichotomy and Other Essays* (Cambridge, MA: Harvard University Press, 2004).

[4] The only argument meant to refute mentalism in this book is the argument provided by the previous chapter, which holds that normative thoughts are too inconsistent to ground political principles. Whether or not they could do so if they were not so inconsistent, and, more importantly, whether they could potentially trump behavioural facts if they were much more consistent than the latter, is not explored here.

[5] G. A. Cohen, 'Facts and Principles', *Philosophy and Public Affairs*, 31:3 (2005), 211–245.

acknowledged. In other words, for the claim that 'in mentalist political philosophy, principles depend upon facts' to mean what I take it to mean, there must be a still deeper principle driving us, such as 'make sure your principles accurately reflect your convictions and beliefs!'. As a result, even if it is just 'a matter of fact' whether or not I have a given set of normative thoughts, that 'fact' could only generate political principles in virtue of a deeper principle of the kind just mentioned. This is a plausible claim, but also a mistaken one. Simply put, even if one held such a principle, it would still, again, be a fact whether or not one held it. At the root of things, therefore, is not a principle, but a truth. Put simply, it is a *truth*, that *thoughts*, like *actions*, are *facts*. Cohen says that 'principles that reflect facts must, in order to reflect facts, reflect principles that don't reflect facts'.[6] My claim is that even if many facts only influence us in virtue of deeper principles, the influence of those principles depends upon facts about our most basic commitments. For example, if I am committed to achieving something like wide reflective equilibrium, then it is a fact that I have that commitment. I do not have it as the result of a deeper principle. I simply *have* it.

Now let's come at this question about facts, principles, thoughts, and behaviour from a broader angle. Imagine here giving the following recommendation to a bear: 'Because there are lots of salmon in the local river for you to eat, you ought to go fishing in that river.' Why would this recommendation have no normative force if we can observe both that the bear would like to eat salmon and that fishing in the river would enable it to do so? Consider in turn a parallel argument with human beings: 'Because you want to avoid famine, war, disease, subjugation, and instability, as revealed by your behaviour, you should try and build what I call a social-liberal-democracy.' Why would this recommendation have no normative force if we observe both (1) that humans want to avoid these things and (2) that building this political system would enable them to do so?

The standard reply the mentalist would offer here, clearly, is that humans are fundamentally different to bears, not to mention the rest of the animal kingdom. But how? For an existentialist, the fundamental point would be that only humans have to answer what I have set out as the 'organising questions' for, separately, moral philosophy and political philosophy: 'how should I live?' and 'how should we live?'. This may well be true, even if it is not clear why *even that* question could not be answered in a normative behaviourist manner. Yet that is not the key argument here. Our focus, instead, needs to be on what I imagine would be a more common mentalist elaboration, and which runs something like this:

---

[6] G. A. Cohen, *Rescuing Justice and Equality*, 232.

human *action*, unlike bear *behaviour*, requires *reasons*. This elaboration, however, turns out to be illogical, and ironically so. It is illogical, and thus unreasonable, in the sense that reasons derive from rather than ground human motivations, and ironic in the sense that that mistake is made in the very name of reason.

To put the point rather grandly, reason, when properly understood, concerns logical connections, without itself providing the values that make those connections significant. This much is clear when we consider all sorts of practical dilemmas. In choosing a partner, a career, a place to live, a selection of music, a restaurant, or a book, is there any meaningful sense in which I could be said to have reasons for a given choice outside of my own pre-existing needs and desires? There is not. I simply have a taste for some things and not others. I simply prefer, say, Kebab vans, grunge, and English villages, to noodle bars, techno, and German cities.

Of course, the term 'simply' is rather misleading. Naturally, I have many 'reasons' for these preferences in the sense of having several motivations at play in each case. For example, it could be my love of tranquillity, country pubs, and having neighbours with whom I can converse in my native tongue, amongst no doubt many other things, that explains my preference for English villages over German cities. More generally, we could also say that I am *only* reasonable if I consider and weigh up all of my existing needs and desires before making the all-important decision of where to live. But that does not change the key point here, given that 'all-importance', again, is still nothing more than a function of the significance of this decision for those same needs and desires. And think carefully about what 'reasonable' means in all these cases. It means nothing more or less than consistent faithfulness to one's pre-existing needs and desires, including their relative strengths and the connections between them.

So, I am illogical, and thus unreasonable, if I eat a food I do not like, provided that there is not some further and more important (to me) need or desire of mine that would be realised by doing so. By contrast, I am logical, and thus reasonable, when I eat something I do like the taste of, provided, again, that there is not some further and more important (to me) need or desire of mine that would be realised by doing so. Reason is thus about logic in the sense that it is about being consistent with and faithful to my pre-existing needs and desires. Eating mud, simply *because* you hate it, is illogical, and thus unreasonable. Eating cheese, simply *because* you like it, is logical, and thus reasonable – provided, again, that there are no further, stronger, and countervailing needs or desires. And so it goes on.

Perhaps some readers will think I have picked easy or misleading cases so far. As a result, let's now look at a second and more complex decision.

Consider here one of the more serious challenges listed earlier – that of choosing a career. And indeed, consider not just any career, but the specific career of a political philosopher. How am I to decide whether or not to become, or indeed continue as, a political philosopher? Again, many factors come into play. If I need an income sufficient to meet my various needs and desires (and it does not matter how one divides needs from desires in this context), then I need to check that political philosophy could provide this. If in order to become a political philosopher I would have to move to another country, then I need to think about whether or not I would be happy to emigrate. If in order to become a political philosopher I would need to spend the best part of a decade earning very little and working very hard with no guarantee of ever earning a full-time position, then I shall need to think again about my various needs and desires in order to assess whether or not it would be wise for me to take this risk.

And these are just the most basic concerns. I might also ask: if I am so concerned about whether or not it is possible to deliver a convincing and meaningful answer to OQ, then might it not prove unwise to be a political philosopher if it also proves impossible to provide that answer? It certainly might. But again, things are *still* more complex than even this question suggests, because if it only becomes clear that it is impossible to provide that answer once I have finished with the argument of this book, and if I only manage to finish this book after having committed ten years of my life to the research that made it possible, then by the time I am finished, I will really only know what I should have done a decade ago, and not what I should do now. My decision *now* has to consider not just all of the aforementioned factors, but also the worsening of my alternative set of options, now that I am too old or too unwilling to train for and embark upon a completely different career. And so the problem goes on.

What's the lesson here? The lesson, once more, is that even in *this* case no consideration came into play that was anything other than either a pre-existing need/desire or an instrumental need/desire derived from one. I only want a given level of income, for example, in order to meet other needs and desires, some of which I only want because they meet yet further needs and desires, and some of which I just *have*. And, once more, it is a matter of *fact* whether or not I have such needs and desires. If we think of reason as the muscle of contemplation, then we can certainly say that we need to exercise it in order to know what to do, just as we can say that we are unreasonable when we fail to take into account all of our needs and desires (with such needs and desires including our normative convictions), together with the connections between them, and the relative strength they have for us, when deciding on any course of action. Neither claim, though, affects the fundamental point, which is that at least some small set of needs and desires are, and must be, prior to whatever reasons we infer from them. Or, alternatively put, reasons are subordinate to, because necessarily derived from, our pre-existing motivations.

This, then, is broadly my case for siding with Hume's famous dictum about reason always being a slave to the passions, as well as Bernard Williams' more recent case for the priority of 'internal' over 'external' reasons.[7] And note, as I have noted once before, that even in the work of someone who has explored more than anyone else the place of 'reasons' in practical reasoning – Joseph Raz – it ultimately proves impossible to eliminate the fundamental role of pre-existing and thus pre-rational motivations (see **1.10**). Even according to his system, in which it is possible to regard something as objectively valuable without having any need or desire for it, and in which all values provide us with, at least potentially, 'reasons for action', it remains impossible to elim-inate pre-existing wants given the *multitude* of such values, and our need to *choose amongst them*, thus leaving us with what he sometimes calls the 'under-determination' of reason. Or, as he illustrates the point on one occasion, 'our chemistry rather than our rationality explains why some like it hot'.[8]

Now let's focus on specifically behavioural facts. What we need to see now is that when a behaviourist political philosopher tells me to pursue x as a means to y, they are actually saying more than a mentalist can manage. In essence, the behaviourist imperative takes the following form: 'you should pursue or support or accept x as a means to y, not just because in practice x tends to be the best means to y, but also because, in practice, y strongly tends to be what you prioritise (or is at least what other human beings, to whom we have every reason to expect you to be similar, strongly tend to prioritise in your situation)'. By contrast, the mentalist often finds himself or herself offering an imperative of the form 'you should do p as a means to q, even though in practice q is not what you prioritise, and even though in practice q might bring with it consequences r which you tend to abhor'. This is important, and it gives us a *prima facie* reason to consider

---

[7] See 'Internal and External Reasons', in B. Williams (Ed.), *Moral Luck* (Cambridge: Cambridge University Press, 1981), 101–113.

[8] See J. Raz, *Engaging Reason: On the Theory of Value and Action* (Oxford: Oxford University Press, 2002), 66. I invoked Raz to the same effect in J. Floyd, 'From Historical Contextualism, to Mentalism, to Behaviourism', in J. Floyd and M. Stears (Eds.), *Political Philosophy versus History: Contextualism and Real Politics in Contemporary Political Thought* (Cambridge: Cambridge University Press, 2011), 59.

behaviourist imperatives as possessing more normative force than their mentalist equivalents.

Except of course some mentalists will still not accept this claim, suggesting instead that we have good reason, whatever that reason might be, for acting on the basis of what we prefer in abstract reflection, rather than on the basis of what we prefer in political practice. Yet this reveals a problem for the mentalist. In short, even if we were to grant that hierarchy for argument's sake, and say that armchair preferences always trump revealed preferences – perhaps because they are made in a calmer or more considered fashion – this would only take us back to the problem demonstrated by the previous chapter, which is that even in the most abstract and reflective corners of our mind, human beings tend to disagree both with each other and within themselves. The choice between acting on mentalist or behaviourist imperatives, therefore, is not just a choice between acting on preferences confirmed by practice and preferences that sometimes clash with practice, but also a choice between relatively consistent preferences, as I hope to show, and deeply inconsistent preferences, as I hope to have shown already, over the course of the previous chapter.

Some elaboration of my use of the term 'imperative' will help to clarify and thus round off this point. Consider Kant's distinction between 'categorical' and 'hypothetical' imperatives. Clearly the kind of imperative discussed here is essentially the latter type, which claims that '*if* you want x, *then* you should do y', although describing it as such might be somewhat misleading. A better description of a normative behaviourist imperative would be a *contingent* imperative. It is a contingent imperative just insofar as it claims '*given* that you have set of preferences x, you *should* adopt or support or accept set of principles y'. It is contingent, then, in the sense that, of course, *if* human beings were wired differently, and displayed different preferences, *then* you might not want to live with such principles, but *given* that you do, and this is just a contingent fact of human nature, you *should* do so. Remember here the crucial truth, as argued earlier, that even before considerations of consistency are taken into account, normative behaviourism and mentalism exist on, at the very least, a level playing field. According to mentalism, it is perfectly fine to issue imperatives of the form 'if you have contingent preferences p, as revealed by reflective thought, then you should be convinced by set of principles q'. As a result, why not also imperatives of the form 'if you have contingent preferences x, as revealed by behaviour, then you should be convinced by set of principles y'? And, indeed, why not imperatives of the latter form if they turn out to offer strongly expressed preferences, whilst the former involve unreliable ones?

3.4   Preliminaries, Part 2: Reasonable Objections, Causes/ Purposes, Reliable Tendencies, and the Case for Experimental Optimism

> What means are there of determining which is the acutest of two pains, or the intensest of two pleasurable sensations, except the general suffrage of those who are familiar with both?[9]
>
> [T]he considered judgment arrived at through real experience instead of through disembodied reflection may be more important, serious and reliable for moral theory than its ideal counterpart.[10]
>
> I like to think that sensible suggestions are local and not easily transportable from one country to another ... though it may happen that some experiments will prove themselves in practice and will become the blueprint for many others. Perhaps this is not really the age for grand theory.[11]

This chapter so far has discussed the general possibility of moving from behavioural facts to political principles, without providing, as yet, the key thing I have promised: a detailed normative behaviourist case for social-liberal-democracy. That case still has to wait. For now we continue the preliminary discussion by (1) providing a first pointer regarding how behavioural facts could translate into a convincing and meaningful answer to OQ, (2) being more specific about the nature of these facts, in terms of the kinds of empirical claims they express, and (3) making a general case for, at least temporarily, a certain experimental optimism when it comes to persevering with normative behaviourism. Remember though, during this section, something that should be clear from the discussion so far: the ultimate goal of all this is to show that people should be convinced by the principles I have in mind only as an entailment of pre-existing needs and desires. They will be convinced, that is, not in the sense that my answer to OQ realises values that *I say they should adopt*, or that I claim they *would adopt under certain hypothetical conditions*, but rather in the sense that it realises, both directly and indirectly, values to which different people *are already attracted or committed*, with such attractions and commitments being revealed by the behaviour they reliably perform. As a result, the goal to keep in mind, at all times, is that of arriving at a position whereby those attractions and commitments clearly entail the conclusion I want to draw as regards the appropriate answer to OQ.

---

[9] J. S. Mill, *On Liberty, Utilitarianism, and Other Essays* (Oxford: Oxford University Press, 2015), 125.

[10] V. Held, *Rights and Goods: Justifying Social Action* (New York: Free Press, 1984), 49–52.

[11] J. Raz, interviewed in R. Farneti, 'Philosophy and the Practice of Freedom: An Interview with Joseph Raz', *Critical Review of International Social and Political Philosophy*, 9:1 (2006), 71–84.

For now, though, as I say, we stick with the preliminaries, and turn next to the 'pointer' just mentioned. This goes as follows. An as yet unmentioned feature of normative behaviourism is that, according to its logic, someone who is *unconvinced* by a particular political system (and I say nothing as yet about the several reasons according to which they might be *convinced*) is still *reasonable* if that system is one with which many people – and perhaps many people at different times and in different parts of the world – have been strongly dissatisfied, as judged by their actions within that system (that is, bearing in mind the previous section, there is no failure of logical reasoning involved in them making this fact the basis of their judgement to this effect, given what I assume to be their pre-existing needs and desires).

This does not mean that that is the only way in which they can stay reasonable and convinced. It means, instead, that that fact would be a sufficient (though unnecessary) condition of that status. As regards other ways in which someone might be both reasonable *and* unconvinced by a given political system, that problem will be discussed later, at the point where we consider just why people with a variety of motivations should be persuaded by the particular political order I have in mind. For now, though, all that matters is that we introduce just one way of being both reasonable and *un*convinced by a given answer to OQ, and a way that operates, not in terms of some pre-adopted principle, or by reference to ordinary language, but rather in terms of objective patterns of behaviour that can be observed in both past and present political systems.

Let me explain this idea. By looking to see, *as a matter of fact*, just what kinds of political arrangements large numbers of people resent, in practice, behaviourist political philosophy is able to get a handle on what would constitute at least one class of reasonable objections, and thus at least one group of reasonable yet unconvinced individuals. Or, put differently, if there is a system, policy, or set of policies, that always produces legal and political non-co-operation on the part of a large number of people, then we can infer that those non-co-operators have a reasonable objection to it. As a result, we would have a set of answers to OQ that are, at least to some people, meaningful but *unconvincing*. And what does that mean? It means that, even if we are not at the point where we are able to justify a particular political system, we are at least able to eliminate some possibilities from the field via reference to observable behaviour. This, then, is a helpful pointer towards the full case for social-liberal-democracy via normative behaviourism – but only that. For now, to repeat, we still have more preliminaries to get through.

The first of these relates to a worry that some readers might have, even at this early stage, as regards my apparent equation of the cause of an action with its purpose. That is, is it true that I equate the guiding *purpose* behind any particular risky, illegal action with the *cause* of that action? It is certainly not necessarily and thus always the case, though just how often it is the case will be a matter for empirical, rather than *a priori*, analysis. For example, although Peter, a poor and petty thief, might risk his life in order to steal money for a new pair of trainers, it does not follow that it is the absence of those trainers that, at root, drives him to theft. Instead, we are rather likely to think that it is the quality and future prospects of his life. Because this pairing of quality and prospects is so demeaning and unappealing, particularly when contrasted with the lives led by various others around him, we are rather likely to think that it is them, and not the trainers, that explain his behaviour. Were Peter's life better, had his life been better to date, he would probably not have arrived at the point of theft. Had he had any chance of decent life prospects, had he had a better childhood, had he been born to better, wealthier, more educated, more stable parents, he would probably not have come to a point where he risked everything for these shoes.

When it comes to normative behaviourism, then, we should not be blinded by what actors describe as their purpose, given how various those purposes can be. What we are interested in, fundamentally, is the kinds of political circumstances that tend to produce insurrection and crime, regardless of the various things people espouse as their motive when performing such behaviour. Consider, for example, that if large numbers of people tend to rebel under set of political conditions X, then they might rise up in the name of, say, religion, or freedom, or nationalism, or communism. As a result, we *could* describe the cause of their actions as, variously, religion, freedom, nationalism, and communism – *or* we could go a little deeper, and see that it is the circumstances that breed the ideologies, even if the question of which ideology is adopted is answered differently in different contexts. Of course, this point only holds if it *is* the case, empirically, that behaviour *does* track such political circumstances rather than being purely a function of varied ideologies – but if it does, then it is those circumstances that concern us, together with the political principles they express. If people tend to pursue insurrection or crime under the rule of particular principles, then we are learning something about the worth of those principles, according to normative behaviourism, and should not be distracted from that lesson by the more particular purposes espoused by the people committing the behaviour in question. You might want to overthrow the government in the name of God, I might want to do it in the name of equality, she might want to do it in the name of nation, he might want to do it in the name of revenge – what matters is that we all hate the government, regardless of the various notions we have as to what constitutes its key vices, or what constitutes its ideal replacement.

This takes us to our next preliminary point, which is that 'tend' and 'likely' are crucial phrases throughout this whole approach. We are interested, as all good social scientists should be, in large-scale, *probabilistic tendencies*, not *iron laws*.[12] And, relatedly, we want to try and draw our behaviourist conclusions from *strong* trends and *long* periods of assessment. Why do these things matter? Because the stronger and more long-standing a trend is, the more likely it is to offer genuine insight into the worth of whatever policy or institutional feature it is supposed to track. For instance, if over a long period of time we find that a particular policy or feature of political institutions correlates very highly with, say, either low or high crime (in the absence of some further likely cause behind both), then that will be an instance when we have good reason to think that we have found a significant normative behaviourist trend.

Strong trends and long periods of assessment are also important because, as one can readily observe, complexities of human nature and personal history being what they are, it is possible for at least a few individuals, from any background, and in just about any circumstance, to come to commit any sort of crime and any kind of act of insurrection – including, as we know, terrorism. In this kind of empirical inquiry, therefore, just as in any other, we have to do as good a job as we can of distinguishing between exceptions and rules, or, better still, between outliers and prevailing patterns. But that is a task I think we can manage. As we will see, the data we already have is of such a kind as to make it very hard indeed to deny the strong causal relationship between 'absence of rebellion' and 'presence of liberal democracy', just as it would be hard, though perhaps not quite as hard, to deny a similar relationship between the level of inequality within a given liberal democracy and the amount of crime it tends to encounter.[13]

There is, of course, always more statistical work that can be done in this vein, and we should be just as wary of moving too hastily from data to inferred trend as we are of moving from trend to principle. As a result, there is still a question here about just what the right epistemological stance is on all this. Should we say that normative behaviourism has all the data and arguments it needs already, and is beyond doubt? Or is it enough

[12] For further comment on this distinction, see the discussion at **3.5**.
[13] For evidence to this effect, see the datasets listed in **3.4**, **3.5**, and **3.6**.

simply to simply show that such work *might* be relevant, that it at least holds the *possibility* of deriving conclusions of real normative significance?

The tone we should strike here is one of cautious optimism, or experimentalism, or open-mindedness. Just pause here for a moment, and remember that we assumed for *centuries* that, beneath the blooming, buzzing confusion of our normative thoughts, there lay an underlying order just waiting to be discovered. From the earliest works of (at least) modern ethics through to the latest treatises in contemporary political philosophy, it was widely assumed that there exists some determinate set of impartial choices or considered judgements or abstract intuitions 'out there' that is, not just universal as regards humanity as such, but also internally consistent. And remember, as noted in the previous chapter, that despite that assumption becoming unsustainable, the specialised and fragmented nature of contemporary normative inquiry has been such as to permit even philosophers who have *never* found what they would consider to be genuine, universal normative principles, to think that somewhere there is work that has been done, or that is being done, or that will be done, that is perfectly capable of producing such things. As a result, the key point here is this: even if we are unsure *right now* about the clarity of the empirical picture *we already have* of political causality in both past and present systems, this would still not be reason to abandon the normative behaviourist enterprise, given how much that picture might still be improved. We should still keep an open mind, and amass as much data as possible, for as long as we can.

Coming at this same point from another angle, all we really need, in order to approach this new way of doing political philosophy in the right frame of mind, is the right working assumption. Instead of persisting in the old, canonical faith expressed by mentalism, we should just try and assume, if only for a few years of experimental endeavour, that human beings are animals possessed of *observable* and *reliable* normative political preferences.[14] Significantly, this does *not* mean denying that humans are animals of a uniquely creative and clever kind. Undoubtedly, they are capable of constructing, pursuing, and convincing their fellows to pursue a variety of wildly different political ideals. We are the creators and followers of memes, as well as the helpless vehicles of genes.

---

[14] Note that by 'experimental endeavour' here, all I mean is that political philosophers should treat political and economic history as, in effect, a dataset of experiments into the relationship between, on the one hand, different policies and institutions, and, on the other, the consequences of those policies and institutions in terms of normatively relevant behaviour. In the future – and I repeat this point later in the chapter – I should also like us to promote new, creative, political endeavours, and to view those endeavours as experiments which themselves are never 'justified' until enough results are in, though that is of course a longer-term project, given the timescales involved.

Nevertheless, we could assume, at least for now, that when given the chance to actually *live* with those ideals, as expressed by a corresponding variety of different regimes, we eventually come to express, over time, universal tendencies towards a preference for one particular type. This assumption – this possibility – is at the heart of normative behaviourism.

Now, one important upshot of all this is that, just as the proof is in the empirical pudding when it comes to social-liberal-democracy as an answer to OQ, so it is for normative behaviourism as a proposed method for justifying that answer. And that's fine. I am happy to grant that, just as we cannot know the measure of a particular kind of political system in the absence of at least a few pieces of empirical data, we will not truly know the value of normative behaviourism until we have really tried it out. But that does mean *really* trying it out, which means in turn, and amongst other things, building up a very large body of work concerned with trying to identify the universally expressed preferences of human beings as regards different political systems and the lives they facilitate. Although I believe – and will try to demonstrate – that we are already in possession of a highly persuasive dataset regarding the observable superiority of social-liberal-democracy, I also accept that there is still more data collection, and more in the way of its analysis (particularly as would be conducted by political philosophers), that could be done.[15]

Concessions and open-mindedness, clearly, are important at this stage, and give us an appropriate sense of fallibility. Yet they should not distract us from something else that matters here: the various powerful motives various scholars have for ploughing the furrow I have in mind. Consider here, for example, that most liberal political philosophers, just insofar as they tend to be liberals of an egalitarian and democratic hue, have a great deal to gain here from this form of inquiry, given that it holds out the possibility of a genuinely universal case in favour of the very institutions to which they are already attracted. Similarly, consider that nearly all political philosophers, just insofar as they tend to be universalists of some kind or other, have something similar to gain, given that normative behaviourism holds out the possibility of genuinely universal normative political principles. I could perhaps go one better here, and say that absolutely all political philosophers, just insofar as they are mentalists, have nothing to

---

[15] For example, political philosophers might want to see if there is an observable relationship between the performance of different social-liberal-democracies and the degree to which they meet various standards of deliberative democracy, or between levels of insurrection and the presence or absence of differentiated legal and political rights for different cultural groups. All manner of different forms and aspects of democracy, different approaches to multiculturalism, and different policies regarding free speech or judicial review could be compared, if only political philosophers interested in these issues would consult or, indeed, both collect and consult the relevant data.

lose but their chains, but that is probably pushing it. So how about nothing to lose but their frustrations?

Perhaps a more powerful motivation is the common ground normative behaviourism shares with some of our heroes. Consider here that one way of stating my position would be to say that, as far as normative behaviourism is concerned, genuine normativity is not something that can be found in venerable armchairs, or indeed in the latest pages of *Ethics, Philosophy and Public Affairs*, or the *Journal of Political Philosophy*. It is, instead, something we induce from political practice, which means in the first instance adopting this working assumption that humans have regular and observable preferences for some systems and policies over others. And is that really such a difficult assumption to hold? It was, after all, held by such venerable figures as Aristotle, Polybius, Machiavelli, and Montesquieu.[16] So, even if our front foot is on new territory, our back foot stands on hallowed ground.

On a similar note, consider further that the assumption I have in mind is also shared by modern social scientists, including the section of that group we call political scientists. And indeed, it is not just a guiding ideal for these subjects, but also, apparently, their *finding*. And why expect otherwise? Human beings just *do* want some things more than others, a fact which when combined with the truth that no large-scale social movement can get going without reliable human dispositions at its root, shows the potential of all behavioural analysis, regardless of whether that analysis be normative or empirical in its ultimate intent.[17] It is hardly astounding to note that for human beings to engage in crime or insurrection, there has to be something they want, and are not currently getting, that explains that action, though again, this need not be the specific thing that they demand (remember here that I might fight *for* communism on

[16] The thought that one can work up normative political principles from an empirical, diachronic, and comparative study of past and present political institutions was one of considerable standing in both the classical and early modern worlds. Each of Aristotle, Polybius, Machiavelli, and Montesquieu, for instance, held it to some or other degree, and not only in order to render pre-existing political ideals more realistic (though they also often did that), but also in order to work out just what those ideals *were*. At the surface, it is true, much of the praise paid to this kind of study derived from the understandably high esteem in which they held the condition of order and stability but, underlying this, there was also the thought that order itself was an indication of some kind of political justice or, perhaps more accurately, political *health*. If one holds this thought, and thinks of long-term stability not as the product of successful political manipulation (for if it was just that, how long could it last?), but rather as an indicator of something fundamentally more normative – say, the genuine satisfaction of a people with its existing political order – it is not hard to see how that tradition of inquiry could be put to all kinds of productive uses, if one would but try.

[17] This truth has been precisely spelled out by Bernard Williams. See B. Williams, *Ethics and the Limits of Philosophy* (Cambridge, MA: Harvard University Press, 1985), 201.

the basis that I am starving and believe that only a communist system would feed me, in which case the key question is where such starvation came from). As a result, the more political science manages to deliver such explanations, the more normative behaviourism becomes an attractive theoretical prospect.

What is astounding is that political philosophers have spent so much time thinking about, for example, our intuitions about fairness, without ever giving due consideration to the fact that illiberal, undemocratic systems tend towards collapse. Or the fact that once prosperity reaches a certain point, democracy is soon demanded. Or the fact that once a small suffrage is permitted, more is soon demanded. Perhaps some political philosophers think that by providing mentalist justifications of particular regimes, they are providing at least part of an explanation for either why that regime has emerged or why its rivals have failed? This is possible, but also, I think, unlikely.

Just consider here that according to the logic of mentalism, it is perfectly conceivable for a just state to be a just state regardless of what most people think of it, and regardless of what its internal political dynamics tend to lead to over time. For example, if libertarian government did turn out to be that form of government *entailed* by our politically relevant judgements and intuitions, then it would be, for mentalists, *ex vi termini*, just. It would be deemed, simply in virtue of that entailment, the right state for us. It could of course *also* be the case that the principles so entailed include a principle of legitimacy which holds that no state could be convincing to any reasonable person which lacked, in practice, widespread support, but that is just a possibility, and does nothing to change the direction in which justification runs. In behaviourist political philosophy, by contrast, the proof is in the empirical pudding, which means that political orders are only proven as good or just or legitimate or right if they have been found as much by those who have had to live with them.

It is to this proof that I am about to turn. In the following section, as has long been mooted, my claim will be that social-liberal-democracies are, simply put, the people's choice. They are their choice in the very basic sense that people find them more bearable than any other attempted type of regime. This is something we know from observing the significantly lower levels of insurrection and crime they experience. Clearly, individuals living under this regime type find their system and the lives it permits and encourages more palatable than the system and lives offered by, say, totalitarianism, fascism, monarchy, aristocracy, and so on. Note, though, that this connection of behaviour and institutions will in the first instance be no more than an empirical picture, as I described the hope earlier. It will not yet be a *theory* of why a particular regime succeeds, or indeed a list of the *reasons*, some of which will be drawn directly from this theory, for why various people should be convinced by it as an answer to OQ. Both of these things will follow the initial picture. The theory, such as it is, will be an empirically supported list of the particular features and dynamics of social-liberal-democracies that cause and thus explain its success, whilst the reasons will be reasons that are capable of taking existing people from their existing motivations to the conclusion as regards OQ that I have been pressing. But we will get to these points, together with a full account of their place in the overall argument, in good time. For now we simply have to see whether the empirical picture regarding social-liberal-democracies is as clear as I have suggested.

3.5   A Normative Behaviourist Argument in Favour of Social-Liberal-Democracies

> Many of the Carthaginian institutions are excellent. The superiority of their constitution is proved by the fact that the common people remain loyal to the constitution; the Carthaginians have never had any rebellion worth speaking of.[18]
>
> [I]t is not possible to preserve for any length of time that which is repugnant to the wishes of so many [and] those who are subdued by fear will, if an occasion arises when they may do so with hope of impunity, rise up against their rulers in a manner which will be all the more ardent the more they have been constrained against their will and through fear alone, just as water, when forcibly compressed, will burst forth all the more vigorously when it finds an outlet.[19]

Given the way the political science research is organised, and given the hierarchical relationship of normative behaviourism's two dependent variables, we begin with insurrection, rather than crime, and liberal democracy, rather than social-liberal-democracy. The key fact here regarding the relationship between these two things is that liberal democracies experience much less insurrection than any other historically tested political regime. This pattern holds regardless of whether one measures in

---

[18] Aristotle, *The Politics and the Constitution of Athens* (Cambridge: Cambridge University Press, 1996), 57. I suppose it might be pertinent to ask here: where, then, did it all go wrong for the Carthaginians? If the answer is that it went wrong at home, and that there was something in the Carthaginian system that led it on the road to ruin, then that is something for a normative behaviourist to take into account. If, however, the problem was simply *Rome*, long after Aristotle's death, then that is no problem at all. The fact that some other power has more soldiers than you, or better generals, or simply better luck, is itself no measure of the political principles expressed by your constitution, provided, of course, that such deficits were things well beyond your political control.

[19] T. Aquinas, *Political Writings* (Cambridge: Cambridge University Press, 2002), 32–33.

terms of 'political collapse', 'political instability', 'civil wars', 'coups', 'rebellions', 'revolutions', 'state failures', or even just 'violence'; regardless of whether one categorises and analyses according to the Polity, ACLP, or Freedom House datasets[20]; and regardless of whether one is looking for the effects of 'democracy', 'freedom', 'good governance',[21] or even, to give just two examples of some of the more unique yet still compatible approaches, 'the absence of extractive institutions' and the 'presence of open-access political institutions'.[22]

[20] The Polity dataset can be found at www.systemicpeace.org/polity/polity4.htm. The ACLP (Alvarez, Cheibub, Limongi, Przeworski) dataset was the basis of A. Przeworski, M. E. Alvarez, J. A. Cheibub, and F. Limongi, *Democracy and Development: Political Institutions and Well-Being in the World, 1950–1990*. The original dataset can be found at http://politics.as.nyu.edu/object/przeworskilinks.html. The Freedom House dataset can be found at www.freedomhouse.org. The equivalence of the three sets is widely recognised, and has been noted in G. Bingham Powell Jr, 'Aggregating and Representing Political Preferences', in C. Boix and S. C. Stokes, *The Oxford Handbook of Comparative Politics* (Oxford: Oxford University Press, 2007), 656.

[21] Perhaps the most important of all such studies is that provided by the Polity Project, which notes that there is seven to ten times less instability in democracies than autocracies. See www.systemicpeace.org/conflict.htm. For studies involving each of the several overlapping conflict variables, and each of the several overlapping institutional variables, see C. A. Crocker, 'Engaging Fragile States', *Foreign Affairs*, 82:5 (2003); F. Fukuyama, *State-Building: Governance and World Order in the 21st Century* (Ithaca, NY: Cornell University Press, 2004); Freedom House, *The Worst of the Worst: The World's Most Repressive Societies* (Washington, DC: Freedom House, 2004); R. Rotberg, *When States Fail: Causes and Consequences* (Princeton, NJ: Princeton University Press, 2003); M. Besancon, 'Good Governance Rankings: The Art of Measurement', in *World Peace Foundation Reports, No. 36* (Cambridge, MA: World Peace Foundation, 2003); J. A. Goldstone, R. H. Bates, T. R. Gurr, M. Lustik, M. G. Marshall, J. Ulfelder, M. Woodward, 'A Global Forecasting Model of Political Instability', paper presented at the *Annual Meeting of the American Political Science Association*, Washington, DC, September 1–4, 2005, 2; H. Hegre, T. Ellingsen, S. Gates, and N. P. Gleditsch, 'Towards a Democratic Civil Peace? Democracy, Political Change, and Civil War, 1816–1992', *American Political Science Review*, 95:1 (2001), 33–48; USAID, 'Measuring Fragility: Indicators and Methods for Rating State Performance' (2006), available at www.usaid.gov/policy/2005_fragile_states_strategy .pdf; S. E. Rice and P. Stewart, 'Index of State Weakness in the Developing World', Brookings Institution (2007); Fund for Peace, 'The Failed States Index', *Foreign Policy* (2008), May/June; J. Di John, 'Conceptualising the Causes and Consequences of Failed States: A Critical Review of the Literature', *LSE Crisis States Research Centre Working Papers*, 25 (2008). For studies that look at conflict and violence more generally, see J. S. Goldstein, *Winning the War on War: The Decline of Armed Conflict Worldwide* (New York: Plume Books, 2011); and S. Pinker, *The Better Angels of Our Nature: The Decline of Violence in History and Its Causes* (London: Allen Lane, 2011).

[22] For the case regarding 'extractive political and economic institutions', and also an argument claiming that the presence of such institutions is the main cause behind the recent 'Arab Spring' uprisings, see D. Acemoglu and J. Robinson, *Why Nations Fail* (Profile Books: London, 2012). For the case regarding 'open-access societies', see D. C. North, J. J. Wallis, and B. R. Weingast, *Violence and Social Orders: A Conceptual Framework for Interpreting Recorded Human History* (Cambridge: Cambridge University Press, 2009).

There are, admittedly, some wrinkles in this mass of studies and datasets that should be noted early on, for the sake of clarity. One is that so-called anocracies or partial democracies – meaning systems that combine elements of democracy and autocracy – can be more prone to insurrection than autocracies, depending on the particular combination involved. Another, as Tocqueville once noted, is that states going through the process of reforming their institutions are more vulnerable to insurrection than they would have been had they stayed with the status quo – though there is some evidence that it is marginally safer to reform in a democratic, rather than autocratic, direction. A third is that the difference in insurrection levels between newly established autocracies and newly established democracies is much less in the short term than in the long term – although, as with the previous two, this wrinkle is really of little relevance given our criteria and the reasoning behind them. Consider here that if a large number of people hate their political system and the lives it facilitates, then the fact that they often have to wait a long time for a good opportunity to express that hatred, and thus incur the risks that such expression involves, is testament only to that state's capacity for organised repression, not its capacity to satisfy the people.

Some further wrinkles involve the likelihood of coups and the influence of prosperity. As regards coups, although the more comprehensive Polity dataset, along with the analyses given in the annual reports based on that data, clearly show that coups are much more likely in autocracies and anocracies than in liberal democracies, the picture is not quite as simple as that trend suggests.[23] Paul Collier, for instance, has noted that in Africa coups are more likely in democracies than in autocracies (although his data, in connection with the point made earlier, do appear to be thrown somewhat by including several partial democracies).[24] But then, even if that is the case, and patterns involving coups turn out to be less clear than those involving other kinds of insurrection, perhaps we should not be too surprised. After all, it takes only a few dissatisfied members of the military or political elite to complete such an operation, and even fewer to plan one.

There might, however, be a significant and potentially troubling economic dimension to this pattern. Consider three trends here: (1) that according to several studies, both (a) poverty and (b) a combination of

---

[23] See www.systemicpeace.org/conflict.htm.

[24] P. Collier, *Wars, Guns, and Votes* (London: Vintage, 2010). Note, though, that the general thrust of this work, as is the case with most research in this area, is that institutions, and not aid or economic policies, are the key. For an illustrative example of that general thrust, see P. Collier, *The Bottom Billion: Why the Poorest Countries Are Failing and What Can Be Done About It* (Oxford: Oxford University Press, 2008).

poverty and wealth-generating natural resources appear to considerably boost the chances of this particular kind of insurrection; (2) that, conversely, once liberal democracies cross a certain income threshold, they become, in Adam Przeworski's phrase, 'all but impregnable'; and (3) that, according to some studies, poverty significantly boosts the likelihood of civil war. Again, though, all three trends ultimately turn out to be more interesting than they are relevant to our case. First of all, even if prosperity were to boost the satisfaction of a given population, and thus reduce its desire for insurrection, it is still not something that individuals could *choose* as part of an answer to OQ – unless of course it were the case that a certain set of political principles hugely boosted the chances of its achievement. On this point, crucially, the data is too unclear for any strong consensus to emerge, although to the extent that it shows any trend, liberal democracy does seem a much better bet than any of its alternatives. But this is still not the key point. The second and crucial point here is that the relative influence of prosperity is just *so much less*, in terms of the likelihood of insurrection, than the influence of regime type. Regardless of a society's point on the income scale, liberal democracies are just much more stable than any other attempted political system.[25]

There are many angles that one could take on this literature. For example, we can say that, in contrast to liberal democracy, all the many forms of totalitarianism, authoritarianism, communism, theocracy, monarchy, and aristocracy that have been tried in the world exhibit strong and clear tendencies towards political collapse. We can also say with some confidence that as a country's income rises, so does the number of subjects or citizens demanding both greater civil liberties and a greater say in the decisions that shape their collective existence – a trend that seems to indicate that the more free time and education people enjoy, and thus the

---

[25] Goldstone et al., for example, estimate that 'the impact of "getting the institutions right" on the risks of violent political crisis is generally five to ten times as large as the impact of levels of poverty or trade'. J. Goldstone, T. Gurr, M. Marshall, and J. Ulfelder, 'It's all about State Structure – New Findings on Revolutionary Origins from Global Data', in *Homo Oeconomicus*, 21:4 (2004), 429–455. See also J. A. Goldstone, R. H. Bates, D. L. Epstein, T. R. Gurr, M. B. Lustik, M. G. Marshall, J. Ulfelder, and M. Woodward, 'A Global Model for Forecasting Political Instability', *American Journal of Political Science*, 54 1 (2010), 190–208. And consider, even beyond debates involving the relative importance of economic and political factors, time and time again, variables involving institutions and governance trump other plausible candidates for primary causal status, including, for example, variables involving the natural environment. See I. Salehyan, 'From Climate Change to Conflict? No Consensus Yet', *Journal of Peace Research*, 45:3 (2008). As Salehyan puts the point, political institutions are just much more important than environmental change in causing conflict as a result of the key fact that 'political processes and institutions ... shape the incentives of actors to engage in violence' (320).

more they know about and are able to influence politics, the more they start to press for liberal democracy.[26] We can also probably say that once even a small amount of suffrage is permitted, very soon more is demanded, perhaps because once a certain amount is deemed justified, it becomes rather difficult to explain why more would not be better.[27] And yet, for all these interesting trends, there is really only one conclusion that we need to hang on to here, which is that, whichever way one looks at it, liberal democracies produce less insurrection than any other political system attempted in human history.

In short, liberal democracies are 'the people's choice', given that every other type of political regime produces enough people with enough motivation to overthrow the system. So what about different kinds of liberal-democracy? That is, what can we say about the best type of liberal-democratic political system, and in particular about more and less social, which is to say more or less egalitarian, variants on that system? The key point on this front is that more equal liberal democracies produce less criminal behaviour than more unequal ones – though we cannot come at this point directly. We need to consider first of all the fact that, despite less than perfect data on the subject (income and equal opportunity patterns are harder to monitor in many countries than distinct political events, such as coups and rebellions), more egalitarian systems of *all* kinds generally seem to do better than their less equal alternatives.

This fact is important, in part because it strengthens my general view that increases in inequality result in increases in dissatisfaction with both the political system and the ways of life it facilitates, but also, and more importantly, because it forestalls any worry we might have that more egalitarian systems, for whatever reason, are more rather than less prone to acts of insurrection. This would be a worry even though, according to normative behaviourism, insurrection trumps criminality in terms of the strength of political dissatisfaction it expresses, and even though regime type, judging from all of the evidence previously cited, is clearly the overwhelmingly crucial factor in explaining the likelihood of insurrection. The problem we would have if rises in inequality actually reduced motivation for insurrection is that we would have to find the optimal trade-off point between the two, and thus potentially identify a combination of

---

[26] For one of the more obvious contemporary illustrations of this process, see 'Charter 08', an unprecedented manifesto for political change in China that was signed by more than 2,000 Chinese citizens. A translation of this document is available at: www.nybooks.com/articles/22210.

[27] For an interesting historical discussion of democracy's development that includes this trend, see R. Wollheim, 'Democracy', *Journal of the History of Ideas*, 19:2 (1958), 231–232.

system and policies which, although it was not perfectly liberal democratic, was nevertheless unequal enough to successfully minimise the
strong level of political dissatisfaction that leads to insurrection (assuming, that is, that one could not achieve that level of inequality from within
a perfectly liberal-democratic system – which is certainly a real
possibility[28]). We would then have a problem similar to that described
by Phillipe Van Parijs in Rawls' *A Theory of Justice*, whereby although
'Justice as Fairness' says that basic liberties and then equal opportunity
have to be maximised before the condition of the worst off can be
optimised, it seems absurd to say that *no* degree of increase in that
condition could justify even the *slightest* incursion into the former pair of
ideals.[29] We should be considerably reassured, therefore, by the fact that,
according to such varied models of state fragility as those produced by
the Fund for Peace, USAID, and the London School of Economics and
Political Science's Crisis States Research Centre, inequality comes up
time and time again as one of several indicators connected to the likelihood of significant levels of insurrection – even allowing for the fact that,
as stated, it is by some way one of the less important ones.[30]

---

[28] It is a real possibility, in part, because there is some evidence that non-democracies
redistribute more than democracies, though this is by no means the full picture. See
J. F. Timmons, 'Does Democracy Reduce Economic Inequality', *British Journal of
Political Science*, 40 (2010), 741–757. Note that when I use the term 'inequality' in this
chapter, I have in mind not just the gap and curve in income between top and bottom in
society, but also the gap in opportunity which, although it is hugely influenced by the gap
in income, is not completely determined by it. This means that although a dictatorship
might generate a better Gini co-efficient than most liberal-democracies, it could nonetheless be a much less socially mobile system, and thus be deemed more unequal than
those systems overall *by the people who have to live with it* (and that is the crucial thing, from
the point of view of normative behaviourism, given that the dissatisfaction of the people,
and not the philosophers, is what ultimately concerns us). Consider also the further
possibility that, as a result of achieving such reduced inequality against a backdrop of
illiberal and undemocratic political conditions, a drop in prosperity occurs, and with it
a rise in poverty for those at the bottom (relative to how they would fare in alternative
systems). This could mean that whatever gains in dissatisfaction and insurrection
resulted from the drop in inequality are now entirely wiped out, if not reversed. For
differences in redistribution between democracies and non-democracies, see Timmons,
'Does Democracy Reduce Income Inequality', but also see R. Wintrobe, 'Dictatorship:
Analytical Approaches', in C. Boix and S. C. Stokes, *The Oxford Handbook of Comparative
Politics*, esp. 390. For an argument to the effect that inequality is a significant and
ineradicable problem in all systems, however much it can be mitigated in both extent
and consequences, see A. Przeworski, *Democracy and the Limits of Self-Government*
(Cambridge: Cambridge University Press, 2010).

[29] P. Van Parijs, 'Difference Principles', in S. Freeman (Ed.), *The Cambridge Companion to
Rawls* (Cambridge: Cambridge University Press, 2003), 200–240.

[30] For the evidence to this effect, see: USAID, 'Measuring Fragility: Indicators and
Methods for Rating State Performance'; Fund for Peace (2008) 'The Failed States
Index', and J. Di John, 'Conceptualising the Causes and Consequences of Failed
States: A Critical Review of the Literature'. An early and pioneering work on this topic

So, with this worry put to one side, we can now look properly at the key trend regarding inequality and criminality, which is that decreases in the former result in decreases in the latter. Numerous studies now show that crime, and in particular violent crime – that type of criminal behaviour that involves more personal risk than any other – is more affected by inequality than any other likely variable, including, for example, something as obvious as absolute poverty levels.[31] It also seems that inequality adversely affects not just the overall level and distribution of political satisfaction with a given political system, but also the way in which that system works, an effect which will, naturally enough, also reduce overall levels of satisfaction.[32] That relationship, however, is only of secondary importance. The key trend – of which that relationship is but one small part – remains that rises in inequality produce rises in, not just the number of people dissatisfied with their political system and the ways of life it facilitates, but also the strength of that dissatisfaction, as expressed through crime – a point that holds regardless of the fact that some small share of those dissatisfied people is upset primarily by the effect of inequality on the political system, rather than its own place within an unequal society and economy.

Looking at this trend from an institutional point of view, a further important finding by political scientists is that inequality, whatever else we might think of it, is fundamentally a political choice.[33] This means that

is T. R. Gurr, *Why Men Rebel* (Princeton, NJ: Princeton University Press, 1970).For more recent accounts of the relationship, see R. Rotberg, *When States Fail: Causes and Consequences*. For a more specific case regarding the relationship between inequality and secessionist conflict, see C. Deiwiks, L. E. Cederman, and K. S. Gleditsch, 'Inequality and Conflict in Federations', *Journal of Peace Research*, 49:2 (2012), 289–304.

[31] R. Wilkinson, 'Why Is Violence More Common Where Inequality Is Greater?', *Annals of the New York Academy of Sciences*, 1036 (2004), 1–12. See also P. Fajnzylber, D. Lederman, & N. Loayza, 'Inequality and Violent Crime', *Journal of Law and Economics*, 45 (2002), 1–40; C. C. Hsieh and M. D. Pugh, 'Poverty, Income Inequality, and Violent Crime: A Meta-analysis of Recent Aggregate Data Studies', *Criminal Justice Review*, 18 (1993), 182–202; United Nations Crime and Justice Information Network, *Survey on Crime Trends and the Operations of Criminal Justice Systems* (New York: United Nations, 2000); Federal Bureau of Investigation, *Crime in the United States* (Washington, DC: U.S. Government Printing Office, 1990–2000). M. Kelly, 'Inequality and Crime', *The Review of Economics and Statistics* 82:4 (2000), 530–539; E. Neumayer, 'Inequality and Violent Crime: Evidence from Data on Robbery and Violent Theft', *Journal of Peace Research*, 42 (2005), 101–112. The most comprehensive study on this topic by some margin is Richard Wilkinson and Kate Pickett's *The Spirit Level: Why More Equal Societies Almost Always Do Better* (London: Allen Lane, 2009).

[32] C. Boix, *Democracy and Redistribution* (Cambridge: Cambridge University Press, 2003); D. Acemoglu and J. Robinson, *Economic Origins of Dictatorship and Democracy* (Cambridge: Cambridge University Press, 2006).

[33] P. Beramendi and C. J. Anderson, *Democracy, Inequality, and Representation* (New York: Russell Sage Foundation, 2008). See also A. Przeworski, *Democracy and the Limits of Self-Government* (Cambridge: Cambridge University Press, 2011), 86–87.

the level of inequality a society permits is ultimately a function of the economic system its politicians introduce and enforce. Rules concerning ownership, investment, competition and monopolies, employment, unionisation, and tax – to take just a few key examples – are all ultimately political choices rather than deviations from some chimerical notion of a free, as in purely unregulated, market. Markets, after all, are systems of rules developed and enforced by states, rather than spontaneous conventions adopted by economic actors, as illustrated by the fact that there would not even be legal enforcement of contracts in the absence of such rules.

This basic point has been central to much post-war political philosophy, including, for example, the likes of Rawls and Dworkin, for whom the idea that societies are always capable of choosing different economic systems was absolutely crucial, given that it was part of the role of a theory of justice to decide just what that system should be. And yet, for all the free reign that political philosophy might appear to enjoy as a result of this capability, regarding both different economic systems and the levels of inequality they produce, it does seem that political science restrains us with at least one crucial caveat. This caveat, as pressed for example by Adam Przeworski, is that it is a great deal easier to prevent rises in inequality than it is to reverse them.[34] Outside of dramatic political and social upheaval, together with all the dissatisfaction and insurrection such upheaval always entails, it appears from the historical record that it is almost impossible to achieve substantial gains in equality once inequality has set in – a sort of ratchet effect that gives a serious note of caution to how states should aim at the social-liberal-democratic answer to OQ that I am claiming normative behaviourism presents.

This caution, however, cannot ultimately amount to anything more than a reasonable wariness regarding exactly how one aims at reducing inequality once it has developed. Provided that attempts to effect such a reduction do not proceed so quickly as to produce greater levels of insurrection and crime than can be offset by improvements in equality levels, there is no reason to regard any country's existing equality level as already the highest it could achieve. Unlike Rousseau, then, who insisted that nations could only be taught when they are young, or Plato, who held much the same thing, we do not need to say that political systems can only be made rationally convincing to all those who live under them when they

---

[34] See A. Przeworski, 'Democracy, Equality and Redistribution', in R. Bourke and R. Geuss (Eds.), *Political Judgement: Essays for John Dunn* (Cambridge: Cambridge University Press, 2009), 281–312.

are started from scratch. All we need to remember is that, in political practice, the twin normative behaviourist targets of minimal insurrection and minimal crime should inform, not just the aims of political endeavour, but also the means employed to achieve them.

Some further insight might be gained here by reflecting on the cause or causes *behind* crime and inequality's causal relationship. We can ask, if rises in inequality produce rises in dissatisfaction with both the political system and the ways of life it facilitates, why exactly is that? One prominent theory in the literature is that rising inequality triggers problems of status and shame for a growing number of the population, with the result that those people turn to crime in an attempt to redeem their social standing, at least in their own eyes.[35] This theory seems to chime with both common sense and the dynamic of the observed relationship. If status is thought of as a positional good or, in effect, a zero-sum game, according to which gains for me mean losses to everyone else, then it would seem to follow that if (a) perceptions of status are bound up with wealth, and (b) differences in wealth grow ever wider, then surely (c) those lower down on the economic ladder will come to seem more and more inferior to those higher up. We do not, however, need to establish here whether or not that theory is true. All that matters is that there is at least one plausible theory regarding the motivational mind-set connecting crime and inequality. This fact reassures us of the apparent causal nature of the correlation between them, and thus in turn the relevance of that trend from the point of view of OQ.

It would, though, be misleading to mention this factor without once again giving prosperity its due. We should not forget, perhaps out of misplaced idealism, just how important a country's wealth is in determining its prospects. As a matter of common sense, for example, we can see clearly that a country's ability to ensure equality of opportunity – say through providing universal education and eliminating corruption from public institutions – is going to depend to a large extent on the resources it has at its disposal. We also know as a matter of statistical fact that democracies in which the average income is $4,000 or more are as good as guaranteed to avoid collapse.[36] And, more impressively still,

---

[35] J. Gilligan, *Violence: Our Deadly Epidemic and Its Causes* (New York: G. P. Putnam, 1996). See also S. Pinker, *The Better Angels of Our Nature*. For further data and links regarding the relationship between crime and inequality, see the website set up by Wilkinson and Pickett's charitable organisation, the Equality Trust.

[36] A. Przeworski, M. E. Alvarez, J. E. Cheibub, and F. Limongi, *Democracy and Development: Political Institutions in the World, 1950–1990* (Cambridge: Cambridge University Press, 2000), 273. See also A. Przeworski, 'Democracy as an Equilibrium', *Public Choice*, 123 (2005), 253–273. As Przeworski puts the point, in developed countries, democracy is all but impregnable.

we know that no democracy has *ever* fallen which had a GDP/capita above \$6,055.[37]

Nevertheless, I am loath, despite this strong trend, to include prosperity as a fourth institutional feature picked out by normative behaviourism, as might be suggested here by some readers. This is in part because prosperity is hardly a unique feature of social-liberal-democracies – oil-rich dictatorships and rapidly growing China spring to mind here – but also because I think there is a strong case to be made for considering prosperity more as a consequence than a cause of social-liberal-democratic government. Yet that case, as noted, is not one on which there is any great consensus in contemporary political science – as one would expect given the short history and small dataset offered by countries that match social-liberal-democracies for wealth without possessing their institutions – which is why I would not want to rest too much importance on its holding true.

Instead, we need to step back a little here and remember, once more, that because we are after a convincing answer to OQ, we are only after things that people could *choose* as the basis for a collectively regulated existence. This means that our focus has to be on political principles and their institutional expressions, for we can no more choose 'prosperity' for a hypothetical regime than we can choose, say, warm weather, mountainous terrain, or a rich musical culture. Now, if it does turn out that certain things, such as prosperity, *are* reliably produced by some regimes and not others, then that will have to come into our considerations, but then what is clear from the empirical data is that to the extent that institutions *do* make a positive difference in terms of prosperity, it is social-liberal-democratic regimes that come out on top. Do bear in mind, though, that the question of whether social-liberal-democracy *boosts* prosperity is different from the question of whether it is *necessary* for any prosperity at all – for we might easily concede that certain alternative systems *can* achieve some or other level of prosperity, given that prosperity might have non-institutional primary causes, without conceding that those systems do a *better* job of advancing that achievement.

But we can do more than make concessions here. We can also strike a more positive note by looking carefully at the findings of a number of recent and innovative studies that put *violence* in all its various shapes and forms at the heart of their analyses. Each of these studies gives us good reason to think that, not just low insurrection and low crime, but also prosperity, *go hand in hand*, and thus that we will not have to make the kind of trade-offs which, for various reasons, would be difficult to both

---

[37] This threshold is provided by the democratic collapse of Argentina in 1975. See A. Przeworski, 'Democracy as an Equilibrium'.

design and justify. To be clear, most of what I want to say about this research will have to wait for the next section, given that it concerns the highly interesting theories of 'success' these authors develop out of their various empirical datasets, but there are still several causal connections worth mentioning in this context.

North, Wallis, and Weingast, for example, in their seminal work *Violence and Social Orders*, establish a number of trends that bear on the questions of equality and prosperity just discussed. Two trends in particular interest me. The first is that high national income tends to go hand in hand with large, though often quite decentralised government.[38] The second is that 'governments that fail to provide prosperity and public goods and services valued by citizens are punished by shrinking economies, lower tax revenues, the exit of mobile factors, and opposition parties that seek to unseat them'.[39] What interests me about these two trends is the institutional causal process they illuminate. In the first case we see a connection not just between prosperity and liberal-democratic government, but also, and in contrast to much of the neo-liberal rhetoric of our time, between prosperity and a more 'social' type of government – understood here as a type of government concerned with the provision of public goods and widespread opportunities. So what do we see in the second? In the second we see again a connection between prosperity and liberal-democratic political systems, just insofar as these systems produce freely contested elections, the upshot of which is that governments are strongly incentivised to deliver as much prosperity as possible.

A second study of interest on this front is the recent *magnum opus* offered by evolutionary psychologist Steven Pinker.[40] In his work, amongst several interesting theories regarding the causes of success for certain regime types, we find a number of empirical trends to add to our picture. One is that different kinds of violence – domestic, criminal, international, and so on – all tend to go down in tandem, a fact which gives much credence to my idea that different kinds of violence-risking behaviour – in my case insurrection and crime – are expressions or at least products of a shared set of factors and preferences.[41] A second trend is that the more peaceable societies tend to be richer, healthier, better educated, better governed, more respectful of women, and more likely to engage in trade.[42] Now, Pinker does admit here, as one would expect, that with so many indicators in play it is difficult to see which happy trends 'got the virtuous circle started and which went along for the ride',[43] but

---

[38] North, Wallis, and Weingast, *Violence and Social Orders*, 11.   [39] Ibid., 133.
[40] S. Pinker, *The Better Angels of Our Nature*.   [41] Ibid., xxii   [42] Ibid., xxiii.   [43] Ibid.

difficult is not the same as impossible, especially when one factor, in this case the rise of the organised state, appears to have been so fundamentally important.[44]

We do, though, need to be at least a little bit cautious here regarding this fascinating picture, which Pinker describes at one point as 'a kind of Whig history that is supported by the facts',[45] given that its ambition from the point of view of political science is actually rather modest. Consider here that whatever behavioural vindication we manage to find in Pinker's case, it has ultimately picked out no institutional formulae more specific than the 'state'. Surely then, given that most of the world's populations now live within and under 'states', despite their institutions differing in so many other ways, we will need to restrict our mining of evidence to much more finely tuned analyses than this one.

Not necessarily, given that yet a third grand study of this kind, in this case provided by the political scientist Francis Fukuyama, points to much the same conclusion.[46] Instead, what we need to recognise is that different states, despite being formally identical, can differ fundamentally in terms of their capacity. If we say, for example, following Weber and most contemporary political science, that the state is defined by its monopoly on the legitimate use of violence, then we can see fairly quickly that different states have very different historical track records when it comes to meeting the goal entailed by that definition. In particular, we can see that states that are widely judged as legitimate by their citizens tend to do a much better job at eliminating both non-state violence and the need to use the state's own coercive muscle. And, in turn, we can see that those states deemed most legitimate by their populations also tend to be, as we would expect, social-liberal-democracies. But there is still more that can be learned here, because, as Fukuyama shows, the connection is not just between *strong* states and *peaceful* societies – where strength is always going to depend hugely on widespread acceptance – but also between strong states and *prosperity*, which suggests yet again that institutional factors more than anything else lie behind the prosperity which, itself, helps to secure social-liberal-democratic orders.[47] In thinking, then, about the central causal importance of a strong state, we always need to remember there must be certain factors lying behind that 'strength', even if those factors are not always themselves the subjects of at least some of the studies we draw on.

---

[44] Ibid., 680.   [45] Ibid., 692.
[46] F. Fukuyama, *The Origins of Political Order: From Prehuman Times to the French Revolution* (London: Profile Books, 2011).
[47] Ibid., 469.

Our conclusion to this section is thus relatively straightforward. It is that the most appreciated political systems in both past and present political life are those that I am calling social-liberal-democracies. But then why, if these systems are so wonderful, have I spent so little time actually spelling out exactly what they are? I have so far been rather vague about this system, and for good reason. This reason is that the system we are trying to define is itself only properly defined by the empirical research. What I have been doing, in essence, is asking which institutions do best, empirically, in accordance with the criteria already laid down. I only *then* use the label social-liberal-democracy for these institutions simply because it is the best that I can muster – not because it has been produced by some prior theory. The proper question to ask here, therefore, is why this label and not another? I respond to this question by assuming, first of all, that the liberal and democratic part of the definition are fairly uncontroversial, given the widespread understanding of those terms utilised in both popular culture and contemporary political science. A state that is liberal is, for present purposes, one that provides certain core freedoms, including of association, speech, political organisation, employment, and political protest. And, in turn, a state that is democratic is simply one in which governments can be changed through regular elections undertaken by a near universally franchised population.

One can, of course, go on endlessly about what exactly I mean by each of the elaborating terms I just used, and then in turn by each of the further terms I might use in order to expand upon that initial elaboration, but I trust that this is not something that most readers will deem vital at this point (even if I would, for pedagogic reasons, be loath to let my own students get away with such a brief description). Instead, I think more attention needs to be paid to my use of the term 'social', even though, again, I only want to offer a very brief account of its intended meaning.

My use of the term 'social' here matches the sense in which it is already used in the concept of 'social democracy', as widely discussed and practised in European political circles. An alternative would have been 'egalitarian', but then, given that that term sounds more like something many political philosophers would like us to try than something many societies have already achieved, I thought it best to avoid the confusion – although, given that there is not much difference between the policies and institutions possessed by many European social democracies and those proposed by egalitarian political theorists (universal education and health care provision, public pension provision, a welfare state which provides support for those who need it), there should not be much cause for confusion. As I hope is already clear, when I use the term 'social' in 'social-liberal-democracy', all I really mean to pick out is political regimes which, in addition to providing democracy and liberty, also try to provide such things as equality of opportunity, a continuous improvement in the condition of the worst off, and a reduction or at least restriction of the level of absolute wealth inequality permitted.

We return, though, now to our conclusion, which is that we can see from all these various studies and datasets that those individuals who inhabit social-liberal-democracies clearly find their political order more bearable than other, rival forms of government, both directly in terms of how they judge the nature of the regime itself, and indirectly in terms of the various ways of life it permits and facilitates. Social-liberal-democracy , we can say, is an *experiment in political living* that *has* worked and *is* working, whereas communism, fascism, aristocracy, monarchy, and theocracy alike are experiments which either *have* failed or, as we speak, *are* failing. But that is still only a *picture*. As yet we do not fully understand either why this experiment is working so well or how these findings translate into reasons for individuals to find social-liberal-democracy a convincing answer to OQ. These two problems are the subject of our next three sections.

3.6   An Explanatory Theory of Social-Liberal-Democracy's Success

> I began by examining men, and I believed that, amidst the infinite diversity of laws and mores, they were not led by their fancies alone. I have set down the principles, and I have seen particular cases conform to them as if by themselves, the histories of all nations being but their consequences.[48]
>
> Violence must be near the heart of any explanation of how societies behave.[49]

We know so far that people *do* prefer social-liberal-democracy, but not *why*. This might seem unimportant. Surely if we know which institutions people find the most satisfying, even if that really means the least dis-satisfying, then that is enough for our argument. After all, if an individual or group can only pick one set of institutions, why *not* pick this one? The problem with this assumption is that unless we are sure that people prefer social-liberal-democracy as a result of goods and processes that can *only* be provided to the requisite degree by social-liberal-democracy, we cannot be sure that there is not some further system, perhaps still untried,

---

[48] Montesquieu, *The Spirit of the Laws* (Cambridge: Cambridge University Press, 1989), xliii.

[49] North, Wallis, and Weingast, *Violence and Social Orders*, 258.

which could deliver those goods and processes to a greater degree despite possessing radically different features. Of course, until that further system *has* been tried we could not be sure that people would really prefer it in practice, but still, just so long as that system appeared to be fairly simple to construct, without any radical leaps into the unknown, there would always be doubt as to which easily conceivable system was really the most convincing.

For example, imagine that the thing people *really* appreciated most about social-liberal-democracies was their production of reality television shows. Imagine also that although people still appreciate their liberties, and still appreciate their democracy, they actually could not give two hoots about the egalitarian character of their system. So, although it might just *happen* to be the case that only social-liberal-democracies have produced these shows so far, it might also be the case that a liberal and democratic system with no egalitarian policies would do just as well according to our two behaviourist measures. Admittedly, there might still be good causal reason for why liberal democracies always tend to be *social-*liberal-democracies – given universal suffrage, there is perhaps always a majority inclination for support of such things – but that would not amount to a behaviourist vindication of the social arm of social-liberal-democracy itself. After all, once enough of the democratic population realises that these reality shows are all that 'really' matters to them, they might quickly vote to shift all those revenues currently 'wasted' on egalitarian measures to the mass production of the television of their dreams.

We might object to this possibility by simply reiterating the fact that, as shown earlier, more egalitarian liberal democracies do better than less egalitarian ones. But that cannot guarantee our argument. It might, after all, be the case that social-liberal-democracies always and necessarily contain welfare states, which in turn produce populations addicted to reality television shows, which are in turn still the principal reason for their contentment. In order, therefore, to know that social-liberal-democracy really is 'the people's choice', we need to know that the things people appreciate about social-liberal-democracies are relatively exclusive to them. This does not automatically mean that the things they appreciate are themselves the broadly social, liberal, and democratic features of the system – although they might be. It could simply be the case that particular and narrower goods (including, say, religious liberties and employment opportunities) social-liberal-democracies provide are much better than those other systems offer. Again, and as I have said throughout this argument, when judging political systems by the standards of normative behaviourism, we judge how palatable people find each system in practice, which, for each individual, will involve both their verdict on the institutions themselves *and* their verdict on the ways of life it permits and facilitates.

With this in mind, consider also a further and related problem, which is that even if we are sure that it is social-liberal-democracy – as opposed to, say, liberal democracies with reality television – that is being vindicated by our empirical picture, we still will not know which of the many features we group under each of the three constituent terms accounts for that vindication. Some liberties, perhaps, are very important for people, whilst others are of no interest at all. And perhaps there are even several optional features of all past and present social-liberal-democracies that actually *lower* general satisfaction with them. In this case, although we know that social-liberal-democracy of the kind experimented with is the best system tried so far, we still will not know which of its features support that success and which *undermine* it, or whether there might be simple ways in which it might be improved in a Pareto-optimal fashion. So, again, we need to come up with plausible explanations of why people prefer social-liberal-democracy, in all three of its dimensions, in order to be sure that the empirical picture described is implying for us just what we have taken it to imply.

All of which takes us to a second reason for developing our theory of social-liberal-democratic success. This reason is that the questions of what large populations tend to prefer and of what individuals 'should' prefer still hold great potential to diverge. It might perhaps be wondered why anyone would want to live in societies that are more crime-ridden and politically unstable than social-liberal-democracies, but we can hardly rule that out from the off, given what we see of human nature and political rhetoric every day. So, although our theory might reassure us that social-liberal-democracy is better than any other readily available political system, in terms of the stated behaviourist criteria, as well as inform us just which of its constituent features account for that success, we will still need to put that theory to work in the production of reasons for why different people with different interests and conceptions of the good – and particularly those with either privileged interests or radical conceptions of the good – should be convinced by it as an answer to OQ. Or, alternatively put, until we have these two things we shall not have crossed all the way from the 'is' of observable behaviour to the 'ought' of a convincing answer to OQ.

But we should not get ahead of ourselves here. In this section we deal solely with the theoretical explanation of social-liberal-democracy's success. This theory has two parts. In the first I set out three arguments in contemporary political philosophy from which we can derive plausible *causes* of the observed institutional success. Here it is hoped that we can move fairly smoothly from proposed justifications for particular principles, which all reasonable people are supposed to accept (even though we know from Chapters 1 and 2 that they do not), to plausible motivations for approximately corresponding large-scale behaviour on the part of different sections of the population, and thus in turn plausible explanations of the overall political effect. The second part, by contrast, draws exclusively on the violence-centric literature discussed in the previous section, and offers both more and less than the first. It offers less just insofar as it only adds one really novel explanatory factor to the set of factors we already have in hand, but also more just insofar as it provides, in addition, a useful framework through which we can aggregate all such factors.

Bear in mind throughout our discussion of this theory that having more explanations is better than having few, even if those explanations do not always appear to be themselves constitutively or causally connected. After all, if social-liberal-democracy is a combination of things that delivers a combination of goods, then we should expect its success to be the product of a combination of causes, just as we would expect different people to find it convincing for different combinations of reasons. Our worry should not, then, be that we have too many explanations, and thus not as clear an explanatory grasp of the situation as we would have hoped, but rather too few, with some people acting in response to more than one of our listed causes, and others acting in response to causes that we have not yet identified. We might also worry here about the related problem of causal regression – i.e. if we say that x causes y, which causes z, do we not also need to know what causes x, or indeed what causes the thing that causes x, and so on? And consider, further, how the line between facts and theories can become quickly blurred. For example, although the fact of democratic superiority is a trend in need of an explanatory theory, it is also a fact capable of explaining itself the particular success of a given set of countries (that is, we could propose a *theory* that they have succeeded because they are democratic). There is no need, though, to get overly concerned by these issues. It is important to bear them in mind, but whatever worries we might have on this front, I will simply say for now that we will be in a much better position to address them towards the end of this section.

At this stage of the argument we need to focus on the detail of our theory, starting with three plausible explanations for the success of social-liberal-democracies, all of which take their lead from particular debates in contemporary political philosophy. The first of these explanations supports the 'social' part of social-liberal-democracy, the second the 'liberal' part, and the third the 'democratic' part.

We start with the 'social' part, and in particular with an explanation that draws on contemporary egalitarian theory.[50] This explanation claims that part of the reason for the success of social-liberal-democracies is the fact that they achieve some sort of *social justice*. Because (a) they provide some not insignificant degree of equality of opportunity across all citizens, (b) they provide a minimal welfare net which keeps the unlucky and the vulnerable away from destitution, and (c) they achieve at least some degree of redistribution via income-proportionate taxation (thus curbing both inequality of wealth and inequality of opportunity), social-liberal-democracies keep more people away from desperate and depressing circumstances than would be the case in, say, a libertarian or feudal economic order. Importantly, these aspects of social justice function as a first set of widely distributed *incentives* capable of accounting for the stability of this kind of regime. The idea, in other words – and not just here but also with the following two explanations – is to extrapolate plausible disincentives for violence-risking behaviour from purported justifications of political principles. Or, more precisely still, by looking closely at the kinds of principles recommended by mentalist political philosophers, we can hopefully better understand and thus better explain the success of a number of institutions and policies which, in addition to producing the observed behavioural success of social-liberal-democracies, are also expressions, however approximate, of the principles in question.

Our second explanation of this kind draws on liberal political theory when it claims that part of the reason for the success of social liberal democracies is the fact that they provide greater personal freedom than would be enjoyed under non-liberal regimes. This is more than mere tautology. Just think of the arguments of the greatest liberal works of the nineteenth and twentieth centuries: Mill's *On Liberty* and Rawls' *A Theory of Justice*. Both of these works, *inter alia*, promote a core set of negative liberties: in the first case because they would be protected by Mill's 'harm principle',[51] and in the second because a particular set of 'basic liberties'

---

[50] For a quick sample of egalitarian positions, see the discussions of Rawls, Dworkin, and Cohen in Chapter 1. For a good collection of essays on the same theme, see: M. Clayton and M. Williams (Eds.), *The Ideal of Equality* (London: Palgrave, 2002). Of course, one could just as easily claim inspiration from the practice of social-democratic political parties over the past sixty years or so, as opposed to these esoteric theorists, but that is not the point here. What really matters is whether or not these ideals are, in practice, appreciated by those who have to live with them. As a result, their *authorship* is ultimately irrelevant. Even so, I still think it's interesting to point out the alignment of the ideals of both groups (theorists and politicians) with the conclusions of normative behaviourism – by explaining how they are part of the story of why social-liberal-democracy does better, comparatively speaking, than other tested political systems. If nothing else, it gives at least some people yet one more reason to give normative behaviourism a chance.

[51] J. S. Mill, *On Liberty*.

would be chosen from the 'original position'.[52] These liberties – of association, speech, employment, and so on – really matter to people. Because they enjoy a greater number of choices regarding how they live their lives, as well as a greater degree of personal 'space' within which they can explore all manner of lifestyles and experiences, these systems make it possible for all sorts of individuals to live what are for them all sorts of meaningful existences. These include a large number of existences which, crucially, they would not be able to pursue under many other kinds of regime, meaning that more individuals are going to be able to do what they *want* to do under them than under other, *less liberal* regimes. Assuming, then, that one finds a range of preferences regarding different ways of life in all populations, whichever system is able to cater to the maximum number of such ways is also going to frustrate – and thus nudge towards insurrection and crime – a minimum number of individuals.

Our third and final explanation of this kind extrapolates from both minimalist and deliberative theories of democracy when it claims that part of the reason for the success of social-liberal-democracies is the fact that they are democratic. Three aspects of this system matter here. First, because elections generate information about aggregate preferences of a sort that is otherwise hard to obtain, they provide a bloodless alternative to war. That is, because they provide information in advance about what the likely outcome of a violent conflict would be, they do away with one primary incentive to initiate such conflict – namely, the thought that you might succeed. As Friedrich Engels once remarked, secret votes are 'paper stones'.[53] Or, as James Fitzjames Stephen once put the point, we count heads in order to avoid breaking them.[54] Second, elections provide a means of both avoiding disastrous policies and getting as close as possible to optimal compromises. Put simply, people get less of what they want to *avoid* and more of what they want to *receive* as a result of regular, popular elections. Third, because liberal democracies (and here I have to combine the liberal and democratic elements of social-liberal-democracy) permit and promote greater dialogue and deliberation amongst the various individuals and groups found in a state, information regarding what both unpalatable options and optimal compromises *would be* is made available to a degree that would be impossible in

---

[52] J. Rawls, *A Theory of Justice*, though a better discussion can be had in *Political Liberalism*, 331–334. For further discussion, including of how Rawls' position evolves in response to an important critique by H. L. A. Hart, see C. Audard, *John Rawls* (London: Acumen, 2007), 95–96; and S. Maffetone, *Rawls: An Introduction* (Cambridge: Polity, 2010), 55–62.

[53] Cited in A. Przeworski and J. Sprague, *Paper Stones: A History of Electoral Socialism* (Chicago, IL: University of Chicago Press, 1986), 1.

[54] J. F. Stephen, *Liberty, Equality, Fraternity* (Indianapolis, IN: Liberty Fund, 1993), 28.

non-democratic orders. Regardless then of whether or not deliberation is so successful as to actually change people's minds about their own political preferences, it does at the very least make available important electoral information regarding both (a) aggregate popular preferences and (b) distributions of preferential hierarchies regarding the relative importance of different policies to different groups and individuals.[55]

We have, then, three partial explanations for the success of social-liberal-democracies, each of which chimes with arguments found in contemporary political philosophy, and each of which already reveals plausible *reasons* for people to support that system, and thus be *convinced* by it as an answer to OQ. But we will get to the full spread of reasons in a moment. For now we need to consider still two further explanations for this success, each of which is drawn from the recent violence-centred literature already discussed.

The first of these, as already noted, identifies yet a further aspect of the system capable of accounting for its success. This aspect, if indeed one can properly call it that, is the fact that social-liberal-democracies are what North, Wallis, and Weingast call 'open access societies'.[56] Open access societies are ones in which both private institutions such as companies and public institutions such as the government or the police are potentially open to anyone who meets the appropriate standards. This kind of society can be compared to what they call 'natural states', in which personal relationships – who one is and who one knows – form the basis of social organisation.[57] In open access societies, by contrast, 'impersonal social relationships' are the order of the day.[58] Important features of such relationships include such things as the rule of law, property rights, and values of fairness and equality, even if it is not primarily with the intrinsic appeal of such things that we are concerned here.[59]

What really matters is the virtuous circle dynamic these scholars describe. For example, although open access societies are peaceful because the police

---

[55] The extent to which any political system, including democracy, can perfectly aggregate preferences is of course highly contestable, and there is certainly no claim here that they do so. My emphasis instead is on the fact that they do it better than other systems, as well as on the fact that they do a good enough job of at least avoiding most of what the electorate have strong preferences *against*, as shown in the work of Robert Dahl, who notes that their key features do at least 'make it rather uncommon for a government to enforce policies to which a substantial number of citizens object'. See R. A. Dahl, *Democracy and Its Critics* (New Haven, CT: Yale University Press). For a useful discussion of the nature of preference aggregation in democratic systems, see G. Bingham Powell Jr, 'Aggregating and Representing Political Preferences', in C. Boix and S. C. Stokes (Eds.), *The Oxford Handbook of Comparative Politics*, 653–677. For a useful discussion of how elections and accountability work, see the chapter by J. M. Maravall in the same volume.

[56] North, Wallis, and Weingast, *Violence and Social Orders*.   [57] Ibid., 2.   [58] Ibid., 12.
[59] Ibid.

maintain order, the police only do this as they should because they are both open access themselves and controlled by a state that is open in the fundamentally important sense that its government can be replaced through free and fair elections which, *in turn*, are facilitated by an open and thus thriving civil society which, *again in turn*, is only able to thrive because (1) it is supported by a thriving economy, which is itself only thriving on account of its open access and thus competitive nature, and (2) the rights that enable it to do so are protected by the police, and so on and so forth. ...[60]

The key idea, therefore, is that the dynamics of open access societies are themselves naturally supportive of open access. North and his colleagues also pick out some of the key upshots of this general process, including what they call 'Schumpeterian creative destruction' in both politics and the economy, and the 'adaptive efficiency' of governments as a result of properly contested elections – though I would assume that the general logic of this process, and how such upshots emerge, is by now fairly clear.[61] There are, though, two further arguments of theirs that need spelling out. The first of these connects to their noted belief that open access economics supports open access politics, and claims that the described virtuous circle, which might also be described as one very successful feedback loop, holds the key to the contested debate, as mentioned earlier, about whether social-liberal-democratic institutions produce prosperity or *vice versa*. The second argument, however, is perhaps the more interesting one. It claims simply that because 'social orders engender different patterns of behaviour, individuals in different social orders come to form different beliefs about how the people around them behave'.[62] This point is important because it enables us to round off our understanding of how the causal logic North and his colleagues describe supports the empirical picture in favour of social-liberal-democracy we are trying to explain. The key argument to be extrapolated for our own concerns, it seems, is that each of the three defining elements of social-liberal-democracy not only supports the other two, but also, more broadly speaking, plays a key role in a system which, at every level, provides not just incentives for people in different positions to serve the interests of others, however indirectly, but also opportunities for almost everyone to occupy those positions.

This logic is, of course, almost as naive as it is compelling, just insofar as there have never been nor ever will be any human societies quite as 'open' as the one just described, but still, given that 'open access' can be a matter of degree, it is worth stressing both (1) that the more open a society is in this sense, the more it seems likely to reduce the kind of behaviour normative behaviourism is interested in, and (2)

---

[60] Ibid., 110.   [61] Ibid., 116–133.   [62] Ibid., 2.

that the more social, liberal, and democratic political systems are, the more likely they are to be open. In other words, we can see both how the pervasive logic of openness within social-liberal-democracies helps to explain their success in normative behaviourist terms, and how the more social, liberal, and democratic they become, the more open, and thus successful, they will be.

All of which takes us to the last of our partial explanations of social-liberal-democratic success. This explanation returns us to the recent work on the history of violence by Stephen Pinker who, with strong echoes of Dawkins' *Selfish Gene*, makes great play of that well-known problem in philosophy and economics, the 'prisoner's dilemma'. The original version of this scenario involves two prisoners who, once separated and charged with the same crime, face a choice between informing on the other prisoner and pleading both innocence and ignorance. The 'dilemma' occurs because although both prisoners would be best off if both of them plead innocence and ignorance, they will be worst off if each of them pleads innocence whilst accusing the other – which is precisely what they do. In short, the mutual mistrust generated in large part by the situation itself proves too much for either party to handle.

Pinker's innovation is to redesign this dilemma with the decision of peace or violence in mind. In this new situation, dubbed the 'pacifist's dilemma', although everyone would be best off if nobody engaged in violence, the worst outcome for each person would be to adopt peace whilst everyone else embarks on violence. The difficulty is that this makes violence the rational choice of each individual, just as accusation was the rational choice in the original scenario involving the prisoners. Yet this difficulty is also an opportunity, at least as far as our theory is concerned, if only because it shows that the challenge of explaining the achievement and maintenance of peace is also the challenge of explaining how this dilemma is overcome.

Now, in order to take advantage of this opportunity, we need to appreciate first just how the framework of options it provides enables us to see how the appeal of different choices within it varies according to the payoffs we attach to each box of the implied decision matrix. This matrix, conceived here for two actors or groups, is as follows:

	Actor 1 attacks	Actor 1 co-operates
Actor 2 attacks	Victory = 10	Victory = 13
	Defeat = 0	Defeat = 0
Actor 2 co-operates	Victory = 13	Peace = 20 for both parties
	Defeat = 0	

Two points should be instantly clear from this table: (1) that the provided payoff figures are somewhat arbitrary, though not inaccurate in their rankings; and (2) that the greatest payoff for both parties lies in mutual non-aggression. The real value of this table, however, together with the framework it represents, is that it helps us to see how changes to the payoffs resulting from each decision can affect the appeal of different choices, and thus move individuals within it from being incentivised to act violently to being incentivised to act peacefully.

How might we alter this distribution of payoffs? As already noted, the biggest alteration we can make to the domestic situation – which, given our concern with OQ, is our real subject here, even if the logic of the change for the so-called security dilemma of international relations theory is perfectly analogous – is to introduce a strong state. This simple, Hobbesian point is already made by both Pinker and Fukuyama, and it is easy to see why. Once a state arrives on the scene (and just how it arrives on the scene need not concern us), a fundamental change occurs to the price of violence, for whereas before you had every chance of acting violently and getting away with it, now you face the strong probability of severe punishment. To act violently and be reprimanded for it, in other words, is now so risky and unappealing a prospect as to severely reduce the appeal of trying to act violently and get away with it (which is not say, of course, that it changes the payoff of successful violence, only that it transforms the chance and negative payoff of being unsuccessful).

Introducing a state, however, is not the only change we can make. As can readily be imagined, the more prosperous a society gets – as Pinker noted under the topic of 'commerce' – the more attractive mutual co-operation becomes. And mutual co-operation of course, as shown by history and distilled by economic theory, becomes an ever more rewarding and enriching affair the more we engage in it. Yet this, as noted earlier, is where the institutional story ends for Pinker. Although he also lists further non-institutional factors contributing to changes in the payoff matrix, including cultural feminisation and a general increase in knowledge regarding the severe costs and rich rewards of the different decisions, his argument has already run its course in terms of our answer to OQ. And that, I would suggest, leaves us with an explanatory shortfall, as noted earlier in our discussion of the importance of 'strong' as opposed to 'weak' states, where it was pointed out that popular appeal or legitimacy plays an absolutely crucial role in generating such strength. What, then, should we do now?

The task now is one of working through those arguments and empirical trends we have already canvassed in order to complete the precise causal picture suggested by the framework just described. This process is a fairly simple one, given that all it really involves is thinking through the ways in which social-liberal-democracies improve the payoffs not just for non-violence, but also, and more generally, for non-engagement in insurrection and crime. Two improvements in particular are worth noting. The first involves the social and liberal aspects of social-liberal-democracy. By thinking through the maximising of choices and opportunities delivered by liberal institutions and policies, together with the elimination of severe poverty and effective facilitating of those opportunities delivered by egalitarian institutions and policies, we can readily see how peaceful behaviour becomes rewarding, not just for the 'haves', but also for the 'have-nots'. If one has no chances in life, and is condemned to a mostly miserable, destitute condition, then one has less to lose from either not co-operating with or actively trying to overthrow the regime under which one lives, and so less disincentive to act in those ways. The second key improvement involves social-liberal-democracy's democratic credentials. All we need to consider here is the fact that, to the extent that governments can both deliver opportunities and relieve the condition of the worst off, they are more likely to do so, and more likely to be informed about how to do so, the more democratic they are. Universal suffrage, that is, gives electoral incentive to political parties to achieve these things, with public debate, itself stimulated by electoral competition, acting in turn to improve elite understanding of how best to do so.

The framework generated by the choice of either co-operation or non-co-operation with a political system provides us, I think, with a useful way of putting together all the various partial explanations of social-liberal-democratic success discussed in this section. Given that we are, fundamentally, trying to explain why people are more likely to co-operate in some situations than in others, it makes sense to think about this problem in terms of a variably incentivised decision as to how appealing and thus rational it is to do so. We can call this decision the 'good citizen's dilemma' – although given the myriad ways in which our choice differs from a time-critical dilemma, that is a little misleading. What matters more is the recognition that this framework, which has already been applied in its general logic to violence in general, and with particular reference to the coercive state, can also be applied to a wider set of decisions, and also a wider and indeed deeper (given that they also explain the 'strength of the state') spread of factors.

Before we round off this theory, however, we need to return briefly to the issue of causal regression noted earlier on. Consider, for example, the claim already discussed to the effect that peace is caused by the presence of strong states. The problem with this claim was that we still have to *explain* the presence of strong states. So what are we to do? We might, of course, say that states are strong when, and only when, they are prosperous social-liberal-democracies. Or, more accurately, we could say that states both *tend to be* and *remain* strong only when they are prosperous social-liberal-democracies. This would be a claim consistent with what we have said so far. But then the question becomes, why is there this tendency? To this we replied earlier that the tendency is a function of various features found in social-liberal-democracies, the upshot of which is that citizens living within them have greater incentive to fully co-operate with them than in any other attempted political system. Yet still the questions keep on coming. Why, for instance, do people prefer liberty and opportunity to, say, martial glory and the building of pyramids?

At some point, I think, there is nothing left for us to say but 'they just do, as a matter of fact, prefer these political institutions and the goods they deliver' – a point that returns us to our earlier discussion surrounding facts and principles. But note, we do not say this simply because we are *tired* of digging ever deeper, or because we have already gone further than is generally *deemed* necessary in social and political science, but rather because, human nature being what it is, there is nothing more to be said about non-derivative, foundational human preferences outside of the fact that they exist and cause effects in the world – or at least nothing outside of certain speculative branches of evolutionary psychology, the normative relevance of which will be hugely constrained by the fact that being told I hold a deep preference for x over y because of evolutionary cause z is itself no motivation for abstaining from x, let alone in favour of y (though this is not to say that is completely irrelevant, depending on the details of the evolutionary story – as discussed in the following section).

What we do have now, though, is not just a clear empirical picture of which institutions and policies do best, but also a reasonably deep theory of why that is. This theory is composed of a number of factors, and has been inspired by both contemporary political theory and the latest findings of social science. It has also been clarified, and rendered more systematic, by way of its assimilation it to an adapted version of what was *already* an adapted version of the prisoner's dilemma. And yet, as has repeatedly been explained, this is still not quite *a convincing answer to OQ*. Although we can already say to any given individual that he or she should adopt social-liberal-democracy as his or her answer to OQ on the basis that it is the system which people generally prefer, in practice, over all attempted alternatives, this will still not be enough to convince those individuals whose conceptions of the good and connected interests attract them towards still other systems, even if some of those systems generally retain much of what social-liberal-democracy has to offer. Our next problem, therefore, and to put it bluntly, is that the rich and powerful, as well as the radically minded, often want a system that is either more or less egalitarian than social-liberal-democracy, more or less liberal, and more or less democratic, if not, of course, completely undemocratic.

3.7   The Relationship between Normative Behaviourism, Psychological Behaviourism, Political Behaviouralism, and Political Science More Generally

> The ultimate aim of scientific generalisations about politics is to increase the determinacy of important political judgements.[63]
>
> [B]y calling Politics a Science we mean no more than this, that there is a constancy and uniformity in the tendencies of human nature which enable us to regard the acts of men at one time as due to the same causes which have governed their acts at previous times.[64]
>
> Easton argued that ... If certain human values and goals were scientifically and demonstrably rooted in universal basic impulses, then it might be argued that only certain institutional arrangements might satisfy these needs.[65]

Before we get to that convincing answer, however, we need to take a small detour. This detour will be of particular interest to those who have been wondering all along just what the connections are between normative behaviourism and those forms of behaviourism and behaviouralism found elsewhere in the natural and social sciences, including most obviously psychological behaviourism and behavioural political science. Not that sating that ambition is my primary aim in what follows. Instead, my hope is that by clarifying where normative behaviourism stands in relation to these other fields of enquiry, together with the bodies of evidence they contain, I will be able to go some considerable way further along the path of defending both its key ideas and its expression in the case for social-liberal-democracy.

We begin this detour by considering very briefly the rather distant relationship between normative behaviourism and psychological behaviourism. There is, perhaps surprisingly, not a great deal to say on this front. In this book I am not defending or indeed relying upon any particular thesis concerning the question of whether mental states are

---

[63] H. Lasswell, cited in J. G. Gunnell, *The Descent of Political Theory: The Genealogy of an American Vocation* (Chicago, IL: University of Chicago Press, 1993), 221.

[64] J. Bryce, cited in P. Lassman, 'Political Philosophy and the Idea of a Social Science', in G. Klosko, *The Oxford Handbook of The History of Political Philosophy* (Oxford: Oxford University Press, 2011), 438. The claim was made in Bryce's American Political Science Association presidential address in 1909, in which he also stated that the 'the data of politics are the acts of men'.

[65] J. G. Gunnell, *The Descent of Political Theory*, 230.

only knowable or describable in behaviourist terms, or on any thesis regarding how human beings learn, or on any particular approach to learning such as operant conditioning. This is not to say that there is *no* common ground. I share with behaviourist psychology, of course, a focus on the causal relationship between stimulus and response, which is to say between the environments in which groups and individuals operate and the observable behaviour produced in them by those environments. But still, in contrast to much behaviourist literature, my assumption that we can learn at least some of the universal political preference hierarchies of human beings, by observing their different behaviour in different political environments, actually suggests the kind of nativism that is more normally associated with the rise of cognitive psychology and neuroscience – fields that have reduced the sway of behaviourism both within psychology and beyond.

And yet, even if I do, to a large extent, side with the idea of internal, hardware-like human biases at the expense of at least some theories of learned preferences, this should not distract from the fact that my direct focus is, as stated, on observable preferences and their environmental triggers, rather than the internal processing dynamics that connect the two. It is worth stressing that there is no real conflict involved in that focus. For example, if I claim that an individual rebelled because of a change in his political system, I have not contradicted the claim that he rebelled because he was angry, or the claim that he rebelled because a local warlord took his livestock, or the claim that he rebelled because human beings have evolved to respond aggressively to threats to their food supply. The issue here is thus more of detail than distinction. One can easily focus on different parts of an individual's chain reaction to a given environmental change according to the nature of one's own research interest. In this case my interest is with the way in which we can learn different political preferences by noting different behavioural responses to different political environments. Of course, if it proved to be the case that, say, emotions and culture produced wildly different responses in different people to different political environments, then that would be a real problem for normative behaviourism, but that is not, fortunately enough, what the evidence suggests.

There is a great deal more to say about the relationship between normative behaviourism and political science than there is about its relationship with psychology. This relationship includes connections with a number of overlapping strains of thought within political science, including comparative, rational choice, institutionalist, and historical approaches to the subject. Most obviously, though, it includes a strong connection with behaviouralism, and it is that connection that we should look at first. Inspired by positivism, and pioneered by the likes of Merriam, Easton, and Dahl, behaviouralism is in reality something of a broad church, and has been defined by some scholars simply in terms of its focus on observable behaviour and its conviction that explanations of that behaviour should be empirically testable.[66] That claim, however, can be misleading, given that its typical focus does diverge somewhat from the concerns of normative behaviourism. Consider here that whilst behavioural political science has, at least historically, tended to move attention away from institutions and towards individual and group behaviour, normative behaviourism keeps institutions front and centre as the key independent variable being investigated (together, of course, with very general policy programmes – liberal or illiberal, egalitarian or inegalitarian, and so on), despite also tracking, as its data, individual and group behaviour – a point which in some ways aligns it with what is often called the post-behaviouralism of the late 1960s and beyond.[67]

But as I say, behaviouralism is at its roots a very broad church, and I would agree with Robert Dahl when he says that, because it established quantitative analysis, the use of empirical data, and hypothesis testing, we are all behaviouralists now.[68] This remark chimes with the position of several other leading figures in political science, including, for example, Samuel Huntington and Arend Lijphart. Huntington, when asked about his methodology, says that he simply looks for empirical generalisations in whatever it is he is looking at, a task that tends to involve, amongst other things, both comparisons and history.[69] Lijphart, in turn, describes his work as an attempt to look for patterns across as much systematic and comparative data as possible.[70] Normative behaviourism is entirely at one with these approaches, given its aim of finding reliable empirical generalisations within rather large patterns of historical and comparative data. To many, of course, this will seem odd, given that behaviouralism has traditionally been seen as a threat to political theory, as a result of its fixation with what can be observed and falsified, and despite the irony that

---

[66] See, for example, G. L. Munck, 'The Past and Present of Comparative Politics', in G. L. Munck and R. Snyder (Eds.), *Passion, Craft, and Method in Comparative Politics* (Baltimore, MD: Johns Hopkins University Press, 2007), 32–62; and D. Sanders, 'Behavioural Analysis', in D. Marsh and G. Stoker (Eds.), *Theory and Methods in Political Science* (London: Palgrave, 2010), 23–41.

[67] Munck, 'The Past and Present of Comparative Politics', 48–49.

[68] R. A. Dahl, 'Normative Theory, Empirical Research, and Democracy', in G. L. Munck and R. Snyder (Eds.), *Passion, Craft, and Method in Comparative Politics*, 124.

[69] S. P. Huntington, 'Order and Conflict in Global Perspective', in G. L. Munck and R. Snyder (Eds.), *Passion, Craft, and Method in Comparative Politics*, 222.

[70] A. Lijphart, 'Political Institutions, Divided Societies, and Consociational Democracy', in G. L. Munck and R. Snyder (Eds.), *Passion, Craft, and Method in Comparative Politics*, 272.

this push for objectivity was to some extent driven by a desire for political science to be more useful to normative political argument, both within and outside of the academy.[71] Normative behaviourism, by contrast, seeks to dissolve both the threat and the irony, given that it attempts to make such objectivity a crucial plank of both normativity and political relevance.

To say, however, that one is adopting a behavioural approach to a certain class of actions – in this case acts of insurrection and crime – is not as yet to specify exactly how one treats the data those actions generate. One could, for example, adopt a comparative, rational-choice, historical, or institutionalist approach to that data, regardless of how the findings of that approach are then converted into a case for why individuals should be convinced by social-liberal-democracy as an answer to OQ. The argument of this book, as is perhaps already clear, shares common ground with all four approaches, and in particular with the first. Normative behaviourism, we can say, is comparative or comparativist just insofar as it compares both insurrection and crime rates in different countries in order to work out the causes of those different rates, and also insofar as it tries to show that political institutions and general policy platforms, and in particular social-liberal-democratic institutions and policy platforms, are the primary cause, if not purely independent variables (for there are always feedback loops), behind the observed variations in those rates.

There is of, course, a live question here regarding the worth of at least some of the studies of these things on which normative behaviourism relies, given debates about the relative strengths of small-N and large-N comparisons. Reliance on a small number of data points – e.g. ten different countries – is often regarded as both the hallmark and the fundamental weakness of comparative politics, though neither point is *necessarily* true.[72] On the one hand, one retains the comparative method

---

[71] For extensive discussion of both this traditional wariness and the noted irony, see the work of John Gunnell, including in particular J. G. Gunnell, *The Descent of Political Theory*, and J. G. Gunnell, *Political Theory and Social Science: Cutting Against the Grain* (London: Palgrave, 2011).

[72] According to David Collier, the comparative method is generally understood in terms of small-N enquiries: D. Collier, 'The Comparative Method', in A. W. Finifter (Ed.), *Political Science: The State of the Discipline II* (Washington DC: American Political Science Association, 1993), 105. But contrast with J. Hopkin, 'The Comparative Method', in D. Marsh and G. Stoker (Eds.), *Theory and Methods in Political Science* (London: Palgrave, 2010), 289; and P. Burnham, K. G. Lutz, W. Grant, and Z Layton-Henry, *Research Methods in Politics* (London: Palgrave, 2008), 69–95. For further discussion of causal conclusions based on small-N comparisons, see S. Lieberson, 'Small N's and Big Conclusions: An Examination of the Reasoning in Comparative Studies Based on a Small Number of Cases', *Social Forces*, 70:2 (1991), 307–320.

whether one is comparing 10 or 10,000 data points, whilst on the other, a small number of countries need not mean low reliability in terms of generalisations, or even, properly speaking, a low number of data points. For example, if one is interested in the presence or absence of civil war, in addition to asking the synchronic question 'which of 100 selected countries currently experience some form of civil war?', one could also ask the diachronic question 'for each of those countries, in which of the past 100 months did civil war occur?'. This would give us 10,000 data points rather than the initial 100, and we would be able to compare all of the country-months in which civil war occurred with each of the country-months in which it did not in order to see which variable or variables lay behind the occurrence of this form of violence.[73] And in turn, rather than testing for a relatively rare class of events, such as coups or revolutionary terrorist attacks, one can also increase the data by subsuming both classes under broader categories such as 'acts of insurrection'.

But still, and as stated on many occasions throughout this book, I am ultimately relying upon, rather than vindicating, these kinds of studies in the course of my argument, and so have no wish to fully wade into the long-standing debate about small-N versus large-N comparisons. There is, though, one further feature of the debate concerning the nature and strength of generalisations in comparative politics that is worth noting here. This feature is the admission that in any realistic study, as noted earlier, one is hoping, again, for probabilistic tendencies rather than iron laws. Talk of 'necessary' and 'sufficient' in comparative politics, as Mahoney and Villegas point out, need not be fully deterministic in order for the induced generalisations to be reliable or useful, and it is easy in many studies, as is standardly the case in statistics, to simply set a quantitative benchmark, such as 'necessary and sufficient 90% of the time'.[74] For example, we can say that smoking makes cancer more likely, even without being able to predict, for any one person, whether or not they'll get cancer from smoking.[75]

One can, of course, always ask if there are further reasons that help to explain why an expected phenomenon does not occur 10 per cent of the time, but even so, given that we are studying human beings capable of everything from suicide bombing in the name of religion to staying at

---

[73] The point that 'comparative historical analysis' can hugely increase the amount of data available to comparativists has also been made by D. Collier, 'The Comparative Method', 105.

[74] See J. Mahoney and C. M. Villegas, 'Historical Enquiry and Comparative Politics', in C. Boix and S. C. Stokes, *The Oxford Handbook of Comparative Politics*, 75.

[75] Diamond and Robinson use this example in J. Diamond and J. A. Robinson, *Natural Experiments of History* (Cambridge, MA: Harvard University Press, 2010), 1–2.

home on election day because of rain, we are still only ever going to
achieve what Stanley Lieberson calls probabilistic rather than deterministic causal propositions.[76] And indeed, there is good reason to think
that such determinism would always be impossible. Just consider, for
example, the fact that, as Lieberson points out, we would not want to
say that a single accident caused by a sober driver disproves the link
between drinking alcohol and dangerous driving.[77] Even if, therefore,
we can say that drinking increases the risk of having an accident, or that
inegalitarian policy platforms increase the chance of each low-income or
unemployed individual committing a criminal act, we will not be able to
say that either pressure is bound to make any one individual produce
either kind of act. What we *will* be able to say, though, is that, over an
entire population, an increase in drinkdriving will produce an increase
in accidents, just as an increase in inequality will produce an increase in
crime – and that is more than enough for normative behaviourism.

A less obvious point of overlap between normative behaviourism and
political science is the world of rational choice theory. This overlap is less
obvious for the simple reason that it is less pronounced. In part, this is
because normative behaviourism owes nothing to any of the theories
actually developed by rational choice scholars in recent decades, such as
the median-voter model, or Anthony Downs' argument regarding how
and when parties move to the centre ground in order to get elected.
But that is not the only reason. There is also a problem of perception.
Consider here one common idea about the difference between behaviouralism and rational choice, which is that whilst the former thinks preferences can be understood by a focus on environmental variables, the latter
takes them as given.[78] This contrast can be misleading given (a) the fact
that we can easily learn preference hierarchies from behavioural observation, and (b) the fact that such learned hierarchies can easily be applied in
any sensible rational choice modelling of a given situation. There is also
the further point that rational choice models only add to our explanatory
grasp of particular behavioural patterns provided that (c) they match for
predictive accuracy whatever set of empirical generalisations we already
have on the topic and (d) they render both more coherent and more
plausible the supposed pattern. In normative behaviourism, for example,
the main reason for turning to the language of incentives and choice
structures employed by rational-choice scholars, in the context of developing a theory of social-liberal-democracy's supposed superior political

---

[76] S. Lieberson, 'Small N's and Big Conclusions', 309.   [77] Ibid., 311.
[78] J. R. Alford and J. R. Hibbing, 'The Origins of Politics: An Evolutionary Theory of
Political Behaviour', *Perspectives on Politics*, 2:4 (2004), 707.

performance, is to increase our confidence in the empirical reality of that superiority (though this is not the only reason – remember that it will also serve to guide our case regarding why particular individuals *should* support social-liberal-democracy).

Consider also some remarks made by Elinor Ostrom on the possibility of combining behavioural work with rational-choice theory. In a discussion of this topic, she makes the point that we need both approaches in order to explain how trust and reciprocity interact in the context of collective action problems.[79] Note, though, that there are in fact two related problems here: (1) What role is played by trust and reciprocity in those situations where collective actions problems have been solved? (2) What role is required of trust and reciprocity in situations where such problems have not been solved? Rational choice theorists are famously better at explaining the second type of situation (why is there is no effective global agreement on reduced carbon emissions?) than they are at explaining the first (why do individuals bother to vote?).

Normative behaviourism, by contrast, has no such difficulties, given what it takes to be the central role played by institutions. That is, institutions help to explain how they are able to trust and reciprocate with each other, and, as a result, how they are able to solve such dilemmas. Institutions, amongst other things, ensure the kind of fairness and connection between effort and reward that makes individual or national sacrifice worthwhile. From the point of view of normative behaviourism, we can say very generally that good political institutions serve to raise the costs of non-cooperation whilst simultaneously increasing the payoff for cooperation. More narrowly, we can say that whilst social-liberal-democratic institutions and policies incentivise peaceful social, economic, and political cooperation, they disincentivise non-cooperative forms of behaviour such as insurrection and crime.

So: is normative behaviourism an institutionalist theory? Or, perhaps more accurately, is it related to what some scholars call the 'new institutionalism'? It is certainly related. Consider here the following pair of remarks by Jack Goldstone, a scholar whose own work on the causes of political instability, together with the work of his fellow contributors at the 'Polity Project', has probably contributed more than any other single source to the empirical side of my case for social-liberal-democracy. He writes that:

[P]eople's behavior is shaped by the institutions under which they live. Good institutions produce good behavior and prosperous societies; bad institutions produce bad behavior and poor societies. Thus the new institutionalists argue

[79] E. Ostrom, *The American Political Science Review*, 92:1 (1998), 1–22.

that changing institutions can, in relatively short order, lead to changes in behaviour – for good or for ill.[80]

And that:

Analyzing failing states, and finding ways to avert failure, thus depends on identifying clusters of institutions and incentives that produce stability, or that undermine stability when they change. The 'tipping' points are not merely shifts in some index – such as employment, or income per capita, or deaths – rather, they are shifts in the perceptions and incentives embodied in institutional arrangements, such that people rather suddenly shift their behavior and allegiances to those institutions. We therefore need to analyze such institutions *as wholes*. When states are failing, lasting stabilization depends on rebuilding institutions in ways that provide lasting incentives for cooperative behavior.[81]

The language used here, of analysing 'clusters of institutions' as 'wholes', and of studying 'lasting incentives for cooperative behaviour', chimes very strongly with my own approach. Treating institutions as independent variables, and different types of behaviour as dependent variables, is as central to this political instability literature as it is to normative behaviourism, which is precisely why I have drawn on it so much in the preceding sections.

It is perhaps more useful to say where my work differs from, if not these studies, then at least institutionalism as a whole. The key point on this front is that whereas many institutionalists would study the internal dynamics of institutions such as the House of Commons or the European Court in order to explain particular political outcomes, my interest is mainly on the effects produced by different institutions as wholes. I am, of course, interested in why different institutions produce different outcomes, in part because I want to be sure that certain noted correlations do involve genuine causation, and in part because I want to know quite how individuals are being incentivised to produce cooperative behaviour, but I am perhaps less interested in these details than I am in the simple facts regarding *which* institutions produce *what* kinds of behaviour.

I am also, as noted, more interested in institutional and policy patterns as wholes, categorised under such broad organising principles as 'democratic', 'liberal', and 'egalitarian', than I am in particular and

---

[80] J. A. Goldstone, 'Pathways to State Failure', *Conflict Management and Peace Science*, 25 (2008). For further examples of this literature, see M. Brinton and V. Nee (Eds.), *The New Institutionalism in Sociology* (Stanford, CA: Stanford University Press, 1998); W. Powell and P. Dimaggio (Eds.), *The New Institutionalism in Organizational Analysis* (Chicago, IL: University of Chicago Press, 1991); and D. C. North, *Institutions, Institutional Change, and Economic Performance* (Cambridge: Cambridge University Press, 1990).

[81] J. A. Goldstone, 'Pathways to State Failure', 25.

distinct institutions and policies. But again, to say that normative behaviourism shares with institutionalism an attention to institutions as causes is *not* to say that it excludes any of the other strains of thought already noted. Contrasts between such things, as has already been noted, often have more to do with matters of emphasis and the particular parts of the causal chain being scrutinised than they do with conflicting epistemological, ontological, or methodological tenets. There should thus be no doubt that normative behaviourism, in addition to borrowing from institutionalism, retains all of the behavioural, comparative, and rational choice flavours already described.

So what about historical approaches to political science? After all, some readers will already have noted here that, apart from anything else, what all of these things share – the comparative, behavioural, rational choice, and institutionalist aspects of normative behaviourism – is an attention to the data produced by political *history*. That attention, however, can be misleading. Although it is as true that, in terms of the nature and amount of data we have to analyse, we are 'at the mercy of history',[82] it is also true that every piece of empirical data ever gathered is, by necessity, already historical. What defines truly historical political science, by contrast, is the fact that, instead of producing wider generalisations, it only seeks to explain particular outcomes.[83]

Or does it? 'Seek', after all is not the same as 'succeed', and we could easily claim here that as soon as historical scholars start to track types of event and types of historical actors, they are right back in the generalisation game, just as we could claim that as soon as they say x caused y, or a produced b and c, they have already implicitly relied on, and perhaps even added support to, generalisations of the form 'x always causes y, all else being equal' or 'a is both a sufficient and necessary cause of both b and c'. Yet that is neither here nor there in this context. Perhaps it would be best to simply say here that as long as historical scholarship confines its attention to specific outcomes, and as long as that work as a whole fails to undermine the kinds of generalisations on which normative behaviourism depends, there is little to connect the two.

Little, but not quite nothing, for there is at least one concept capable of adding some helpful detail to the normative behaviourist framework. This is the concept of a 'critical juncture'. Critical junctures are a certain type of event with long-term consequences, the explanatory function of which is that they capture rather well the ways in which different institutions,

---

[82] A. Przeworski, 'Is the Science of Comparative Politics Possible?', in C. Boix and S. C. Stokes, *The Oxford Handbook of Comparative Politics*, 167.
[83] J. Mahoney and C. M. Villegas, 'Historical Enquiry and Comparative Politics', in C. Boix and S. C. Stokes, *The Oxford Handbook of Comparative Politics*, 74.

ideas, or even whole societies, manage to change direction quite radically in between periods of relative inertia.[84] In the specific context of normative behaviourism, the main value of critical junctures is that they help us to explain the fact that certain political regimes, despite being of a type that has historically tended towards collapse, do nevertheless persist over the short or medium term. As for which of many possible factors – international pressures, abundant natural resources, nuclear weapons, etc. – served to sustain a particular regime over a given period of time, that will, of course, vary from case to case, but that is hardly the point. The point here is that we can recognise that, once a certain opportunity comes along, both the pressure of bad institutions and the appeal of good institutions instantly exert themselves. For example, although we might say that it was the end of the Cold War that caused the apartheid system in South Africa to end *when* it ended, this would not change the fact that it did *ultimately* end simply because it was a regime that was deemed deeply unpalatable by a majority of its adult population.

To say, however, that normative behaviourism enjoys *support* from all of these sub-fields within political science is not to say that it enjoys the unequivocal support of the field as a *whole*. Clearly, some scholars would say that culture matters more than the institutional complex I have described, others that the age of the institutions matters more than their nature, and others still that economic factors trump all such political considerations.

Let's consider, then, first of all, the argument from culture. This argument holds that the survival of liberal-democratic institutions depends crucially on the extent to which a given population adheres to democratic principles, rather than being a simple function of the quality of the institutions involved.[85] One obvious implication of this approach is that it holds institutional approaches to be mistaken in their assumption that political motivations vary only as a response to political institutions.[86] Yet normative behaviourism need not deny the importance of culture in making social-liberal-democracies successful. Instead it points to the evidence gathered earlier regarding the dominant influence of institutional design on individual behaviour and political outcomes, and claims

---

[84] On the importance of 'critical junctures', see ibid., 79–80. The now-classic application of the concept is R. B. Collier and D. Collier, *Shaping the Political Arena: Critical Junctures, the Labour Movement, and Regime Dynamics in Latin America* (Princeton, NJ: Princeton University Press, 1991). For an application of the concept closer to the concerns of normative behaviourism, see D. Acemoglu and J. M. Robinson, *Why Nations Fail*, 432.
[85] C. Welzel and R. Inglehart, 'Mass Beliefs and Democratic Institutions', in C. Boix and S. C. Stokes (Eds.), *The Oxford Handbook of Comparative Politics*, 297.
[86] Ibid., 311.

only that getting the *right* culture is itself a product of *institutional* design. That is, even if social-liberal-democratic success requires the right social-liberal-democratic background culture, it is only a matter of time, provided that one has the right institutions and policies, before that culture develops. There is thus the potential for an historical lag between getting the institutions right and seeing the right behaviour, just as there is the potential, as noted a moment ago in the context of 'critical junctures', for an historical lag between the introduction of bad institutions and the insurrection needed to topple them, even though in both cases it is still, ultimately, the institutions that are producing the observed behaviour.

Normative behaviourism is thus able to accommodate culture as a mechanism between institutions and behaviour, and also as an explanation regarding whatever time delays sometimes occur between the two, without accepting the point that culture is in any sense a rival causal force to institutions. There is also a further point here regarding whether or not culture could ever be normatively relevant, regardless of its causal role. Consider here the classic work of political culture research, Almond and Verba's *The Civic Culture*. This work claims that the right political culture is needed for democracy to be as stable as possible, but then, even if that is true, in what sense would we be able to choose such a culture as part of our answer to OQ? Consider also the facts that (a) non-democracies are hardly preferable to any full democracies, even if some democracies are stronger than others given the strong cultural roots they have been able to put down, and (b) such culture may well *only* be possible as a product of, not just time, but also the right liberal-democratic institutions.[87] All of which means that, even if we need a strong social-liberal-democratic culture in order to produce the lowest levels of insurrection and crime possible under any set of institutions, we still have no choice but to start with social-liberal-democratic institutions.

This takes us up to our second counter-thesis, about which much less has to be said. This thesis chimes with the earlier concession regarding historical lags when it claims that the statistically induced stability of social-liberal-democratic institutions is actually an illusion produced by the fact that so many of the countries with these institutions managed to establish them a long time ago, and under very different conditions. New democracies, proponents of this argument claim, are a different breed

---

[87] Both Mill and Rawls, perhaps the two most influential figures in the history of liberal political philosophy, considered social pluralism and a vibrant civil society the inevitable result of liberal political institutions, though note that whilst Mill celebrated that connection, Rawls worried about its implications for the justification of those very institutions, given the sheer variety of political viewpoints liberal freedoms tend to produce. See J. S. Mill, *On Liberty*, and J. Rawls, *Political Liberalism*.

altogether.[88] But again, normative behaviourism need not deny that newer democracies are likely to be much less stable than older ones, any more than it has to deny the role culture plays in explaining the superiority of those older variants. The point, once more, is simply that we cannot choose, as a society, and thus as part of an answer to OQ, to adopt an 'old democracy', any more than we can choose to have the world's first democracy. This is not, of course, to say that the findings of this literature should be ignored by normative behaviourists any more than they should be ignored by societies at large. If it is true, for example, and as these scholars suggest, that in newer democracies a special effort should be made to involve minorities in the deliberative process, then that effort should certainly be made.[89] Yet even so, the point that it takes civilians in new democracies a long time to come to trust one another, and ultimately 'learn to lose' when that is what happens to their parties in a free and fair election, is not one with any real normative bite.[90] Even if we need to proceed with caution, that is no reason to change direction.

A more troubling counter-thesis, by contrast, is the one that has already been discussed at several points throughout this chapter – the case from economics. Consider here two related and powerful arguments. The first is well expressed by Steven Pincus, who writes that 'Democracy persists only when the state has insufficient resources to survive unless it negotiates with the bourgeoisie and international economic interests.'[91] The second is well expressed by a group of authors led by Paul Collier, who write that 'Countries with low, stagnant, and unequally distributed per capita incomes that have remained dependent on primary commodities for their exports face dangerously high risks of prolonged conflict.'[92] These claims are rather at odds with the more common case, as discussed already, that prosperity is as at least as important as institutions in achieving what normative behaviourism considers good political results (i.e. low insurrection and crime rates). Instead, these authors suggest that you can also have too much wealth, or at least wealth of the wrong sort, and owned by the wrong people.

We might respond to this case in two ways. We could either question the empirical case these authors make or question its normative relevance.

---

[88] See Anderson and Mendes, 'Learning to Lose: Election Outcomes, Democratic Experience and Political Protest Potential', in *British Journal of Political Science* (2006).
[89] Ibid.   [90] Ibid.
[91] S. Pincus, 'Rethinking Revolutions', in C. Boix and S. C. Stokes (Eds.), *The Oxford Handbook of Comparative Politics*, 412.
[92] P. Collier, V. L. Elliott, H. Hegre, A. Hoeffler, M. Reynal-Querol, and N. Sambanis, *Breaking the Conflict Trap: Civil War and Development Policy* (Washington, DC: World Bank and Oxford University Press, 2003), 53–54. See also S. N. Kalyvas, 'Civil Wars', in C. Boix and S. C. Stokes (Eds.), *The Oxford Handbook of Comparative Politics*, 416–434.

It is enough here to adopt the second response, given that it makes the first unnecessary. The key point here, once more, is that, like a strong civic culture, or popular faith in democracy, or old democratic institutions, we just cannot *choose* whether or not to have poor natural resources, any more than we can choose to have economic resources of a kind that the state finds impossible to monopolise. For example, despite the fact that natural resources seem to be a bonus to established social-liberal-democracies (e.g. Norway or the United Kingdom), and despite the fact that we can choose to adopt principles that preclude the monopolising of such resources by any future governments, it is still just as impossible for any pre-existing society to choose to live in a state bereft of oil as it is to live in a land free of mountains, or lakes, or high levels of precipitation.

This does not mean, of course, that we have to deny the point that Przeworski has made on many occasions, and which has already been acknowledged, namely that rising prosperity (from perhaps not too low levels, and of the right uncontrollable kind) within an established democracy tends only to strengthen that democracy. As he writes: 'There is no doubt that the probability that democracy survives increases with per capita income. You can control it for everything from the kitchen sink to the grandmother's attic. That relationship will survive anything. It is monotonic and strong, unbelievably strong. I have no shred of doubt about that.'[93] But again, you cannot choose such prosperity as part of an answer to OQ any more than you can choose the presence or absence of natural resources, and to the extent that you can choose its preconditions, the evidence points squarely in the direction of social-liberal-democratic institutions.

Or, if that is too strong, it is nonetheless true that the debate about which institutions do best in terms of producing economic growth is really a debate between those who defend institutions of this kind and those who, like Przeworski, say we just do not know.[94] And, if that is right – that is, if we really do not know either way about the causes of prosperity – then what possible reason could we have, given the overwhelming evidence we already possess regarding the lower levels of insurrection and crime produced by social-liberal-democracies, for adopting another kind of system? If there is no evidence to suggest that taking another path would make us so rich as to be ambivalent about, for example, living under a dictatorship, then it is unclear what further case we have to answer. Przeworski suggests that the reason democracies become more

[93] A. Przeworski, 'Capitalism, Democracy, and Science', in G. L. Munck and R. Snyder (Eds.), *Passion, Craft, and Method in Comparative Politics* (Baltimore, MD: Johns Hopkins University Press, 2007), 470.
[94] Ibid., 474–475.

stable as they become richer is that people have ever more to lose in the event of revolution, but that only strengthens our argument.[95] Social-liberal-democracies, we can say, are not only more stable and content than any other kind of system, but also only get better and richer the longer they exist, so why choose anything else?

And indeed, why choose anything else given the fact that there is still further though indirect evidence to support our case regarding both the general political stability of social-liberal-democracies, and the claim that they enjoy this stability as a result of doing better at satisfying both the institutional and the personal preferences of their citizens (where institutional preferences are understood as preferences for one or other kind of political system, and personal preferences are understood as preferences regarding the goods and ways of life that system facilitates)? This evidence, although it is not relied on by normative behaviourism, is nonetheless useful given that it both provides extra support for our case for social-liberal-democracy and helps to illuminate some of the many reasons for that system's claimed political success.

Some of this evidence stays fairly close to our two normative behaviourist variables (insurrection and crime) and thus to the evidence on which we have already drawn. For example, when writing about the findings of their well-known civil war dataset, Fearon and Laitin say that 'Our theoretical interpretation is more Hobbesian than economic. Where states are relatively weak and capricious, both fears and opportunities encourage the rise of would-be rulers who supply a rough local justice while arrogating the power to "tax" for themselves and, often, for a larger cause.'[96] In this case, then, although we are only interested in civil war as just one kind of insurrection, and need to be wary of borrowing too much from this particular work given the degree of relevance it does place on economic factors, we can still take support from the general conclusion that the most important factor in triggering a certain kind of conflict is the nature and quality of political rule.

Other kinds of evidence are considerably more removed from the direct concerns of normative behaviourism. We might, for example, point to the fact that democracies are less likely to undertake international wars,[97] the fact that when democracies do experience civil wars those wars involve on average less than half the battle deaths of civil wars

---

[95] Ibid., 471.

[96] For a recent discussion of these trends in the nature and causes of civil wars, see S. Pinker, *The Better Angels of Our Nature*, 297–319.

[97] This is the much contested claim at the heart of 'democratic peace theory'. For a useful discussion, see N. P. Gleditsch and H. Hegre, 'Peace and Democracy: Three Levels of Analysis', *The Journal of Conflict Resolution*, 41:2 (1997), 283–310.

in non-democracies,[98] and even the fact that liberal-democracies are less likely to involve famines.[99] All such trends chime strongly with our running argument here which holds that democracies are not just preferred by their citizens to the alternatives, but also preferred, in part, as a result of the fact that that system actually and intentionally tracks both the political and non-political preferences of those citizens.

All of which leaves with just one last body of evidence worth considering. This evidence is made up of a number of studies, the common element of which is that they provide support for several of our causal political claims by drawing on evolutionary theory. In general, what drives these studies is the hope or belief that political preferences are at least partly shaped by evolutionary forces and thus genetic heritage.[100] Such theory, it has been claimed, has the potential to unite the social sciences, though we are not interested here in those kinds of ambitions.[101] Instead, we need to look more closely at how this theory binds together, and especially at how one particular variant of the theory – dubbed 'wary cooperation' – could give further support to the normative behaviourist argument in favour of social-liberal-democracies that we have been developing all this time.

This variant, developed by Alford and Hibbing, draws on established evolutionary theory in order to generate a very general political prediction that, despite the problems posed by insecurity and collective actions in a state of nature, human beings will be both politically cooperative and at the same time highly intolerant of traitors and free riders.[102] This intolerance is in some ways especially important, according to these authors, who write that 'the existence of political institutions may in large part be attributed to people's intense desire for sanctions to be brought against noncooperators'.[103] This argument resonates at both a general and a particular level with normative behaviourism. It resonates at a very general level with the institutionalist side of our case, when Alford and Hibbing claim that the theory predicts and is thus supported by a very general trend we see in the world, namely, that human beings exhibit different behaviour under different political systems.[104] Yet that, as it

---

[98] B. Lacina, 'Explaining the Severity of Civil Wars', *Journal of Conflict Resolution*, 50 (2006), 276–289. See also Gleditsch, who writes that democracies only 'rarely experience large-scale civil wars', in N. P. Gleditsch, 'The Liberal Moment Fifteen Years On', *International Studies Quarterly*, 52 (2008), 691–712. For an even more recent discussion of these trends in the nature and causes of civil wars, see S. Pinker, *The Better Angels of Our Nature*, 297–319.

[99] A. Sen, 'Democracy as a Universal Value', *Journal of Democracy* 10:3 (1999), 3–17.

[100] J. R. Alford and J. R Hibbing, 'The Origins of Politics: An Evolutionary Theory of Political Behaviour', *Perspectives on Politics*, 2:4 (2004), 707.

[101] Ibid., 707.   [102] Ibid., 708.   [103] Ibid., 712.   [104] Ibid.

turns out, is not the most interesting connection. As far as we are concerned, the more interesting possibility, which Alford and Hibbing do not consider, is that this theory also seems to imply a particular prediction that human beings would have a preference for both order in general and egalitarian orders in particular given that only under such conditions would the number of people both exploiting and being exploited by the system be minimised – a preference which, again, we can also claim to already observe independently of the theory.

So, if behavioural observation is already able to tell us just which political-environmental factors generate what kinds of behaviour, then perhaps evolutionary theory can provide support for the credibility of those observations and the generalisations we make from them by telling us just why we would have the preferences required to drive that behaviour. Consider here Jon Elster's point that a theory can get support from above or below.[105] If it seems as though certain political environments cause certain kinds of dissatisfaction, as expressed by certain kinds of behaviour, then we can be all the more sure of those causal connections not just (1) if we can provide a theory based in what we know of contemporary human nature that chimes with that behaviour (as we have already done), but also (2) if we can draw on yet a further body of evidence to suggest that that theory, rather than being some culturally biased misunderstanding, is in fact just what we would expect given the dynamics of human evolution. Or, in short, the more bits of theory and bodies of evidence we can tie together into one overarching argument, the stronger that argument becomes.

We do need to be cautious here, however, and remember that we are not fundamentally relying upon this theory as part of our overall case in the sense that if the former was falsified, so would the latter. All we are really relying upon in *that* sense is the claim that different kinds of political system produce different patterns of insurrection and crime to the degree described earlier. We also need to be cautious here given both further arguments presented by Alford and Hibbing and arguments raised against their entire project. As regards the first, it is worth noting here that a further part of their theory is that different individuals will have different political preferences from each other as a result of possessing different genes.[106] Yet this is not *quite* as troubling an idea as it might

---

[105] J. Elster, *Explaining Social Behaviour: More Nuts and Bolts for the Social Sciences* (Cambridge: Cambridge University Press, 2007), esp. 18–19.
[106] See J. Alford, C. Funk, and J. R. Hibbing, 'Are Political Orientations Genetically Transmitted?', *American Political Science Review*, 99:2 (2005), 153–167. It is worth noting that Alford and his colleagues only say that particular combinations of genes make certain behaviours more likely, not inevitable (163).

seem. All I really need to claim is that the preferences of such individuals are uniform or mostly uniform regarding some of the biggest political issues, such as the choice of political system, and the overall egalitarian/inegalitarian character of both that system and the policies it deploys. And indeed, we might also consider the fact that many genes require certain environmental triggers in order to produce particular behaviours, which means that the variables of how and where one is raised are still likely to play a key role in explaining different preferences in much the same way as has always been assumed to be the case.

A more worrying set of issues is raised by Evan Charney, who questions the whole project of trying to work out how different political ideologies, let alone just one ideology, could be inherited.[107] The heart of Charney's argument involves pointing out just how hopeless the idea is that our ancestors could have had, say, 'liberal genes', given (1) that there was no discussion of such ideas when they were alive, and (2) given that there would have been no political problems or institutions, and probably no social or economic problems or institutions, of the kind needed to trigger one. Instead, he claims, our ideals have evolved historically, through ideas designed to address a sequence of historically specific situations. Why, though, couldn't a very general idea or inclination, such as 'wary coopera- tion', survive down the ages either in terms of being always present, or at least in the sense that it would always manifest itself given the right political conditions (which in turn might only present themselves subject to the right level of technological or agricultural or economic advance- ment, or perhaps simply when population density and thus human inter- action crosses a certain threshold)?

For example, if a child in 1980 complains that he is treated unfairly because his sibling has a Rubik's Cube whilst he does not, and a child in 2000 complains that she is unloved because her sibling has a Buzz Lightyear whilst she does not, do we really want to say that nothing connects the two claims? Of course we can laugh at the idea that there is a genotype for wanting a Rubik's Cube or a Buzz Lightyear, but such events need not be categorised so specifically, and it is not hard to see how there could be some sort of a covering ideal type, i.e. 'don't give one child more than another without a reason they could come to accept'. Nor is it hard to see that their complaint could be understood as invoking a principle of roughly this sort. And indeed, nor is it hard to see that if they simply said nothing, but just threw themselves on the floor and held their breath, then that could also be treated as an action expressing just such a principle (of a sort, we might then say, for further support, that they

---

[107] E. Charney, 'Genes and Ideologies', *Perspectives on Politics*, 6:2 (2008), 299–319.

have articulated in the past, or perhaps that others have articulated in highly similar situations, or of a sort that we can work out by looking at the precise conditions under which such tantrums do and do not occur).

As I say though, we are not *relying* on this connection between evolutionary theory and political behaviour in the course of the normative behaviourist case for social-liberal-democracy presented in this book. It is enough for now to simply note how that theory might provide extra support, not just for normative behaviourism in general – via the idea that human beings might well have evolved to hold reliable and regular preferences for certain kinds of political kinds of institution – but also for the case for social-liberal-democracy in particular – via (1) the possibility that those preferences, which could be independently though perhaps imperfectly observed, might pick out social-liberal-democratic institutions as an optimal choice, and (2) the possibility that some particular evolutionary theory of political behaviour, such as 'wary cooperation', somehow manages to roughly predict those preferences directly.

We are almost at the end of our detour, with just one final issue to consider: the issue of whether we could go even further than the case for social-liberal-democracy developed so far. That is, rather than worry about whether there is enough evidence in contemporary political science to support the claims already made about the levels of insurrection and crime and produced by social-liberal-democracies, perhaps we should be worrying about whether we can pick out even more specific institutions and policies from within this very broad ideal. Two debates in particular are worth looking at here: The debate about presidentialism versus parliamentarism and the debate about proportional representation versus majoritarianism.

As regards the first of these two, presidentialism seems to collapse more than parliamentarism in a mild way, meaning that although there is a slightly stronger tendency for *governments* in that system to fail, the *system* as a whole is no more likely to fall than a parliamentary order.[108] This, unfortunately, does not tell us very much, given that we are only interested in either complete political collapse, understood as a function of insurrection, or unsuccessful efforts to achieve the same end. And indeed, who is to say that systems in which governments last longer are really doing better in terms of satisfying their citizens? It might just be that the institutional set-up is unduly biased towards the status quo. The key

---

[108] See D. Samuels, 'Separation of Powers', in C. Boix and S. C. Stokes, *The Oxford Handbook of Comparative Politics*, 703–726. It is probably fair to say that there is a tendency within the literature to prefer parliamentary systems, even if the evidence remains unclear as to how the two systems differ in the presence of other variables, and even if that preference has itself little to do with the concerns of normative behaviourism.

point is that, if they really doing much better or worse, we would expect to see that played out in the insurrection and crime statistics. For now, though, there is little to choose between these two variants on liberal democracy from the point of view of normative behaviourism.

So how about proportional representation versus majoritarianism? As with the presidentialism/parliamentarism debate, there are many arguments here, and we shall have to confine ourselves to those which bear on the concerns of normative behaviourism. Of these, perhaps the most interesting is a case to the effect that proportional systems tend to be dominated by centre-left governments, whilst majoritarian systems tend to be dominated by centre-right ones, the upshot of which is that the former tend to redistribute more.[109] This trend, if reliable, would certainly be relevant, given that it suggests an institutional and not merely ideological basis to a given state's position on the egalitarian/inegalitarian spectrum. We would be able to say, that is, not just that societies should adopt a social-liberal-democratic answer to OQ, with that answer then interpreted on the ground as faithfully as possible in the light of whatever constraints and empirical information are to hand, but also that they should adopt, in particular, a liberal democracy based on proportional representation as an explicit part of that interpretation.

But we should not get carried away here, in part because studies of this kind are relatively young and thin on the ground – and thus less reliable than much of the insurrection and crime literature relied on previously – but also because, at least in this case, they imply no real change to the social-liberal-democratic answer to OQ already developed. Certainly there is good reason to do more work on this front with the concerns of normative behaviourism in mind, just as there is good reason to look at similar arguments, such as the claim that proportional systems are less socially divisive,[110] and thus potentially less insurrection and crime-generating than their alternatives, but for now that is all it is – a good reason for more work. For now it is enough to console ourselves with the answer we already have, together with the political science we have already used. Further studies, just like the extra data they will have to rely on, are matters for the future, not the present.

---

[109] See, for example, T. Iversen and D. Soskice, 'Electoral Institutions, Parties, and the Politics of Class: Explaining the Formation of Redistributive Coalitions', in P. Beramendi and C. J. Anderson (Eds.), *Democracy, Inequality, and Representation* (New York: Russell Sage Foundation, 2008), 93–126.

[110] See A. Lijphart, 'Political Institutions, Divided Societies, and Consociational Democracy', in G. L. Munck and R. Snyder (Eds.), *Passion, Craft, and Method in Comparative Politics*, 271; and L. Diamond, *Developing Democracy: Towards Consolidation* (Baltimore, MD: Johns Hopkins University Press, 1999).

3.8   Reasons to Be Convinced by Social-Liberal-Democracy

We are looking, remember, for a convincing and meaningful answer to OQ, which means an answer that is not just politically determinate in terms of its principles and institutions, but also rationally compelling to those individuals who would have to live with it. In one sense, this is a problem that takes us from the perspective of the political philosopher to the perspectives of different individuals and social groups. It is also a problem that requires me to emphasise once again the claim that I am not, contrary to what some might suspect, working with the assumption that if one could but find that political system capable of satisfying the highest number of people in one society, then that would, *ipso facto*, be the system for them to adopt. Clearly, if I were to make that assumption I would be in grave trouble, and not just because I would have slipped into utilitarian terrain, but also because I would have placed myself firmly, though blindly, on planet mentalism.

Happily enough, we can now present four new arguments for why a range of different individuals should be convinced by social-liberal-democracy as an answer to OQ, and thus avoid the kind of mentalism with which some readers will have already thought me flirting. Remember, though, that we have *already seen* that most people do, in practice, prefer social-liberal-democracy to its alternatives. Yet we want to convince *as many people as possible*. As a result, what we are trying to do here is find *yet further reasons* for those people we still expect to remain unpersuaded of social-liberal-democracy's merits, as explained so far.

Now, as noted earlier, the best way of conceiving of these further individuals is to organise them into two groups – the rich and the radical – neither of which is necessarily exclusive of the other, even if in practice almost nobody is a member of both – such are the beasts we live with. Our task with these groups, as explained, is to find extra ways of persuading them in terms of motivations that at least some of their members can already be expected to hold. As a result, our task is to show that these people should be convinced by social-liberal-democracy as an answer to OQ, by combining such motivations with either points we have already noted about the described political system and its products, or new points that could be deduced from the old.

The first of these arguments is of particular relevance to the rich, given that the more you have, the more you have to lose. It says that, if you care about your security, then you should be attracted to social-liberal-democracy, given that this is the political system best able to provide it. This is an openly Hobbesian case. If what you want is a state capable of keeping you safe from violent conflict, then surely you want whatever state is going to breed the least amount of crime and rebellion. You want to inhabit a type of state which, in addition to being perfectly bearable in every other way, is also able to guarantee your personal safety to a greater degree than any other tried and tested political possibility. Although it might tax you, although it might tell you to keep your hedges trimmed below a certain level, although you might not agree with this or that aspect of its constitution and these or those of its current policies, you do at least know that you will be safer in this state than in any other. And, in turn, because you know that you live in an interdependent world in which pretty much every individual is capable, should they wish it, of killing any other individual (a condition we might call *Hobbesian equality*), you also know that a state capable of easing your vulnerability, *as well as* the vulnerability of your friends and family, would be very much in your interest. So, because your survival, as well as the survival of your nearest and dearest, matters to you, the type of state most capable of guaranteeing it is a very attractive and, for many, convincing proposition.

This takes us to our second argument, and a case that appeals more to the idealistic than the privileged. This argument claims that if you, like Richard Rorty (see **1.12**), want to prioritise the avoidance of cruelty, then surely you want to support that state which produces, directly and indirectly, and by both acts and omissions, the least cruelty, where cruelty is very broadly understood to mean anything (a) that one person or group causes to happen to another person or group, and (b) which we know from observation would cause anyone to suffer. This argument, we might say, appeals to the better angels of our nature, though that does not mean anybody who simply 'wants to be good' should be convinced by it – for if we were to say that, then that would change radically the meanings of 'should' and 'convince' we have been employing to date. We are not practising covert mentalism here, and saying that, if everyone consults their normative thoughts, then they will realise that they are committed to a particular idea of 'being good', and this is what it entails in practice. The fact remains that arguments are only convincing to people if they draw on motivations they already have, which means that this argument, like the one before it, will never convince everyone. But this, again, is fine. All that matters is that we have a reason capable of persuading yet another part of the population, however small, of the wisdom of social-liberal-democracy as an answer to OQ.

Now we come to our third argument, which runs as follows: if what you want is to see people flourish, then surely what you want is that system in which as many people as possible live what are, for them, meaningful lives. As a result, because normative behaviourist political philosophy tells us that this system is social-liberal-democracy, that is the system you should support. And note, flourishing is not just something you simply want other people to experience, just as cruelty is not just something you want others to avoid, for it is also something you are likely to want for yourself. This is important, and it connects to one of the key conclusions to be drawn from recent work on the connections between egalitarian politics and individual well-being – the conclusion that all individuals, regardless of circumstance, are likely to do better by their own lights under social-liberal-democratic systems. Or, as one reviewer writes: '[the] rational conclusion to be drawn from the mass of evidence ... assembled is that all of us, irrespective of income, have much to gain from the creation of a more equal society'.[111] Of course, 'all of us' is a little strong, which is why the clause 'likely' in my own rendering of the point is so important. We have to remember here that, in this section, our concern is primarily with those who, due to either well-heeled personal circumstances or ideals that differ radically from those achieved by social-liberal-democracy, fail to be convinced by the mere fact that most people will do better under that system than others, as demonstrated by that system's historical record of encountering minimal expressions of dissatisfaction. This argument, then, such as it is, will again only convince a fraction of the population. It will convince those who want to see others flourish, as well as those whose flourishing requires the presence of a particular kind of politics.

All of which takes us to our fourth argument, which revisits the idea of behaviourist reasonableness originally used earlier on this chapter as a 'pointer' towards how we might move, in very general terms, from the facts of political history to the principles of political philosophy. In this context I have a narrower idea in mind. Here the claim is that those who care about achieving and maintaining a political system which no person could reasonably reject have themselves every reason to support social-liberal-democracy. This reason stems from the fact that we know, from our analysis of history, that fewer people find social-liberal-democracy *unbearable* than any other attempted system. A reasonable objection here, as we said earlier on, is an objection against a system that we know from history has been found unbearable by many different people. Reasonable objections are thus contrasted with idiosyncratic ones, with history providing the means for differentiating one from the other. This means that regardless of anybody else's motivation, and regardless of whether they would describe their own concern as a kind of fairness, or even as an expression of Rawls' principle of 'liberal legitimacy', for those individuals

[111] R. Hattersley, 'Review of the Spirit Level: Why More Equal Societies Almost Always Do Better', *The New Statesman*, 26 March 2009.

who *are* motivated by this concern, social-liberal-democracy is clearly the most convincing answer to OQ available.

Consider here that if it *is* the case that, whenever a certain political system is established, a large section of the population turns to crime, it can hardly be said that their behaviour is unreasonable, for it would always be the case that those who do not commit the crime, had they been born in the same social circumstances as the criminals, would very likely do much the same thing. If the difference between two political systems is that, in one, 0.5 per cent of the populations turn to crime and, in another, 20 per cent does, we cannot say that, in both cases, the causes are genetic (or at least purely genetic, in the unlikely event that only some part of the population, and perhaps exactly 20 per cent, are capable of such action in any circumstances). Clearly the real difference is that the latter set of institutions and policies provides fewer incentives for peaceful, law-abiding social cooperation. Clearly the latter system is one to which, because it provides demonstrably sub-standard well-being to so many people, we can reasonably object. If, then, what liberals want is legitimacy born of an absence of reasonable objections, they should turn to normative behaviourism, because only by looking at patterns of behaviour will they be able to distinguish between all the various demands made by both citizens and philosophers alike.

Some readers, however, will think that the justificatory waters are now very murky indeed. Having said throughout this book that I am after a convincing and meaningful answer to OQ, it is perhaps no longer clear just what I mean by such a thing, or indeed just how normative behaviourism is able to deliver one. I have, after all, listed a great many things that might be taken as reasons to be convinced by social-liberal-democracy as an answer to OQ. Earlier on in this chapter, having already noted that social-liberal-democracy is the political system that breeds the least amount of dissatisfaction amongst its citizens, I set out some of the factors that I took to explain that success. These factors were features of social-liberal-democracy which, in virtue of either their existence or their products, gave individuals good *reason* to support that regime. But then, surely if these are the principal causes behind the fact that individuals *are already* satisfied by social-liberal-democracy, they must also be the principal reasons for why they would be convinced by it as answer to OQ. After all, what further proof could we need that something is capable of motivating people to support a given answer to OQ than the fact that it is, in behavioural terms, *already* doing so? To deny such capability, it seems, would be deeply illogical, given that it appears to deny that we can move, not from 'is' to 'ought', or indeed from 'ought' to 'can', but rather from 'has done' to 'can do'.

But we are not denying any such thing. There are two things to appreciate here. First off, for an individual to be convinced by a given answer to OQ, it need not be true that he or she is convinced for just one reason. He or she will often have several reasons for being convinced, all of which might be necessary for him or her, even if not one of them is sufficient by itself. Second, for an individual to be convinced by a given combination of reasons, it need not be the case that all other individuals are convinced by the same combination. And indeed, just because two or more individuals are convinced by the same answer to OQ, it need not follow that they share even one reason for that common conviction.

Taken together, these points mean that we can now clarify quite easily the relationship between the various claims made in this chapter as to why individuals are or should be convinced by social-liberal-democracy as an answer to OQ. Different factors motivate different people, which means that the more reasons we can provide in favour of a given system, the more chance that system has of being rationally convincing to all those who would have to live with it. Explanations of why people *already* support social-liberal-democracy, and new reasons for why they *should* support it, are complementary when it comes to the task of providing an answer to OQ that is rationally compelling to all those who have to live with it. Whilst some will be convinced by social-liberal-democracy on account of its provision of opportunities for all, others will be more motivated by its alleviation of the condition of the worst off. Whilst some will be persuaded by that system's provision of various liberties, still others will be attracted to the peaceful way in which it democratically manages transitions between different political elites. And indeed, remember that normative behaviourism tracks not just the opinion people have of those institutions which together make up their political system, but also the opinion they have of the ways of life those institutions permit and facilitate. This means, for example, that although particular individuals might consider social-liberal-democracy's liberal pedigree vital to their own way of life, perhaps because they are of some minority sexual or religious persuasion, they might still *not* be convinced by that system were it not for the fact that it also gave them their best opportunity of being, say, a television talk-show host, or professional tennis player, and so on.

So: explanation, theory, justification, reason, and persuasion – it all points in the same direction. Everything we can say in favour of social-liberal democracy serves both (1) to explain its behavioural success and reassure us of the reality of the trends we (think we) observe, whilst also (2) providing reasons for real individuals today, with particular ideologies, and particular vested interests, to support it as a political system, whether it's already their status quo or something into which their current political system could be transformed. We could, of course, just say to people, 'look, you already prefer this system, whether you realise it or not, because if you lived 1,000 lives in each of 1,000 systems, this is the one your behaviour would pick out as the best', but we don't have to leave it at that. We can also say, more elaborately, 'look, you are likely to prefer this system in practice, right now, to its alternatives, given that it delivers A, B, C, D, and so on, all of which you are likely to care about, and we know that you are likely to care about them given the way, in general, human beings (like you) behave'. That is what we are trying to do here.

Nevertheless, there is still good reason for differentiating between the new reasons introduced in this section and those implied by the theory of the earlier sections, which is that even if most people are already satisfied by social-liberal-democracy for the reasons captured by that theory, there will still be some who, either out of riches or radicalism, remain unconvinced. The hope here has been that, for those unconvinced by various features of social-liberal-democracy's social, liberal, and democratic aspects, these further reasons might just tip the balance. They will be convinced, perhaps, on grounds of security, on account of the fact that social-liberal-democracy is that system in which they are least likely to be harmed or killed. Or they will be convinced out of compassion, on the grounds that social-liberal-democracy is that political system in which the least cruelty and suffering occurs. Or they will be convinced out of a desire to see others flourish, on the grounds that social-liberal-democracy is the system in which that will happen for the maximum number of people. Or they will be convinced out of an ideal of reasonableness, on the basis that social-liberal-democracy is the political system for which people have the least grounds for rejection.

But then, even if we add these reasons to the mix, is it not naive to say that *all* will be convinced by social-liberal-democracy as an answer to OQ? This is where we need to make an important distinction between 'will be convinced by' and 'should be convinced by', even if that distinction is not of the kind usually employed in mentalist political philosophy. This distinction makes use of a very rational, self-interested 'should'. Consider here that even if you do not care about liberal legitimacy, or the avoidance of suffering, or the maximisation of flourishing, you really should care about the first reason mentioned in this section – security – because you should care about your own survival.

Whoever you are – be you beggar or queen – you are vulnerable, and, because you are vulnerable, it is in your interest to live in that state most capable of ensuring your safety. As a result, it is in your interest to recognise that the requirements of survival are numerous. If you are poor, for example, then social-liberal-democracy will feed, clothe, and house you. Or, if we forget about the poor, who already, and most obviously, have so much to gain from this system, then think only of the richest and most powerful. Consider here that if you are a leader of thugs, or a dictator, or even a queen, then a social-liberal-democratic state, unlike whatever state you currently inhabit, will keep you safe, or at least safer, throughout your life. It will not totter, collapse, and lead to a dangerous environment. It will not, if you are a good citizen, hang you from a lamppost, or have you shot for crimes against humanity. Or, more prosaically, if you are a business owner, and perhaps of a broadly libertarian mind-set, the fact remains that if you live in a social-liberal-democracy, you will be safer from crime than in a libertarian utopia. Although it will rankle with you, because your taxes are pooled with the taxes of others in the common cause of social justice, that revenue will serve to reduce what would otherwise be widely held motivations to vandalise, rob, hijack, rape, and murder either you or those you care about.

Now, of course, this last character, the libertarian, might say – as indeed might a communitarian, or more radical egalitarian – that this is not *my morality*. He or she will say, 'I do not think theft fair; I do not think tax fair; I do not think this state fair.' And, in a very deep sense, this is, of course, a matter for *their* judgement. If they prefer libertarian anarchy to the safety of social-liberal-democracy then that is, when all has been said and done, *their* preference. We can, however, still say to them the following things. First: what *you* think is fair is not what *all* people consider fair. Or, more generally put, what you take to be universal morality is in fact something else: it is particular, partial, partisan, and personal, as discussed over the course of Chapters 1 and 2. There is also a good chance that the things you consider *moral truths* fail to cohere with each other. But again, this may still not convince you, which is why it becomes so important for you to recognise that, just as you cannot fall back on mentalist strategies to rationally ground your position, you have no good reason to expect others – including poor, desperate, uneducated, predated-upon and badly raised others – to adopt it themselves.

If it is really not enough that social-liberal-democracy provides other people with meaningful options in life; if it is not enough that it saves them from horrors; if it is not even enough that it gives *you* your best chance of survival, there is little more that can be said. Clearly, you want to gamble, but, if that is so, you should also realise this: that you cannot come running when you have been harmed. You cannot come running because you cannot complain, and you cannot complain not just because you cannot say that you would never have done what *they* did had *you* been born in their shoes, and not just because such things will be always be more likely under non-social-liberal-democratic regime types, but also because if you are harmed under such a regime, and if that harm is of a kind that is made more likely by that regime (as opposed, say, to an outraged spouse who just discovered your affair), there is simply no rational argument available that would entail that your assailant should be content with the life their political regime has offered them.

So, whilst most people will be convinced by social-liberal-democracy on account of those reasons produced by the theory that sought to explain that system's success, and whilst still others will be convinced by the four new reasons listed, there will always be some for whom social-liberal-democracy is just too unattractive. For this remainder, the ultimate point is that if they do not care that their own preferred system is or will be unbearable for many people, and if they do not care that their own system cannot possibly convince those same people, then they cannot complain either if social-liberal-democracy is forced upon them or if they come to harm as a result of getting their own way.

They might however be tempted if, for whatever reason, they already have some kind of a desire to find and then support a convincing answer to OQ! Perhaps they are even reading this book in order to find one. If so, they should see that social-liberal-democracy is *that* answer because, on the one hand, it provides good things for everyone and a better life for many than they would have under any other system, and on the other hand, mentalist justification simply does not work.

Yet this is *still* not all we can say here, at least as regards the contrast between mentalist and behaviourist political philosophy. Consider finally that, when we initially contrasted the two, we noted that whilst the former looks for patterns in our thoughts, the latter looks for patterns in our actions. At this stage of the argument, we should note that very few mentalists, as a matter of fact, ever pause to worry about why we should be *motivated* by the normative preferences uncovered by their enquiries if our own pre-existing interests point in a different direction, even assuming that those preferences were consistent and coherent in the required fashion. As a result, in order to do *better* than mentalist political philosophy, we could simply have left the matter where it stood earlier on in the chapter, and not worried at all about what is often called the problem of 'moral motivation'. After all, if it is fine to ground political principles in normative thoughts that we believed to be held without contradiction by the vast majority of individuals, then why not in expressed political preferences held by a similar percentage?

Unfortunately, even if this was 'fine' for some, it would still be philosophically and politically unsatisfying. Part of the point of this book, once more, is to convince as many people as possible of a single answer to OQ, which means initially looking to see what *already convinces*. We then tried to see what else could be said in favour of this system to convert the unpersuaded remainder. And then, finally, we said that to those who are still not persuaded, you really *should* be, not just because it is in your interest, or because a commitment to having a convincing answer means a commitment to adopting that answer which convinces the most people, but also because if you are harmed as a result of getting your way, you have no mentalist, or what you would probably call moral, comeback. Beyond that however, for the unconvinced, there is nothing left to say.

3.9   Normative Behaviourism Defended against Five Objections

We come, then, to the final part of this chapter. The intention here is to defend both normative behaviourism and its application in favour of social-liberal-democracy by arguing against those objections it is most likely to encounter. Although Mill was wrong about the mentalist version of this kind of argument, he remains right in general that, in normative matters, you cannot successfully make your case without anticipating and responding to the objections of others.[112]

Objection 1: It is not clear what you are doing. Are you justifying social-liberal-democracy? If so, surely that justification is grounded, tacitly, in some further principle. But then if that is true, are you not as a result just doing sub-standard mentalist political philosophy, i.e. extrapolating higher principles from lower thoughts or principles without any argument in favour of those thoughts or principles, or indeed even any mention of them?

It was, I think, Bertrand Russell – Mill's Godson – who remarked somewhere that the deepest convictions of philosophers are seldom contained in their formal arguments: fundamental beliefs, comprehensive views of life, are like citadels which must be guarded against the enemy.[113]

There are many ways of responding to this objection, several of which have already been spelled out. Perhaps a good starting place would be to repeat the simple observation that human beings are animals that (not *who*) exhibit observable patterns of regular behaviour. That is, they exhibit identifiable, perennial tendencies, and not just as individuals, but also

---

[112] Mill puts the point as follows: 'when we turn to subjects infinitely more complicated, to morals, religion, politics, social relations, and the business of life, three-fourths of the arguments for every disputed opinion consist in dispelling the appearances which favour some opinion different from it'. J. S. Mill, *On Liberty*, 98.

[113] I. Berlin, *Four Essays on Liberty* (Oxford: Oxford University Press, 1969), 200.

as groups. Consider here that one of the key claims of this chapter has been that, amongst these tendencies, one of the most important, politically speaking, is the exhibited preference for social-liberal-democracy. So far so clear – but also so *empirical*, given that these are all, apparently, purely factual claims, with little hint so far as to how they can lead into the land of normativity. This is what many readers will still be puzzling over. They will say, even if we accept these few claims for argument's sake, what we would like to know is: (1) even if most people do prefer social-liberal-democracy in practice, why *should* they do so? and (2) why should people who do *not* currently prefer it *change* their mind about that preference?

Let's address these questions one at a time. As regards the first, which inquires as to whether people *should* support social-liberal-democracy, it will often be enough to say simply that many people just *do* prefer it, just as they prefer eating chocolate to eating coal – though this point does have one important caveat. This caveat is that when we say that the vast majority of people prefer social-liberal-democracy, what we really mean is that the reactions people give to different regime types, including social-liberal-democracy, demonstrate indirectly that the latter is the preferred political system. We have to remember that the vast majority of people *have not had the chance* to experience several different political systems for a sustained period of time, which means that our expressed preferences, such as they are, are being extrapolated from the different experiences of different people, not from the similar experiences of everyone. Yet this should not be taken as a weakness of the finding or its connected argument, given that we can say to the vast majority of people that *had they had the chance* to experience multiple political systems, social-liberal-democracy would be their preference. And note: the fact that there *are* these strong trends across time, place, and culture, as discovered by the various studies covered in this chapter, shows that this assumption of equivalence across different individuals and populations – that you would probably have felt and acted in the same way as X, had you been in born in X's shoes – is a safe one to make.

But that is still not enough. We still have to provide something extra than that which is provided by the language of 'most', 'majority', and 'would', given that there might still be some for whom it will simply *not* be true that, had they experienced all the many different political systems experimented with in political history, social-liberal-democracy would be their preference. This is why I have tried to show that, *almost* regardless of their ideals and social position, these individuals still have sufficient reason to change their mind, and thus really *should* be convinced, given a number of motivations they are highly likely to already possess. These motivations include the desire for personal security and the security of one's friends and family; the desire to live in a political order to which nobody can reasonably object; the desire to live in a political order which provides extensive opportunities for others to flourish; and the desire to live in a political order in which the least amount of cruelty and suffering occur.

And, on top of these motivations, we also noted a few further points. These points all connect to the fact that successful mentalist arguments in favour of any meaningful and thus distinctive answer to OQ are unavailable. The first of these points, simply enough, is that at least one reason for supporting political systems *other* than social-liberal-democracy is *gone*, given that mentalist justification for such systems is impossible. The second is that, given the failure of mentalism, any individual possessed of a desire to live in accordance with the most convincing answer to OQ available (a desire that is close but not identical to the desire to live under a system to which a minimum number of people would object) should now be persuaded of the superiority of social-liberal-democracy. The third is that you cannot complain with quite the indignation you might assume if you are robbed or harmed under alternative political systems, given that (a) you cannot be sure that you would not have done the same thing had you been born in your assailant's shoes, and (b) there is no mentalist argument available to you that involves the claim 'you have violated the rules of a just system'. This is not, of course, to suggest that murder or even theft is 'right', or 'permissible', or even that its 'wrongness' is not one of the few things that mentalist argument *could* successfully prove – the point is simply that at least one instinctive and common line of complaint is completely unavailable.

This argument also reinforces itself in at least three parallel aspects. First, as a matter of logic, the more people who are convinced by our recommended answer to OQ, the fewer people there are to object to it, and thus the more reasonable and convincing that system becomes to those who desire a reasonable and convincing system (some of whom will then promptly move from the camp of objectors to the camp of the convinced, and thus perpetuate yet further that same dynamic). Second, as more people are convinced by this system, fewer individuals have sufficient motivation to engage in acts of violent non-co-operation. This means that the level of security provided by the system is improved, and thus in turn the ability of the system to motivate people already possessed of the desire for such security. Third, as the number of people convinced by the system increases, so will the number of people capable of living flourishing lives within it increase, if only because some individuals are no longer likely to live out unfulfilling lives as a result of their efforts to fundamentally change the status quo. We have then not just a number of reasons capable of convincing a number of different people, but also a number of reasons which, the more they succeed in convincing people, the more convincing the system becomes to those who are as yet unconvinced.

The nature and content of this argument should, I think, be perfectly clear by now, if not perfectly convincing. It might, though, become just a little bit more convincing with just a little bit more clarification. This is why we should point out at least one further upshot of our case: that it is perfectly possible for the number of people who describe social-liberal-democracy as their first-choice system to decrease just as the number of people who *should* be convinced by it increases. Consider the following dynamic: (1) As social-liberal-democracy convinces more and more societies living under alternative regimes to adopt its principles, the more social-liberal-democracies there will be in the world; (2) as social-liberal-democracy becomes both widely established and established for a long period of time, the fewer people there will be who have had to live with alternative systems; (3) as the number of people who have only ever known social-liberal-democracy increases, so will the number of people yearning after some other set of ideals – at least potentially – increase, even though (4) the more social-liberal-democracy establishes itself in the world, the more it is able to prove its ability to deliver on all the things I have already claimed for it. And so, even though prosperous social-liberal-democracies might breed a significant number of people yearning for, say, martial glory, religious homogeneity, or communist equality, the case against those yearnings will only have been strengthened by the peaceful, comfortable success that bred them in the first place.

I describe this dynamic only in order to illuminate the nature of our case, which we can still summarise with the following two points: (1) *given* the facts of human behaviour, including facts about the different consequences produced by different political systems, it would be a good idea for human beings, *given* what their behaviour tells us they prefer, to support social-liberal-democracy; (2) for those who remain unconvinced, there are still further reasons, each of which combines a particular behavioural pattern with a particular pre-existing motivation (the existence of which can also be behaviourally observed), for why they should be convinced by that system. This is, remember, normative *behaviourism*.

By contrast, there is not even the slightest hint in my argument of what might be called the 'requirements of morality'. Nor as a result is there any need for talk of whether morality is regulative or all-encompassing, or of whether it is overriding and primary, or optional and only suggestively normative. Nor is there any need to talk about the difficulties of either accounting for or overcoming the problems of moral motivation. What I am doing here is providing a set of behavioural patterns, together with a set of reasons tied to those patterns, for why (1) most people would be convinced by social-liberal-democracy were they to have the chance of experimenting with every possible variation on every political system so far attempted in human history, and (2) almost all of those who would not be so convinced should be, given the possession of any one of a number of pre-existing motivations. The 'ought' that I offer here, therefore, is, as already noted, an instrumental or 'contingent' one which claims only that 'it is incredibly likely to be the case that you will be better off, by your own lights, in a social-liberal-democracy'.

People are, of course, still free to ignore this advice just insofar as there is no way in which I can force people with rare and radical motivational hierarchies to change their mind about those things. I could, of course, hold them at gunpoint in order to make them say that they have changed their mind, but that is a very different thing, even if having to go through that experience would perhaps, in several cases, change their deep-set priorities as regards the choice between enjoying personal security and pursuing unpopular radicalism. We just have to accept that there will always at least potentially be an unconvincable minority. But that should not worry us too much. As long as we remember (1) that these people will never be more than a small minority spread out within a larger political society for which only one answer to OQ can be instantiated at any time, (2) that they are providing no convincing answer of their own, given the failures of mentalism, and also (3) that they obviously do not even care that much whether or not people could be convinced by their own proposed principles. If we remember this, I think, then we will also realise that despite our own concern to deliver a system that provides ample reason for them to cooperate, there is no reason for us to feel too bad about forcing the best possible answer to OQ upon them.

Objection (2): Am I not just saying, whatever humans do, that is fine? Surely they do all sorts of different things. How then can we read off normativity from behaviour?

an argument from the Practise of men, that have not sifted to the bottom, and with exact reason weighed the causes, and nature of Common-wealths, and suffer daily those miseries, that proceed from the ignorance thereof, is invalid. For though in all places of the world, men should lay the foundation of their houses on the sand, it could not thence be inferred, that so it ought to be.[114]

---

[114] T. Hobbes, *Leviathan* (Cambridge: Cambridge University Press, 1996), 145.

Although it is true that human beings pursue all sorts of different things for all sorts of different reasons, that truth can mislead us. What matters here is the bigger picture, which is that, when observed in large numbers, and over long periods of time, human *political preferences* are more regular than day-to-day life – or indeed novels, cultural anthropology, or history – suggests. At this macro level, although humans certainly do try all sorts of things, their reactions to those efforts are considerably more uniform. We therefore 'read off' normativity from behaviour by reading off the political preferences expressed by the behaviour of large groups of people over long periods of time. We look to see just how people get on with their particular political system once they have got used to it, and once the institutional consequences of that state have fully fed through to the population. For example, although communist states may well be popular in theory, and even popular in practice at their inception, it is not long before all sorts of internal power dynamics, together with all sorts of failures to deliver various private and public goods, lead these states towards rebellion and collapse. By the end of their existence, as history shows us, they have long become detestable to too large a section of the population (notwithstanding the kernel of truth in what can easily become a 'no true Scotsman' fallacy, namely, that we have yet to see *real* communism. Naturally, if we do ever *see* it, and it *works*, over a *long* period of time, then normative behaviourism changes its recommendation).

As to whether I say 'whatever people do is ok', that would be a gross misinterpretation. For example, although I have not had cause to discuss such things in the context of this book, I do not take it to be an implication of normative behaviourism that it would be ok to be, say, a jihadist terrorist in a social-liberal-democracy. Putting issues of foreign policy to one side, it would hardly be right for such a terrorist to carry out his or her acts of violence simply in order to defeat that state's liberal ideals. Nor would there be reason for a normative behaviourist to condone, say, the actions of the Baader-Meinhoff gang in 1970s Germany. This is because those political actors were engaging in acts of violent non-co-operation against the best system that humanity has developed so far. We have to look, according to the logic of this approach to political philosophy, at the big, indicative patterns.

For example, in an empire, lots of people rob, vandalise, rape, enslave, and pillage. This is because empires offer scant personal security, set up the wrong dynamics, contain the wrong structure of incentives, and dissatisfy and anger too many people. In short, we can say that empire is a type of political system that fails to *fit* human nature, as expressed by the aggregate behaviour of this species over a suitable period of time. As a result, empire is an easy contrast to social-liberal-democracy – a system that experiences relatively, and tellingly, little in the way of crime, rebellion, and collapse.

Acts of terrorism and resistance within *this* system are the exception rather than the rule, which means, as far as normative behaviourism is concerned, they are not an indictment of the system that experiences them. So, what we do *not* do is base normativity on outliers. That there *are* terrorists does not, *ipso facto*, make a system wrong. That there are a *million* does.

We could put this same point another way. Consider here, in abstraction, someone who is engaged in armed resistance against a state, but not in violent attacks on its citizens. We might want to know: should we call that individual a terrorist or a freedom fighter? From the point of view of normative behaviourism, the difference between the two labels here, assuming that citizens are kept out of it, is *numbers*. We look for clear and strong trends. If someone says something is unacceptable, we defer our judgement. If a million say the same thing, and express that judgement by way of various actions and risks, then we need very good reasons to doubt it (though this is not to say that the precise boundary line is simple – the Sorites problem applies just as much here as it does to the question of how many grams, hairs, or millimetres one has to gain before becoming fat, hairy, or tall).

Now let's think about some more examples. Looking at local support patterns, as well as trends elsewhere in response to equivalent regimes, perhaps we could distinguish, in the manner described, between the military efforts of the Mujahidin/Taliban against the Soviets and their efforts against their own, post-invasion, democratic government? Or, more controversially, perhaps we could distinguish between the behaviour of the Irish Republican Army in Ireland and the United Kingdom from that of the African National Congress in apartheid South Africa? Consider here that whilst the former killed roughly 3,700 people throughout Ireland and the United Kingdom, despite people in Northern Ireland having the same rights as other British citizens, and despite a majority of people in Northern Ireland wanting to stay part of the UK, black South Africans were forced to accept less of just about every recognised social good, and were restricted to unambiguously second-class citizenship, in addition to being often brutally treated by both white citizens and the various arms of the law.[115] Remember, we know from behaviour *elsewhere*

---

[115] To be clear, I am not taking a stand here on whether there was a non-violent alternative to armed resistance in South Africa, or on whether the IRA, via Sinn Fein, had a perfectly valid, and non-violent, political case to make. Nor am I saying that terrorism in the sense of attacks on citizens is ever defensible, no matter how bad the regime – the claim that the existence of a million 'terrorists' indicts a particular system does not amount to a claim that even one of those individuals is justified in, say, blowing up the Houses of Parliament (and indeed, terrorism in the sense of political violence against civilians may well be one of the things on which most mentalists agree). My focus here is simply on armed resistance to states, understood as a form of insurrection, but also as something that often comes in a form called 'terrorism' by the states in question. With

just how much these things matter to people, just as we know from behaviour *in these countries* just how many people wanted to risk their lives in the relevant conflicts. Once again, then, when it comes to armed resistance, just as with other forms of insurrectionary behaviour, we follow large-N trends, not violent outliers.

We should not, of course, get carried away here, if only because this way of evaluating violence is neither a central argument of the book nor an argument upon which the case either for normative behaviourism or social-liberal-democracy depends. My point is simply that a commitment to normative behaviourism *need not entail* a commitment to a completely laissez-faire morality. The objection considered was that it must be impossible to read off normativity from behaviour given the variation, capriciousness, malleability, and goodness knows what else of human nature. It therefore seemed as though either everything or nothing was justified. As explained though, that is not the case. Whilst we can see on the one hand that human beings exhibit regular and strong tendencies in their political behaviour, and not at all the kinds of variety we might assume from focusing on the wrong things, we can see on the other that there is at least the potential for taking those tendencies and using them to distinguish between what we tend to call moral and immoral, justifiable and unjustifiable, legitimate and illegitimate, and right and wrong forms of individual behaviour.

Objection (3): Is this order not too static? We would never have achieved social-liberal-democracy without complaint and creativity, so are we now never to improve?

I want to admit to a nagging worry: even if the metaphysical aspiration to eternity is to have no role in a proper conception of reason, could it still have been a necessary element in the historical formation of those universalist moral traditions that are ours today? Could we have gotten to where we are now only if we had not reasoned as I am urging we now should, only if instead we had imagined this morality was the voice of reason itself?[116]

There is no reason not to expect things to improve. After all, before we even consider radical constitutional change, we should see that social-liberal-democracies are themselves always trying to improve, at least over

this focus in mind, I am exploring the legitimacy of such resistance from the point of view of normative behaviourism, and saying that it seems to come down to (1) the scale of support *in other contexts* (other countries, etc.) for fighting against the system that is being fought against locally and (2) the scale of *local support* for fighting against that system. If in both cases support is low, then such resistance looks on shaky ground.

[116] C. Larmore, *The Morals of Modernity* (Cambridge: Cambridge University Press, 1996), 64.

the long term. This much is clear in light of the theory of social-liberal-democratic success advanced earlier, and particularly in light of the contribution made to that theory by the work of North, Wallis, and Weingast, the upshot of which is that a crucial part of the *explanation* of the *contentment* generated by that system is the fact that it is always open to being significantly altered by means of law-abiding, peaceful political campaigns.

Significantly, this is just one aspect of their ability to self-improve. In addition to their openness to the domestic pressure of voters and civil society, there is also their openness to new ideas. Consider here that democracies all over the world are experimenting all the time with new and different policies – that much is obvious. What is perhaps less obvious is that this trend benefits not just the country doing the experimenting, but also every other democracy. By studying the different consequences of different policies in different states, we soon come to discover all sorts of ways of tackling both old and new political problems – and indeed, from the point of view of normative behaviourism, all sorts of new indications of expressed preferences. This means that one social-liberal-democracy can, and often does, learn as much from the successes and failures of another as it does from the creativity and electoral verdicts of its own people. So, as a result of being open enough to both generate and import new ideas, and as a result of being democratic enough to foster genuine electoral competition, social-liberal-democracies are always able to improve, and thus avoid becoming easy prey for either steady decay or violent revolution.

There is even a place for the workings of mentalist political philosophy within this dynamic. The generating, refining, and critiquing of different political principles, each of which could be experimented with in political practice, provides social-liberal-democracies with both new ideas and information as to how those ideas might play out in practice.[117] For example, although the fact that a principle is attractive in theory offers no guarantee of how it will perform in practice, we can be sure that if a principle is flawed in theory, then it will also be flawed in practice. This means that political philosophy can help democracies to avoid at least some of the mistakes that come with political experimentation by spotting those mistakes in advance.

---

[117] It is also rather fitting, given this contribution to political innovation, that one finds more political philosophy in social-liberal-democracies than in any other kind of political system. I would, however, be rather wary of adding it to the list of features which, when aggregated together, explain social-liberal-democracy's political success – though I would be delighted if that were the case...

But, as I say, political philosophers can also perform a more creative role. Consider, for example, the prospect of politically instantiating what we might call Michael Walzer's 'spherical integrity' principle, according to which it is forbidden for goods accrued in one sphere to dominate access to the goods of another.[118] For example, money should not dictate access to political office, just as personal connections should not dictate access to money. This is an interesting and tempting principle, but it is unlikely that we would be aware of it, or least in so refined a form, were it not for the creative efforts of political philosophy. And note, the role of that subject is not merely creative, but also, to some extent, indicative of likely popularity, because even if the mentalist philosophical endeavour is entirely unable to *prove* the value of different principles by itself, the fact that certain political principles appear to garner more academic support than others, and indeed more intuitions and considered judgements, certainly makes it more likely that they will be appreciated in practice. This means that mentalist political philosophy, in addition to safety-testing certain principles before they leave the theoretical factory – a crucial role in guiding democratic debate – is also able to generate and even recommend new principles *worth experimenting with*, even if those recommendations cannot ever turn into something we could call proof, or grounds, or justification.

The way in which political philosophy refines and distils principles is also worth expanding on. Consider here that when assessing political success or failure in normative behaviourist terms, we need to know just what it is that has succeeded or failed. This means establishing just which principles were being practised in the form of the various institutions and policies that led to that success or failure. For example, if we look back at twentieth-century political history in the West, we could say that we have generally *approved* of the application of Mill's harm principle to our criminal laws. Or, to give a more recent example, we could say that at this very moment wide swaths of people are arriving at a *negative* verdict regarding at least one aspect of Rawls' difference principle. Large numbers of individuals, that is, are coming to decide, particularly in the wake of recent financial crises, that absolute inequality *does* matter, even if the bottom *are* being raised up by, allegedly, the industry and enterprise of those at the top. Of course, only time will tell as regards how people's

---

[118] M. Walzer, *Spheres of Justice: A Defense of Pluralism and Equality*. Some readers will think this an odd choice, given how little has been said about this notion, relatively speaking, in the annals of political theory. My own view is that it would hold considerable appeal to the wider public as an ideal around which one could organise various policies and institutions – though, of course, it's the long-term behaviour that matters, and not short-term popularity.

preferences pan out, just as only time will tell what sorts of new policies are attempted in response to this new demand, and what sorts of responses they, in turn, incur. Yet the key idea remains: political philosophy helps to serve the cause of improvement in social-liberal-democracies, not just by proposing and critiquing different principles, the like of which we might want to experiment with, but also by helping us to understand the successes and failures we already observe.

Consider further the role that more empirically minded investigations of political principles might play in this wider project.[119] Surveys of political attitudes towards social justice, philosophical treatises regarding what sorts of trade-offs we might feasibly put together, and empirical studies regarding the political preferences triggered by different instantiated principles, can all help us devise new, experimental policies. The acid test of these policies and ideals remains, of course, that of how large groups of people respond to them over time – that point does not change. Remember here that whereas mentalist political philosophy seeks to justify political orders on the basis of reflective normative thought, behaviourist political philosophy seeks to justify it on the basis of how those orders fare in practice. Nevertheless, existing forms of empirically minded political theory, just like their more abstract counterparts, could continue, even given the truth of normative behaviourism, to play a key part in selecting and guiding the experiments we put into practice, even if they cannot themselves be the final word on their wisdom.

The fundamental point, therefore, is that there is always room for improvement. We try things out, we experiment, we analyse which policies and constitutional features are working and which are not, and, to the best of our abilities, we try to work out *why*. Our aim should always be to establish why people reject or dislike a particular policy in order to avoid replacing it with something else they also dislike. That is, if we can pinpoint that particular aspect of a policy which accounted for its failure, we will also be able to rule out all those policies which contain that aspect.

---

[119] At the more traditional, politico-philosophical end of the scale, see D. Miller, *Principles of Social Justice*. For relevant surveys of contemporary political attitudes, see V. Murphy-Bernan and J. J. Berman, 'Cross-Cultural Differences in Perceptions of Distributive Justice', *Journal of Cross-Cultural Psychology* 33:2 (2002): 157–170; and K. Tornblom, 'The Social Psychology of Distributive Justice', in K. Scherer, *Justice: Interdisciplinary Perspectives* (Cambridge: Cambridge University Press, 1992). As regards more social-scientific approaches to the different consequences of different instantiated principles, see, for example, the now well-established work on the differing performance of different variants of liberal democracy. Two good examples are A. Lijphart, *Patterns of Democracy: Government Forms and Performance in Thirty-Six Countries* (New Haven, CT: Yale University Press, 1999); and T. Vanhanen, 'A New Dataset for Measuring Democracy, 1810–1998', *Journal of Peace Research*, 37:2 (2000), 251–265.

But either way, there is always room for progress, *even if* that progress takes us beyond the point where what we now consider the best system tested so far can no longer be accurately labelled 'social-liberal-democracy', and *despite the fact* that we cannot give our final verdict as to whether or not something deserves that label until a sufficient amount of time has passed. Yet that we cannot give our final normative behaviourist verdict until our political efforts have run their course should not discourage us from experimenting. In this respect behaviourist political philosophy is like gastronomy. That is, although various chefs experiment all the time with all sorts of various dishes, we do not judge a cake by the principles applied in its construction. Instead, we judge it only in terms of the verdicts of those who have eaten and – crucially – fully digested a representative slice of its contents. Liking it today is not enough. It's important that you don't throw it up tomorrow.

There is, however, still a nagging worry regarding our history, as captured by Larmore's remarks above. Put bluntly, what good would normative behaviourism have done us in the past, and perhaps especially the distant past, when there was such scant 'data' to go on? Would it have recommended empires or monarchies? Would it have recommended aristocratic city-states or even hunter-gathering tribes? Surely, for so many of our ancestors, if you had offered them normative behaviourism, they would have said something like: don't give me the past as a guide to political ideals, when 'history is a nightmare from which I am trying to wake'.[120]

There are, I think, three possible responses to this retrospective doubt. First, we might say, hey, perhaps mentalism would also struggle with this, so let's not get too cut up about it. Second, we might say, well, even if it couldn't deliver the goods, it certainly can now. Third, and this is the key reply here, we could say, even when there is less data to go on, there is always *some* data, and no matter how much data there is, there is *still* always reason to experiment in the manner described.

For examples of such experimentation, though rather Western-centric ones, we might think here of the rivalry of Greek city-states in the period running from Homer to Aristotle, or of European states during the Renaissance and beyond, though that still rather invites the response: what would we have done before that? Well, perhaps examples from Chinese civilisation, or ancient Egypt, or even Mesopotamia. But again we have to ask: what about before that? The further back we go, I would suggest, the clearer it becomes that the idea of experimentation is crucial. Yes, normative behaviourism and social-liberal-democracy are natural

---

[120] So says James Joyce, through the mouth of Stephen Dedalus, in *Ulysses*.

bedfellows, given that (1) the social part maximises the number of available and articulate voices, (2) the liberal part allows those voices to be heard and their views discussed, and (3) the democratic part allows those views to be put into practice – but there is always reason to experiment, even outside of this system. There is *always* reason to try something new, and, as soon as one has done so, there is data to consider. We got where we are today, at least in part, though sticking with what works and abandoning what fails, and despite the depressing fact that some failures lasted for millennia, whilst many successes were killed off by others before they got a chance.[121]

Objection (4): *Human beings are driven by all sorts of ideas, of which only some are those which led, in the West, to universal suffrage and human rights. What makes these ideas so special?*

Indifference to East Asian political thought – more generally, to non-Western political theory – has been the blind spot of contemporary Western, especially Anglo-American, political theory.[122]

What makes these ideas special is the fact that they are clearly preferred to others by the people who have to live with them. By the same token, if non-Western ideas come to pass this test, then they in turn become the special ones. Monarchy has failed. Feudalism has failed. Empire has failed. Soviet communism has failed. Modern dictatorships – whether African, European, Latin American or south-east Asian – have all failed or are failing. Even Chinese communism, despite the distortion caused to Western views of it by competitive fear, combined with a good dose of cultural relativism, is stumbling and, indeed, already transforming itself, under all sorts of liberal-democratic pressures bubbling away beneath the surface.

What we need to remember, when it comes to normative behaviourism, is that we measure ideas not simply by their consequences, but, more precisely, by the verdicts given to them, over time, by entire populations. This is how we distinguish between successful (or, in the terms of the

---

[121] This point has been covered before, but it's worth repeating: what matters is the response of 'the people', over time, to their system. The fact that a neighbouring empire might roll into town and subjugate all and sundry might be international reality, or just historical bad luck, but it is still no indictment of the system in question, unless there was something tied to that system that always invited such invasions. The fact that Poland lies between Germany and Russia is no fault of Polish constitutions, any more than the lack of disease-resistance was a failure of Meso-American civilisations at the time of European colonialism.

[122] D. Bell, 'East Asia and the West: The Impact of Confucianism on Anglo-American Political Theory', in J. Dryzek, B. Honig, and A. Phillips (Eds.), *The Oxford Handbook of Political Theory* (Oxford: Oxford University Press, 2006), 263.

question, *special*) and failed ideas. Successful ideas should not be thought of as those ideas which most easily motivate people at their inception, or which are most likely to organise vast numbers of people into revolution, but rather those which do better than previous ideas according to the two measures of insurrection and crime. Failed ideas are those which have proven themselves worse than others by the same standards.

Consider again modern China. Anyone who has read, say, Jung Chang's *Wild Swans*, or who knows just a little of the history of Mao's rule, knows (1) what horrors and predations were visited upon the Chinese people by those ideas and (2) what degree of misinformation and secret policing was required to maintain the political stability of that system. That China will only survive as a cohesive, peaceful political society by granting stronger individual rights, greater freedom of speech, and full universal suffrage, should be clear to anyone who takes a longer view than just the past twenty years.[123] Relatedly, it will also only survive in this form if it educates its people in such a way as to ensure that they do not use these tools to tear themselves apart. Of course, political prophecy is a mug's game, but even so, if I had to bet on the matter, I would still say that fear of this latter danger, the strength of which is so apparent from existing legislation, combined with short-term efforts to shore up public opinion by way of media regulation and the restriction of dissidents, will not keep the pressure of tens and eventually hundreds of millions of people at bay for ever. Admittedly, I read this line back to myself in a year in which Donald Trump became the American president, Britain voted to leave the European Union, and Leicester City won the Premier League, but even so, what is one's neck for if not occasionally putting it on the line?

In any case, to reiterate the key point, I do not need to deny, and am not denying, that people are swayed by all sorts of ideals, including, for example, various ideals of liberty, equality, and national and religious fraternity. All I deny is that the final measure of those ideals should be anything other than their record in political practice. We are interested in large-scale, clear political trends and, in particular – given their centrality to everything else – the empirical records of fundamentally different types of political orders. Even if we are often going to struggle, through lack of

---

[123] I do not mean to be too gung-ho here. Clearly, even if everyone, in every society in the world, had a 'vote', those votes would still be filtered in different ways in different systems, such is the nature of democracy. Cabinets, parties, parliaments, councils, and other representative institutions, always lead to divergences of practice and political consequence. Though of course, observing such deviation over time could itself encourage long-term convergence, provided that something emerges that most people deem 'good' or 'even' best practice. I do not take any stance here, though, on whether or not that is likely. My case here is unaffected either way.

information, to explain or predict particular instances of public dissatisfaction or collapse, we are still, I think, able to pull together enough clear
tendencies to construct a fairly determinate picture of what constitutes
the best system developed so far. Simply put, social-liberal-democracies
experience less crime than non-democracies, illiberal democracies, and
more libertarian democracies. If that is right, then it is a clear indicator of
the relative success of that particular answer to OQ, given everything
I have said so far.

It might also help to consider here again, and in isolation, the fact no
liberal democracy (egalitarian, libertarian, or otherwise) with a GDP/
capita of $6,055 or above has ever failed. Again, I think this is a clear
indicator of the success of that type of political system as a whole.
Even allowing for its relative historical youth (it is, broadly speaking,
a twentieth-century achievement), the relevant social-scientific data is
highly persuasive. And, more to the point, we cannot make any claim of
this positive sort in favour of any *other* fundamentally different kind of
political order. So, even if we do struggle for detail, even if we do struggle
to distinguish slightly better from slightly worse, and even if we do
struggle to explain all sorts of political phenomenon, normative behaviourism is still capable of delivering what it tries to deliver, just so long
as there are at least a few trends generating the kind of clarity just
mentioned. Or, more generally put, provided that it can identify enough
of these trends, normative behaviourism is capable of delivering a fairly
clear picture of what constitutes the best system developed so far for
human beings, and, as a result, a convincing and meaningful answer
to OQ.

Objection (5): *How can you read off expressed preferences from collective dynamics?*
    Surely unintended consequences and collective action problems mean that you are
    often wildly misinterpreting what you take to be people's real preferences?

Seven years had passed. The storm-tossed sea of European history had subsided
within its shores and seemed to have become calm. But the mysterious forces that
move humanity (mysterious because the laws of their motion are unknown to us)
continued to operate.[124]

It is certainly true that unintended consequences and collective action
problems constitute a large part of any proper analysis of the success or
failure of different political institutions and policies. But that should not
distract us. What matters here is that regime types that tend to lead to
disastrous consequences, however indirectly those consequences are

---

[124] L. Tolstoy, *War and Peace: Volume 3* (London: Everyman's Library, 1992), 409.

produced by the cumulative effects of the acts of their citizens, are bad states, by my criteria as much as anyone else's. States are measured in normative behaviourism by their consequences, which means, amongst other things, by the consequences of the dynamics which tend to develop within them. It makes no difference whether or not the political effects of a crime, or the coup that follows a protest, or indeed the civil war that follows the coup, are intended or unintended. Nor does it make any difference if the people whose actions led to the collapse of the regime actually wanted that regime to survive. From the point of view of normative behaviourism, all that matters is whether or not the consequences of behaviourist import – insurrection and crime – are attributable to the presence of a particular set of political institutions and policies, and not, for example, attributable to foreign pressures that are neither regularly triggered by that regime type nor so common as to regularly undermine it, regardless of their connection to the system in question. For if either of those things *were* true, that would give the principles instantiated by that system a very different historical record and, as such, a very different value from the point of view of normative behaviourism.

Constitutions that permit or facilitate disastrous dynamics are ultimately indicted by them. For example, a constitution which tends to lead, or indeed, which can be seen *right now* as tending to lead to the destruction of the natural environment of its people will not survive. It should as such be condemned from the perspective of normative behaviourism. Or, as a second example, consider a constitution which, despite the best of intentions, allowed great and rigid inequalities to build up, just as properties build up on a monopoly board (and *this* lesson was the very point of *that* game). This system will, again, experience serious insurrection and, perhaps in time, collapse, which means again that it ought to be condemned. These are the kinds of consequences we look for when we evaluate states, regardless of how indirect or unintended they may be. Consider here that just as we would not want to be driven in a bus that regularly crashed, despite the intentions of the designer, or by a driver that regularly caused accidents, despite his or her best intentions, so do normative behaviourists want to avoid political systems which, despite the best intentions, always tend to fail their citizens.

Of course, some people might want to return us to objection (3) here, by objecting to this last line of reasoning on the grounds that studying the behavioural consequences of different historical institutions and policies only tells us how human beings behave under *those* institutions and policies, and nothing of what human nature would be like under *other*, as yet untried, regimes. But this is nonsense. As Bernard Williams once wrote:

[T]he structuralists ... cannot deny the existence and causal role of dispositions. No set of social structures can drive youths into violence and football games except by being represented, however confusedly or obscurely, in those youths' desires and habits of life.[125]

Saying that studying institutions and their consequences tell us nothing about human nature is tantamount to saying that if you replaced the human in those institutions with monkeys, you would get the same result. Of course we are conditioned, of course we are influenced, and of course we are pressured. The point is that we are also creatures regular enough to be both effectively conditioned and productively studied. Collective action problems, for example, would simply cease to exist if human beings were more like angels, or hive-dwelling insects, and so on.

Consider the prisoner's dilemma one last time. It only works as a model of human behaviour so long as the individuals involved are both mistrustful and untrustworthy (bearing in mind that the latter always tend towards the former). The same could be said of any economic theory under the sun about competition. Such theories assume a certain motivational set which, if absent, would prevent the competition from ever beginning. Or consider Hobbes' theory regarding individuals in a state of nature. We will only see the war of all against all that he describes if, and only if, human beings are already mistrustful, fearful, and maybe also glory-seeking, in the way that he insists.

To be clear, I am not trying to assert or subscribe to any one of these theories. My point is rather the simple one that for any such theory to be true – by which I mean *any* theory claiming that human nature changes as institutions change – it must also be true (1) that there is some deeper nature upon which those institutions act, in order to produce more visible changes in something we had previously described as 'nature', and (2) that we could only know of both this deeper nature, and its surface variations according to institutional context, by studying human behaviour under those very institutions. In short, what starts off as critical theory, in the objection under consideration, soon becomes critical behaviourism, and in turn failed behaviourism, given that it would have to rely on the same body of evidence – as gathered from human history and contemporary political science – that tells us that human beings are more content under social-liberal-democracy than any other attempted system. So, again: does that mean that things can never improve? Or that human

---

[125] B. Williams, *Ethics and the Limits of Philosophy*, 201. This also connects to my case against 'pure' interpretivism in the history of ideas. For ideas to somehow 'catch on' with human beings, it seems to me, they need to find purchase in a set of needs of desires we somehow already have. See J. Floyd, 'Why the History of Ideas Needs More than Just Ideas', *Intellectual History Review*, 21:1 (2011), 27–42.

beings could not still further improve their behaviour under improved though as yet unimagined political institutions? Of course not, as has already been shown in response to objection (3). The key point, once more, is that although human *nature*, properly understood, is a constant, at least at its core, and although *justification* ultimately rests on proven experimentation, that is still no reason not to innovate, provided one does so in a way that avoids making any of the mistakes we should already have learned from in the past.

3.10   Conclusions

I have argued in this chapter (1) that we should look for patterns in our behaviour, rather than our normative thoughts, and thus adopt normative behaviourism as a new approach to political philosophy; (2) that this approach picks out social-liberal-democracy as the most convincing of all the meaningful answers to OQ currently available; and (3) that it can be defended against all of the main objections to which it is initially likely to be subjected. So where does that leave us? For now, it leaves us with a new approach to political philosophy that is, if not perfectly defended, then at least minimally defensible. As for where this pairing of approach and defence leaves us in a more general sense – I have more to say about that in a moment.

Conclusion

Overview

I always tell students: *never put anything new in a conclusion*. Admittedly, the subject of that advice tends to be the final paragraph of a 2,000–3,000-word essay, rather than the closing chapter of a 140,000-word book, but even so, I still think it should apply, in essence, to the latter. As a result, instead of introducing any fundamentally new arguments, what I want to do here is simply reiterate and hopefully further clarify the preceding arguments by comparing them to a variety of other strains of thought with which they might still be confused. So, for those who have skim-read, and not quite understood, as well as those who have read meticulously, yet still find me unclear, perhaps the following and final set of contrasts between my argument and those advanced by others will make all the difference.

I also want to try and connect here with scholars who stand, if not close to normative behaviourism, then at least only a short walk away from it. Sometimes I will try to bring them closer to my position by saying something of the form: if you think this, then why not that? Sometimes I will try to show that normative behaviourism solves problems they struggle with in their own arguments. Sometimes I will try to show that it solves arguments they have not even seen. In the course of doing all this, I also hope to show that several leading scholars, who perhaps some readers consider non-mentalist, or maybe even something close to normative behaviourist, really *are* part of the mentalist project, despite whatever signs there are to the contrary. The overall point of this conclusion, however, remains the same: to further clarify the central arguments of this book by comparing and contrasting them to a number of arguments in which, I assume, many readers will already be interested. Naturally enough, there will be some concessions and further attempts to reach out to other political philosophers at the very end of the chapter, but even so, these should in no way be misconstrued either as new arguments or as changes to the ones that precede them.

Reiteration: Out of the Cave and on the Way to Denmark

I start this clarification with simple reiteration. That is, before coming to what I hope is a set of illuminating contrasts, I just want to restate, in as clear a form as possible, the central claims already made in this book. The first of these was that political philosophy should be understood in terms of what I call its organising question – how should we live? At first glance, one might think this question too open (it seems to include every aspect of our life), or too personal (it seems to include private matters that many would consider no business of political philosophy), though neither worry proves warranted. Instead, this question-based definition (1) includes what we would want to include in any such definition; (2) excludes what we would want to exclude, and also (3) starts us off on the right path, just insofar as it gives us the framework we need to approach both arguments in political philosophy in general and the argument of this book in particular. It is also a framework that launches us up to the vantage point provided by the guiding question of this book as a whole: is there a convincing and meaningful answer to political philosophy's organising question?

My answer to this question came in three long chapters. In the first, I concluded (1) that there is no convincing and meaningful answer already 'out there' in existing debates; (2) that, judging from the way in which arguments in those debates are carried out, there is no prospect of such an answer ever emerging, and also (3) that, despite the apparent impossibility of success in political philosophy, it is also impossible to avoid that subject, just insofar as it is impossible to avoid 'living out', in every part of the world, some or other answer to its organising question. If you're living, then you're living with other people; if you're living with other people, then you're living with politics; if you're living with politics, then you're living with political philosophy.

In the second chapter I attempted to explain the first of these two impossibilities by arguing that all modern political philosophy, and perhaps *all* past political philosophy, fails to deliver the answer we need as a result of adhering to a model of enquiry I call *mentalism*. Mentalist political philosophy, I say, tries to move us from what we already think to what we are supposed to think. That is, it tries to derive political principles from patterns in our pre-existing normative thoughts in much the same way as natural scientists try to derive causal principles from patterns in the wider, physical universe. Yet that method, I argue, just will not work, on account of the fact that the thoughts mentalist political philosophy tries to work with are just too inconsistent to reveal the kinds of patterns, and thus principles, required. So what are we to do instead?

In the third chapter I argued that rather than looking for patterns in our thought, we should look for patterns in our behaviour. That is, we should look to see whether the actions with which human beings express their strongest political preferences give a better and clearer picture than the kinds of thoughts with which political philosophers have so far been, at a fundamental level, exclusively concerned. So: if mentalism explains contemporary political philosophy's stalemate, then what I call *normative behaviourism* breaks it – or so I hope. To give a little more detail, the argument holds (1) that a set of political principles I call *social-liberal-democracy* produces less insurrection and crime, in practice, than any other type of political regime, and (2) that this fact underpins a set of reasons which, when taken together, mean that just about anyone should be convinced by it as an answer to political philosophy's organising question. So, we need to move away from mentalism and towards this new way of doing political philosophy which, as far as I can tell, picks out social-liberal-democracy as the best available political system. Or, put differently, out of the cave and on the way to Denmark.[1] Of course, if you want more detail than this, you shall have to return to the book proper. Or is *detail* not the problem? Perhaps instead you have already read the rest of the book, yet remain confused. In that case, my hope is that the following set of contrasts manages to provide, one way or another, the required elaboration.

Clarification by Way of a New Set of Comparisons

Let's look first at three positions, all of which appear to say something similar to normative behaviourism. These three are Alan Gewirth's 'principle of generic consistency', Brian Barry's 'empirical approach' to social justice, and David Miller's blend of social justice and social science. The reason I did not discuss these positions earlier is that, despite a handful of similarities to normative behaviourism, they are actually mentalist to the core.

---

[1] This is a rather obscure remark. The idea is that whilst the cave represents mentalism, Denmark represents social-liberal-democracy. As most readers will probably guess, the metaphor of the cave is borrowed from Plato's *Republic*. As probably won't be guessed, the idea of 'on the way to Denmark' comes from a paper written by two social scientists at the World Bank. Its original title was 'Getting to Denmark'. Its eventual and tragically more academic title was 'Solutions when the Solution Is the Problem: Arraying the Disarray in Development' (Center for Global Development Working Paper 10, 2002). The idea behind the original title was that Denmark is often taken as an exemplar of 'good' political and economic institutions. I know this only from reading F. Fukuyama, *The Origins of Political Order: From Prehuman Times to the French Revolution* (London: Profile Books, 2011), 14 (and fn. 25).

Consider Gewirth. He writes that 'every agent, by the fact of engaging in action, is logically committed to the acceptance of certain evaluative and deontic judgments and ultimately of a supreme moral principle'.[2] Andrew Vincent recently interpreted this idea as: 'Every agent, when acting in the world, is consequently committed to a determinate normative content.'[3] Yet Gewirth does not mean that by performing a *particular* action, you are committing to a *particular* normative content. He means that if you perform *any* action, you are committing to the particular content he has in mind. More precisely, he thinks that by performing any action, we are committing to its presuppositions, which include, initially, our own well-being and freedom, but also, by extension, the freedom and well-being of everybody else in the world. The gap, however, between my performing any action, and all of us being required to adopt particular principles, is unbridgeable, and not just because Gewirth fails to bridge it, but also because it would require all human beings to share some prior principle (and thus prior *normative thought*) of the form 'always grant to others whatever is required for your own plans'.

It is telling, I think, that even the most optimistic of mentalist political philosophers have avoided trying to make something like *that* stick. In contrast, my argument is that whatever *you* do, and whatever *your* actions presuppose, if a given political system always produces significant levels of insurrection and crime, then that fact, when combined with a range of pre-existing human motivations, provides sufficient reason for nearly all people to want to avoid it. My focus is thus exclusively on the particular beliefs and motivations people express by way of particular actions, not on whatever presuppositions appear to be made by all human action, or on the 'moral' significance of those presuppositions given the purported existence of some prior, and allegedly universally shared, 'moral' principles.

Consider second Brian Barry's proposals regarding an 'empirical method' of studying social justice. This method certainly *sounds* promising, but in practice turns out to involve studying what people happen to believe and disagree about in societies that already fit the *independent requirements* of Scanlonian contractualism[4]. As a result, we might already put it to one side. But that would be a mistake. Rather more promising than this idea, in light of the extra attention it appears to pay to behaviour, as opposed to just 'belief', is his use of the history of modern India to undermine the principles of *modus vivendi*.[5] Given the focus normative

---

[2] A. Gewirth, *Reason and Morality* (Chicago, IL: University of Chicago Press, 1978), x.
[3] A. Vincent, *The Nature of Political Theory* (Oxford: Oxford University Press, 2004), 5.
[4] B. Barry, *Justice as Impartiality* (Oxford: Oxford University Press, 1995), 196–197.
[5] Ibid., 38.

behaviourism applies to the political histories of different political systems, his general claim here that history both undermines 'justice as mutual advantage' and supports 'justice as impartiality' is a welcome one.[6] Again, though, he still only judges the consequences of different political systems in terms of principles that are themselves solely supported by mentalist endeavours. So, whereas I judge political principles by political behaviour, Barry does the reverse. That is, he takes a set of political principles that he considers adequately justified by mentalist means, and then studies the consequences of their different expressions in political practice in order to get a better sense of what those principles require at the level of concrete political policy.

As it turns out, perhaps the only serious points of overlap between what I do and what he writes come (1) in his claim that all societies need rules to minimise mutual frustration[7] and (2) his description of the way in which some utilitarians assess the worth of different constitutions.[8] The first of these claims connects to normative behaviourism without adding to it, just insofar as it chimes with the claim that just about everyone, regardless of circumstance, has good reason to want a political system in which such 'frustration' is minimised. The second, in turn, is of less help, because even if utilitarian principles did turn out to offer the most persuasive answer to OQ – and they do not – the account a normative behaviourist gives for that persuasiveness would be completely different to that given by a mentalist like Barry.

Consider third David Miller's argument. When he says that 'empirical evidence should play a significant role in justifying a normative theory of justice',[9] normative behaviourism pricks up its ears. But what does he mean by 'empirical evidence'? As he says straightaway: 'such a theory is to be tested, in part, by its correspondence with our evidence concerning everyday beliefs about justice'.[10] Swift therefore has it right when he says that, for Miller, 'justice can only be popular opinion corrected by commonly accepted modes of reasoning'.[11] Yet that, to be clear, is just mentalism with a focus on *other people's* minds. That is, whereas most mentalist political philosophers are happy to say 'we', when what they mean is 'myself and other decent people I know', Miller makes the effort to find out what vast numbers of ordinary people think about the

---

[6] Ibid., 102–103, 111, 114, 205–206.   [7] Ibid., 201.   [8] Ibid., 80.

[9] D. Miller, 'Review of K. Scherer (Ed.) Justice: Interdisciplinary Perspectives', *Social Justice Research*, 7 (1994), 177.

[10] Ibid., 177.

[11] A. Swift, 'Public Opinion and Political Philosophy: The Relation between Social-Scientific and Philosophical Analyses of Distributive Justice', *Ethical Theory and Moral Practice*, 2:4 (1999), 358.

questions at the heart of social justice (including things like the relevance and nature of desert, need, and equality). Nevertheless, like all mentalists, Miller remains exclusively concerned with thoughts and the patterns across them. He has no interest, as a normative behaviourist does, in actions or the preferences they express, or indeed the principles those preferences might express or underpin.

The most telling thing Miller says on this front, I think, is that his aim is 'to discover the underlying principles that people use when they judge some aspect of their society to be just or unjust, and then to show that these principles are coherent'[12]. It would be hard, I think, to find a more explicit subscription to mentalist political philosophy than that. As a result, from my point of view, perhaps this is ultimately the most interesting aspect of Miller's work, given that he makes, in my judgement, a perfectly appropriate use of the term 'empirical evidence' when describing *the contents of other people's minds*. He sees mentalist political philosophy, it seems, including his own variant upon it, with a degree of clarity others lack. And that's important. Mentalism in general, as explained in the previous chapter, is on something of a sticky wicket when it clings to both a clear fact/principle separation and a reliance on thoughts as, in effect, a data-set open to philosophical mining. Sometimes one wants to ask, for example, whether liberty is a value when I think about it but a fact when you think about it. But let's not get distracted. What ultimately matters here is that yet another apparently 'empirical' approach to political philosophy is, in truth, mentalist through and through.

That's three contrasts out of the way. Now let's consider a much larger set of claims which, although they are only minor notes in the arguments from which they are taken, do nonetheless make the normative behaviourist think, 'if only you had taken that idea further, or in a different direction, then perhaps you too would have ended up where I have'. Consider Rawls, first of all, when he says, in *The Law of Peoples*, that a 'realistic utopia' concerns not just the 'practically possible' given human nature, but also the practically possible given the 'historical conditions' of our age.[13] Or, better yet, consider his discussion of the 'facts of human psychology' and the 'strains of human commitment' in *A Theory of Justice*.[14] Here one wants to say, if one should only choose principles of justice for a realistic utopia that would pass the test of what we know of observable patterns of political commitment and human psychology, then why not choose those principles picked out by normative

---

[12] D. Miller, *Principles of Social Justice* (Cambridge, MA: Harvard University Press, 1999), ix.

[13] J. Rawls, *The Law of Peoples* (Cambridge, MA: Harvard University Press, 1999), 11–12.

[14] J. Rawls, *A Theory of Justice* (Cambridge, MA: Harvard University Press, 1971), 145.

behaviourism? Surely a rational and (given the veil of ignorance) impartial chooser of political principles would pick whichever set minimises their chances of ending up in a position where they feel no choice but to turn to crime or insurrection? Of course, a normative behaviourist would want to completely change the tenor of the argument, and ask instead, 'is there a set of political principles which many *different* people would choose, given the motivational sets they *already* possess?', but that is irrelevant. What matters here is the possibility (1) that Rawls' argument and normative behaviourism could converge on the same set of principles, and (2) that they would do so for at least some of the same reasons (i.e. the reality of the different behaviour patterns produced by different political systems, and the rationality of wanting to avoid some of those patterns).

A more surprising note of overlap with normative behaviourism, given his usefulness to our exploration of mentalism in Chapter 2 (**2.3**), and also his staunch position on the irrelevance of human nature to political philosophy,[15] can be found in the work of David Estlund. Estlund says several things of encouragement for the normative behaviourist. He says that it's odd that deliberative democracy defends deliberation whilst denying deliberation-independent standards of good decisions.[16] He says that 'much of democracy's promise derives from our historical experience'.[17] He says that we should avoid a democratic system based on contractualist procedures given that those procedures have 'no tendency to produce the decisions necessary to avoid (avoidable) famine'.[18] And he says that we should evaluate democracy's performance in terms of what he calls 'primary bads', such as war, famine, economic collapse, political collapse, epidemic, and genocide.[19]

Why, then, does he refuse to find out whether, in practice, democracies actually *do* produce fewer of these 'bads'? He says that we will not pursue 'with any specificity' whether democratic arrangements would perform well with respect to them,[20] and that 'while such performance is, in principle, an empirical question, it is a very difficult one to confront with good empirical evidence'.[21] As a result, he thinks the real question is 'not how a given regime does perform in our experience, but how we would expect it to perform'.[22] He then gives a list of reasons for why we should expect good political performance from democracies,[23] and they are certainly good reasons – though for a normative behaviourist, they

---

[15] D. Estlund, *Democratic Authority: A Philosophical Framework*, esp. 258–276; D. Estlund, 'Human Nature and the Limits (if Any) of Political Philosophy', *Philosophy and Public Affairs*, 39:3 (2011), 207–237.
[16] D. Estlund, *Democratic Authority*, 30.   [17] Ibid., 186, and again on 204–205.
[18] Ibid., 239.   [19] Ibid., 163.   [20] Ibid., 165.   [21] Ibid., 167.   [22] Ibid.   [23] Ibid., 176.

would be treated, not as justifications of a given answer to political philosophy's organising question, but rather as part of an explanatory theory for what I take to be an already excellent data-set. Estlund writes at one point that in traditional 'normative democratic theory [the] merits of democratic decisions are held to be entirely in their past'.[24] Yet for the normative behaviourist, as should now be clear, there is an entirely different way in which such decisions could be judged by their past. Rather than relying on the supposed legitimacy of the procedure that produces them, we could say that our faith in future democratic decisions lies entirely in democracy's past, or what Estlund would call its 'historical promise', just insofar as we can see, throughout history, that people have expressed less discontent with the workings and products of that system than with any of its alternatives.

Perhaps we should say here (though I would not adopt the term) that normative behaviourism is a kind of 'epistemic consequentialism', as opposed to Estlund's 'epistemic proceduralism', just insofar as it tells us that, yes, as revealed by political science and history, democracy does make the best decisions, given that the key consequence of those decisions is a minimising of insurrection and crime. So why does Estlund not take this route? That is an impossible question to answer. We could point, perhaps, to his wariness of consequentialism, as illustrated throughout *Democratic Authority*, or his commitment to mentalism, as illustrated in Chapter 2 of this book. We could also point, naturally, to his belief that we lack any good data of the kind required. But this gets us nowhere. What matters from the point of view of normative behaviourism is that whilst Estlund believes (1) that facts are irrelevant to political philosophy, and (2) that democracy is justified by being better at making decisions, I believe (3) that you cannot stick to (2) without relying on the facts of democracy's superior historical track record, and thus violating (1).

An even more surprising 'note' of normative behaviourism, given everything he says about the separation of facts from principles – as noted in the previous chapter (3.3) – can be found in the work of G. A. Cohen. Cohen says that sometimes 'responses to actual facts reveal our principles better than our responses to hypothesised facts'.[25] This, I think, is a fascinating idea. Bearing it in mind, we might now ask here: if my emotional response to something I witness tells me that I have just seen an injustice, and thus informs me that I subscribe to a principle regarding the avoidance of all such acts, then why not a similar response

---

[24] Ibid., 98.
[25] G. A. Cohen, *Rescuing Justice and Equality* (Cambridge, MA: Harvard University Press, 2008), 247.

on the part of another person? That is, if my reliable response to a given phenomenon is supposed to ground a principle *for me*, then why not a similar response on the part of other people? Or, more importantly, if my or your emotional response is capable of revealing a principle to which you or I already, though unwittingly, subscribed, then why not a particular *behavioural* response, given that many kinds of behaviour are easily recognised as expressions of particular emotions? And indeed, could it not even be the case that my or your behavioural response to actual conditions does a better job of revealing our principles than armchair-bound, emotional responses to actual conditions, not to mention, as is more often the case in moral and political philosophy, hypothetical responses to hypothetical conditions?

A standard technique in mentalist political philosophy is to map out our safe, armchair-bound feelings of injustice in response to different actual and hypothetical conditions in order to map out, and thus unearth, the principles that govern those responses. By contrast, and unlike Cohen, who does not consider this possibility, normative behaviourism makes the study of real behavioural responses to real political conditions absolutely central. And why is that? In part because our idle and reflective normative thoughts are unreliable, given that they conflict both within one and the same person and between different people; in part because clear patterns can be found in our behavioural responses to different political conditions; and in part because those responses can be considered, for various reasons, a much stronger expression of our normative preferences, given the degree of commitment, and thus consideration, required of, for example, the act of political rebellion.

Some notes of normative behaviourism are even weaker than these. Consider, for example, Thomas Christiano when he writes of 'ideas that require empirical testing', including 'the fruitfulness of debating opposite points of view in the democratic forum as well as the idea that people can see that they are being treated publicly as equals in a democratic society'[26]; or Amy Gutmann and Dennis Thompson, when they write of the provisionality and similarity to hypotheses of political principles within their theory of normative democracy[27]; or Philippe Van Parijs, when he writes of the need to investigate whether a basic-income society would be sustainable in the long term.[28] Each of these arguments finds

---

[26] T. Christiano, *The Constitution of Equality: Democratic Authority and Its Limits* (Oxford: Oxford University Press, 2008), 7.

[27] A. Gutmann and D. Thompson, *Why Deliberative Democracy?* (Princeton, NJ: Princeton University Press, 2004), 122.

[28] P. Van Parijs, *Real Freedom for All: What (if Anything) Can Justify Capitalism?* (Oxford: Oxford University Press, 1995), 38.

some parallel in normative behaviourism without sharing any of its essential claims. Take Christiano first. Although he thinks empirical work should be undertaken in order to see how extrapolations of fundamental principles play out in the real world, he is clear that that work has no power to affect those principles. As he writes at one point: 'political philosophy must . . . provide the underlying ideas of justice and the good and . . . a map that gives us pointers as to what kinds of empirical research needs to be done'.[29] He does at another point say that '[the fact that] well-being is a fundamental good can be seen from the fact that societies are devoted to realising the common good and that the common good is to be understood in terms of well-being', which hints at the intriguing possibility of political principles being justified by their behaviourally expressed popularity – but it is no more than a hint.[30] The rest of his work gives no sign of him believing such a thing even remotely possible.

We can say much the same thing of the parallel with, on the one hand, Gutmann and Thompson, and, on the other, Van Parijs. Although normative behaviourism shares with Gutmann and Thompson's theory of deliberative democracy a belief in the provisionality of political principles – for there will always be new historical evidence regarding both old and new principles – it opposes their belief that fundamental principles can only be adequately justified by mentalist means, as well as their belief that principles are only amenable in terms of further mentalist arguments. Admittedly, they would describe such talk of 'fundamental' and 'mentalist' as misleading, but I disagree. They *claim* that *all* principles are provisional, and talk of 'arguments' rather than 'thoughts', but the truth is that certain ideas, such as 'mutual respect' and 'reasonable rejection', are treated as effectively fundamental, whilst the arguments they have in mind run solely along mentalist lines.

As for Van Parijs, he is only really interested here, as Christiano was, in issues of feasibility rather than justification. In this they are like most theorists who come within driving distance of normative behaviourism. That is, although they are genuinely interested in empirical research into the political performance of different institutions, they are only interested as thinkers who worry about 'ought implies can', not as thinkers who contemplate, as I do, any serious moves from 'is' to 'ought'. This, I think, is a mistake, and not just because, as I see it, normative behaviourism succeeds where mentalism fails, but also because, if one *can* produce a successful move from 'is' to 'ought', in which the 'is' in question is an historically tested political policy or institution, then the former worry

---

[29] Ibid., 7.   [30] Ibid., 18.

becomes irrelevant – for we are seeing, at one and the same time, both that the principle we have in mind is *good*, and that it *works*.

Let me give three last examples. First, Russell Hardin, who works in general with an argument that we cannot say that we *ought* to have liberal democracy if it turns out to be *unworkable*, and in particular with an argument that history and political science reveal that that system *only* works when it serves the interests of key social groups.[31] Second, Richard Bellamy, who uses historical evidence to both undermine legal constitutionalism and support what he calls political constitutionalism.[32] Third, Jonathan Wolff, who thinks that we need to begin with the study of existing political problems, and avoid using top-down theories to give solutions from on high.[33] Wolff also says several other things of interest here. He says at one point that inconsistency is not as fatal in politics as it is in philosophy, and that an inconsistent policy set will often be better than a consistent set given the way in which people respond to each in practice.[34] He says that sometimes a law is ignored, simply because people will not behave in the way it requires, which then leads to a damaging undermining of the law as a whole.[35] He says that 'applied political philosophy' badly needs to understand human motivations.[36] And he says that often our intuitions and strong judgements are unreliable, though he is unsure, in light of this, whether there is anything else that we can use.[37]

In response to that last point, clearly, I would suggest that Wolff considers normative behaviourism as his alternative, though that is not our main concern here. The main point, just as it was a moment ago, is that all of these arguments, despite going further than just 'ought implies can', still fundamentally rely on mentalism. Although they are prepared to use empirical evidence in order to choose between two or more second-order political principles, they are not prepared to apply it to what might be called, in this context, foundational political principles. For example, although Bellamy is happy to use history in order to undermine legal constitutionalism, his support for political constitutionalism still fundamentally depends on a prior set of republican

---

[31] R. Hardin, *Liberalism, Constitutionalism, and Democracy* (Oxford: Oxford University Press, 1999).

[32] R. Bellamy, *Political Constitutionalism: A Republican Defence of the Constitutionality of Democracy* (Cambridge: Cambridge University Press, 2007). For an example of the kind of empirical work on which Bellamy relies in his argument, see J. M. Maravall and A. Przeworski (Eds.), *Democracy and the Rule of Law* (Cambridge: Cambridge University Press, 2003). One of the key claims bridging empirical and normative concerns in this work is that the rule of law only survives in democracies.

[33] J. Wolff, *Ethics and Public Policy: A Philosophical Enquiry* (London: Routledge, 2011).

[34] Ibid., 198.   [35] Ibid., 60.   [36] Ibid., 127.   [37] Ibid., 190.

principles for which only mentalist argument is offered. The idea is thus to ground republican principles in whatever combination of our normative thoughts (intuitions, considered judgements, impartial choices, and so on) is deemed appropriate, before then working out what the best expression of those principles is in practice. Empirical patterns of behaviour are then only deemed relevant at the point at which one wants to apply political principles to political practice, including questions of institutional design.

Away from these individual examples, there are also three larger debates which, again, appear to bear on at least some of normative behaviourism's concerns. The first two of these – realism versus moralism, and ideal versus non-ideal theory – are closely related, despite being carried out, for reasons that relate in part to how contemporary political philosophy is organised, in relative isolation from one another. I touched on realism in Chapter 1 (1.14), in the context of whether it provides a convincing answer to political philosophy's organising question, but now we have different concerns. In this context we are interested in how both debates go about trying to solve their shared central problem – that of whether and how abstract political principles apply to the real, contemporary world.

Where normative behaviourism differs from all positions advanced in these two debates is in its belief that certain facts about the observable political world – when combined with certain facts about pre-existing and observable human motivations – are capable of grounding ultimate political principles. In contrast, realists tend to say (1) that order, peace, or legitimacy matters more than justice, and (2) that certain political 'realities' make pursuit of the latter, especially as expressed by abstract principles, both impossible and, in many cases, dangerous. Non-ideal theorists, in turn, say either that those realities require a further set of principles in order for visions of 'pure justice' to be properly translated into practice, or that they require some minor moderation to the content of those visions. So, whereas some of these thinkers disagree about ultimate values (e.g. peace versus justice), and others about how abstract political principles need to be moderated or translated in light of practical concerns, nobody considers the possibility that certain facts about the political world might switch us entirely from one set of ultimate values to another. As a result, and just as was the case a moment ago with Christiano and Van Parijs, the focus here is only on 'ought implies can', not on 'is' to 'ought'. Despite their disagreements about feasibility, legitimacy, and applicability, and even about ultimate values, there is no disagreement, as far as I can tell, that only mentalist arguments have the power to rank those values. Much as I am tempted, then, to describe normative behaviourism as a kind of 'political political philosophy'[38] which somehow meets all of realism's concerns – by magically converting political facts into theoretical truths, and settling all questions of 'ought' to 'can' by way of a new position on 'is' to 'ought' – it remains, methodologically speaking, a very different proposition.

The third debate, or rather literature, is moral psychology. This literature is, in many ways, more promising than the previous two, which is unsurprising given how much I drew on it in Chapter 2 in my case against mentalism. In its blending of, amongst other things, meta-ethics, evolutionary theory, and experimental ethics, it provides a naturalistic approach to normativity that has more resonance with normative behaviourism than anything currently on offer within political philosophy itself. It is also striking that three of the leading lights in this field – Joshua Knobe, Shaun Nichols, and Walter Sinnott-Armstrong – all say that they want to return to a tradition in which philosophy was not cut off from history, psychology, and political science, amongst other things.[39] Nevertheless, it is just as striking that, in all their considerations of how empirical research in general, and moral psychology in particular, should affect the world of philosophy, they do not even mention, let alone consider, political philosophy.

Just as was the case with the moralism/realism and ideal/non-ideal theory debates, this says more about how modern scholars are organised than the contents of their arguments. But is there no overlap? Perhaps the closest thing to normative behaviourist political philosophy found in this area is the kind of 'ethical naturalism' described by, for example, Flanagan, Sarkissian, and Wong.[40] Yet even here, it turns out, there is a problem, at least as far as normative behaviourism is concerned, because although the position on the separation of facts from values is close to that adopted by normative behaviourism, and although most of the thinkers in this area treat thoughts as 'facts' in much the same way as I would, there is

---

[38] This phrase is adapted from J. Waldron, 'Political Political Theory', *Journal of Political Philosophy*. Note, though, that whereas he wants to take mentalist political philosophy and expand it, so that it takes in choices between concrete institutions as well as between abstract principles, I want to replace or at least supplement it with a different way of doing things altogether – normative behaviourism. Of course, I do happen to think normative behaviourism serves this aim rather well – given its focus on how we respond, in practice, to particular institutions – but that still leaves me with a very different way of doing things to Waldron.

[39] J. Knobe and S. Nichols, 'An Experimental Philosophy Manifesto', in J. Knobe and S. Nichols (Eds.), *Experimental Philosophy* (Oxford: Oxford University Press, 2008), 3; W. Sinnott-Armstrong, 'Introduction', in W. Sinnott-Armstrong (Ed.), *Moral Psychology*, vol. 1 (Cambridge, MA: MIT Press, 2008), xiii.

[40] O. Flanagan, H. Sarkissian, and D. Wong, 'Naturalizing Ethics', in W. Sinnott-Armstrong (Ed.), *Moral Psychology*, vol. 1 (Cambridge, MA: MIT Press, 2008), 1–26.

still no desire to consider, in the quest for principles, anything other than mental phenomena. As a result, however much they rail against the kind of thought experiments and intuitions moral and political philosophers use, it remains the case that the kinds of facts they *do* want to turn into values are themselves still only another kind of thought or mental state, depending on the argument in question. There is never any consideration of behaviour as being itself expressive of our moral psychology, let alone of our wider personal and political preferences.

Interestingly enough, we might get more traction by considering, not the place where evolutionary psychology meets experimental ethics, but rather the place in which evolutionary theory meets human nature more generally considered. The best example of this, famously enough, is Richard Dawkins' *The Selfish Gene*.[41] Dawkins shares several positions in common with the normative behaviourist, including the belief that the 'prisoner's dilemma' captures a central dynamic of human interaction, though that is not our focus here. Of more interest is his invention of the concept of a 'meme' (an idea that has become a 'meme' in its own right, especially where the Internet is concerned). Memes, he tells us, are ideas with survival value, as shown by their ability to replicate and spread.[42] His examples of such ideas include tunes, catch-phrases, ways of making pots, and even the idea of God.[43] So what about political principles? That is, if ideas can spread from mind to mind, and thus from generation to generation, provided that they have some kind of psychological appeal to those who carry them, then why not certain political principles, given that, if those principles serve their hosts well, those hosts might do better than other hosts, and thus in time only further the spread of the principles in question? Dawkins also points out that different memes often cluster together when they reinforce each other,[44] so why not those different parts of social-liberal-democracy? Given that, as shown in Chapter 3, the social, liberal, and democratic elements of this set of principles all provide mutual support for one another, might this not be part of the story of their success as an emerging and flourishing meme?

The problem with these suggestions, and indeed this general way of looking at things, is that it is unclear just how much memes, as opposed to genes, actually have to do with the kind of political behaviour normative behaviourism studies. The reaction of an individual to a given regime, as expressed through an act of insurrection, is ultimately more like a reaction to a bad food or an unpleasant noise than it is to, for example, the 'sin' of

---

[41] R. Dawkins, *The Selfish Gene* (Oxford: Oxford University Press, 1999).   [42] Ibid., 195.
[43] Ibid., 192–193.
[44] Ibid., 192. Fittingly enough, given his later writings, he gives the examples of the idea of God, the idea of hellfire, the idea of everlasting life, and the idea of priests.

usury. That is, even if we have never heard or read about a given regime before we had to live with it, and thus not been the recipient of any pre-existing meme, we are still repulsed by it, just as we are naturally repulsed by the smell of rotten eggs, or the sound of nails being dragged down a chalkboard. This does not, of course, mean that good political principles cannot be spread in just the way that other successful memes are spread, only that the ultimate reason for their political 'success' has nothing to do with the meme itself, in terms of its intuitive or even aesthetic appeal. It's also worth stressing here that if there was no way in which one could transmit the memes of good political principles, or indeed the meme of normative behaviourism, then there would be little point in writing this book! Nevertheless, we should not forget that political philosophy is ultimately no more responsible for the way in which political institutions work than astronomers are for the way in which stars move.

If that is true, however, perhaps it would make more sense to consider institutions, rather than ideas, as the proper unit of evolution, at least as far as normative behaviourism is concerned? We might say, that is, that institutions, understood here as expressions of particular political princi-ples, are adaptations to an *already* adapted, *fully* formed, and, within the context of political history, entirely *fixed* human nature (given that the entire history of political institutions is just the blink of an eye, as far as human evolution is concerned). As a result, we might talk of the 'selfish state' rather than, for example, 'the selfish philosophical argument', if indeed it is the interaction of political institutions, rather than our dis-cussion of that interaction, that ultimately drives their development.

Again, though, such talk is more than a little misleading. Although it is true that social-liberal-democracies appear to have thrived and become preponderant since their relatively recent historical emergence, it is also true that normative behaviourism concerns more than mere survival. Admittedly, survival is an excellent proxy for political success in norma-tive behaviourist terms, but it is still only a proxy. Although we would always expect institutions that breed high levels of discontent amongst their citizens to fail sooner or later, it is the fact that they fail through insurrection and crime, and not just, say, nuclear obliteration by a distant dictator, that ultimately matters, given that the particular *causes* of success and failure are central to the particular *reasons* individuals have for why they should be convinced by a particular set of principles.

There is, however, a risk, despite this dismissal of the many false parallels between normative behaviourism and evolutionary theory, that this last contrast obscures more than it illuminates, which is why I now want to return to political philosophy proper. In particular, I want to look again at some of the key objections to my argument against mentalism.

These objections are well presented in an illuminating article by Adam Swift[45] – though he was not, to be clear, writing with my own work in mind. In this article, Swift anticipates many of the key points found in the moralism/realism and ideal/non-ideal theory debates, despite predating them by almost a decade, but also makes several claims of direct relevance to my own project. First, he writes that 'the mere existence of disagreement about which conception of justice is right cannot warrant the conclusion that no such conception could be'.[46] Second, he says that this inference 'perhaps gains plausibility from the observation that people seem to disagree not only with one another but also with themselves'.[47] Third, he says that it remains a mistake, even if 'one can understand why those who spend their time wading through the contradictions and confusions in ordinary minds should grow doubtful of the claim that there is a coherent, albeit possibly complex, philosophical "truth"' to be apprehended'.[48]

Why, though, would it be a mistake to use facts about people's internal and inter-personal disagreements about normative matters as part of a case against the existence of the kind of coherent, philosophical truth Swift describes? Two further things he says are telling here. First, he points out that it is always unclear in survey questionnaires on popular morality whether social scientists are discovering and comparing views on morality in general, or on justice in particular, or on particular economic distributions, or on something else altogether.[49] This is an important point about 'discovered' contradictions, given that it might well turn out to be the case that, even if people disagree about all sorts of normative matters, they do still agree somewhere 'higher up', at some more general point of abstraction from which lower conflicts can then be resolved. Second, there is the problem that the average person's opinion, uninformed by as many possible resolutions to a given problem as might be considered, and unsorted by as keen a critical knife as a philosopher might wield, is perhaps unrepresentative of what *would* be believed after what Swift calls 'a dose of philosophical education'.[50] So what should we conclude here? According to Swift, we should conclude that although popular opinion is important for questions of feasibility and legitimacy, it has no part to play in the justification of principles of justice.[51]

My own argument both contradicts and deviates from Swift's. As regards popular opinion polls regarding justice, I agree that they can be misleading,

---

[45] A. Swift, 'Public Opinion and Political Philosophy: The Relation between Social-Scientific and Philosophical Analyses of Distributive Justice', *Ethical Theory and Moral Practice*, 2:4 (1999), 337–363.
[46] Ibid., 339.   [47] Ibid., 341.   [48] Ibid.   [49] Ibid., 343, 347.   [50] Ibid., 348.
[51] Ibid., 351, 361.

but they are only a small part of the story. Of more relevance, I think, are popular opinion polls regarding the decisions individuals would make in different abstract dilemmas, given that those answers are often meant to form the basis of what we *should* think about things like justice. Swift's objections do not apply to these, given the supposed purity of the presented choices. Yet even this is still only *part* of the story. The real trick in the case against mentalism, as explained in Chapter 2, is to realise (1) that there are ultimately three types of normative thought of relevance to the political philosopher, and (2) that not one of these is fit for purpose. These three types, remember, are 'impartial choices of "ideal state", "considered judgements", and "intuitive responses to abstract dilemmas"', and I can repeat the difficulties with each. The problem with the first is that, barring controversial restrictions on choice, different people choose different states. The problem with the second is that such judgements are either universal but politically indeterminate (meaning that they cannot solve political philosophy's problems), or highly varied across different individuals. The problem with the third is that, in addition to different people agreeing about the right choice in a given dilemma, one and the same person will disagree on the right answer according to how that choice is framed (and perhaps also other factors, such as the order in which situations are presented to the chooser, or their mood, etc.).

Swift, it is worth emphasising, is like all mentalists, just insofar as he thinks that the way to justify political principles is to try and derive them, one way or another, from normative thoughts we already have. In this he is no different from any other conventional political philosopher, or indeed any other conventional moral philosopher. Philippa Foot once wrote that 'there is worked into our moral system a distinction between' – the quote is cut short because I am only interested in the first six words. They capture perfectly the assumption central to all mentalist endeavour, namely, that human beings already possess some kind of near-perfectly working moral system. This makes the task of the philosopher (1) to work out what it is and how it works, and (2) to work out what it entails for complicated and controversial areas such as politics.

Now consider something Hilary Putnam says about Hume. He writes that Hume held 'the comfortable eighteenth-century assumption that all intelligent and well-informed people who mastered the art of thinking about human actions and problems impartially would feel the appropriate "sentiments" of approval and disapproval in the same circumstances unless there was something wrong with their personal constitution'.[52]

---

[52] H. Putnam, *The Collapse of the Fact/Value Dichotomy and Other Essays* (Cambridge, MA: Harvard University Press, 2002), 20.

Well, it seems to me that there is something wrong either with most of us, or with all of political philosophy, and I am currently more persuaded of the latter possibility. The instinctive reaction of most political philosophers to my case against mentalism, I believe, as noted in Chapter 2, and expressed in one form here by Swift, would be to say that 'we do not care how people *do* think; only how they *should* think'. Yet that just will not cut it, because in trying to tell us what we should think, political philosophers *always* rely on claims about what we *already* think that *always* turn out to be false. Of course, we can try to make life easier for ourselves by focusing only on what intelligent or even philosophical people think, but even there we fail, for there is still too much disagreement in all the relevant places.

Bearing this disagreement in mind, let's consider one last comparison here. In 'speech act' theory people say that when you or I *say* something, we are also *doing* something. In normative behaviourism, by contrast, I claim that when you're doing something, you're also saying something. Actions, I believe, are often better guides to preferences, including political preferences, than either the things people say, or indeed, in many cases, the things people think. Living with and reacting to a given political system is in many ways a more telling process than simply reflecting from a distance on either real or hypothetical states of affairs. For example, in the British soap opera *Eastenders*, there used to be a character called Sayed. Over and over again, Sayed tells both others and himself that he is heterosexual, even though we know, from his actions, that he is not. In this context, we might say, behaviour trumps thoughts. That is, because what Sayed thinks and says at any given time will often contradict, not just what he does, but also what he thinks and says at other times, his actions prove a more reliable guide to his preferences.

Now consider a second example. If someone who has never experienced apartheid says that it is a perfectly pleasant system to live with, whilst many who have had to live with it decide to commit acts of insurrection, and thus risk their own lives, in order to try to end it, who should we take as a more *reliable* guide to the tolerability of that regime to the average human being? Note here that I do not say 'all human beings'. It is enough for normative behaviourism to identify the system that a minimum number of people find unbearable, just as it is enough for many people to know what that system is in order to be convinced by it as the best answer to political philosophy's organising question. Again though, many but not *all*, which is why in Chapter 3 I distinguish between the *evidence* for social-liberal-democracy being the kind of regime described, and the *reasons* for why almost any rational person, given a range of different pre-existing human motivations, would be so convinced by it.

For example, even those attracted to libertarian political principles tend to prefer, in practice, a system which, although it takes more money from them via taxation than would be the case in an anarchist utopia, does provide a great deal more safety (by way of reduced motivation for theft) and protection (by way of a strong and widely supported legal system) for both themselves and their loved ones. History, via Hume, bears witness to this point. In medieval England, under the reign of Edward I, when the clergy demanded exemption from all taxes, they were granted it, but at the same time they were told that they would from now on be exempt from all support and protection from the state. As a result, life soon because so unbearable for those 'enjoying' that exemption, that they quickly withdrew their demand. Andy Sabl neatly captures the libertarian flavour of this policy when describing it as 'Those who live by autonomy and anarchy should be left to die by it.'[53] So what does that mean for political philosophy in general and normative behaviourism in particular? It means that the experience of living with libertarianism hugely reduces the rational appeal of its central principles. Or, put differently, it means that the experience of clergy in thirteenth-century England says more, ultimately, about the worth of those principles than anything Robert Nozick could say about the analogies between taxation and slavery.

Concessions and Reflections

'[M]orality makes people think that, without its very special obligation, there is only inclination; without its utter voluntariness, there is only force; without its ultimately pure justice, there is no justice. Its philosophical errors are only the most abstract expressions of a deeply rooted and still powerful misconception of life.'[54]

A final reiteration: I argued in Chapter 1 that debates in contemporary political philosophy are interminable; in Chapter 2 that methodological adherence to mentalism is the cause of that interminability; and in Chapter 3 (a) that an alternative method, normative behaviourism, could lead us out of the quagmire, and (b) that this method picks out social-liberal-democracy as the best political system developed so far.

With that reiteration in mind, let's revisit once more some of our central problems. For the purposes of simplicity, we can start by saying that the

---

[53] For both the quote and the example, see A. Sabl, 'History and Reality: Idealist Pathologies and 'Harvard School' Remedies', in J. Floyd and M. Stears (Eds.), *Political Philosophy versus History: Contextualism and Real Politics in Contemporary Political Thought* (Cambridge: Cambridge University Press, 2011), 168–169.

[54] B. Williams, *Ethics and Limits of Philosophy* (Cambridge, MA: Harvard University Press, 1985), 196.

problem with political philosophy is mentalism. Mentalists are, in a way, modern-day alchemists who for years have sought to convert the impure metals of human normative thought into the gold of universal political principles. This is no great slight on their efforts. After all, we forget that Newton was an alchemist, and perhaps the 'peerless alchemist of Europe', in addition to having authored some rather less exotic work on the laws of motion.[55] It is hindsight that reveals the latter as his enduring contribution, and in time I hope we will say much the same thing as regards, on the one hand, that vast array of political principles that philosophers proposed during their mentalist period and, on the other, the final justifications they provided for them. As Nietzsche once wrote, 'Do you believe ... that the sciences would ever have arisen and become great if there had not beforehand been magicians, alchemists, astrologers and wizards, who thirsted and hungered after abscondite and forbidden powers?'[56]

My hope is that, in proposing no end of ingenious principles and policies, political philosophers have rendered humanity the great service of both distilling existing practices into intelligible forms and providing new ideas open to testing in future political practice. And that is just part of the service. They have also warned us of some of those principles that are best left untried, or at least unrepeated, given that many awful conflicts can already be seen in advance – which is to say, *in theory*, given the predictable trade-offs and costs involved in the instantiation of certain political ideals.

It is only in their justifications that mentalists have let us down. Mentalist justifications of political principles fail because there is no coherent, underlying framework of normative thought lying hidden in the human mind, just waiting to be captured by political philosophers. But again, the fact that what mentalists took themselves to be doing was a lie should not detract from the majesty of their heritage. No doubt some version of Mill's Harm Principle, some twist on Rawls' difference principle, some variation on Walzer's ideal of spherical integrity, and some model of deliberative democracy are all going to have their place in the best political system we can design today. Presumably some or other conception of tolerance, some or other vision of social justice, some or other ideal of autonomy, and some or other programme of rights will have a place alongside them. So: even if it is time to leave their *method* behind, we are as indebted today to the creativity of the mentalists as we ever were. And consider, just as we depend in the here and now on those ideas granted to us by past political philosophers, via the benefits we derive from laws and institutions guided by their work, so shall we continue to

[55] See, for example, J. Gleick, *Isaac Newton* (London: Fourth Estate, 1998), 101–108.
[56] F. Nietzsche, *The Gay Science* (Cambridge: Cambridge University Press, 2001), 170.

depend on such creativity in the future. Proposing new laws and policies fit for political testing is as important a task now as it ever was.

Of course, no part of this concession should detract from the fact that, in my view, political philosophy, as it stands right now, needs a paradigm shift from mentalism to behaviourism. Let me borrow for a moment the language of mentalism – which loves so dearly to take us from a little of how we do think to a lot of how we should think – and repeat a metaphor I provided earlier. We do not, I take it, judge a cake by the principles that went into its construction, but rather by the verdicts of those who have tasted and fully digested the complete combination and treatment of its ingredients. Well, as with cakes, so with states. The acid test of political principles, according to the view expressed in this book, is their record in political power. We gauge the ultimate worth of answers to political philosophy's organising question by monitoring the responses human beings give to them in political practice. If the answers lead to greater discontent – as measured principally by insurrection and crime – then they are bad, and if they lead to the opposite, then they are good. Political philosophy should not obsess about either self-interest – for we want many things, and we only know what we want to avoid the most by looking at behaviour – or about morality – for our 'moral' thought exists in a state of fundamental dissonance. Instead, it should become more empirical and, in particular, more social-scientific. It is often said that political philosophers need to reacquaint and reconnect themselves with politics and practice. Well, this is how they should do it.

Of course, every one of these claims is, in its own way, vulnerable. That is only to be expected, and I suppose my most resilient hope throughout this entire book has been simply that readers will find enough of inspiration and potential in my arguments to try and develop and strengthen them themselves. After all, normative behaviourism, as a *collective* enterprise, has yet to be born. Perhaps I might even return, with some irony, to Derek Parfit's claim that because non-religious ethics is such a young subject, we should not judge it prematurely (see **1.13**).[57] I was unconvinced by that claim

---

[57] D. Parfit, *Reasons and Persons* (Oxford: Oxford University Press, 1984), 454. We might also note James Rachels' claim to the same effect. He writes, in one of the most popular moral philosophy textbooks of recent years, that because 'civilization is only a few thousand years old', we should be optimistic about the future of our subject, despite the flaws each thinker always finds in the work of his or her fellows. There is, however, one caveat a normative behaviourist would appreciate, as expressed by his claim that 'If we do not destroy ourselves, then the study of Ethics has a bright future.' As far as the normative behaviourist is concerned, it would be better to begin by looking at those political systems that *do* have observable or predictable tendencies to destroy themselves, and then work your way in. See J. Rachels and S. Rachels, *The Elements of Moral Philosophy* (New York: McGraw-Hill, 2010), 183.

because however old we take secular ethics to be, it is more than old enough to know better. Similarly, I am unconvinced by an alternative version of this claim invoking 'professional' ethics, because even if we have only had this for around fifty years, that is still more than enough time to stick with a tree that just will not yield fruit – and especially so when one considers that it involves, in today's world, thousands of thinkers at hundreds of institutions. By contrast, normative behaviourism, as a serious proposition, is no older than this book.[58] It is a millennial meme, and like most millennials, has yet to find permanent employment. As a result, we should at least give it an internship.

Let's not get carried away though. Like Hume, I find it hard to put away the fear that 'an hypothesis, so obvious, had it been a true one, would, long ere now, have been received by the unanimous suffrage and consent of mankind'.[59] Similarly, I am sympathetic, as noted through the last chapter, to his remark that:

I am apt ... to entertain a suspicion that the world is still too young to fix many general truths in politics, which will remain true to the latest posterity. We have not as yet had experience of three thousand years; so that not only the art of reasoning is still imperfect in this science, as in all others, but we even want sufficient materials upon which we can reason.[60]

What, then, should one think? I would say that, if I have cast enough doubt upon mentalism, and lent enough of an air of potential to normative behaviourism, then that is surely enough for now. And who knows? Maybe normative behaviourism is everything, maybe it's nothing, or maybe it's just a tie-breaker when mentalism breaks down. Again though, don't be misled. I am, at the least, more confident than the second of those maybes suggests. Yet that doesn't really matter now. This book is finished, which means it's not up to me anymore.

---

[58] This was true when I wrote the sentence, and only slightly less true now, given my recent attempt to 'apply' normative behaviourism to questions of global political theory: J. Floyd, 'Normative Behaviourism and Global Political Principles', *Journal of International Political Theory*, 12:2 (2016), 152–168. To situate this attempt alongside other attempts to render global political theory 'more realistic', see J. Floyd, 'Should Global Political Theory Get Real?', *Journal of International Political Theory*, 12:2 (2016), 93–95.

[59] D. Hume, *An Enquiry concerning the Principles of Morals* (Oxford: Oxford University Press, 1998), 79.

[60] D. Hume, *Selected Essays* (Oxford: Oxford University Press, 1998), 49. Perhaps I should also add William James' claim that there can be no 'final truth in ethics ... until the last man has had his experience and said his say'. W. James, *The Will to Believe, And Other Essays in Popular Philosophy* (Cambridge, MA: Harvard University Press, 1979), 141. He also once wrote, perhaps even more encouragingly, that 'Everywhere the ethical philosopher must wait on facts.' See W. James, 'The Moral Philosopher and the Moral Life', *International Journal of Ethics*, 1:3 (1891), 330.

Index